DEAR STUDENT/TEACHER

MORE INFORMATION AND FREE MATERIAL AT:

ibmathworkbooks.webnode.es

FIRST EDITION COPYRIGHT ©

ALL RIGHTS RESERVED. PERMISSION IN WRITING MUST BE OBTAINED FROM THE WRITER BEFORE ANY PART OF THIS PUBLICATION MAY BE REPRODUCED OR TRANSMITTED IN ANY FORM OR BY ANY MEANS, ELECTRONIC OR MECHANICAL. INCLUDING PHOTOCOPY, RECORDING OR ANY INFORMATION STORAGE OR RETRIEVEL SYSTEM.

CONTENTS

CHAPTER 1 – ALGEBRA

1.1 Order of operations...5
1.2 Introduction to fractions..10
1.3 Decimals and fractions..33
1.4 Types of numbers..38
1.5 Exponents..45
1.6 Roots and rationalization...51
1.7 Percentages..53
1.8 Evaluating expressions..62
1.9 Expanding and factoring...63
1.10 Ratios...67
1.11 Equations of the first degree...69
1.12 Systems of equations first degree...77
1.13 Interval notation and inequalities..88
1.14 Equations of the second degree..97

CHAPTER 2 – GEOMETRY

2.1 Introduction to geometry...106
2.2 Angles 109
2.3 Triangles..114
2.4 Distance and midpoint...128
2.5 Quadrilaterals..132
2.6 Circles and complex shapes..139
2.7 3D geometry volume and surface area...144
2.8 Geometric transformations..151
2.9 Congruent and similar triangles..161

CHAPTER 3 – FUNCTIONS

3.1 Introduction to functions..166
3.2 Linear functions..175

CHAPTER 4 – STATISTICS

4.1 Introduction to statistics..207
4.2 Bivariate data and scatter plots...212
4.3 Mean, Median, Mode and Frequency diagrams.................................221
4.4 Probability...227

CHAPTER 5

5.1 International system of units...229
5.2 Common errors...231

ANSWER KEY

Chapter 1 – ALGEBRA

1.2	Order of operations	234
1.2	Introduction to fractions	237
1.3	Decimals and fractions	254
1.4	Types of numbers	257
1.5	Exponents	261
1.6	Roots and rationalization	267
1.7	Percentages	269
1.8	Evaluating expressions	274
1.9	Expanding and factoring	275
1.10	Ratios	278
1.11	Equations of the first degree	279
1.12	Systems of equations first degree	283
1.13	Interval notation and inequalities	289
1.14	Equations of the second degree	294

Chapter 2 – GEOMETRY

2.1	Introduction to geometry	299
2.2	Angles	300
2.3	Triangles	304
2.4	Distance and midpoint	312
2.5	Quadrilaterals	314
2.6	Circles and complex shapes	319
2.7	3D geometry volume and surface area	322
2.8	Geometric transformations	326
2.9	Congruent and similar triangles	331

Chapter 3 – FUNCTIONS

3.1	Introduction to functions	334
3.2	Linear functions	340

Chapter 4 – STATISTICS

4.1	Introduction to statistics	355
4.2	Bivariate data and scatter plots	360
4.3	Mean, Median, Mode and Frequency diagrams	366
4.4	Probability	371

Chapter 5

5.1	International system of units	373
5.2	Common errors	375

CHAPTER 1 - ALGEBRA

1.1. – ORDER OF OPERATIONS

1. The correct order of operations is:

    a. P_____

    b. E_____

    c. M_____ or D_____

    d. A_____ or S_____

2. Given the product $3 \cdot 2$ which of the following is a good model for this product, explain.

3. Given the product $4 \cdot 2$ which of the following is a good model for this product, explain.

4. Given the product $3 \cdot 3$ which of the following is a good model for this product, explain.

5. Given the following model, write the corresponding product sentence, is it the only possible one?

6. Given the following model, write the corresponding product sentence, is it the only possible one?

7. Calculate the following products, remember the correct order of operations

    a. $3 \cdot 8 =$

    b. $3 \cdot (-5) =$

    c. $(-9) \cdot (-3) =$

    d. $(-3) \cdot 7 =$

    e. $-(-2) \cdot (-3) =$

    f. $-(-11) \cdot 3 =$

    g. $6 \cdot (-6) =$

    h. $-(-23) \cdot (-3) =$

8. Calculate the following, , remember the correct order of operations

    a. $(-3) \cdot (-3) =$

    b. $-3 \cdot (-3) =$

    c. $3 \cdot (-3) =$

    d. $(-3) \cdot 3 =$

    e. $-3 \cdot 3 =$

    f. $3 \cdot 3 =$

9. Given the division $10 \div 2 = 5$, build a model that fits this sentence

10. Given the division $15 \div 3 = 5$, build a model that fits this sentence

11. Given the division $6 \div 6 = 1$, build a model that fits this sentence

12. Calculate the following, , remember the correct order of operations

    a. $12 \div 3 =$

    b. $20 \div (-5) =$

    c. $-38 \div 2 =$

    d. $(-42) \div (-7) =$

    e. $-36 \div (-12) =$

    f. $-(-75) \div 5 =$

13. Given the following expression: $6 - 4/2 =$ ___ which of the following is the same sentence: $6 - \dfrac{4}{2} =$ $\dfrac{6-4}{2} =$ Find its value

14. Given the following expression: $(17 - 6)/6 =$ ___ which of the following is the same sentence: $17 - \dfrac{6}{6} =$ $\dfrac{17-6}{6} =$ Find its value

15. Given the following expression: $3 \cdot 5 + 12/3 =$ ___ which of the following is the same sentence: $15 + \dfrac{12}{3} =$ $\dfrac{15-12}{3} =$ Find its value

16. Given the following expression: $18/2 - 5 =$ ___ which of the following is the same sentence: $\dfrac{18}{2} - 5 =$ $\dfrac{18}{2-5} =$ Find its value

17. $-2 - 3 = 6$ True or False
18. $-2(-3) = 6$ True or False
19. $0 \cdot a = a$ True or False
20. $0 + a = a$ True or False
21. $1 + a = a$ True or False
22. $\dfrac{a}{a} = a \div a$ True or False
23. $\dfrac{a}{a} = 1$ True or False

24. $a \cdot a = (-a)(-a)$ True or False
25. $-a \cdot b = (-a)(-b)$ True or False
26. $-a \cdot (-b) = ab$ True or False
27. $a \cdot (-b) = -a - b$ True or False
28. $a \div b = b \div a$ True or False
29. $ab = ba$ True or False
30. $a + b = b + a$ True or False
31. $a - b = b - a$ True or False

Calculate the following; remember the correct order of operations

32. $5 + 3 \cdot 2 =$

33. $5 - 3 \cdot 2 =$

34. $3 \cdot 7 - 6 =$

35. $2 \cdot 3 - (-3) =$

36. $-(-4) \cdot 3 - (-3) =$

37. $-(-2) \cdot (-5) - (-6) =$

38. $-(-4) \cdot 3/2 - (-3)(-3) =$

39. $-5 \cdot 5 - (-8) \cdot 2 =$

40. $-2 - 5 - (-2) + 2 =$

41. $(-2)(-5) - (-2) \cdot 2 =$

42. $25 \cdot 2 - 7 =$

43. $15 + 4/2 =$

44. $14 \div 7 + 3 \cdot 6 =$

45. $5/5 - 30/2 \cdot 5 =$

46. $1 + 4/2 - 8/4 \cdot 5 =$

47. $20/4/2 + 4 =$

48. $12 \cdot (2+3) =$

49. $5(3 \cdot 2/3 \cdot 2) + 2 =$

50. $1/2 + 3/2 =$

51. $6/3 - 20 \div 10 =$

52. $5(1 + 3 \cdot 2) + 2/2 - 8/4 =$

53. $(15+3) \cdot 2 - 2 =$

54. $0/5 + 3 \cdot 2 =$

55. $5/0 + 3 \cdot 2 - 1 =$

56. $(1+1) \cdot (2-2) \cdot (4 \cdot 5 \cdot 5) =$

57. $(5+3) \cdot 2 =$

58. $(5 \cdot 3) \cdot 2 =$

59. $5 \cdot (3 \cdot 2) =$

60. $5 \cdot 3 \cdot 2 =$

61. $100/2 + 21/3 =$

62. $(2+1) \div 3 + 13 =$

63. $2(-(-3) \cdot 3 - 4/2) - 1 \cdot 3 =$

64. $3(1 - 4/2) - 15 \div 3 =$

65. $10(16/2 - 1 + 1)/2 =$

66. $2 + 3(2 - 20/4) - (25+3) \div 2 =$

67. $5/0 =$

68. $0/4 =$

69. $0/0 =$

70. $(2+4) \cdot 25 - 2/2 =$

71. $-3 \cdot 5 - 2 + (-3)(-2)(-2) =$

72. $(-2 \cdot 2 - 2 \cdot 3) \cdot (-2) =$

73. $(4 - 5 \cdot 2)/2 - 1 =$

Fill the blank

74. $\_\_ \cdot 2 = 8$

75. $\_\_ / 2 = 8$

76. $\_\_ + 2 = 8$

77. $\_\_ - 2 = 8$

78. $\_\_ \cdot 3 = 7$

79. $\_\_ / 6 = 3$

80. $\_\_ + 7 = 7$

81. $\_\_ - 12 = 1$

82. $5 \cdot \_\_ = 10$

83. $-15 / \_\_ = 3$

84. $7 + \_\_ = 1$

85. $25 - \_\_ = 30$

86. $12 / \_\_ = -4$

87. $\_\_ + 2 = -8$

88. $\_\_ \cdot (-3) = 33$

89. $(-21) / \_\_ = -7$

Fill the blanks with 2 different options for solutions:

90. $\_\_ + 2 / \_\_ = 1$ $\_\_ + 2 / \_\_ = 1$

91. $\_\_ \cdot 2 / \_\_ = 1$ $\_\_ \cdot 2 / \_\_ = 1$

92. $\_\_ - 2 / \_\_ = 1$ $\_\_ - 2 / \_\_ = 1$

93. $\_\_ + 4 / \_\_ = 3$ $\_\_ + 4 / \_\_ = 3$

94. $\_\_ + 12 \cdot \_\_ = 3$ $\_\_ + 12 \cdot \_\_ = 3$

95. $\_\_ - 6 / \_\_ = 11$ $\_\_ - 6 / \_\_ = 11$

96. $\_\_ + 3 / \_\_ = 2$ $\_\_ + 3 / \_\_ = 2$

97. $\_\_ - 5 / \_\_ = 22$ $\_\_ - 5 / \_\_ = 22$

98. $4 \cdot \_\_ + \_\_ - 5 = 6$ $4 \cdot \_\_ + \_\_ - 5 = 6$

99. $\_\_ / 5 + \_\_ = 4$ $\_\_ / 5 + \_\_ = 4$

100. $\_\_ + 1 / \_\_ = 12$ $\_\_ + 1 / \_\_ = 12$

101. $\_\_ / 5 + \_\_ = 4$ $\_\_ / 5 + \_\_ = 4$

102. $\_\_ - 6 + \_\_ = 6$ $\_\_ - 6 + \_\_ = 6$

1.2. – FRACTIONS

1. Given the following circle, divide it to 2 equal pieces and shade $\frac{1}{2}$

2. Given the following circle divide it to 3 equal pieces and shade $\frac{1}{3}$

3. Given the following circle, divide it to 4 equal pieces and shade $\frac{1}{4}$

4. Given the following circle, divide it to 5 equal pieces and shade $\frac{1}{5}$

5. Given the following circle, divide it to 6 equal pieces and shade $\frac{1}{6}$

6. Given the following circle, divide it to 7 equal pieces and shade $\frac{1}{7}$

7. Given the following circle, divide it to 8 equal pieces and shade $\frac{1}{8}$

8. Given the following circle, divide it to 9 equal pieces and shade $\frac{1}{9}$

9. Given the following circle, divide it to 10 equal pieces and shade $\frac{1}{10}$

10. Given the following circle, divide it to 3 equal pieces and shade $\frac{2}{3}$

11. Given the following circle, divide it to 4 equal pieces and shade $\frac{2}{4}$

12. Given the following circle, divide it to 4 equal pieces and shade $\frac{3}{4}$

13. Given the following circle, divide it to 5 equal pieces and shade $\frac{2}{5}$

14. Given the following circle, divide it to 6 equal pieces and shade $\frac{5}{6}$

15. Given the following circle, divide it to 8 equal pieces and shade $\frac{5}{8}$

16. Given the following circle, divide it to 5 equal pieces and shade $\frac{4}{5}$

17. Given the following circle, divide it to 9 equal pieces and shade $\frac{4}{9}$

18. What fraction of the following circle is shaded:

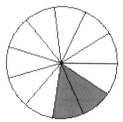

19. What fraction of the following circle is shaded:

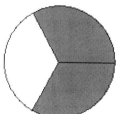

11

20. What fraction of the following circle is shaded:

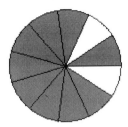

21. What fraction of the following circle is shaded:

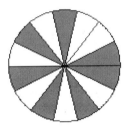

22. What fraction of the following circle is shaded:

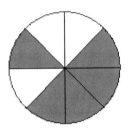

23. What fraction of the following circle is shaded:

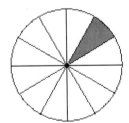

24. What fraction of the following table is shaded:

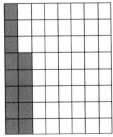

25. What fraction of the following table is shaded:

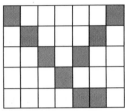

26. What fraction of the following table is shaded?

27. What fraction is shaded?

28. What fraction is shaded?

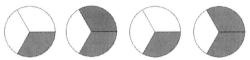

29. What fraction is shaded?

30. What fraction is shaded?

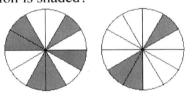

31. There were 12 cookies in the jar. John ate 7, write down the fraction of cookies john ate and the fraction that is left in the jar.

32. Lia ate 3 cookies that represented $\frac{3}{4}$ of the cookies in the jar. Write down the number of cookies in the jar before she ate. Make a sketch to show answer.

33. Rami ate $\frac{2}{5}$ of the cookies in the jar, Melissa ate $\frac{1}{4}$ of the cookies. Who ate more? Invent an imaginary jar with a number of cookies that will make the problem easy to solve.

34. How much is $\frac{1}{2}$ of 2? Shade to show your answer:

35. How much is $\frac{1}{3}$ of 2? Shade to show your answer:

36. How much is $\frac{1}{4}$ of 2? Shade to show your answer:

37. How much is $\frac{1}{5}$ of 2? Shade to show your answer:

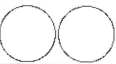

38. How much is $\frac{1}{3}$ of 5? Shade in 2 different ways to show your answer:

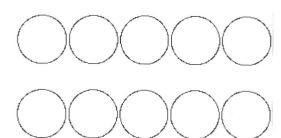

39. How much is $\frac{2}{5}$ of 4? Shade in 2 different ways to show your answer:

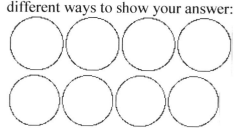

40. Sketch $\frac{3}{2}$ circles:

41. Sketch $\frac{5}{3}$ circles:

42. Sketch $\frac{7}{4}$ circles:

43. Sketch $\frac{8}{4}$ circles:

44. Sketch $\frac{7}{5}$ circles:

45. Sketch $\frac{8}{3}$ circles:

46. Nathan ate $\frac{2}{7}$ of the cookies in the jar, Melissa ate $\frac{1}{3}$ of the cookies. Who ate more? Invent an imaginary jar with a number of cookies that will make the problem easy to solve.

47. Write down the missing number(s) between 0 and 1:

48. Write down the missing number(s) between 0 and 1:

49. Write down the missing number(s) between 0 and 1:

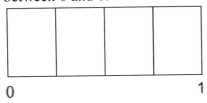

50. Write down the missing number(s) between 0 and 1:

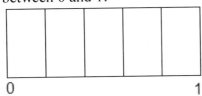

51. Write down the missing number(s) between 0 and 1:

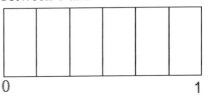

52. Write down the missing number(s) between 0 and 2:

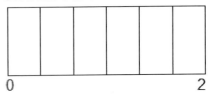

53. Write down the missing number(s) between 0 and 2:

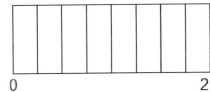

54. Write down the missing number(s) between 0 and 2:

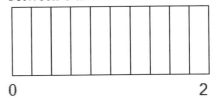

55. Write down the missing number(s) between 2 and 3:

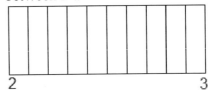

56. Write down the missing number(s) between 2 and 4:

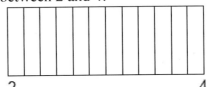

57. Write down the missing fractions(s):

58. Write down the missing fractions(s):

59. Write down the missing fractions(s):

60. Write down the missing fractions(s)::

    [0] ———————————————————— [1/5]

61. Write down the missing fractions(s):

    [1/8]   [1/2]

62. Write down the missing fractions(s):

    [1]   [3/2] [5/3]

63. Write down the missing fractions(s):

    [13/7] [2]   [20/7]

64. Write down the missing fractions(s):

    [26/9]   [3]   [10/3]

65. Write down the missing fractions(s):

    [-10/9] [-1]   [-4/9] [-1/3]

66. Write down the missing fractions(s):

    [-4]   [-2] [-8/5] [-6/5]

67. Write down the missing fractions(s):

    [3/4] [3/2] [9/4] [3]   [6] [27/4] [15/2]

68. Write down the fractions in different ways:

    $\dfrac{1}{2} =$ $\dfrac{1}{3} =$ $\dfrac{1}{4} =$ $\dfrac{9}{4} =$ $\dfrac{2}{3} =$ $\dfrac{11}{8} =$

    $\dfrac{a}{b} =$ $\dfrac{2a}{a} =$ $\dfrac{x+13}{13+x} =$ $\dfrac{x}{3x} =$ $\dfrac{a-b}{b-a} =$

Fill the blank to make the fractions equal:

69. $\dfrac{a}{2} = \dfrac{}{4}$

70. $\dfrac{a-b}{4} = \dfrac{}{12}$

71. $\dfrac{a}{b} = \dfrac{}{2b}$

72. $\dfrac{1}{a} = \dfrac{}{5a}$

73. $\dfrac{1}{3} = \dfrac{}{\_a}$

74. $\dfrac{a-b}{} = 1$

75. $\dfrac{2-a}{} = \dfrac{a-2}{2}$

76. $\dfrac{2a}{b} = \dfrac{}{4b}$

77. $\dfrac{x^2}{2xy} = \dfrac{}{4y^2}$

78. $\dfrac{2a}{7x} = \dfrac{}{14x^2}$

79. Circle the fractions that are greater than 1: $\quad \dfrac{7}{6}, \dfrac{6}{7}, \dfrac{35}{34}, \dfrac{21}{7}, \dfrac{10001}{10000}$

80. A fraction will be greater than 1 if _____

81. Circle the fractions that are greater than 2: $\quad \dfrac{50}{26}, \dfrac{60}{30}, \dfrac{35}{40}, \dfrac{20}{7}, \dfrac{20001}{10000}$

82. A fraction will be greater than 2 if _____

83. Circle the fractions that are greater than 5: $\quad \dfrac{50}{10}, \dfrac{47}{9}, \dfrac{100}{6}, \dfrac{28}{3}, \dfrac{1201}{300}$

84. A fraction will be greater than 5 if _____

85. Circle the fractions that are smaller than $\dfrac{1}{2}$: $\quad \dfrac{1}{3}, \dfrac{2}{3}, \dfrac{4}{9}, \dfrac{28}{29}, \dfrac{34}{60}, \dfrac{23}{51}, \dfrac{17}{32}, \dfrac{34}{67}$

86. A fraction will be smaller than $\dfrac{1}{2}$ if: _____

87. Circle the fractions that are smaller than $\dfrac{1}{3}$: $\quad \dfrac{2}{7}, \dfrac{5}{9}, \dfrac{4}{11}, \dfrac{13}{29}, \dfrac{24}{75}, \dfrac{3}{11}$

88. A fraction will be smaller than $\dfrac{1}{3}$ if: _____

Fill the blank with: <, > or =, assume a, b, n are positive constants:

89. $\dfrac{1}{2}$ — $\dfrac{1}{3}$

90. $\dfrac{1}{2}$ — $\dfrac{1}{3}$

91. $\dfrac{1}{3}$ — $\dfrac{1}{4}$

92. $\dfrac{2}{5}$ — $\dfrac{3}{7}$

93. $\dfrac{5}{8}$ — $\dfrac{7}{11}$

94. $\dfrac{12}{7}$ — $\dfrac{13}{8}$

95. $\dfrac{21}{8}$ — $\dfrac{13}{5}$

96. $\dfrac{35}{8}$ — $\dfrac{17}{4}$

97. $\dfrac{a}{b}$ — $\dfrac{a}{b+1}$, $a, b > 0$

98. $\dfrac{a}{b}$ — $\dfrac{a+1}{b+1}$, $a, b > 0$

99. $\dfrac{1}{n+1}$ — $\dfrac{1}{n}$, $n \geq 0$

100. $\dfrac{1}{n^2}$ — $\dfrac{1}{n}$, $n \geq 1$

101. $\dfrac{1}{a}$ — $\dfrac{1}{b}$, $b > a > 0$

102. Indicate the location of the fractions on the number line: $-\dfrac{7}{6}, -\dfrac{6}{7}, \dfrac{17}{34}, \dfrac{-1}{7}, \dfrac{10001}{5000}$

103. Indicate the location of the fractions on the number line: $-\dfrac{1}{6}, -\dfrac{8}{7}, \dfrac{20}{9}, \dfrac{-10}{20}, \dfrac{99}{50}$

104. Indicate the location of the fractions on the number line: $-\dfrac{4}{5}, -\dfrac{3}{2}, \dfrac{5}{2}, \dfrac{9}{8}, \dfrac{100}{33}$

105. Indicate the location of the fractions on the number line: $-\dfrac{7}{5}, -\dfrac{9}{3}, \dfrac{2}{3}, \dfrac{1}{10}, -\dfrac{66}{32}$

106. Indicate the location of the fractions on the number line: $-\dfrac{7}{8}, -\dfrac{6}{13}, \dfrac{11}{21}, \dfrac{-2}{17}, \dfrac{100}{501}$

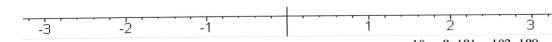

107. Indicate the location of the fractions on the number line: $-\dfrac{10}{6}, -\dfrac{8}{7}, \dfrac{181}{90}, \dfrac{-102}{200}, \dfrac{189}{60}$

108. Indicate the location of the fractions on the number line: $-\dfrac{6}{5}, -\dfrac{5}{2}, \dfrac{2}{5}, \dfrac{90}{80}, \dfrac{33}{100}$

109. Indicate the location of the fractions on the number line: $-\dfrac{12}{5}, -\dfrac{6}{3}, \dfrac{11}{6}, \dfrac{11}{10}, -\dfrac{37}{12}$

110. Indicate the location of the fractions on the number line: $-\dfrac{10}{4}, -\dfrac{2}{10}, \dfrac{64}{33}, \dfrac{21}{10}, -\dfrac{3}{1}$

ADDING AND SUBTRACTING FRACTIONS

Write the corresponding addition sentence:

1.

2.

3.

4.

5.

6.

7.

8. In order to add or subtract fractions they must have _____

9. $\dfrac{1}{2}+\dfrac{1}{2}=$

10. $\dfrac{1}{3}+\dfrac{1}{3}=$

11. $\dfrac{2}{4}+\dfrac{3}{4}=$

12. $\dfrac{2}{4}-\dfrac{5}{4}=$

13. $\dfrac{8}{7}-\dfrac{5}{7}+\dfrac{6}{7}=$

14. $\dfrac{17}{11}-\dfrac{2}{11}-\dfrac{1}{11}=$

15. $\dfrac{1}{2}+\dfrac{1}{2}+\dfrac{1}{2}+\dfrac{1}{2}+\dfrac{1}{2}+\dfrac{1}{2}=$

16. $\dfrac{1}{7}-\dfrac{20}{7}-\dfrac{3}{7}+\dfrac{5}{7}=$

17. $\dfrac{21}{17}-\dfrac{5}{17}-\dfrac{13}{17}+\dfrac{25}{17}=$

18. $\dfrac{1}{3}+\dfrac{1}{2}=$

19. $\dfrac{2}{3}-\dfrac{1}{4}=$

20. $\dfrac{2}{5}+\dfrac{3}{2}=$

21. $\dfrac{3}{4}-\dfrac{1}{2}=$

22. $\dfrac{2}{3}+\dfrac{3}{5}=$

23. $\dfrac{2}{3}-\dfrac{5}{6}=$

24. $\dfrac{3}{4}+\dfrac{3}{7}=$

25. $\dfrac{3}{8}-\dfrac{3}{4}=$

26. $\dfrac{5}{8}+\dfrac{4}{5}=$

27. $\dfrac{5}{7}+\dfrac{4}{14}=$

28. $\dfrac{1}{2}+\dfrac{1}{3}+\dfrac{1}{4}=$

29. $\dfrac{1}{2}+\dfrac{3}{4}-\dfrac{2}{5}=$

30. $\dfrac{2}{3}-\dfrac{3}{4}+\dfrac{3}{5}=$

31. $\dfrac{1}{2}+\dfrac{3}{4}+\dfrac{5}{6}=$

32. $\dfrac{3}{2}-\dfrac{2}{3}-\dfrac{4}{5}=$

33. $\dfrac{4}{5}+\dfrac{1}{6}+\dfrac{5}{7}=$

34. $\dfrac{7}{4}-\dfrac{7}{8}-\left(-\dfrac{7}{12}\right)=$

35. $\dfrac{1}{2}-\left(-\dfrac{5}{8}\right)-\dfrac{9}{10}=$

36. $-\dfrac{3}{2}-\dfrac{3}{4}-\dfrac{9}{16}=$

37. $\dfrac{2}{3}+\dfrac{5}{6}+\dfrac{-11}{12}=$

38. $\dfrac{7}{8}-\dfrac{-5}{6}+\dfrac{7}{10}=$

39. $\dfrac{3}{8}+\dfrac{3}{16}-\dfrac{7}{32}=$

40. $\dfrac{1}{a}+\dfrac{1}{a}=$

41. $\dfrac{2}{a}-\dfrac{7}{a}=$

42. $\dfrac{5}{a}-\dfrac{b}{a}=$

43. $\dfrac{c}{a}+\dfrac{b}{a}=$

44. $\dfrac{5}{a}-\dfrac{b}{a}+\dfrac{c}{a}=$

45. $\dfrac{2b}{a}-\dfrac{3c}{a}+\dfrac{c}{a}=$

46. $\dfrac{1}{a}+\dfrac{1}{b}=$

47. $\dfrac{2}{a}-\dfrac{1}{b}=$

48. $\dfrac{c}{a}-\dfrac{d}{b}=$

49. $\dfrac{c}{a}-\dfrac{d}{b}+\dfrac{5}{b}=$

50. $\dfrac{c}{a}-1+\dfrac{5}{b}=$

51. $\dfrac{1}{ab}+\dfrac{1}{a}+\dfrac{1}{b}=$

52. $\dfrac{1}{ab}+\dfrac{1}{ab}+\dfrac{1}{b}=$

53. $\dfrac{1}{ab}+\dfrac{1}{ab}+\dfrac{1}{ab}=$

54. $\dfrac{c}{ab}+\dfrac{1}{b}+\dfrac{1}{a}=$

55. $\dfrac{c}{ab}-\dfrac{1}{b}+\dfrac{2}{a}=$

56. $2+\dfrac{1}{x}=$

57. $\dfrac{5}{2x}-\dfrac{1}{x}=$

58. $2-\dfrac{3}{x}=$

59. $\dfrac{x}{3}-2=$

60. $\dfrac{2}{5}-\dfrac{7}{2x}=$

61. $\dfrac{3}{5x}-\dfrac{1}{2x}=$

62. $a-\dfrac{1}{2}=$

63. $\dfrac{1}{1+x}-1=$

64. $2-\dfrac{4}{2+x}=$

65. $\dfrac{2x}{3}-\dfrac{x}{2}-\dfrac{x}{6}=$

66. $\dfrac{2x}{3}-\dfrac{x+1}{4}-\dfrac{3x}{8}=$

67. Jeff spent $\frac{1}{5}$ of his savings and later spent $\frac{1}{4}$ of his savings, what fraction of his savings did he spend in total? What fraction of his savings is left?

68. Lia walked $\frac{2}{3}$ of the distance home and stopped to rest. Later she walked a $\frac{1}{4}$ more. What fraction of the distance did she walk in total? What part she still needs to walk?

69. Dina ate $\frac{1}{9}$ of the cookies in the jar, Dan ate a $\frac{1}{6}$ and Ben $\frac{2}{11}$. What fraction of the cookies is left in the jar? Which one of the 3 ate more cookies?

70. Robyn did $\frac{5}{6}$ of her HW. Later she did $\frac{1}{13}$ of the HW. What part of her HW she still needs to do.

True or False:

71. $\dfrac{a+b}{c} = \dfrac{a}{c} + \dfrac{b}{c}$

72. $\dfrac{a+b}{c+d} = \dfrac{a}{c} + \dfrac{b}{d}$

73. $\dfrac{a+b}{a} = 1 + \dfrac{b}{a}$

74. $\dfrac{a-b}{b-a} = -1$

75. $\dfrac{a}{c+d} = \dfrac{a}{c} + \dfrac{a}{d}$

76. $\dfrac{c-d}{d} = c$

77. $\dfrac{c-d}{d} = -1 + c$

78. $\dfrac{ab}{ad} = \dfrac{b}{d}$

79. $\dfrac{a(c-d)}{a} = c - d$

80. $\dfrac{ac-d}{c-d} = a$

81. $\dfrac{2a+d}{d-2a} = -1$

MULTIPLYING FRACTIONS

1. $\dfrac{1}{1} \cdot \dfrac{1}{2} =$

2. $\dfrac{2}{1} \cdot \dfrac{1}{2} =$

3. $\dfrac{a}{1} \cdot \dfrac{1}{a} =$

4. $\dfrac{3}{1} \cdot \dfrac{1}{1} =$

5. $(-4) \cdot \dfrac{1}{2} =$

6. $6 \cdot \dfrac{1}{3} =$

7. $20 \cdot \dfrac{1}{5} =$

8. $\dfrac{1}{2} \cdot \dfrac{1}{2} =$

9. $\dfrac{1}{2} \cdot \left(-\dfrac{1}{3}\right) =$

10. $\dfrac{1}{2} \cdot \dfrac{1}{4} =$

11. $\dfrac{1}{2} \cdot \dfrac{1}{5} =$

12. $\dfrac{1}{3} \cdot \dfrac{1}{10} =$

13. $\dfrac{2}{3} \cdot \dfrac{6}{1} =$

14. $\left(-\dfrac{4}{5}\right) \cdot \dfrac{7}{-8} =$

15. $\dfrac{2}{5} \cdot \dfrac{3}{4} =$

16. $\dfrac{8}{5} \cdot \dfrac{17}{-2} =$

17. $\dfrac{9}{5} \cdot \dfrac{4}{9} =$

18. $\dfrac{12}{15} \cdot \dfrac{15}{9} =$

19. $-\dfrac{8}{a} \cdot \dfrac{a}{7} =$

20. $\dfrac{12}{a} \cdot \dfrac{a}{27} =$

21. $\dfrac{-x}{a} \cdot \dfrac{-a}{x} =$

22. $\dfrac{y}{b} \cdot \dfrac{b}{x} =$

23. $\dfrac{1}{2}$ of 50 is _____

24. $\dfrac{1}{3}$ of 66 is _____

25. $\dfrac{1}{4}$ of 48 is _____

26. $\dfrac{2}{5}$ of 20 is _____

27. $\dfrac{7}{9}$ of 81 is _____

28. $\dfrac{1}{2}$ of $\dfrac{3}{-2}$ is _____

29. $\dfrac{1}{2}$ of $\dfrac{3}{4}$ is _____

30. $\dfrac{2}{7}$ of $\dfrac{6}{5}$ is _____

31. $\dfrac{4}{3}$ of $\dfrac{2}{3}$ is _____

32. $\dfrac{10}{3}$ of $-\dfrac{2}{5}$ is _____

33. $\dfrac{8}{7}$ of $\dfrac{13}{4}$ is _____

34. $\dfrac{11}{2}$ of $\dfrac{12}{7}$ is _____

35. $\dfrac{1}{2}$ of $\dfrac{1}{2}$ of $\dfrac{1}{2}$ is _____

36. $\dfrac{1}{3}$ of $\dfrac{3}{4}$ of $\dfrac{3}{4}$ is _____

37. $\dfrac{2}{3}$ of $\dfrac{3}{4}$ of $-\dfrac{4}{5}$ is _____

38. $\dfrac{4}{3}$ of $\dfrac{3}{4}$ of 6 is _____

39. $\dfrac{5}{6}$ of $\dfrac{7}{4}$ of $\dfrac{12}{7}$ is _____

40. $\dfrac{8}{3}$ of $\dfrac{5}{3}$ of 10 is _____

41. $\dfrac{5}{3}$ of $\dfrac{8}{3}$ of 10 is _____

42. $\dfrac{a}{b}$ of $\dfrac{b}{3}$ of $\dfrac{2}{a}$ is _____

43. Jim ate 220 grams of pasta. Lily ate $\frac{2}{3}$ of Jim, find the amount of pasta Lily ate.

44. Jessica walks $2\frac{2}{3}$ miles every morning. Marc walks $\frac{4}{5}$ of Jessica, find the distance Marc walks every morning.

45. Michael ate $\frac{1}{3}$ of the 66 cookies in the jar, how many cookies did he eat?

46. Lisa climbed 130 meters. Mervin climbed $\frac{2}{5}$ more than Lisa. Find the distance Mervin climbed.

47. Juan ate $\frac{2}{3}$ of $\frac{2}{5}$ the 50 cookies in the jar, how many cookies did he eat?

48. Paul bought 5 Kg of fruit. He ate $\frac{3}{8}$ of the fruit. Ruth ate $\frac{2}{7}$ of Paul.
   a. How many Kg of fruit did Paul eat?
   b. How many Kg of fruit did Ruth eat?
   c. How many Kg of fruit is left?

49. Raquel walked 10 miles on Monday and $\frac{1}{6}$ more on Tuesday. How many km did she walk on Tuesday?

50. Liam's height is 186 cm. Daphne's height is $\frac{1}{12}$ less. Find Daphne's height.

51. Ben's weight is 66 kg. Lana's weight is $\frac{2}{11}$ more. Find Lana's weight.

52. Rafa drove 500 km his 3 day trip. $\frac{2}{5}$ of the trip in day 1 and $\frac{5}{12}$ in day 2.
    a. How many km did he drive in day 1?
    b. How many km did he drive in day 2?
    c. How many km did he drive in day 3?
    d. What fraction of the way was driven in day 3?

53. To <u>increase</u> an amount x by a fraction $\frac{a}{b}$ we can operate in the following ways:

    a. Find first _____ and than using addition: _____

    b. Using multiplication directly: _____

54. To <u>decrease</u> an amount x by a fraction $\frac{a}{b}$ we can operate in the following ways:

    a. Find first _____ and than using subtraction: _____

    b. Using multiplication directly: _____

DIVIDING FRACTIONS

1. How many halves fit into 1? _____ in consequence $1 \div \frac{1}{2} =$

2. How many thirds fit into 1? _____ in consequence $1 \div \frac{1}{3} =$

3. How many halves fit into 2? _____ in consequence $2 \div \frac{1}{2} =$

4. How many thirds fit into 2? _____ in consequence $2 \div \frac{1}{3} =$

5. How many quarters fit into 2? _____ in consequence $2 \div \frac{1}{4} =$

6. How many fifths fit into 4? _____ in consequence $4 \div \frac{1}{5} =$

7. How many quarters fit into half? _____ in consequence $\frac{1}{2} \div \frac{1}{4} =$

8. How many quarters fit into three halves? _____ in consequence $\frac{3}{2} \div \frac{1}{4} =$

9. How many sixths fit into two thirds? _____ in consequence $\frac{2}{3} \div \frac{1}{6} =$

10. In general $\frac{a}{b} \div \frac{c}{d} = \frac{\left(\frac{a}{b}\right)}{\left(\frac{c}{d}\right)} =$

11. $\frac{7}{9} \div \frac{2}{5} =$

12. $12 \div \frac{3}{5} =$

13. $\frac{12}{7} \div \frac{5}{6} =$

14. $\frac{2}{3} \div 7 =$

15. $\frac{11}{3} \div \frac{12}{5} =$

16. $\frac{2}{7} \div \frac{3}{8} =$

17. $11 \div \frac{3}{7} =$

18. $\frac{9}{7} \div 11 =$

19. $\frac{\left(\frac{7}{12}\right)}{\left(\frac{9}{5}\right)} =$

20. $\frac{\left(\frac{2}{11}\right)}{\left(\frac{3}{5}\right)} =$

21. $\frac{4}{\left(\frac{3}{5}\right)} =$

22. $\frac{2}{\left(\frac{2}{7}\right)} =$

23. $\frac{\left(\frac{7}{12}\right)}{2} =$

24. $\frac{\left(\frac{2}{3}\right)}{4} =$

25. $\frac{\left(\frac{a}{2}\right)}{\left(\frac{a}{3}\right)} =$

26. $\dfrac{a}{\left(\dfrac{a}{5}\right)} =$

27. $\dfrac{2}{\left(\dfrac{2}{b}\right)} =$

28. $\dfrac{\left(\dfrac{4}{a}\right)}{\left(\dfrac{5}{a}\right)} =$

29. $\dfrac{\left(\dfrac{2}{3}\right)}{2} =$

30. $\dfrac{\left(\dfrac{a}{b}\right)}{a} =$

31. $\dfrac{\left(\dfrac{2x}{5}\right)}{(4x)} =$

32. $\dfrac{(x)}{\left(\dfrac{4x}{5}\right)} =$

33. $\dfrac{\left(\dfrac{3x}{7}\right)}{\left(\dfrac{4x}{11}\right)} =$

34. $\dfrac{\left(\dfrac{x}{12}\right)}{(3x)} =$

35. $1 + \dfrac{2}{3} =$

36. $\dfrac{5}{6} + \dfrac{2}{3} =$

37. $\dfrac{2}{7} - \dfrac{1}{6} =$

38. $5 \cdot \dfrac{3}{8} - \dfrac{2}{12} =$

39. $\left(\dfrac{2}{14} - \dfrac{3}{7}\right) \cdot \dfrac{2}{9} =$

40. $\left(\dfrac{7}{2} - \dfrac{4}{3}\right) \cdot \dfrac{1}{5} =$

41. $\dfrac{5}{6} + \dfrac{2}{3} - 6 =$

42. $\dfrac{1}{a} + \dfrac{1}{a} =$

43. $\dfrac{1}{d} + d =$

44. $\dfrac{1}{a} + \dfrac{a}{1} =$

45. $\dfrac{1}{b+1} + b =$

46. $\dfrac{a}{b} + \dfrac{1}{b} =$

47. $\dfrac{a}{b} + \dfrac{d}{b} =$

48. $\dfrac{a}{c} + \dfrac{d}{b} =$

49. $\dfrac{a+b}{b} + \dfrac{d}{b} + 2 =$

50. $\dfrac{\left(\dfrac{a}{b}\right)}{b} =$

51. $\dfrac{a}{\left(\dfrac{a}{b}\right)} =$

52. $\dfrac{\left(\dfrac{b}{a}\right)}{b} =$

53. $\dfrac{\left(\dfrac{b}{a}\right)}{1} =$

54. $\dfrac{\left(\dfrac{1}{a}\right)}{b} =$

55. $\dfrac{\left(\dfrac{b}{1}\right)}{b} =$

56. $\dfrac{1}{\left(\dfrac{a}{b}\right)} =$

57. $\dfrac{\left(\dfrac{a}{b}\right)}{\left(\dfrac{a}{b}\right)} =$

58. $\dfrac{\left(\dfrac{b}{a}\right)}{\left(\dfrac{a}{b}\right)} =$

59. $\dfrac{\left(\dfrac{a}{1}\right)}{\left(\dfrac{a}{b}\right)} =$

60. $\dfrac{\left(\dfrac{a}{b}\right)}{\left(\dfrac{1}{b}\right)} =$

61. $\dfrac{\left(\dfrac{c+1}{d}\right)}{\left(\dfrac{1}{d}+d\right)} =$

62. $\dfrac{1}{d} + \dfrac{2}{d^2} + \dfrac{1}{d^3} =$

63. $\dfrac{2}{3} + \dfrac{3a}{c} - \dfrac{b}{2} =$

64. $\dfrac{\left(\dfrac{4}{b} - \dfrac{a}{7}\right)}{2} =$

65. $\dfrac{a}{c(c+1)} + \dfrac{d}{c+1} =$

66. $\dfrac{\left(2x + \dfrac{1}{x}\right)}{\left(1 + \dfrac{1}{x}\right)} =$

67. $\dfrac{12}{2a} \times \dfrac{a+1}{6} =$

68. $\dfrac{12}{2a} \div \dfrac{a}{6} =$

69. $3 \times \dfrac{4}{3} =$

70. $3 \div \dfrac{4}{3} =$

71. $12 - \dfrac{4}{3} =$

72. $a \times \dfrac{b}{3c} =$

73. $\dfrac{b}{3a} \div 3a =$

74. $\dfrac{b}{3a} \times 3a =$

75. $\dfrac{\left(\dfrac{1}{3}+\dfrac{2}{5}\right)}{\left(\dfrac{5}{3}-\dfrac{1}{3}\right)} =$

76. $\dfrac{\left(\dfrac{b}{3c}\right)}{2} =$

77. $\dfrac{\left(\dfrac{1}{2}\right)}{2\left(\dfrac{2}{3c}\right)} =$

78. $\dfrac{\left(\dfrac{1}{2}\right)}{2} =$

79. $\dfrac{\left(\dfrac{2}{7}\right)}{3} =$

80. $\dfrac{2}{\left(\dfrac{2}{7}\right)} =$

81. $\dfrac{3}{\left(\dfrac{a}{7}\right)} =$

82. $\dfrac{6}{\left(\dfrac{8}{3}\right)} =$

83. $\dfrac{\left(\dfrac{4}{3}\right)}{\left(\dfrac{3}{4}\right)} =$

84. $\dfrac{\left(\dfrac{2}{3}\right)}{\left(\dfrac{4}{5}\right)} =$

85. $\dfrac{\left(\dfrac{2}{3}\right)}{\left(\dfrac{2}{3}\right)} =$

86. $\left(\dfrac{a}{b}\right) \cdot \left(\dfrac{c}{a}\right) =$

87. $\left(\dfrac{2}{c}\right) \cdot \left(\dfrac{c}{7}\right) =$

88. $\left(\dfrac{b+1}{3}\right) \cdot \left(\dfrac{2}{b}\right) =$

89. $\left(\dfrac{z+1}{z-2}\right) \cdot \left(\dfrac{4}{z+1}\right) =$

90. $\left(\dfrac{3a+6}{5}\right) \cdot \left(\dfrac{1}{a+2}\right) =$

91. $\left(\dfrac{2c-4}{c}\right) \cdot \left(\dfrac{2c}{4c-8}\right) =$

92. $\dfrac{1}{\left(\dfrac{2}{4}\right)} \cdot \left(\dfrac{2}{3}\right) =$

93. $\dfrac{\left(\dfrac{3}{4}\right)}{\left(\dfrac{a}{2}\right)} \cdot \left(\dfrac{2}{3}\right) =$

95. $\dfrac{\left(x + \dfrac{1}{x}\right)}{\left(1 - \dfrac{1}{x}\right)} =$

94. $\dfrac{\left(\dfrac{1}{a}\right)}{\left(\dfrac{2}{a}\right)} + 2 =$

96. $\dfrac{\left(\dfrac{1}{1+x} + 1\right)}{\left(x - \dfrac{2}{x}\right)} =$

97. Juan has 40 cookies. He wants to share the cookies with his classmates. There are 25 students in hiss classroom, how should Juan split the cookies?

98. Gina has an 120 m² field. She wants to grow carrots on a third of the field, potatoes on a fifth and use the rest as a playground. How many square meters should she use in each case?

99. Lia has needs two fifths cup of sugar to bake a cake. If she has three cups of sugar how many cakes can she bake?

100. In the construction of a new road twenty five kilometers long a sign should be put every 100 m (1km = 1000m). Find the number of signs that should be put along the road. If the cost of each sign is 50$, find the total cost.

101. A quarter of a kilogram of fruit costs 2$. Find the cost of three and a half Kg of fruit.

102. A can of drink contains 400ml (1 Liter = 1000ml). Find the number of cans that can be filled with 500 liters of drink.

103. How many $\frac{2}{5}$ kg of meat are needed to feed a certain animal that needs to eat 8 kg of meat a day?

1.3. – DECIMALS AND FRACTIONS

Write the fractions as decimals:

1. $\dfrac{1}{10} =$
2. $\dfrac{1}{100} =$
3. $\dfrac{1}{1000} =$
4. $\dfrac{1}{10000} =$
5. $\dfrac{2}{10} =$
6. $\dfrac{7}{100} =$
7. $\dfrac{-29}{1000} =$
8. $\dfrac{966}{10000} =$
9. $\dfrac{75}{10} =$
10. $\dfrac{101}{100} =$
11. $\dfrac{-135}{1000} =$
12. $\dfrac{30000}{10000} =$
13. $\dfrac{1}{2} =$
14. $\dfrac{1}{5} =$
15. $\dfrac{1}{4} =$
16. $\dfrac{1}{3} =$
17. $\dfrac{1}{8} =$
18. $\dfrac{1}{9} =$
19. $\dfrac{2}{5} =$
20. $\dfrac{2}{4} =$
21. $\dfrac{3}{5} =$
22. $\dfrac{4}{5} =$
23. $\dfrac{3}{4} =$
24. $\dfrac{7}{5} =$
25. $\dfrac{5}{4} =$
26. $\dfrac{9}{5} =$
27. $\dfrac{2}{9} =$
28. $\dfrac{1}{20} =$
29. $\dfrac{3}{20} =$
30. $\dfrac{8}{5} =$
31. $\dfrac{18}{10} =$

Write the decimals as fractions:

32. $0.3 =$
33. $0.2 =$
34. $0.1 =$
35. $0.01 =$
36. $0.02 =$
37. $0.11 =$
38. $0.24 =$
39. $1.3 =$
40. $1.57 =$
41. $0.011 =$
42. $0.418 =$
43. $0.17 =$
44. $1.4 =$
45. $2.043 =$
46. $75.2 =$
47. $4.12 =$
48. $1.307 =$
49. $1.111 =$
50. $132.87 =$
51. $6.234 =$

Perform the operations <u>using fractions only</u>; give the answer as a decimal and fraction:

52. $40 \cdot 0.1 =$
53. $95 \cdot 0.01 =$
54. $46 \cdot 0.001 =$
55. $7 \cdot 0.0001 =$
56. $8345 \cdot 0.001 =$
57. $962 \cdot 0.01 =$
58. $14 \cdot 0.001 =$
59. $-6423 \cdot 0.0001 =$
60. $3117 \cdot 0.1 =$
61. $1053 \cdot 0.01 =$

62. $3500 \cdot 0.001 =$

63. $0.17 \cdot 0.0001 =$

64. $13 \cdot 1.2 =$

65. $24 \cdot 0.22 =$

66. $2.5 \cdot 1.7 =$

67. $7.1 \cdot 8.8 =$

68. $0.14 \cdot 2.01 =$

69. $87.4 \cdot 0.2 =$

70. $30.5 \cdot 0.3 =$

71. $0.211 \cdot 1.38 =$

72. $0.4 \cdot 1.23 =$

73. $1.03 \cdot 2.5 =$

74. $31.7 \cdot 0.19 =$

75. $21.1 \cdot 1.13 =$

76. $0.41 \cdot 5.56 =$

77. $3.1 \cdot 0.641 =$

78. $13.6 \cdot 8.9 =$

79. $1.08 \cdot 0.03 =$

Perform the operations <u>using fractions only</u>; give the answer as a decimal and fraction:

80. $\dfrac{1}{0.1} =$

81. $\dfrac{4}{0.01} =$

82. $\dfrac{-57}{0.001} =$

83. $\dfrac{-2.4}{0.01} =$

84. $\dfrac{7}{0.1} =$

85. $\dfrac{0.51}{0.01} =$

86. $\dfrac{-31.7}{0.001} =$

87. $\dfrac{0.024}{0.01} =$

88. $\dfrac{15}{0.01} =$

89. $\dfrac{-216}{0.01} =$

90. $\dfrac{-45.7}{0.001} =$

91. $\dfrac{-12.4}{0.01} =$

92. $\dfrac{1}{0.02} =$

93. $\dfrac{-2}{0.03} =$

94. $\dfrac{-4.7}{0.05} =$

95. $\dfrac{-1.2}{0.06} =$

96. $\dfrac{1}{0.25} =$

97. $\dfrac{-2}{0.9} =$

98. $\dfrac{-5.1}{0.2} =$

99. $\dfrac{-1.3}{0.05} =$

100. $\dfrac{1}{0.015} =$

101. $\dfrac{-12}{0.6} =$

102. $\dfrac{-14}{0.003} =$

103. $\dfrac{-0.3}{0.02} =$

104. Write down the number that is 0.2 units on the left of −1: _____

105. Write down the number that is 0.5 units on the left of −3: _____

106. Write down the number that is 0.3 units on the right of −1: _____

107. Write down the number that is 0.4 units on the right of −2: _____

108. Write down the number that is 0.8 units on the left of −9: _____

109. Write down the number that is 0.2 units on the left of 0: _____

110. Write down the number that is 0.9 units on the right of −9: _____

111. Write down the number that is 0.2 units on the right of −4: _____

112. Write down the number that is 0.21 units on the left of −1: _____

113. Write down the number that is 0.51 units on the left of −2: _____

114. Write down the number that is 0.32 units on the right of −1: _____

115. Write down the number that is 0.06 units on the right of −10: _____

116. Write down the number that is 0.11 units on the right of −1: _____

117. Write down the number that is 0.01 units on the right of −2: _____

118. Write down the number that is 0.36 units on the right of 9: _____

119. Write down the number that is 0.06 units on the right of 10: _____

120. Write down the number that is 0.17 units on the right of −9: _____

121. Write down the number that is 0.53 units on the left of −3: _____

122. Write down the number that is 0.01 units on the left of −7: _____

123. Write down the number that is 0.02 units on the right of −1: _____

124. Write down the number that is 0.002 units on the right of −10: _____

125. Write down the number that is 0.111 units on the right of −1: _____

126. Write down the number that is 0.021 units on the right of −2: _____

127. Write down the number that is 0.4 units on the right of 9: _____

128. Write down the number that is 0.04 units on the right of 10: _____

129. Write down the number that is 0.202 units on the right of −9: _____

130. Write down numbers that are very close to 2 on its left: _____ right: _____

131. Write down numbers that are very close to 1 on its left: _____ right: _____

132. Write down numbers that are very close to 0 on its left: _____ right: _____

133. Write down numbers that are very close to −1 on its left: _____ right: _____

134. Write down numbers that are very close to −7 on its left: _____ right: _____

135. Write down numbers that are very close to −12 on its left: _____ right: _____

136. Write down numbers that are very close to −2 on its left: _____ right: _____

137. Write down numbers that are very close to −10 on its left: _____ right: _____

138. Write down numbers that are very close to 9 on its left: _____ right: _____

139. Write down numbers that are very close to 100 on its left: _____ right: _____

140. Write down 2 numbers between 3 and 3.1: _____, _____. Write the same numbers as fractions: _____, _____

141. Write down 2 numbers between 6.2 and 6.3: _____, _____. Write the same numbers as fractions: _____, _____

142. Write down 2 numbers between 6.2 and 6.21: _____, _____. Write the same numbers as fractions: _____, _____

143. Write down 2 numbers between −5.2 and −5.3: _____, _____. Write the same numbers as fractions: _____, _____

144. Write down 2 numbers between 0.25 and 0.251: _____, _____. Write the same numbers as fractions: _____, _____

145. Write down 2 numbers between 1.11 and 1.111: _____, _____. Write the same numbers as fractions: _____, _____

146. Write down 2 numbers between 0.21 and 0.22: _____, _____. Write the same numbers as fractions: _____, _____

147. Write down 2 numbers between 5.99 and 5.999: _____, _____. Write the same numbers as fractions: _____, _____

148. Write down 2 numbers between 6 and 6.01: _____, _____. Write the same numbers as fractions: _____, _____

149. Write the value of each position shown on the number line:

150. Write the value of each position shown on the number line:

151. Write the value of each position shown on the number line:

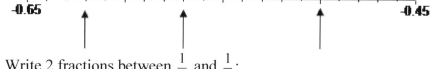

152. Write 2 fractions between $\frac{1}{2}$ and $\frac{1}{3}$: _____

153. Write 2 fractions between $-\frac{1}{10}$ and $-\frac{1}{11}$: _____

154. Write 2 fractions between $\frac{2}{7}$ and $\frac{3}{7}$: _____

155. Write 2 fractions between $-\frac{3}{22}$ and $-\frac{2}{11}$: _____

156. Write 2 fractions between $\frac{5}{3}$ and $\frac{16}{9}$: _____

1.4. – TYPES OF NUMBERS

Natural Numbers (N):   N = {__, __, __, __, __ ...}

Integers (Z):   Z = {...,__, __, __, __, __, 0, __, __, __, __, __ ...}

Rational Numbers (Q): $Q = \{\frac{a}{b}, a, b \in Z\}$

Numbers that **can** be written as _____ being both the

numerator and the denominator _____.

Examples: $\frac{1}{1}, \frac{2}{3}, \frac{-7}{3}, \frac{4}{-1}, \frac{}{}, \underline{}, \underline{} ...$

Irrational Numbers (Q'): $Q' \neq \{\frac{a}{b}, a, b \in Z\}$ Numbers that _____ be written as

fractions, being both the _____ and _____ Integers.

Examples: $\sqrt{2}, \sqrt{3}. \pi$ ...º

Real Numbers (R):   R = Q + Q' (Rationals and Irrationals)

Represented in a Venn diagram:

Fill the blanks with the corresponding letter and name

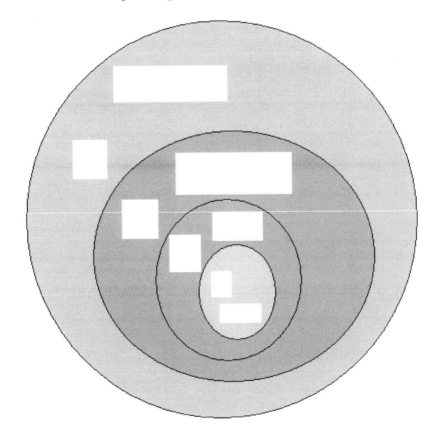

1. Natural numbers are contained in the _____ numbers.

2. Integer numbers are contained in the _____ numbers

3. Rational numbers are contained in the _____ numbers.

4. Irrational numbers are located _____.

5. Shade the area in which the irrational numbers are located:

6. True or False:

    a. Some Integers are also Natural: ____

    b. All Real numbers are Integers: ____

    c. All Rational numbers are Real: ____

    d. Some Real numbers are Rational: ____

    e. All Integer numbers are Rational: ____

    f. All Real numbers are Irrational: ____

    g. Some Irrational numbers are Real and some are not: ____

    h. Some Irrational numbers can be written as fractions using Integers: ____

    i. Some integers are negative: ____

    j. Some Irrationals are negative: ____

    k. Some Natural numbers are negative: ____

7. Write the value of the numbers with 10 decimal places (use a calculator)

    $\sqrt{2} =$ $\sqrt{3} =$

    $\sqrt{4} =$ $\sqrt{5} =$

    $\dfrac{5}{6} =$ $\dfrac{43}{27} =$

    $\dfrac{122}{90} =$ $\dfrac{158}{990} =$

    $\pi =$ $\sqrt{\pi} =$

    Write a conclusion: _____

8. Write down all the Natural numbers smaller than 3.01: _____

9. Write down all the Integer numbers between $-\dfrac{5}{2}$ and $\dfrac{3}{2}$: _____

10. Write down a Rational number between $\dfrac{1}{100}$ and $\dfrac{1}{10}$: _____

11. Write down a positive Rational number smaller than $\dfrac{1}{137}$: _____

12. Write down an Integer that is not a Natural : _____

13. Write down a Natural that is not an Integer: _____

14. Write down a Rational number that is not an Integer: _____

15. Circle the irrational numbers:

    0.56734   0.121231234…

    0.1212212221...   0.8719

    0.333…   0.226666…

    $\pi^2 =$ $\sqrt{\pi} =$

16. Estimate the following numbers with 1 decimal, follow the example:

    $\sqrt{3} \approx 1.7 \quad \sqrt{1}<\sqrt{3}<\sqrt{4} \Rightarrow 1<\sqrt{3}<2; 1.6\cdot 1.6=2.56; 1.7\cdot 1.7=2.89; 1.8\cdot 1.8=3.24 \Rightarrow 1.7<\sqrt{3}<1.8$

    $\sqrt{5} \approx$

    $\sqrt{6} \approx$

    $\sqrt{7} \approx$

    $\sqrt{8} \approx$

    $\sqrt{10} \approx$

    $\sqrt{55} \approx$

    $\sqrt{245} \approx$

17. Locate the following numbers on the number line without finding their exact value:

$$\sqrt{245}, \sqrt{45}, \sqrt[3]{100}, \sqrt{24}, \sqrt{5}, \sqrt{75}, \sqrt{62}, \pi, \pi^2$$

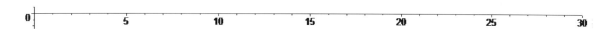

18. Locate the following numbers on the number line without finding their exact value:

$$\sqrt{\frac{1}{2}}, \sqrt{\frac{10}{3}}, \sqrt[300]{100}, \sqrt[3]{9}, \sqrt[4]{83}, \sqrt{\pi}, \sqrt{6}$$

19. Fill the table with yes or no (follow the example):

Number	Natural	Integer	Rational	Real
−3	no	yes	yes	yes
π				
−3.66776677...				
−25.56				
$\sqrt{31}$				
$-5\frac{2}{3}$				
$\sqrt[3]{8}$				

20. Fill the numbers column with appropriate numbers and yes or no.

Number	Natural	Integer	Rational	Real
	no	yes		
		no	yes	yes
	yes	yes	yes	
			no	yes
		no	yes	yes
			yes	
	no			
		yes	no	

21. If possible, convert the following numbers into the form: $\dfrac{n}{m}$

a. $0.333\ldots =$

b. $1.050050005\ldots =$

c. $2.4 =$

d. $1.1818\ldots =$

e. $-2.4545\ldots =$

f. $37.29 =$

g. $12.377377\ldots =$

h. $-30.32 =$

i. $0.325325\ldots =$

m. $1.654654\ldots =$

j. $3.12331233\ldots =$

n. $1.2131313\ldots =$

k. $7774.21 =$

o. $1.55747474\ldots =$

l. $78.253 =$

p. $5.333123123\ldots =$

22. Given the following diagram:

Write the following numbers in the appropriate location in the diagram:

a. 3.2
b. $0.1234\ldots$
c. -2
d. 13
e. $\dfrac{1}{2}$
f. 2π
g. 1
h. -7.3
i. $1.222\ldots$
j. $\dfrac{1}{\sqrt{5}}$
k. $\sqrt{2} + 1$
l. $\dfrac{8}{2}$

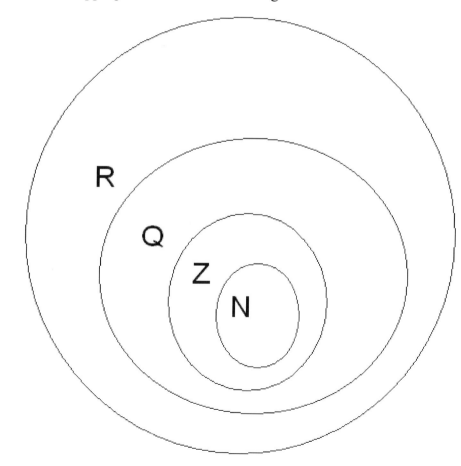

Circle the right option

23. The number –1 is:

    a. Integer and Natural.
    b. Positive
    c. Integer and Rational
    d. Natural and Real
    e. Natural and Rational
    f. None of the above

24. The number 2.0414141..... is:

    a. Integer and Natural.
    b. Natural
    c. Integer and Real
    d. Rational and Integer
    e. Rational
    f. None of the above

25. The number 5.001 is:

    a. Integer and Natural.
    b. Integer
    c. Rational and Real
    d. Integer and Real
    e. Rational and negative
    f. None of the above

26. The number $\sqrt{3}$ is:

    a. Integer and Natural.
    b. Integer
    c. Decimal
    d. Integer and Real
    e. Rational
    f. Irrational

27. The number 5555 is:

    a. Natural.
    b. Integer
    c. Real
    d. Integer and Natural
    e. Rational and Natural
    f. All of the above

1.5 – EXPONENTS AND SCIENTIFIC NOTATION

Product:

$a^0 = $ ___ $a^1 = $ ___ $a^2 = $ ___ × ___
$a^3 = $ ___ × ___ × ___
$a^3 a^2 = $ _____ = ___

$$a^m a^n = \underline{\hspace{2cm}}$$

Division:

$\dfrac{a^5}{a^3} = \dfrac{\underline{\hspace{2cm}}}{\underline{\hspace{1cm}}} = \dfrac{\underline{\hspace{1cm}}}{} = $ ___

$\dfrac{a^2}{a^5} = \dfrac{\underline{\hspace{2cm}}}{\underline{\hspace{1cm}}} = \dfrac{\underline{\hspace{1cm}}}{} = $ ___

$$\dfrac{a^m}{a^n} = \underline{\hspace{1cm}}$$

Power:

$(a^2)^3 = $ _____ = ___

$\left(\dfrac{a^2}{b}\right)^3 = \dfrac{\underline{\hspace{2cm}}}{\underline{\hspace{1cm}}} = \dfrac{\underline{\hspace{1cm}}}{}$

$$(a^m)^n = \underline{\hspace{1cm}}$$

$$\left(\dfrac{a^m}{b^k}\right)^n = \dfrac{\underline{\hspace{2cm}}}{\underline{\hspace{1cm}}}$$

Radicals:

$(a^3)^{\frac{1}{2}} = $ ___ = ___

$(a^4)^{\frac{1}{7}} = $ ___ = ___

$$(a^m)^{\frac{1}{n}} = \underline{\hspace{1cm}} = \underline{\hspace{1cm}}$$

Exercises

Write in all possible forms and evaluate without using a calculator (follow example):

1. $4^{-1} = \dfrac{1}{4} = 0.25$
2. $10^0 = $
3. $10^1 = $
4. $10^3 = $
5. $10^{-1} = $
6. $10^{-2} = $
7. $10^{-3} = $
8. $10^{-4} = $
9. $2^0 = $
10. $2^1 = $
11. $2^{-1} = $
12. $2^{-2} = $
13. $2^{-3} = $
14. $2^{-4} = $
15. $(-1)^0 = $
16. $-1^0 = $
17. $(-1)^1 = $
18. $-1^1 = $
19. $(-1)^{-1} = $
20. $-1^2 = $

21. $(-1)^2 =$

22. $-1^2 =$

23. $(-1)^{-2} =$

24. $-1^{-2} =$

25. $(-3)^0 =$

26. $(-3)^1 =$

27. $-3^1 =$

28. $(-3)^2 =$

29. $-3^2 =$

30. $(-3)^{-1} =$

31. $-3^{-1} =$

32. $(-3)^{-2} =$

33. $-3^{-2} =$

34. $9^{\frac{1}{2}} =$

35. $4^{\frac{1}{2}} =$

36. $16^{-\frac{1}{2}} =$

37. $8^{\frac{2}{3}} =$

38. $27^{-\frac{4}{3}} =$

39. $125^{-\frac{1}{3}} =$

40. $16^{\frac{3}{4}} =$

41. $(2^{-1})^2 =$

42. $(-8^{-3})^{\frac{2}{3}} =$

43. $(-27^{-1})^{\frac{2}{3}} =$

44. $(16^{-1})^{-\frac{3}{2}} =$

45. $\left(\frac{1}{2}\right)^0 =$

46. $\left(\frac{1}{2}\right)^1 =$

47. $\left(\frac{1}{2}\right)^{-1} =$

48. $\left(\frac{1}{2}\right)^2 =$

49. $\left(-\frac{1}{2}\right)^{-\frac{5}{3}} =$

50. $\left(-\frac{2}{3}\right)^{-2} =$

51. $\left(\frac{2}{5}\right)^1 =$

52. $\left(\frac{100}{9}\right)^{-\frac{3}{2}} =$

53. $\left(\frac{6}{7}\right)^2 =$

54. $\left(\frac{a}{b}\right)^{-1} =$

55. $\left(\frac{1}{b}\right)^{-1} =$

56. $b^{-1} =$

57. $\left(\frac{-7}{2}\right)^{-2} =$

58. $\left(\frac{3}{-2}\right)^1 =$

59. $\left(\frac{-1}{\sqrt{2}}\right)^{-2} =$

60. $\left(\frac{5\sqrt{6}}{2}\right)^2 =$

61. $\left(\frac{-\sqrt{3}}{2}\right)^{-2} =$

62. $\left(\frac{1+3\sqrt{2}}{-2}\right)^2 =$

63. $\left(\dfrac{-5}{3-\sqrt{2}}\right)^{-2} =$

64. $\left(\dfrac{3+\sqrt{3}}{3}\right)^{2} =$

65. $\left(\dfrac{-2-\sqrt{5}}{2+\sqrt{2}}\right)^{-2} =$

66. $\left(\dfrac{-27}{8}\right)^{\frac{2}{3}} =$

67. $\left(\dfrac{16}{9}\right)^{\frac{3}{4}} =$

68. $\left(\dfrac{1}{2}\right)^{\frac{3}{2}} =$

69. $\left(\dfrac{9}{16}\right)^{\frac{1}{2}} =$

70. $\left(\dfrac{8}{27}\right)^{-\frac{1}{3}} =$

71. $a^{-2} =$

72. $a^{-\frac{1}{2}} =$

73. $a^{-\frac{2}{7}} =$

74. $5^2 5^{-11} =$

75. $4^{34} \cdot 2^{-70} =$

76. $9^{-3} \cdot 3^{-9} =$

77. $a^b a^{-b} =$

78. $(-125)^{\frac{2}{3}} =$

79. $\dfrac{5^7}{5^4} =$

80. $\dfrac{3^8}{9^2} 3^{-2} =$

81. $\dfrac{3^1 \, 3^{-\frac{1}{2}}}{9^{\frac{1}{4}}} =$

82. $\dfrac{\sqrt{2}\cdot 8^2}{2^{\frac{3}{4}}} 2^{-\frac{1}{2}} =$

83. $\dfrac{a^{-1}}{a^{-2}} =$

84. $\sqrt{\dfrac{a^{-8}}{a^{-10}}} =$

85. $\sqrt{\sqrt{a}} =$

86. $a\sqrt{a} =$

87. $\sqrt{\sqrt[3]{a}} =$

88. $\dfrac{1}{\sqrt[4]{\sqrt{\sqrt{a}}}} =$

89. $\sqrt{\sqrt{\sqrt[7]{a^2}}} =$

90. $\sqrt{a\sqrt{a^2}} =$

91. $\dfrac{2\sqrt{a}}{\sqrt{2a}} =$

92. $\dfrac{\sqrt{a}}{\sqrt[3]{a}} =$

93. $\dfrac{a\sqrt{a}}{\sqrt[5]{a}} =$

94. $\dfrac{\sqrt{8}\sqrt{a}}{\sqrt{2}\cdot a} =$

95. $\sqrt{\dfrac{\sqrt{a}a^{-1}}{a\sqrt{a^{-2}}}} =$

96. $\dfrac{a}{\sqrt{2a^{-1}}} =$

97. $\dfrac{\sqrt{\dfrac{1}{a}}}{\sqrt{aa^{-2}}} =$

98. $\left(\dfrac{2}{5}\right)^3 \times \left(\dfrac{5}{3}\right)^4 =$

99. $\left(\dfrac{4}{7}\right)^2 \div \left(\dfrac{9}{7}\right) =$

100. $\sqrt{\left(\dfrac{7}{5}\right)^6 \div \left(\dfrac{49}{125}\right)^3} =$

101. $\left(\dfrac{2}{5}\right)^3 \cdot \left(\dfrac{3}{5}\right)^{-2} =$

102. $\left(\dfrac{4^2}{5^{-1}}\right)^2 \cdot \left(\dfrac{25^{-1}}{64}\right)^2 =$

103. $\left(\dfrac{3^{-5}}{4^2}\right)^2 \div \left(\dfrac{9^{-1}}{2^3}\right)^3 =$

104. $\left(\dfrac{3}{4}\right)^5 \div \left(\dfrac{9}{64}\right)^2 =$

105. $\sqrt[3]{\left(\dfrac{3}{4}\right)^5 \div \left(\dfrac{9}{64}\right)^2} =$

106. $\left(\dfrac{2^{-3}}{3^{-2}}\right)^3 \cdot \left(\dfrac{4}{27}\right)^2 =$

107. $2^{-1} + 1 =$

108. $3^{-1} - 3^{-2} =$

109. $5^{-1} - 5^{-2} =$

110. $3^{-2} + 2^{-2} =$

111. $3^{-1} + 4^{-2} =$

112. $7^{-1} + 2^{-2} =$

113. $8^{-2} - 3^{-1} =$

114. $7^{-2} - 2^{-3} =$

115. $a^{-1} + a^{-1} =$

116. $ba^{-1} + a^{-1} =$

117. $2x^{-1} + x^{-2} =$

118. $a^{-1} - ba^{-1} =$

119. $(ba)^{-1} + a^{-1} =$

120. $\dfrac{1}{x} + x^{-2} =$

Write in Standard notation:

1. $7 \cdot 10^2 =$ _____
2. $6.3 \cdot 10^{-2} =$ _____
3. $2 \cdot 10^{-1} =$ _____
4. $3 \cdot 10^3 =$ _____
5. $12 \cdot 10^{-3} =$ _____
6. $156 \cdot 10^4 =$ _____
7. $91.43 \cdot 10^7 =$ _____
8. $78.0101 \cdot 10^{-5} =$ _____
9. $78818.112 \cdot 10^5 =$ _____
10. $782 \cdot 10^{-9} =$ _____

Write in scientific notation:

11. $0.135 =$ _____
12. $0.071 =$ _____
13. $0.0000001 =$ _____
14. $91.2 =$ _____
15. $12.02 =$ _____
16. $10000 =$ _____
17. $0.0000114 =$ _____
18. $0.006023 =$ _____
19. $0.0155 =$ _____
20. $0.000204 =$ _____
21. $101000 =$ _____
22. $11.01 =$ _____
23. $2022 =$ _____
24. $251 =$ _____
25. $101.102 =$ _____
26. $9.200 =$ _____
27. $230.80 =$ _____
28. $209.1 =$ _____
29. $24.18 =$ _____
30. $5500 =$ _____
31. $65000 =$ _____
32. $0.00545 =$ _____
33. $0.000015 =$ _____
34. $0.0505 =$ _____
35. $0.005045 =$ _____

Calculate

36. $5 \cdot 10^7 \cdot 7 \cdot 10^3 =$
37. $6 \cdot 10^{-7} \cdot 12 \cdot 10^3 =$
38. $\dfrac{10 \cdot 10^{-3}}{5 \cdot 10^{-6}} =$
39. $15 \cdot 10^{-6} \cdot 2 \cdot 10^{-3} =$
40. $1.5 \cdot 10^{-16} \cdot 20 \cdot 10^{13} =$
41. $5 \cdot 10^{-12} - 8 \cdot 10^{-12} =$
42. $\dfrac{6 \cdot 10^{-7}}{12 \cdot 10^3} =$
43. $12 \cdot 10^{-10} + 18 \cdot 10^{-10} =$
44. $2 \cdot 10^{-19} - 80 \cdot 10^{-20} =$

45. $7.1 \cdot 10^{-7} - 20 \cdot 10^{-9} =$

46. $12 \cdot 10^{13} \cdot 2.5 \cdot 10^{13} =$

47. $15 \cdot 10^{-6} \cdot 21 \cdot 10^{6} =$

48. $\dfrac{120 \cdot 10^{-22}}{1.1 \cdot 10^{-19}} =$

49. In a chemical experiment there are 30 million reactions. In a later experiment there are 6 million reactions. Find, using scientific notation how many more reactions take place in the first experiment.

50. The number of US citizens is approximately 300 million. The number of Chinese citizens is approximately 5 times bigger.

   a. Write the number of US and Chinese citizens in scientific notation.
   b. How many citizens in both countries together.

51. The number of molecules in 1 gram of water is approximately $1.08 \cdot 10^{25}$. Find the number of molecules in 1 litre of water.

52. The speed of light is approximately 300 million meters per second. The speed of sound is approximately 300 meters per second.

   a. Write the speed of light and sound in scientific notation.
   b. By what factor is the speed of light faster than the speed of sound?
   c. The sun is 150 million km away from earth, how long does it take the light to travel from the earth to the sun. Write your answer in scientific notation.
   d. What distance can sound reach in one minute? Write your answer in scientific notation.

1.6. – ROOTS AND RATIONALIZATION

Simplify as much as possible:

1. $\sqrt{0} =$

2. $\sqrt{1} =$

3. $\sqrt{4} =$

4. $\sqrt[3]{8} =$

5. $\sqrt{16} \cdot \sqrt{25} =$

6. $\sqrt[4]{2} \cdot \sqrt[4]{8} =$

7. $\sqrt{-1} =$

8. $\left(\sqrt{4}\right)^2 =$

9. $\left(\sqrt{-6}\right)^2 =$

10. $\left(-\sqrt{5}\right)^2 \cdot \left(\sqrt[3]{3}\right)^3 =$

11. $\left(\sqrt{532}\right)^2 =$

12. $\left(\sqrt{a}\right)^2 \left(\sqrt[n]{a}\right)^n =$

13. $\sqrt{\dfrac{a^2}{9}} =$

14. $\sqrt{\dfrac{8}{200}} =$

15. $\sqrt{3} + \sqrt{3} =$

16. $\sqrt{2} + \sqrt{2} + \sqrt{2} =$

Write as fractions and find the root:

17. $\sqrt{0.01} =$

18. $\sqrt{0.25} =$

19. $\sqrt{2.25} =$

20. $\sqrt{0.16} =$

21. $\sqrt{0.36} =$

22. $\sqrt{0.0081} =$

23. $\sqrt{6.25} =$

24. $\sqrt{20.25} =$

Simplify:

25. $\sqrt{2} + \sqrt{8} + \sqrt{2} =$

26. $\sqrt{4} + \sqrt{2} + \sqrt{8} =$

27. $\sqrt{9} + \sqrt{12} + \sqrt{27} =$

28. $\sqrt{50} + \sqrt{75} + \sqrt{12} =$

29. $\sqrt[3]{16} + \sqrt[3]{54} =$

30. $\sqrt[4]{32} - \sqrt[4]{162} =$

31. $\sqrt{27} + \sqrt{81} + \sqrt{48} =$

32. $\sqrt{200} + \sqrt{50} - \sqrt{18} =$

33. $\sqrt{20} + \sqrt{80} - \sqrt{125} =$

34. $\sqrt{10}\sqrt{10} =$

35. $\sqrt[3]{a} \cdot \sqrt[3]{a} \cdot \sqrt[3]{a} =$

36. $\sqrt{3}\sqrt{9}\sqrt{3} =$

37. $\dfrac{\sqrt{50}}{\sqrt{2}} =$

38. $\dfrac{\sqrt{72}}{\sqrt{2}} =$

39. $\sqrt{15}\,\dfrac{\sqrt{75}}{\sqrt{5}} =$

40. $\sqrt{3}\,\dfrac{\sqrt{24}}{\sqrt{2}} =$

41. $\sqrt{x}\sqrt{x} =$

42. $\sqrt{x} + \sqrt{x} =$

Rationalize the denominator:

43. $\dfrac{1}{\sqrt{23}} =$

44. $\dfrac{3}{\sqrt{2}+1} =$

45. $\dfrac{-7}{\sqrt{3}-2} =$

46. $\dfrac{\sqrt{2}+3}{-5} =$

47. $\dfrac{\sqrt{2}+3}{\sqrt{5}-5} =$

48. $\dfrac{\sqrt{2}}{\sqrt{6}+\sqrt{7}} =$

49. $\dfrac{\sqrt{2}-1}{2\sqrt{6}-\sqrt{3}} =$

50. $\dfrac{-1}{2\sqrt{a}+b} =$

51. $\dfrac{3\sqrt{a}-b}{2\sqrt{a}+\sqrt{b}} =$

Rationalize the numerator:

52. $\dfrac{\sqrt{16}}{\sqrt{5}} =$

53. $\dfrac{3-\sqrt{5}}{\sqrt{5}+1} =$

54. $\dfrac{-7}{\sqrt{5}-2} =$

55. $\dfrac{\sqrt{2}+3}{\sqrt{6}-5} =$

56. $\dfrac{\sqrt{2}}{\sqrt{2x}+\sqrt{3}} =$

57. $\dfrac{\sqrt{b}-a}{\sqrt{a}-\sqrt{3}} =$

58. $\dfrac{-3\sqrt{7}+4}{2\sqrt{5}+7} =$

59. $\dfrac{\sqrt{a}-2\sqrt{b}}{2\sqrt{a}+\sqrt{b}} =$

1.7. – PERCENTAGES

1. A percentage is a way to represent _____ we sometimes use _____ or _____ for that purpose.

2. Write as a fraction and as a decimal:

   a. 1% = _____
   b. 10% = _____
   c. 79% = _____
   d. 100% = _____
   e. 101% = _____
   f. 110% = _____
   g. 200% = _____

   h. 0.1% = _____
   i. 0.14% = _____
   j. 0.06% = _____
   k. 0.072% = _____
   l. 1.02% = _____
   m. 7.056% = _____
   n. 5356% = _____

A PERCENTAGE OF AN AMOUNT (same as a fraction of an amount)

3. Find (write the expression and simplify it to get a final answer):

   a. 1% of 800 = _____
   b. 2% of 800 = _____
   c. 3% of 800 = _____
   d. 10% of 800 = _____
   e. 15% of 800 = _____
   f. 20% of 800 = _____
   g. 25% of 800 = _____
   h. 35% of 800 = _____

   i. 100% of 600 = _____
   j. 101% of 600 = _____
   k. 110% of 600 = _____
   l. 120% of 600 = _____
   m. 125% of 600 = _____
   n. 140% of 600 = _____
   o. 200% of 600 = _____
   p. 300% of 600 = _____

4. Find (write the expression and simplify it to get a final answer):

   a. 1% of 60 = _____
   b. 2% of 60 = _____
   c. 10% of 110 = _____
   d. 15% of 7 = _____

   e. 20% of 130 = _____
   f. 25% of 450 = _____
   g. 35% of 3100 = _____
   h. 100% of 1356 = _____

i. 101% of 530 = _____   m. 140% of 910 = _____

j. 110% of 160 = _____   n. 200% of 2400 = _____

k. 120% of 122 = _____   o. 300% of 110 = _____

l. 125% of 250 = _____   p. A% of M = _____

5. Johann scored 170 out 200 in a test, find his score in percentage?

6. Given that in a group of 20 students, 2 are taller than 188cm. Write down the percentage of student shorter than 188cm _____

7. Nina scored 75 out 80 in a test, find her score in percentage?

8. Given a square with side x. Inside it a smaller square is drawn with side length of 80% of x. Find the percentage of the area that is shaded and not shaded.

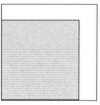

9. In a certain box of cookies there are 90 cookies of 3 colours: white, brown and black. 20% of the cookies are white, 15 cookies are brown and the rest are black.

    a. Find the percentage of brown and black cookies in the box and the number of cookies of each type.

    b. Dani ate 2 cookies of each colour; find the new percentages of each kind.

10. Jeff bought a car for 5000$ and sold it for 5750$, Find his benefit in percent.

11. Jessica bought a car for 3400$ and sold it for 3000$, Find her lost in percent.

12. Given the rectangle, write down the percentage of it that is shaded : _____

    Write the percentage as a fraction and decimal: _____

13. Given the following square. Write down the percentage of it that is

    shaded: _____, Write the percentage as a fraction and decimal: _____

14. It is known that the area shaded is 20% of 70% of the circle. Find the percentage of the circle that is shaded and not shaded. Write your answer as a fraction, decimal and percentage.

    Shaded: _____   Not Shaded: _____

15. It is known that 10% of 75% of a population of 5000 students usually do sports. How many students usually do sports?

16. It is known that 5% of 40% of a certain amount is 30 euros, find the amount.

17. It is known that 60% of 30% of a certain amount is 10 euros, find the amount.

18. Find 10% of 20% of 30% of 500: _____

19. Find 10% of 30% of 30% of 200: _____

20. Find 70% of 130% of 4000: _____

55

21. Find 90% of 130% of 70% 600: _____

22. It is known that 30% of 30% of a certain amount is 63 euros, find the amount.

23. It is known that 10% of 30% of 5% of a certain amount is 45 euros, find the amount.

INCREASE OR DECREASE BY A PERCENTAGE

24. The price of a Car is A $. In case the price increases by:

    a. In case the price increases by 1%, state the new price in terms of A _____
    b. In case the price increases by 2%, state the new price in terms of A _____
    c. In case the price increases by 3%, state the new price in terms of A _____
    d. In case the price increases by 5%, state the new price in terms of A _____
    e. In case the price increases by 8%, state the new price in terms of A _____
    f. In case the price increases by 10%, state the new price in terms of A _____
    g. In case the price increases by 18%, state the new price in terms of A _____
    h. In case the price increases by 30%, state the new price in terms of A _____
    i. In case the price increases by 50%, state the new price in terms of A _____
    j. In case the price increases by 58%, state the new price in terms of A _____
    k. In case the price increases by 90%, state the new price in terms of A _____
    l. In case the price increases by 100%, state the new price in terms of A _____
    m. In case the price increases by 101%, state the new price in terms of A _____
    n. In case the price increases by 108%, state the new price in terms of A _____
    o. In case the price increases by 110%, state the new price in terms of A _____
    p. In case the price increases by 200%, state the new price in terms of A _____
    q. In case the price increases by 228%, state the new price in terms of A _____
    r. In case the price increases by 300%, state the new price in terms of A _____

25. The price of a Stock is A $.

   a. In case the price decreases by 1%, state the new price in terms of A _____

   b. In case the price decreases by 2%, state the new price in terms of A _____

   c. In case the price decreases by 3%, state the new price in terms of A _____

   d. In case the price decreases by 5%, state the new price in terms of A _____

   e. In case the price decreases by 8%, state the new price in terms of A _____

   f. In case the price decreases by 10%, state the new price in terms of A _____

   g. In case the price decreases by 18%, state the new price in terms of A _____

   h. In case the price decreases by 30%, state the new price in terms of A _____

   i. In case the price decreases by 50%, state the new price in terms of A _____

   j. In case the price decreases by 58%, state the new price in terms of A _____

   k. In case the price decreases by 90%, state the new price in terms of A _____

   l. In case the price decreases by 100%, state the new price in terms of A _____

   m. In case the price decreases by 101%, state the new price in terms of A _____

   n. In case the price decreases by 110%, state the new price in terms of A _____

26.
   a. To increase an amount by 10% we multiply it by _____

   b. To increase an amount by 25% we multiply it by _____

   c. To increase an amount by 7.2% we multiply it by _____

   d. To decrease an amount by 12% we multiply it by _____

   e. To decrease an amount by 35% we multiply it by _____

   f. To decrease an amount by 5.1% we multiply it by _____

   g. To decrease an amount by 100% we multiply it by _____

   h. To increase an amount by 100% we multiply it by _____

   i. To increase an amount by 200% we multiply it by _____

   j. To increase an amount by M% we multiply it by _____

   k. To decrease an amount by S% we multiply it by _____

27. The price of a shirt is 50 $. In case the price increases by 14% find the new price.

28. The price of a toy is 40 $. In case the price decreases by 8% find the new price.

29. Danni's height was 150 cm. His height increases by 16%, find his height.

30. George can kick a football 60m. His young brother can kick the ball 18% less. How far can his brother kick the ball?

31. The price of a product was 38 euros after a 5% discount was applied to it, find the price before discount.

32. The price of a TV after it increased by 15% was 437$ find the price before the increase.

33. 2 years old Xavier height is 100 cm, it increased by 10% in one year and 5% more in the next year. Find his height.

34. The price of a bike after a 4% discount was 120$ find the price before discount.

35. The price of a shirt is B $. In case the price increases by 10% and then decreases by 10%, state the new price in terms of B _____ and the overall change in the price (as a percentage).

36. The price of a shirt is C $. In case the price increases by 20% and then decreases by 30%, state the new price in terms of C _____ and the overall change in the price (as a percentage).

37. The price of a shirt is D $. In case the price decreases by 20% and then decreases by 60%, state the new price in terms of D _____ and the overall change in the price (as a percentage).

38. The price of a shirt is E $. In case the price increases by 70% and then increases by 60%, state the new price in terms of E _____ and the overall change in the price (as a percentage).

39. The price of a shirt is E $. In case the price increases every month by 3%, write the expression for the price after 48 months: _____

40. The price of a shirt is M$. In case the price decreases every month by 11%, write the expression for the price after 12 months: _____

41. The price of a shirt is M$. In case the price decreases every month by 7.2%, write the expression for the price after 16 months: _____

42. The price of a shirt is M$. The price increases by x% every month. State its price in terms of M and x after n months: _____

BIGGER OR SMALLER BY A PERCENTAGE

43. Find the percentage by which:

    a. 5 is bigger than 4: _____

    b. 4 is smaller than 5: _____

    c. 11 is bigger than 10: _____

    d. 10 is smaller than 11: _____

    e. 51 is bigger than 50 : _____

    f. 40 is smaller than 45: _____

    g. 2 is bigger than 1 : _____

    h. 1 is smaller than 2: _____

    i. 3 is bigger than 1 : _____

    j. 1 is smaller than 3: _____

    k. 10 is bigger than 1 : _____

    l. 1 is smaller than 10: _____

    m. 1000 is bigger than 200 : _____

    n. 200 is smaller than 1000: _____

    o. A is bigger than B: _____

    p. x is smaller than y: _____

44. Alexandra runs 12km a week. David Runs 6km a week. By what percentage does Alexandra run more than David? By what percentage does David run less than Alexandra?

45. Yael dedicates 90 minutes to do her HW every day. Alex dedicates 80 minutes to do his HW every day. By what percentage does Yael dedicate more time than Alex? By what percentage does Alex dedicate less time than Yael?

46. Ricardo drives to work 40% less than Rhona. Rhona drives to work 10% more than Alex who drives 500 km per week.

   a. How many km does Rhona drive to work per week?

   b. How many km does Ricardo drive to work per week?

   c. By what percentage does Ricardo drive more or less than Alex?

47. Michael spends 1 hour every day in the Gym. Toni Spends 2 and half hours every day in the Gym. By what percentage does Toni dedicate more time than Michael? By what percentage does Michael dedicate less time than Toni?

1.8. – EVALUATING EXPRESSIONS

Evaluate the expression given the value of x:

1. $x = 2$, $x^2 + x =$

2. $x = -4$, $x^2 + x =$

3. $x = -2$, $5x^2 + 3x =$

4. $x = -4$, $x^{-1} =$

5. $x = -2$, $x^3 =$

6. $x = -3$, $x^{-3} =$

7. $x = -9$, $2x^{-2} =$

8. $x = 4$, $x^{-2} + x =$

9. $x = -4$, $2x^2 + \dfrac{x}{2} =$

10. $x = -2$, $\dfrac{1}{x} + \dfrac{x}{2} =$

11. $x = 4$, $\dfrac{1}{x-3} + \dfrac{x}{2} =$

12. $x = 8$, $\dfrac{8}{x-4} + \dfrac{x-2}{2} =$

13. $x = -1$, $7x^{-3} + 2x^{-1} + 1 =$

14. $x = 3$, $x^{-2} + x + x^2 =$

15. $x = 2$, $x^{-3} + x^{-2} + x^{-1} + x^0 =$

16. $x = 2$, $2x^{-2} \cdot x^{-1} =$

17. $x = -1$, $x^{-200} - 2x^{501} =$

18. $x = -5$, $5x^{-2} - x^2 =$

19. $x = -2$, $2^x =$

20. $x = -2$, $3^x =$

21. $x = -2$, $2^{2x+1} =$

22. $x = -1$, $2^{3x-1} =$

23. $x = 2$, $2^{\frac{3}{x}} =$

24. $x = -\dfrac{1}{2}$, $4^x =$

25. $x = -\dfrac{2}{3}$, $8^x =$

26. $x = -\dfrac{2}{3}$, $27^{-x} =$

1.09. – EXPANDING AND FACTORING

Expand:

1. $(x+1)^2 =$
2. $(x-1)^2 =$
3. $(x+2)^2 =$
4. $(x-2)^2 =$
5. $(a+b)^2 =$
6. $(a-b)^2 =$
7. $(2a+b)^2 =$
8. $(a-3b)^2 =$
9. $(2x+3)^2 =$
10. $(4-2x)^2 =$
11. $(x+2)(x-3) =$
12. $(x-2)(x+2) =$
13. $(3+x)(x-7) =$
14. $(x+3)(x-3) =$
15. $(2x+2)(x-5) =$
16. $(2x+4)(2x-4) =$
17. $(3x-1)(x+2) =$
18. $(x+4)(x^2-4x+3) =$
19. $(5x+6)(5x-6) =$
20. $(x+6)(x^5-6x^2-3x+1) =$
21. $(x-a+2)(x+2a+b) =$

22. $(\sqrt{a}-\sqrt{b})(\sqrt{a}+\sqrt{b}) =$
23. $(2x-3c)(2x+3c-1) =$
24. $x(x+8)^2 =$
25. $(x-6)^2 \cdot 3x =$
26. $2-(x+1)^2 =$
27. $(x+3)^2 - (x+2)^2 =$
28. $(x-2)^2 + (x+2)^2 =$
29. $(x-\sqrt{2})^2 =$
30. $(x-\sqrt{2})(x+\sqrt{2}) =$
31. $5(x-\sqrt{a})(x+\sqrt{a}) =$
32. $(\sqrt{a}-\sqrt{b})^2 =$
33. $2(x-\sqrt{10})(x+\sqrt{10}) =$
34. $(x-\dfrac{2}{x})^2 =$
35. $(x-\dfrac{2}{\sqrt{x}})^2 =$
36. $(3x-\dfrac{2}{3\sqrt{x}})^2 =$
37. $2(\sqrt{a}-\dfrac{1}{\sqrt{a}})^2 =$
38. $(\sqrt{a}-\dfrac{1}{\sqrt{a}})(-\sqrt{a}-\dfrac{1}{\sqrt{a}}) =$
39. $(x^2-y^2)^2 =$

40. $(2x^3 - 3y^4)^2 =$

41. $(2^x + 2^{-x})^2 =$

42. $(4^{2x} + 2^{-x})^2 =$

43. $(3^{2x} + 3^{-2x})^2 =$

44. $(7^x - 7)^2 =$

45. $(a^{nx} - b^{nx})^2 =$

46. $(x^2 - y^2)(x^2 + y^2) =$

47. $(x^3 - y^3)(x^3 + y^3) =$

48. $(x^n - y^n)(x^n + y^n) =$

49. $(a^x - b^x)^2 =$

50. $(a^{mx} - a^{-mx})^2 =$

51. $(a^{mx} - a^{-mx})(a^{mx} + a^{-mx}) =$

Given the following polynomials, obtain the maximum possible common factor:

1. $x - ax =$
2. $3x - x - ax =$
3. $-x + ax =$
4. $xy + 2x =$
5. $8xy - 2y =$
6. $-6x + 12xy =$
7. $12xyz + 2xy =$
8. $14xy - 2yz =$
9. $12xz + 14xyz =$
10. $xy + 4y^2 + 5y =$
11. $z - 4z^2 + 8zy =$
12. $-8x^3 - 4xyz =$
13. $-6x^4 + x^2y^2 + x^2 =$
14. $-9x^7y^3 + 3x^3y =$
15. $-90x^{10}y^5 - 3x^3y^4 =$
16. $-80x^4y^6z^8 + 8x^{12}y^4z^6 =$
17. $xyz + 2x^2y^2z^2 + 3x^3y^3z^3 =$
18. $10x^3y^2z^4 + 2x^2y^6z^4 - 5x^2y^4z^2 =$
19. $20x^{30}y^{20}z^{40} - 2x^{20}y^{60}z^{40} - 2x^{20}y^{40}z^{20} =$
20. $ax^m + x^m =$
21. $ax^{m+1} + x^m =$
22. $ax^m + x^{m-1} =$
23. $ax^m - x =$
24. $-ax^m - x^{2m} =$
25. $z^{n+1} - z^{n+2} =$
26. $ax^{m+2} + x^{m-1} =$

Given the following polynomials factor, if possible.

1. $x^2 - 6x + 9 =$
2. $x^2 - 5x + 6 =$
3. $x^2 + 4x + 10 =$
4. $-x^2 - x + 6 =$
5. $x^2 + x - 6 =$
6. $x^2 + 5x + 6 =$
7. $-x^2 + 7x - 10 =$
8. $x^2 - 6x + 12 =$
9. $x^2 + 3x + 2 =$
10. $x^2 - x - 2 =$

11. $-x^2 + 4x =$

12. $-x^2 + 4x - 10 =$

13. $x^2 + x - 2 =$

14. $x^2 + 3x + 7 =$

15. $x^2 - 3x + 2 =$

16. $x^2 - x + 7 =$

17. $x^2 + 5x + 9 =$

18. $-x^2 - 5x + 6 =$

19. $x^2 - 2xa + a^2 =$

20. $x^2 - a^2 =$

21. $c^2 - a^2 =$

22. $x^2 - x =$

23. $2x^2 - x =$

24. $2x^2 + 3x =$

25. $x^2 + 5x =$

26. $x^2 - 7x + 12 =$

27. $2x^2 - 4x =$

28. $x^2 - 7x + 10 =$

29. $x^2 - 7x + 6 =$

30. $x^2 - x - 12 =$

31. $x^2 + x - 12 =$

32. $x^2 - 3x - 10 =$

33. $x^2 - 8x - 9 =$

34. $x^2 - 1 =$

35. $x^2 + 1 =$

36. $x^2 - 2 =$

37. $x^2 - 3 =$

38. $x^2 - 4 =$

39. $-x^2 + 1 =$

40. $-x^2 + 2 =$

41. $-x^2 + 3 =$

42. $-x^2 + 4 =$

43. $-x^2 + 13 =$

44. $-x^2 + 49 =$

45. $2x^2 - 72 =$

46. $-x^2 - 2 =$

47. $5x^2 - 125 =$

48. $-x^2 + 81 =$

49. $-3x^2 + 27 =$

50. $2x^2 - 6 =$

51. $3x^2 - 1 =$

52. $-2x^2 - 3 =$

53. $5x^2 - 6 =$

54. $4x^2 - 2 =$

55. $-8x^2 - 1 =$

56. $x^2 - b =$

57. $ax^2 - b =$

58. $-ax^2 + b =$

59. $2x^2 - 4x + 2 =$

60. $3x^2 - 3x - 18 =$

61. $-4x^2 + 20x + 24 =$

62. $7x^2 + 7x - 630 =$

63. $-5x^2 + 10x + 75 =$

64. $3x^2 - 12x - 63 =$

65. $2x^2 + 2x - 112 =$

66. $2x^2 - 12x - 14 =$

67. $-5x^2 + 15x + 90 =$

68. $-3x^2 - 12x - 12 =$

69. $-2x^2 - 26x - 84 =$

70. $6x^2 + 48x + 72 =$

Factor and simplify:

1. $\dfrac{x^2-6x+9}{x^2-7x+12} =$

2. $\dfrac{x^2-5x+6}{x^2+x-6} =$

3. $\dfrac{x^2-9}{x^2-7x+12} =$

4. $\dfrac{x^2-1}{x^2-2x+1} =$

5. $\dfrac{x^2-6x+8}{x^2-4x+4} =$

6. $\dfrac{x^2-16}{x^2+5x+4} =$

7. $\dfrac{x^2-x-2}{x^2+6x+5} =$

8. $\dfrac{3x+9}{x^2-9} =$

9. $\dfrac{x^2-6x}{x^2-7x+6} =$

10. $\dfrac{x^2-x}{x^2+x-2} =$

11. $\dfrac{x^2-4}{x^2+x-2} =$

12. $\dfrac{4-x}{x-4} =$

13. $\dfrac{x^2-x}{1-x} =$

14. $\dfrac{2x-1}{4x^2-4x+1} =$

15. $\dfrac{x^2-2x}{x^2-4} =$

16. $\dfrac{4x^2+4x+1}{2x^2+5x+2} =$

17. $\dfrac{3x^2+4x+1}{9x^2-1} =$

18. $\dfrac{4x^2+4x-3}{2x^2-13x+15} =$

19. $\dfrac{4x^2+4x-3}{2x^2+13x+15} =$

20. $\dfrac{5x^2-12x+4}{10x^2+16x-8} =$

1.10. – RATIO AND PROPORTION

1. The ratio between 2 and 12 is the same as between _____ and a 120.

2. The ratio between 1 and 7 is the same as between _____ and 35.

3. The ratio between 2 and 24 is the same as between 6 and _____

4. The ratio 2:3:7 is the same as _____

5. Divide 180 in the ratio 2:3

6. Divide 2800 in the ratio 3:4

7. Divide 180 in the ratio 2:3:4

8. Divide 720 in the ratio 2:5:8

9. Divide 30 in the ratio 1:2:3

10. The diagram representing an apartment has the scale 1:60. The dimensions of a bedroom in the diagram are 7 x 8 cm. Find the dimensions, perimeter and area of the bedroom.

11. To make a chocolate cake the ingredients needed are 2 eggs, 1 cup of sugar and 3 cups of flower. Find the ingredients needed to make:
    a. A cake half as big.
    b. A cake 2.5 times as big.

12. In a certain family with 2 children the parents eat twice as much as the kids. The family ordered 900g of Pasta, find the amount of pasta each one of the family members will eat.

13. The scale of a map is 1:600000. Find the real distance represented by:

    a. 1 cm

    b. 9 cm

    c. The distance in the map that represent 10km

    d. The distance in the map that represent 50km

14. The scale of a map is 1:1000000. Find the real distance represented by:

    a. 1.5 cm

    b. 10 cm

    c. The distance in the map that represent 20km

    d. The distance in the map that represent 120km

15. The ratio between students that choose Math, Science and English is 10:12: 9. How many students will choose each subject in a school with 1550 students?

1.11. – EQUATIONS OF THE 1ˢᵀ DEGREE

1. In real life we sometimes use equations to solve a _____. For example: We want to use tiles to pave our garden. We know that the size of the garden is 20 m² and that every tile is 100 cm², how many tiles should we buy? (Ignoring the shape of the garden)

   Since 20 m² = 200000 cm² $100 \cdot n = 200000$
   (n is the number of tiles)   n = 2000 tiles.

2. When solving any equation the central idea is to _____ on both sides of the equation.

3. A linear equation, sometimes called an equation of the 1ˢᵗ degree is an equation in which the variable is _____

4. An equation may have a _____ but not always. For example the equation

   x + 1 = x   _____ and the equation

   x + 1 = x + 1   _____

1ˢᵗ Degree Equations

1. $x + 1 = 2$

2. $x + 2 = x$

3. $x - 1 = -1$

4. $x - 1 = -x$

5. $x - 2 = 2 - x$

6. $-x - 2 = 1 - x$

7. $-x - 2 = -2 - x$

8. $-5x - 12 = (3 - 3x)2$

9. $5x - 3 = -3x + 2$

10. $2 - 4x - 22 = 2(4 + 3x)$

11. $x - 1 = 4 - x$

12. $7 - (12x - 2) = -7x + 2$

13. $\dfrac{1}{x} = 5$

14. $\dfrac{4}{x} = 12$

15. $\dfrac{2}{x} = \dfrac{1}{2}$

16. $\dfrac{5}{x} = 1$

17. $\dfrac{x}{12} = 5$

18. $\dfrac{x}{7} + 2 = 5$

19. $\dfrac{2x}{7} + 2 = 5 - 3x$

20. $\dfrac{2x}{7} + \dfrac{2}{5} = -2x + 1$

21. $\dfrac{x}{2} + \dfrac{3}{4} = 1$

22. $\dfrac{2x+1}{7} + \dfrac{2}{5} = \dfrac{x-2}{5} + 1$

23. $\dfrac{2-x}{6} + \dfrac{x+4}{12} = x - 8$

24. $\dfrac{3x-5}{20} = \dfrac{x}{10}$

25. $\dfrac{x}{7} - \dfrac{1-x}{6} = 2$

26. $\dfrac{2x-2}{6} - \dfrac{6-3x}{24} = x - 6$

27. $\dfrac{9-x}{5} - \dfrac{5x-2}{3} = -x - 1$

28. $\dfrac{2x-1}{x} = 3$

29. $\dfrac{x+2}{2x} = 5$

30. $\dfrac{x-2}{2x-1} = 6$

31. $\dfrac{2x-2}{x+1} = -2$

32. $\dfrac{2x}{7} + 1 = \dfrac{-5x}{7}$

33. $\dfrac{2x}{7} + 4 = \dfrac{3x}{2}$

34. $\dfrac{2}{x} - 3 = \dfrac{3}{2x}$

35. $\dfrac{2}{x-2} - 3 = \dfrac{3}{x-2}$

36. $\dfrac{-2}{x} = \dfrac{3}{x-2}$

37. $\dfrac{4}{x+1} = \dfrac{4}{x+2}$

38. $\dfrac{2}{x+1} = \dfrac{4}{x+2}$

39. $-\dfrac{2}{2x+1} - 2 = \dfrac{4}{2x+1}$

40. $\dfrac{x}{2} - \dfrac{x}{5} = 3$

41. $\dfrac{2}{x} + \dfrac{3}{5} = 3$

42. $\dfrac{2x-7}{2} - \dfrac{3x}{5} = x$

43. $1 - \dfrac{1}{x} = 7 - \dfrac{3x+1}{x}$

44. $3 - \dfrac{2x}{x-2} = 7 - \dfrac{2x+1}{x-2}$

45. $\dfrac{2-x}{x-2} = 1$

46. $\dfrac{2-x}{x-2} = -1$

47. $\dfrac{5-7x}{3x-2} = -1 + \dfrac{5}{3x-2}$

48. $\dfrac{15-x}{3-x} = 7 - \dfrac{5x}{3-x}$

49. Write an equation of the form $\dfrac{ax}{5} = 1$ whose solution is 1

50. Write an equation of the form $\dfrac{x+k}{6} = 2$ whose solution is 4

51. Write an equation of the form $\dfrac{ax+k}{5} = 10$ whose solution is 3

52. Write an equation of the form $\dfrac{ax+k}{8} = 4$ whose solution is -1

Isolate x

1. $\dfrac{4}{x} = \dfrac{a}{x+6}$

2. $\dfrac{14}{x+2} = \dfrac{a}{x+2} - a$

3. $\dfrac{2}{x+3} - a = \dfrac{a+b}{x+3}$

4. $\dfrac{5}{2x+1} - 3a = \dfrac{b}{2x+1}$

5. $\dfrac{-2x}{a+3} = \dfrac{x+2}{2a-1}$

6. $\dfrac{-5x+1}{2a} = \dfrac{bx}{3a+2}$

7. $\dfrac{a}{x+2} = \dfrac{b}{x+2} - b + 1$

8. $\dfrac{b}{2x-4} - 3 = \dfrac{b}{2x-4} - b + 1$

9. $\dfrac{1}{ax+2} = \dfrac{b}{x+a}$

10. $\dfrac{1}{ax+2} = \dfrac{b}{ax+2} - 3$

11. $3\dfrac{x}{ax+2} = 3$

12. $-3\dfrac{2x}{ax+3} = b$

13. $\dfrac{2x-3}{2ax+5} = -3b$

14. $\dfrac{x}{ax+2} = \dfrac{2}{a} - 3$

15. $\dfrac{bx}{x+2} = 3 - b$

16. $\dfrac{b+x}{x-3} = \dfrac{b}{x-3} + a$

17. $\dfrac{bx}{a} = 2x + 8$

18. $\dfrac{ax+b}{dx+2} = c - g$

19. $\dfrac{1}{x+2} + \dfrac{1}{b} = 2$

20. $\dfrac{1-a}{x} + \dfrac{2a}{x} = 2b$

21. $x - \dfrac{2+ax}{b} = 2x+3$

22. $\dfrac{7-2ax}{x+1} = 2+b$

23. $\dfrac{3-2x}{2x-3} = a$

24. $\dfrac{2}{1-x} = \dfrac{2a}{x-1} - a$

25. $\dfrac{3}{a-2x} = \dfrac{b}{2x-a} - c$

26. Complete the RHS of the equation so its solution is a

$x + 3 =$ _____

27. Complete the RHS of the equation so its solution is a

$2x - 5 =$ _____

28. Complete the RHS of the equation so its solution is a

$\dfrac{2x+3}{2} =$ _____

29. Complete the RHS of the equation so its solution is a

$\dfrac{x+1}{xa} - 1 =$ _____

1.12. – SYSTEMS OF EQUATIONS OF THE 1ST DEGREE

1. One equation with 1 variable may have _____ or _____ or _____ solutions. Give examples:

2. One equation with 2 two variables may have _____ or _____ or _____ solutions. Give examples:

3. Equations of the first degree are equations in which_____
   Give examples with 1,2 and 3 variables:

4. Equations of the 2nd degree are equations in which_____
   Give examples with 1 and 2 variables:

5. The solution to one equation of the first degree with 2 variables from a graphical point of view, is a _____. The collection of points will form a _____.

6. Write a system of 2 equations whose only solution is $x = 1, y = 2$. Is this a unique system? Explain

7. Write a system of 2 equations whose only solution is $x = 0, y = -2$.

8. Write a system of 2 equations whose only solution is $x = -3, y = \frac{1}{2}$.

9. Write a system of 2 equations whose only solution is $x = 15, y = -6$.

10. Write a system of equations that has no solutions

11. Write a system of equations that has infinite solutions

12. Given the equations I) $2x + y = 3$, II) $2y - x = 4$

   a. Write a few solutions of each one of the equations:

   I) (__, __), (__, __), (__, __)

   II) (__, __), (__, __), (__, __)

   b. Show the solutions on the graph.

   c. Draw a conclusion:

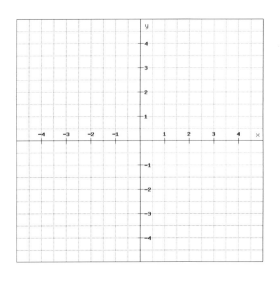

13. Given the equations I) $4x + 2y = 3$, II) $y + 2x = 8$

   a. Write a few solutions of each one of the equations:

   I) (__, __), (__, __), (__, __)

   II) (__, __), (__, __), (__, __)

   b. Show the solutions on the graph.
   c. Draw a conclusion:

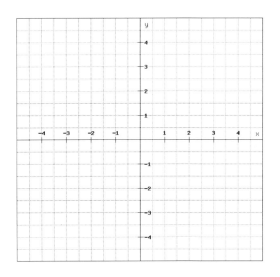

14. Given the equations I) $6x - 2y = 2$, II) $y - 3x = -1$

   a. Write a few solutions of each one of the equations:

   I) (__, __), (__, __), (__, __)

   II) (__, __), (__, __), (__, __)

   b. Show the solutions on the graph.
   c. Draw a conclusion:

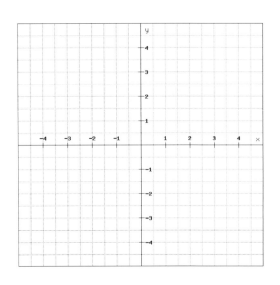

Solve each system using both substitution and elimination; verify that the same solution is obtained in both cases. Graph both equations to illustrate the solution found.

15. $x + y = 2$
    $2x - y = 1$

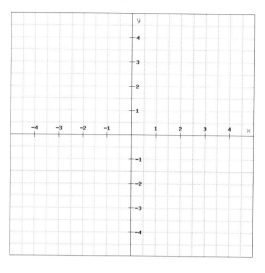

16. $x + y = 2$
    $2x + 2y = 1$

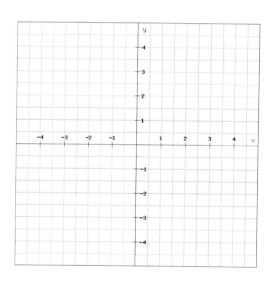

17. $\begin{array}{l} 4x + 2y = 6 \\ 6x + 3y = 9 \end{array}$

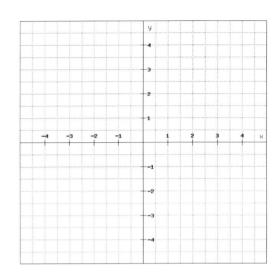

18. $\begin{array}{l} x - y = 1 \\ 3x - 2y = 4 \end{array}$

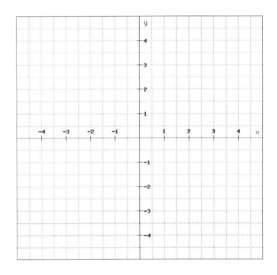

19. $\begin{array}{l} 2x - 5y = 1 \\ 3x - 7y = 2 \end{array}$

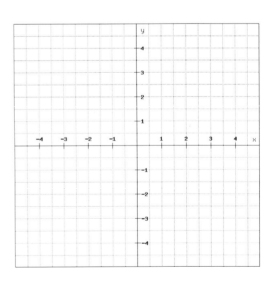

20. $\begin{aligned} 2x - 5y &= -8 \\ 3x - 2y &= -1 \end{aligned}$

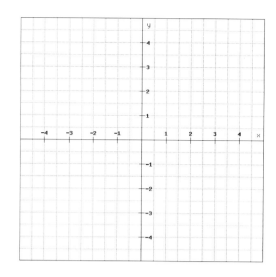

21. $\begin{aligned} 9x - 2y &= -11 \\ 8x - 3y &= -22 \end{aligned}$

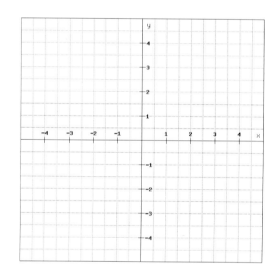

22. $\begin{aligned} 5x + 1 &= 2y \\ 4y + x - 3 &= 0 \end{aligned}$

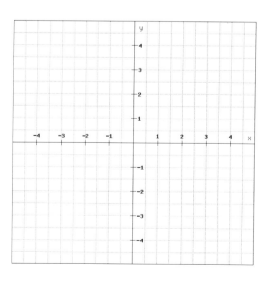

23. $\begin{aligned} 5x + 3y &= 2 - 2y \\ -y + 2x - 5 &= 0 \end{aligned}$

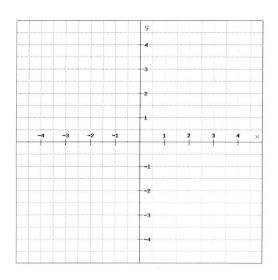

24. $\begin{aligned} 5x &= 2y \\ -y + 2x &= 0 \end{aligned}$

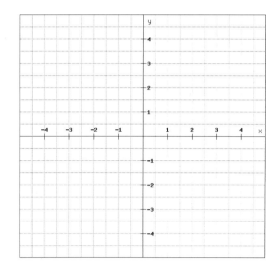

25. $\begin{aligned} x &= 2y - 7 \\ 4y - 2x &= 0 \end{aligned}$

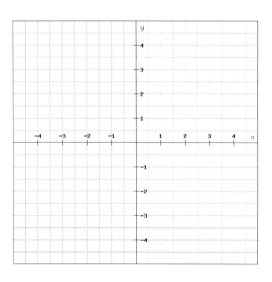

26. $\begin{aligned}-5x+1&=2y\\-4y+x-3&=x\end{aligned}$

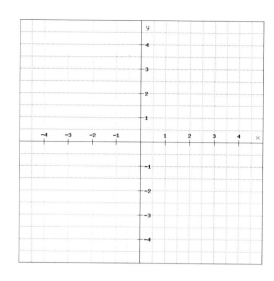

27. $\begin{aligned}5x+1&=2y\\10y-25x&=10\end{aligned}$

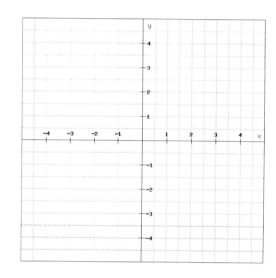

28. $\begin{aligned}2x+1&=2y\\-4y+4x+2&=0\end{aligned}$

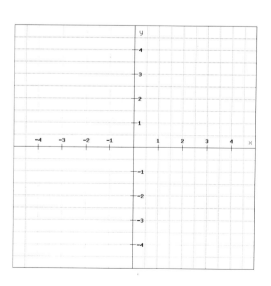

29. $\begin{aligned} x+1&=2y \\ 4y-2x-3&=0 \end{aligned}$

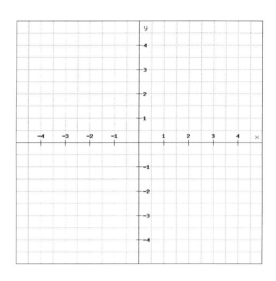

30. $\begin{aligned} 4x&=y \\ 3y-12x&=0 \end{aligned}$

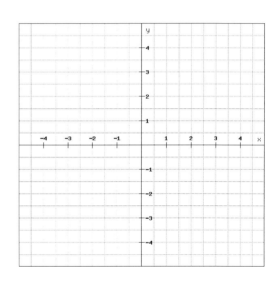

31. $\begin{aligned} 2x+7y&=4 \\ 3y-5x-3&=0 \end{aligned}$

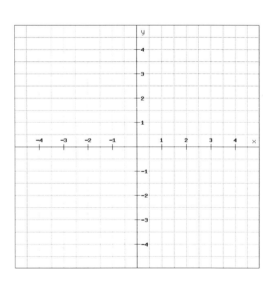

Solve each system using both substitution and elimination; verify that the same solution is obtained in both cases

32. $\dfrac{x}{5} + 1 = 2y$
    $\dfrac{y}{3} + \dfrac{x}{2} - 3 = 0$

33. $\dfrac{x}{5} + 2 = 6y$
    $-3y + \dfrac{x}{10} + 1 = 0$

34. $\dfrac{x}{2} + 1 = \dfrac{y}{3}$
    $-2y + 3x + 6 = 0$

35. $\dfrac{2x}{3} - 2 = -y$
    $\dfrac{y}{2} + \dfrac{x}{3} - 3 = 0$

36. $\dfrac{x}{5} = 1 + \dfrac{y}{10}$
    $\dfrac{-y}{2} - \dfrac{x}{2} = -10$

37. $\dfrac{x}{4} = \dfrac{y-1}{2} + 2$
    $\dfrac{x+2}{2} = 5 - \dfrac{y-1}{2}$

38.
$$1 - \frac{3x}{2} = \frac{y-1}{3}$$
$$3x - 2 = \frac{2-2y}{3}$$

39.
$$\frac{2x}{7} = \frac{2y-5}{14} - 2$$
$$8x = 4y - 1$$

40. Given that in a parking lot the total number of wheels is 88 and that in total there are 25 cars and motorbikes. Write 2 equations representing this information. Find the number of cars and motorbikes in the parking lot.

41. The company Sweetday makes 2 kinds of chocolates: Dark and white. The price of dark chocolate bar is 1.2$ and white 1.4$. In one day the company sold 3000 chocolate bars and made 3960$. How many bars of each type were sold?

42. The sum of 2 numbers is 100. If we divide the first number by 3 and the second by 4 the sum obtained is 65. Find the numbers.

43. The perimeter of a rectangular field is 80 meters. If the field is divided in 2 equal rectangles along one of its sides the new perimeter is 70 meters. Find the dimensions of the field and show how it was divided.

44. Jeff played soccer for 0.5 hours and later basketball for 1 hour. He burned 500 calories in total. Dina played soccer for 1 hour and later basketball for 0.5 hour. She burned 550 calories in total. Find the number of calories burned in 1 hour of a soccer game and 1 hour of basketball game.

1.13. – INTERVAL NOTATION AND INEQUALITIES

$x \in (a, b]$ or $\{x|\ a < x \leq b\}$ means x is between a and b, not including a and including

Exercises:

1. Represent the following Intervals on the real line:

a. $x \in (1, 4]$

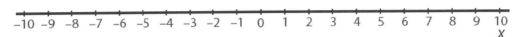

b. $x \in (4, 7)$

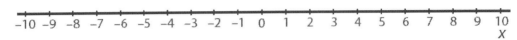

c. $x \in [-6, 8]$

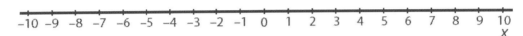

d. $x \in [-7, 0)$

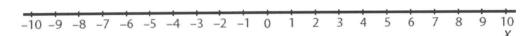

e. $x \in [-\infty, -2)$

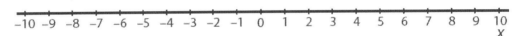

f. $x \in [-\infty, 3]$

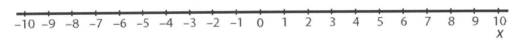

g. $x \in (5, \infty)$

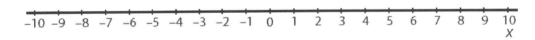

h. $\{x|\ 8 < x < 10\}$

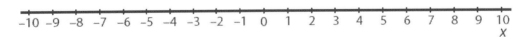

i. $\{x|\ -8 < x < -3\}$

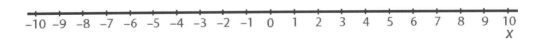

j. $\{x|\ 0 < x < 1\}$

```
-10 -9 -8 -7 -6 -5 -4 -3 -2 -1  0  1  2  3  4  5  6  7  8  9  10
                                                                 x
```

k. $\{x|\ \infty < x < 2\}$

```
-10 -9 -8 -7 -6 -5 -4 -3 -2 -1  0  1  2  3  4  5  6  7  8  9  10
                                                                 x
```

l. $\{x|\ 2 < x < \infty\}$

```
-10 -9 -8 -7 -6 -5 -4 -3 -2 -1  0  1  2  3  4  5  6  7  8  9  10
                                                                 x
```

2. Write each one of the Intervals using all types of notations:

a. $x \in (5, 6)$

```
-10 -9 -8 -7 -6 -5 -4 -3 -2 -1  0  1  2  3  4  5  6  7  8  9  10
                                                                 x
```

b. $x \in (-\infty, 4)$

```
-10 -9 -8 -7 -6 -5 -4 -3 -2 -1  0  1  2  3  4  5  6  7  8  9  10
                                                                 x
```

c. $x \in (2, 3)$

```
-10 -9 -8 -7 -6 -5 -4 -3 -2 -1  0  1  2  3  4  5  6  7  8  9  10
                                                                 x
```

d. $x \in (5, \infty)$

```
-10 -9 -8 -7 -6 -5 -4 -3 -2 -1  0  1  2  3  4  5  6  7  8  9  10
                                                                 x
```

e. $x \in\ ]-4, 10]$

```
-10 -9 -8 -7 -6 -5 -4 -3 -2 -1  0  1  2  3  4  5  6  7  8  9  10
                                                                 x
```

f. $x \in [-9, -2[$

```
-10 -9 -8 -7 -6 -5 -4 -3 -2 -1  0  1  2  3  4  5  6  7  8  9  10
                                                                 x
```

g. $\{x|\ 6 < x < 8\}$

```
-10 -9 -8 -7 -6 -5 -4 -3 -2 -1  0  1  2  3  4  5  6  7  8  9  10
                                                                 x
```

h. $\{x|\ -3 < x < 2\}$

```
-10 -9 -8 -7 -6 -5 -4 -3 -2 -1  0  1  2  3  4  5  6  7  8  9  10
                                                                 x
```

3. Solve the following inequalities and shade the solution on the given diagram:

   a. $-x \leq 2$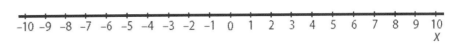

   b. $5 - x \leq 0$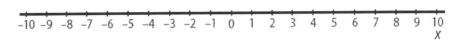

   c. $8 - 2x \leq 2$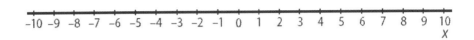

   d. $-2x \leq 3 - 2x$

   e. $7 + x \leq x + 1$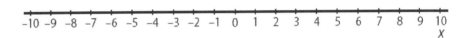

   f. $-2x \leq 2x + 4$

   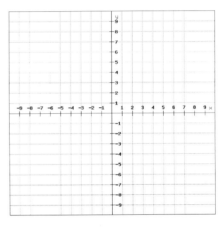

   g. $-3x \leq 2x$

   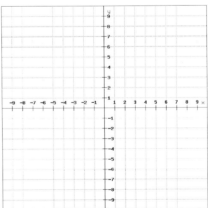

h. $-5x + 3 \leq 2x - 6$

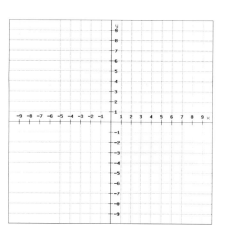

i. $3x \leq 4 + 3x + 1$

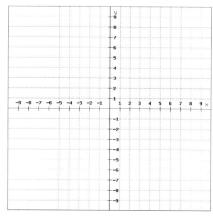

j. $\dfrac{x}{2} \leq x + 4$

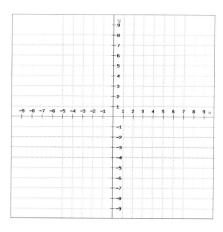

k. $\dfrac{x}{3} \leq \dfrac{x}{12} + 2$

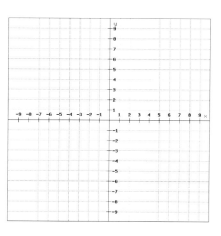

l. $\dfrac{2x-4}{6} \leq x-4$

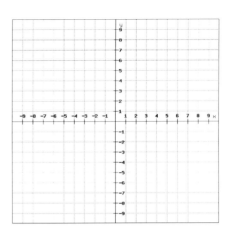

m. $\dfrac{2-x}{5} \geq \dfrac{x-2}{5} - 2$

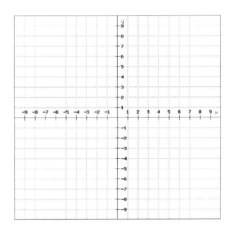

n. $\dfrac{11-2x}{5} \geq \dfrac{2x}{3} - \dfrac{x-1}{2}$

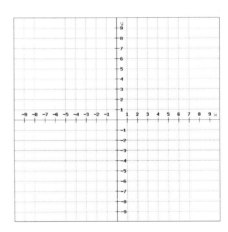

o. $\dfrac{-x}{5} + \dfrac{1}{4} \leq \dfrac{x-2}{4} - \dfrac{x-1}{2}$

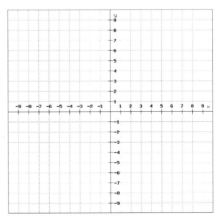

p. $\dfrac{y+8}{6} \le -y-1$

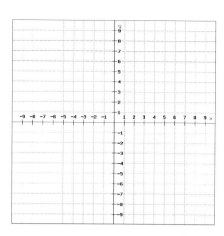

q. $\dfrac{2-2y}{2} \le \dfrac{2y}{4} - 2$

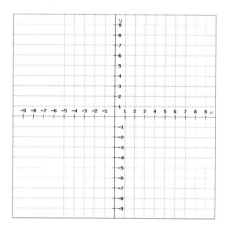

r. $\dfrac{4-y}{5} \le \dfrac{2y}{2} - 2y$

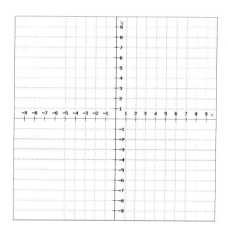

s. $\dfrac{1+y}{5} - 1 \le y - \dfrac{2y-2}{2}$

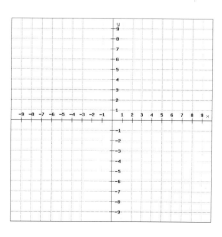

t. $-2 \leq 2x \leq 1$

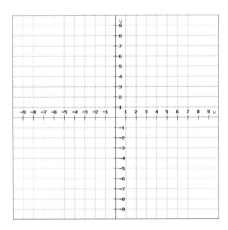

u. $-8 \leq \dfrac{-6x+3}{4} \leq 7$

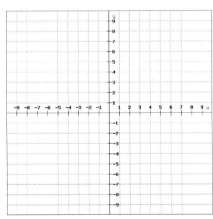

v. $-10 \leq 4y+2 \leq 9$

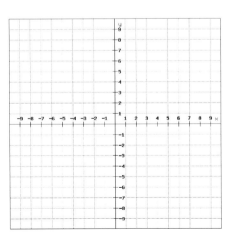

w. $0 \leq \dfrac{y+2}{3} \leq 2$

4.

   a. Solve the inequality $2x \leq 4$

   b. Solve the inequality $-x < 3$

   c. Represent both solutions on the real line:

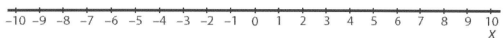

   d. State their intersection: _____ .

5.

   a. Solve the inequality $2x - 2 \leq 4$

   b. Solve the inequality $-3x + 4 > -2$.

   c. Represent both solutions on the real line:

   d. State their intersection: _____ .

6.

   a. Solve the inequality $x - 2 \leq -7$

   b. Solve the inequality $-2x + 10 \leq -2$.

   c. Represent both solutions on the real line:

   d. State their intersection: _____

7.
   a. Solve the inequality $3x - 10 \leq 2$

   b. Solve the inequality $-x < -3$.

   c. Represent both solutions on the real line:

   d. State their intersection: _____.

8.
   a. Solve the inequality $5x - 3 \leq 2$

   b. Solve the inequality $-2x + 2 > -2$.

   c. Represent both solutions on the real line:

   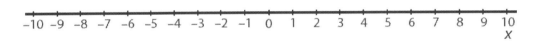

   d. State their intersection: _____.

9.
   a. Solve the inequality $2x - 2 \leq -12$

   b. Solve the inequality $-2x - 8 \leq -2$.

   c. Represent both solutions on the real line:

   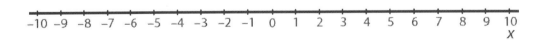

   d. State their intersection: _____

1.14. – EQUATIONS OF THE 2ND DEGREE

1. The solution of the equation $A \cdot B \cdot C \cdot ... = 0$ is _____ or _____ or _____ ...

2. Write an equation whose solutions are 1 and 2: _____

3. Write an equation whose solutions are -3 and 7: _____

4. Write an equation whose solutions are $\frac{1}{2}$ and b: _____

5. Write an equation whose solutions are a and b: _____

Solve:

6. $(x-5)(x+8) = 0$

7. $2(x-15)(x+58) = 0$

8. $(x-\frac{1}{2})(x+22.3) = 0$

9. $3(x-\sqrt{5})(x+\sqrt[5]{8}) = 0$

10. $c(x-a)(x+b) = 0$

11. $x(2x-4)(3x+\frac{7}{3}) = 0$

12. $(5x-1)(\frac{x}{13}+22)x = 0$

13. $x(3x+7) = 0$

14. $(2x-5)x = 0$

15. $3(2x-1)(3x+1)(2x-3) = 0$

16. $(2x-4)x(5x-\dfrac{1}{2}) = 0$

17. $(\dfrac{2}{x}-4)x = 0$

18. $6(\dfrac{1}{2x}-3)(\dfrac{x}{2}+1)(\dfrac{2}{x}-1)x = 0$

19. $-5(\dfrac{3}{2x}-1)(\dfrac{ax}{b}+c)(\dfrac{1}{x}+1)x = 0$

20. $-5(\dfrac{2}{x}+2)(\dfrac{a}{x}+c)(\dfrac{5}{x}+10)x = 0$

21. $-50(x+2)^{10}(\dfrac{1}{x}+7)^{120} = 0$

22. $16(2x-0.2)^{10}(\dfrac{3}{2x}+5)^{10} = 0$

23. $x(x-a)^{10}(a+x)^{10} = 0$

Factor and Solve:

24. $x^2 - 6x + 9 = 0$

25. $x^2 - 5x + 6 = 0$

26. $-x^2 - x + 6 = 0$

27. $x^2 + x = 6$

28. $x^2 + 5x + 6 = 0$

29. $-x^2 + 7x - 10 = 0$

30. $x^2 + 3x + 2 = 0$

31. $x^2 - x - 2 = 0$

32. $-x^2 = -4x$

33. $x^2 + x - 2 = 0$

34. $x^2 - 3x = -2$

35. $-x^2 - 5x + 6 = 0$

36. $x^2 - 2xa + a^2 = 0$

37. $x^2 = a^2$

38. $x^2 - x = 0$

39. $2x^2 - x = 0$

40. $2x^2 + 3x = 0$

41. $x^2 + 5x + 2 = 2$

42. $x^2 - 7x = -12$

43. $2x^2 - 4x = 0$

44. $x^2 - 6x+ = -10 + x$

45. $x^2 - 7x + 6 = 0$

46. $x^2 - x - 12 = 0$

47. $x^2 + 3x - 1 = 2x + 11$

48. $x^2 - 3x - 10 = 0$

49. $x^2 - 6x = 9 + 2x$

50. $x^2 - 1 + x = x$

51. $x^2 - 2 = 0$

52. $x^2 - 3 = 0$

53. $x^2 - 4 = 0$

54. $-x^2 + 1 = 0$

55. $-x^2 + 2 = 0$

56. $-x^2 + 3 = 0$

57. $-x^2 + 4 = 0$

58. $-x^2 + 13 = 0$

59. $-x^2 + 49 = 0$

60. $2x^2 - 72 = 0$

61. $-x^2 - 2 = 0$

62. $5x^2 - 125 = 0$

63. $-x^2 + 81 = 0$

64. $-3x^2 + 27 = 0$

65. $2x^2 - 6 = 0$

66. $3x^2 - 1 = 0$

67. $5x^2 - 6 = 0$

68. $4x^2 - 2 = 0$

69. $x^2 - b = 0$

70. $ax^2 - b = 0$

71. $-ax^2 + b = 0$

72. $2x^2 - 4x + 2 = 0$

73. $3x^2 - 3x - 18 = 0$

74. $-5x^2 + 10x + 75 = 0$

75. $3x^2 - 12x - 63 = 0$

76. $2x^2 + 2x - 112 = 0$

77. $2x^2 - 12x = 14$

78. $-5x^2 + 15x + 90 = 0$

79. $-3x^2 - 12x - 12 = 0$

80. $-2x^2 - 26x - 84 = 0$

81. $6x^2 + 48x + 72 = 0$

Solve by taking the square, cubic or other root, factor if possible:

82. $x^2 = 2$

86. $x^2 - 8 = 1$

83. $x^4 - 8 = 28$

87. $2x^5 - 5 = 1$

84. $2x^3 = -2$

88. $2 - x^{11} + 4 = 1$

85. $3 - x^2 = -6$

89. $20 - 3x^2 - 227 = 1$

90. Draw a conclusion about equations of the form $x^n = c$ (same as $x^n - c = 0$)

91. Draw a conclusion about equations of the form $x^2 = bx$ (same as $x^2 - bx = 0$)

92. Given the equations $x^2 = -1$, $x^2 = 1$
    a. Explain why one of them cannot be solved by taking the square root while the other can.

    b. Can that equation be solved by factoring? Explain

93. Given the equation $(x-1)^2 = 0$
    a. Solve it by taking the square root.

    b. Can the equation be solved by factoring?

94. Draw a conclusion about the number of solutions of quadratic equations

95. Given the equation $(x-\pi)(x+\sqrt{2})=0$
    a. Its solutions are _____ and _____
    b. In case the equation is expanded the following equation is obtained: $x^2 - x(\pi - \sqrt{2}) - \pi\sqrt{2} = 0$ The solutions of this equation are _____ and _____.
    c. Conclusion: In general _____ equations are easier to solve. When an equation is not factorised it may be difficult to find its solutions.

96. The product of 2 consecutive numbers is 56. Write a quadratic equation that represents the numbers. Solve the equation by factoring to obtain all the possible solutions.

97. The Area of a square field is 4 km². Write a quadratic equation that represents the information. Solve the equation by factoring and find the perimeter of the field.

98. When the side of a square is increases by 2 its area increases by 40cm^2. Write a quadratic equation that represents the information. Solve the equation and find the perimeter of the square.

99. One side of a rectangular field is 2 m longer than the other. It is known that the area of the field is 360 m^2. Write a quadratic equation that represents the information. Solve the equation by factoring and find the perimeter of the field.

CHAPTER 2 - GEOMETRY

2.1. – INTRODUCTION TO GEOMETRY

POINTS: elements that have no area or volume nor can be split into smaller parts

1. Indicate the following points on the plane: A(1,5), B(–1, 4), C(–3, –7), D(6,–5), E(–1, –1), F(2, 0), G(0,–4), H(–4, 0)

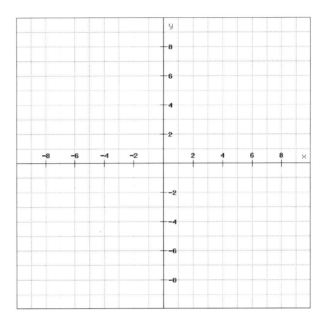

LINE: a collection of points organized in a "row", it has no area or volume

2. Indicate the following points on the plane: A(0,0), B(1, 1), C(–2, –2), D(6,6)

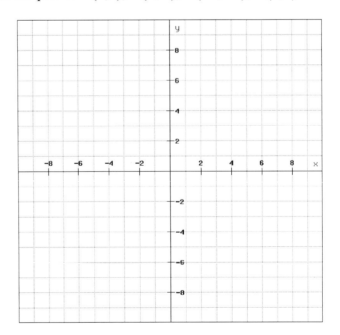

    a. What do these points have in common?

    b. Could you describe all the points that satisfy this property? How?

3. Indicate the following points on the plane: A(0,0), B(1, 2), C(–2, –4), D(4,8)

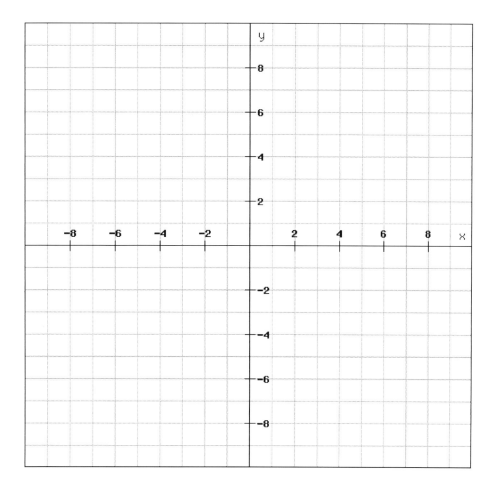

a. What do these points have in common? Use a ruler to draw the line that connects them.

b. Could you describe all the points that satisfy this property? How?

c. On the same graph sketch the following points E(0,1), F(1, 3), G(–2, –3), H(4,9)

d. What do these points have in common? Use a ruler to draw the line that connects them. What is the relation between this line and the previous line?

4. Indicate the following points on the plane: A(0, –2), B(1, 1), C(2, 4), D(–2, –8)

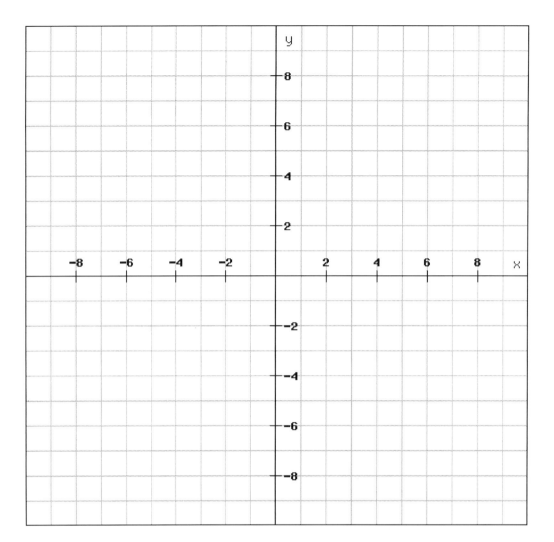

    a. What do these points have in common? Use a ruler to draw the line that connects them.

    b. Could you describe all the points that satisfy this property? How?

    c. On the same graph sketch the following points E(0,1), F(1, 4), G(–2, –5), H(2, 7)

    d. What do these points have in common? Use a ruler to draw the line that connects them. What is the relation between this line and the previous line?

2.2. – ANGLES

1. An angle is the figure formed by _____ lines called _____ that start at a common point.

   For example:

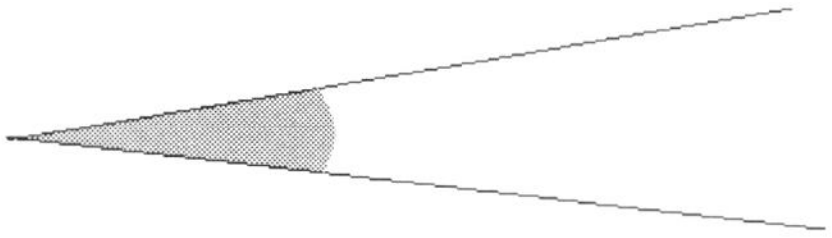

2. A straight angle is: _____

3. An acute angle is: _____

4. A right angle is: _____

5. An obtuse angle is: _____

6. A reflex angle is: _____

7. Given the following diagram:

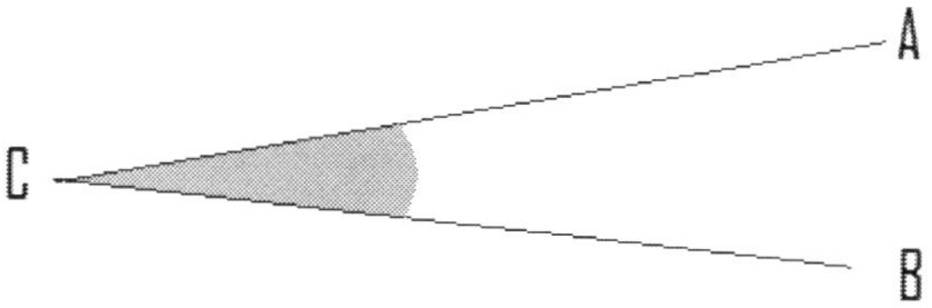

   a. CA and CB are _____

   b. The shaded angle can be called _____ or _____

8. We say that the following angle has a size of _____ degrees or _____°

9. Use the following square to sketch an angle of 45° degrees:

10. Two angles are complementary if their sum is _____

11. Two angles are supplementary if their sum is _____

12. The complementary of 20° is _____. The complementary of x° is _____

13. The supplementary of 20° is _____. The supplementary of x° is _____

14. The complementary of 42° is _____. The complementary of x° is _____

15. The supplementary of 126° is _____. The supplementary of x° is _____

16. The complementary of 81° is _____. The complementary of x° is _____

17. The supplementary of 0° is _____. The supplementary of x° is _____

18. Find all the unknown angles: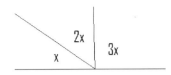

19. Find all the unknown angles: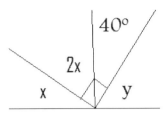

20. Straight lines are _____ or _____

21. Given the following diagram:

   a. The angles x and y are _____

   b. The angles x and a are _____

   c. The angles y and b are _____

22. Given the following diagram: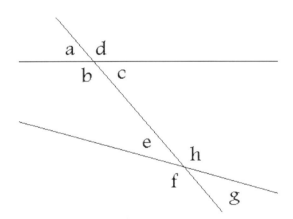

   a. The angles a and e are _____

   b. The angles b and e are _____

   c. The angles b and f are _____

   d. The angles c and e are _____

   e. The angles h and b are _____

   f. The angles e and g are _____

   g. The angles c and h are _____

   h. The angles g and h are _____

   i. The angles b and d are _____

   j. Which angle is a corresponding angle pair with g? _____

   k. Which angle is an alternate angle pair with g? _____

   l. Which angle is a co-interior angle pair with e? _____

110

23. Given the following diagram in which the transversal intersects 2 parallel lines:

   a. The angles a and e are _____
   b. The angles b and e are _____
   c. The angles b and f are _____
   d. The angles c and e are _____
   e. The angles h and b are _____
   f. The angles e and g are _____
   g. The angles c and h are _____

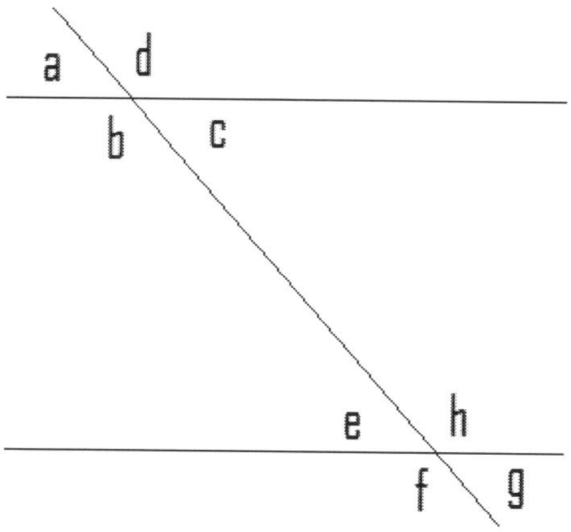

24. Determine if the lines are parallel, explain why: 100°, 79°

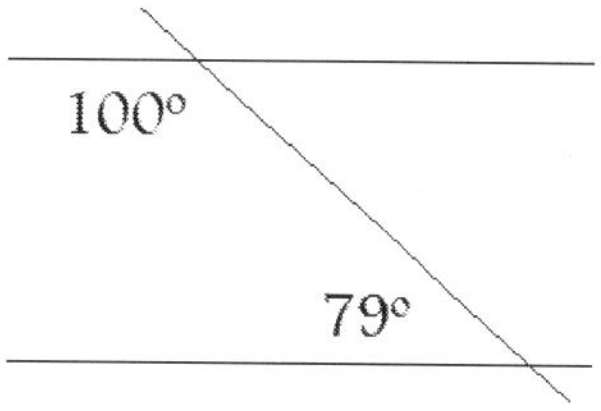

25. Determine if the lines are parallel, explain why: 100°, 100°

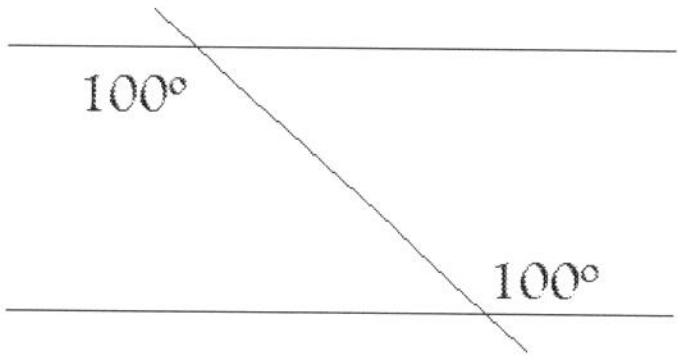

26. Determine if the lines are parallel, explain why: 50°, 50°

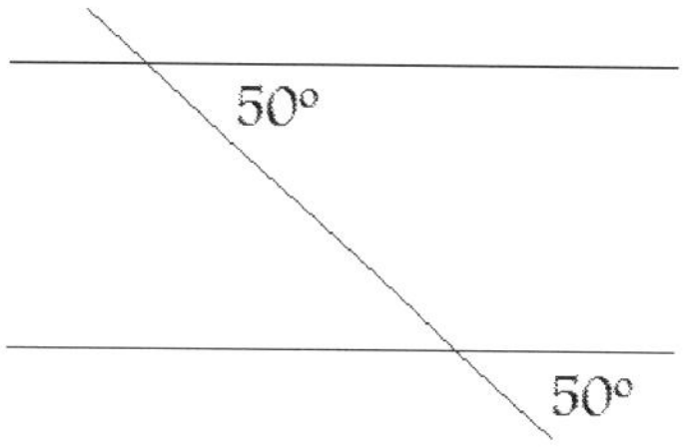

27. Sketch corresponding angle:

28. Sketch alternate interior angles:

29. Sketch alternate exterior angles:

30. Given the AB is parallel to CD, find the angles a, b, c, d, e.

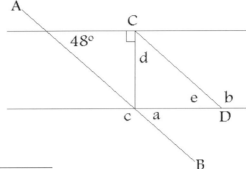

31. The sum of the angles in a triangle is _____

32. The sum of the angles in a square is _____

33. The sum of the angles in a rectangle is _____

34. The sum of the angles in a quadrilateral is _____

35. The sum of the angles in a pentagon is _____

36. The sum of the angles in an hexagon is _____

37. The sum of the angles in an heptagon is _____

38. The sum of the angles in an octagon is _____

39. The sum of the angles in a shape with n sides is _____,

    the reason is that _____

40. Find the regular polygons with which you can fill the floor with tiles. Explain why does this happen.

41. Find all the unknown angles:

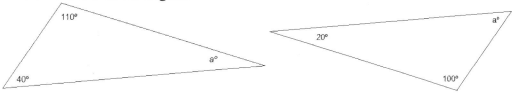

42. Find all the unknown angles:

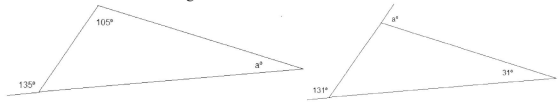

43. Find all the unknown angles:

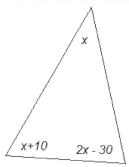 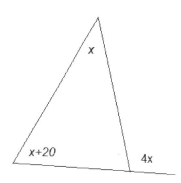

44. Find all the unknown angles:

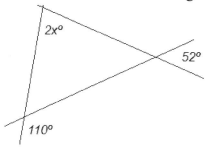 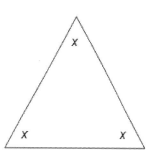

45. Find all the unknown angles:

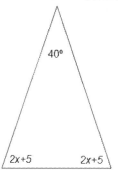 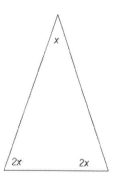

2.3. –TRIANGLES

1. Indicate the following points on the plane: A(0, 6), B(6, 0), C(0, 0)

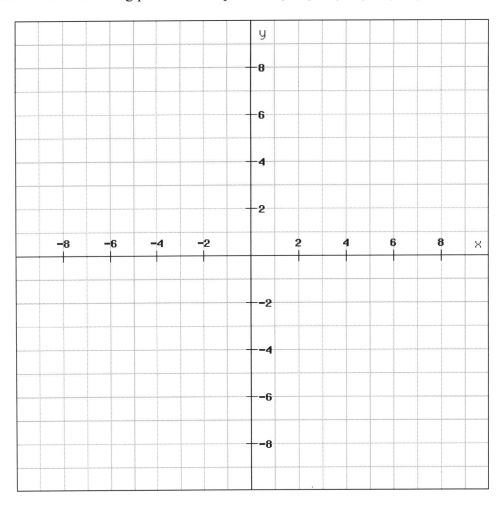

   a. Use a ruler to draw the line that connects each pair of points to form a triangle.

   b. Find all the angles of the triangles you can.

   c. This kind of triangle is called _____ and _____

   d. Write down the length of the 2 equal sides: _____

   e. Write down the Pythagorean Theorem: _____.

   This theorem is only true in _____ triangles.

   f. Use P. Theorem to find the length of the third side of the triangle.

   g. Add the point D(6, 6) to the graph. The form ABCD is a _____. The area of this shape is _____

   h. Use the area of the square to find the area of the triangle.

2. Indicate the following points on the plane: A(–4, 0), B(2, 6), C(8, 0)

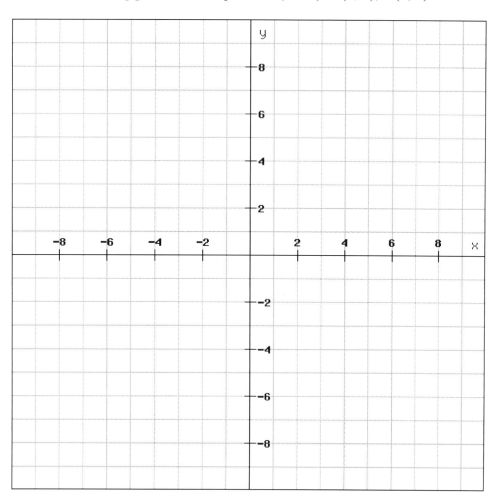

a. Use a ruler to draw the line that connects each pair of points to form a triangle.

b. This kind of triangle is called _____

c. Write down the Pythagorean Theorem: _____.

   This theorem is only true in _____ triangles.

d. Add the point D (2, 0) to the graph. The triangle ABD is _____.

e. The length of AD is _____. The Length of BD is _____. Use P. Theorem to find the length of AB.

f. In consequence state the length of BC: _____.

g. The perimeter of the triangle ABC is _____

h. Add the point E (–4, 6) to the graph. The shape AEBD is a _____. The area of this shape is ____. Use this area to find the area of the triangle ABD and ABC.

3. Indicate the following points on the plane: A(–6, 0), B(3, 6), C(5, 0)

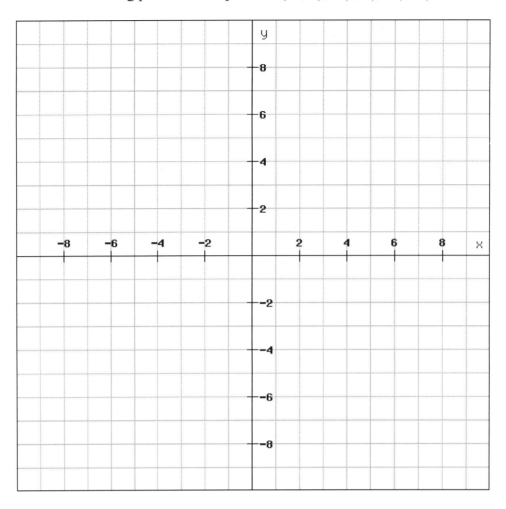

a. Use a ruler to draw the line that connects each pair of points to form a triangle.

b. Is this triangle isosceles or right angled?

c. Add the points D (–6, 6) and E (5, 6) to the graph. The shape ADEC is a _____

 The area of this shape is _____.

d. Add the point F (3, 0) to graph and use the corresponding theorem to find the

 length of AB: _____ and BC _____.

e. The perimeter of the triangle ABC is _____

f. The line BF is called the _____ of the triangle.

g. Every triangle has ___ heights. A height is a lines that starts at a _____

 and ends at _____ forming an angle of _____ with it.

h. Find the area of the triangles ABF, FBC and ABC.

116

4. Indicate the following points on the plane: A (–5, 0), B (5, 0), C (0, $\sqrt{75}$)

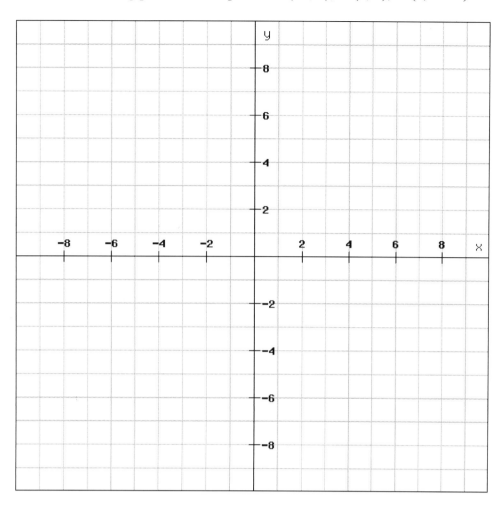

a. Use a ruler to draw the line that connects each pair of points to form a triangle.

b. Add the points D (0, 0) to the graph and use the corresponding theorem to find length of AB: _____ and BC _____.

c. What kind of triangle is this? _____

d. What can you say about the angles of this triangle?

e. The perimeter of the triangle ABC is _____

f. Find the area of the triangle ABC.

5. Define and sketch an example, include all the known angles and lengths of sides in your example.

   a. Equilateral triangle:

   c. Right angled triangle:

   b. Isosceles triangle:

   d. Right angled and isosceles triangle:

6. Given the following right angled triangle, find the missing side, perimeter and area of the triangle.

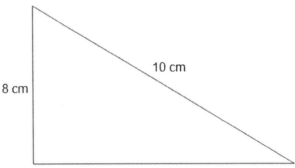

7. Given the following right angled triangle, find the missing side, perimeter and area of the triangle.

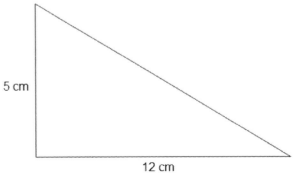

8. Given the following right angled triangle, find the missing side, perimeter and area of the triangle.

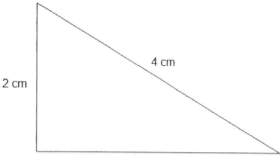

9. Given the following right angled triangles, find the missing sides, perimeter and area of the triangle.

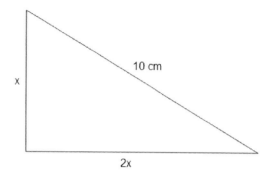

10. The vertex angle of an isosceles triangle is 42°, find the size of its base angle.

11. The vertex angle of an isosceles triangle is 110°, find the size of its base angle.

12. The base angle of an isosceles triangle is 50°, find the size of its vertex angle.

13. The base angle of an isosceles triangle is 33°, find the size of its vertex angle.

14. Given the isosceles triangle:

    y = ___ a = ___ b = ___

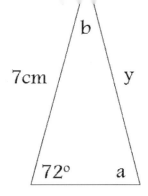

15. Given the diagram, find:

    x = ___ y = ___ a = ___ b = ___

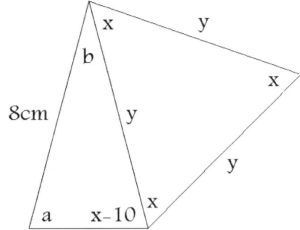

16. The base of an isosceles triangle is 10 cm, its side is 12 cm. Find its perimeter and area.

17. The base angle of an isosceles triangle is 5x + 7, the vertex angle is 2x − 2; find the size of the angles.

18. The base angle of an isosceles triangle is 9x – 10, the vertex angle is 12x – 10; find the size of the angles.

19. Given the following triangle, it is known that AB = 10cm, AD = 7cm and DC = 4cm. Angle CDB = 90°. Find:

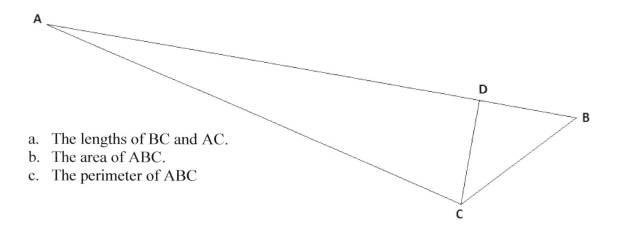

   a. The lengths of BC and AC.
   b. The area of ABC.
   c. The perimeter of ABC

20. Given the following triangle, it is known that AC = 13cm, DB = 4cm and DC = 5cm. Angle CDB = 90°. Find:

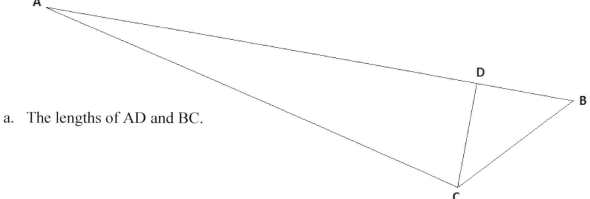

   a. The lengths of AD and BC.

   b. The area of DCB.

   c. The perimeter of ABC

21. Given the following triangle, it is known that AC = 20cm, DB = 10cm and DC = 11 cm. Angle CDB = 90° and angle CEA = 90°. Find:

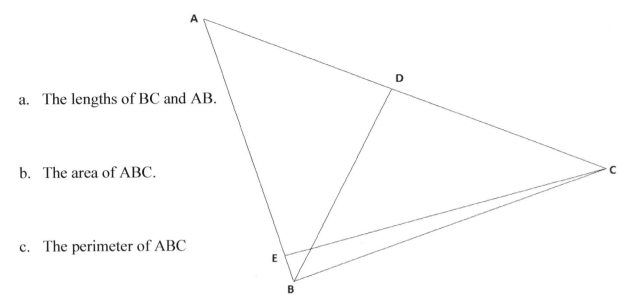

a. The lengths of BC and AB.

b. The area of ABC.

c. The perimeter of ABC

d. What do EC and BD have in common?

e. The lengths of EC, EB and AE

22. Find the perimeter and area of an isosceles right angled triangle whose leg is 10cm.

23. Find the perimeter and area of a right angled triangle whose sides are $6, x, 10$

24. Find the perimeter and area of an isosceles right angled triangle whose sides are $\sqrt{x}, \sqrt{x}, \dfrac{x}{2}$

25. Find the perimeter of an isosceles right angled triangle whose area is $20 cm^2$.

26. Find the area of an equilateral triangle whose perimeter is 30cm.

27. Given a right angled isosceles triangle whose longest side is 10 cm long.

   a. Sketch the triangle.
   b. Find the perimeter of the triangle.
   c. Find the area of the triangle.

28. Given a right angled isosceles triangle whose smallest side is X cm long.

   a. Sketch the triangle.
   b. Find the perimeter of the triangle in terms of X.
   c. Find the area of the triangle in terms of X.

29. Given an equilateral triangle whose side is 20 cm long.

   a. Sketch the triangle.
   b. Find the perimeter of the triangle.
   c. Find the area of the triangle.

30. Given an equilateral triangle whose side is X cm long.

   a. Sketch the triangle.
   b. Find the perimeter of the triangle in terms of X.
   c. Find the area of the triangle in terms of X.

31. Find the perimeter of an isosceles triangle whose base is half of its side and its area is 20 cm^2

32. Find the perimeter of an isosceles triangle whose base is six fifths of its side and its area is 12 cm^2.

33. Find the perimeter of a right angled triangle in which 1 leg is 10% <u>longer</u> than the other and whose area is 55 cm^2.

34. Find the area of a right angled triangle in which 1 leg is 25% <u>shorter</u> than the other and whose perimeter is 24cm

35. Given the following diagram (not to scale), BD = 8 cm, AD = 17 , DC = 104 cm,

   a. Find the perimeter and area of ABC

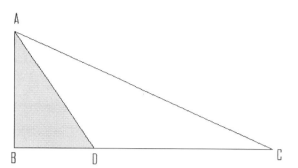

   b. Find the perimeter and area of ABD.

   c. Find the perimeter and area of ADC.

   d. Determine the percentage of the area that is shaded.

   e. Determine the percentage by which the area of ABC is bigger than ABD

   f. Determine the percentage by which the area of ABD is smaller than ABC

   g. Determine the percentage by which the Perimeter of ABC is bigger than ABD

   h. Determine the percentage by which the Perimeter of ABD is smaller than ABC

2.4. – DISTANCE AND MIDPOINT

1. Indicate the following points on the plane: A(2,3), B(6, 9), C(–3, –7), D(6,–5)

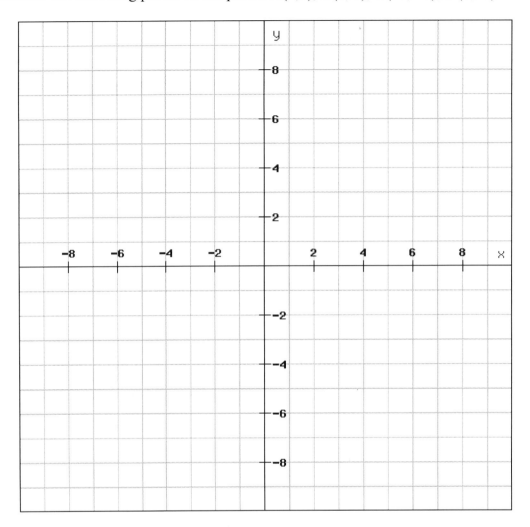

   a. Add the point (6, 3) and use Pythagorean Theorem to find the distance between the points A and B.

   b. Add the point (–3,–5) and use Pythagorean Theorem to find the distance between the points C and D.

   c. Find the distance AC

   d. Find the midpoint between AB (help: the midpoint x coordinate is the "average" of the x coordinates and the y coordinate is the "average" of the y coordinates)

   e. Find the midpoint between CD

   f. Find the midpoint between AC

2. Find the distance between (1, 3) and (7, –3), find the mid point. Show on diagram.

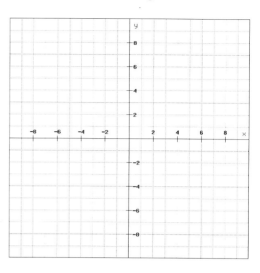

3. Find the distance between (–5, –4) and (2, –9), find the mid point. Show on diagram.

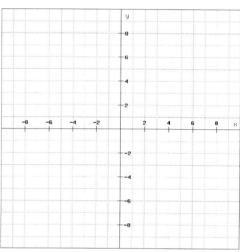

4. Find a point whose distance to the point (2, 1) is 7. Show on diagram.

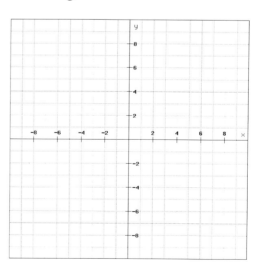

5. Find 3 points in the first quadrant whose distance to the point (4, 2) is 3; can you draw a conclusion about the location of such points in general. Show on diagram.

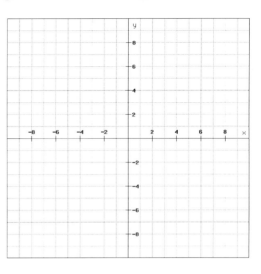

6. The midpoint between the points (*a*, 5) and (–2, b) is (0, 0) find *a* and b. Show on diagram.

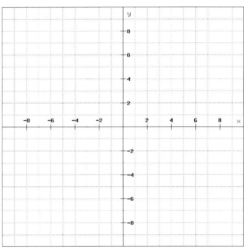

7. The distance between the points (*c*, 4) and (0, 0) is 5 find *a*. Show on diagram.

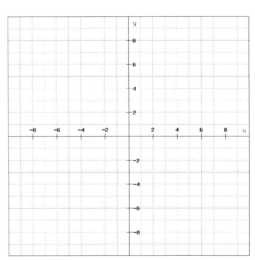

8. The distance between the points (1, –2) and (6, b) is 13 find *b*. Show on diagram.

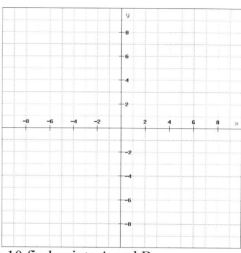

9. The distance between the points A(0, *a*) and B(2*a*, 0) is 10 find points A and B. Show on diagram.

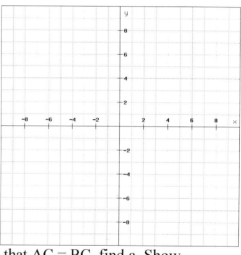

10. Given points A(3, –2), B(6, 1) and C(0, a). It is known that AC = BC, find a. Show on diagram.

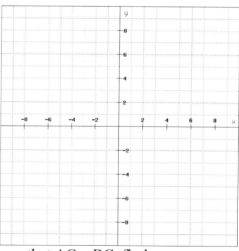

11. Given points A(–12, –8), B(–4, 7) and C(a, 0). It is known that AC = BC, find a.

2.5. – QUADRILATERAS

1. Given the following table, fill the blank using *a, b, c, d, h, r*

	Shape	Area	Perimeter
Square			
Rectangle			
Parallelogram			
Isosceles Trapezoid			
Trapezpezoid			
Rhombus			
Kite			

2. Given the following quadrilaterals. Write the name of each one of them:

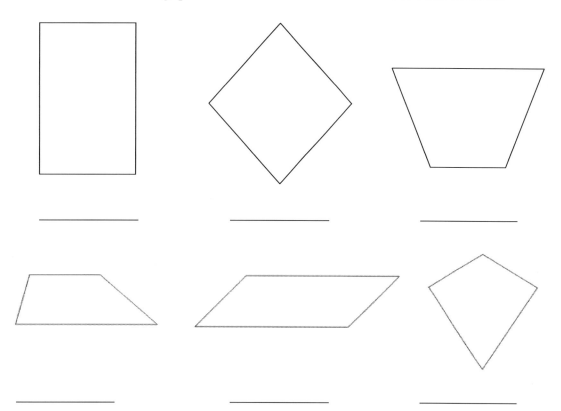

3. Given the following table, fill the blanks with yes or no.

	Shape (sketch)	Only 1 pair of parallel sides	2 pairs of parallel sides	1 pair of equal sides	2 pairs of equal sides	4 equal sides
Square						
Rectangle						
Parallelogram						
Isosceles Trapezoid						
Trapezoid						
Rhombus						
Kite						

4. True or False

   a. A square is also a parallelogram   True / False

   b. A square is also a rectangle   True / False

   c. A square is also a trapezoid   True / False

   d. A parallelogram is also a square   True / False

   e. A rectangle is also a square   True / False

   f. A rhombus is always a parallelogram   True / False

   g. A parallelogram is always r rhombus   True / False

   h. A parallelogram is sometimes a rhombus   True / False

   i. A rhombus is always a kite   True / False

   j. All the shapes above mentioned are quadrilaterals   True / False

5. Given the following table, fill the blanks with yes or no.

	Shape (Sketch diagonals as well)	Diagonals are perpendicular	Diagonals are equal	Diagonals bisect angle	Diagonals bisect each other
Square					
Rectangle					
Parallelogram					
Isosceles Trapezoid					
Trapezoid					
Rhombus					
Kite					

6. Given a square with diagonal of 4 cm, find its area and perimeter.

7. Given a square with diagonal of a cm, find its area and perimeter.

8. Given a rectangle with diagonal of 7m and one side is twice as large as the other, find its area and perimeter.

9. Given a rectangle with diagonal of 20m and one side is twice as large as the other, find its area and perimeter.

10. Given the following parallelogram. ABC is isosceles and right angled. AB = 2cm, CD = 5cm (Diagram not to scale). Find:

    a. The area and perimeter of the parallelogram
    b. The area and perimeter of ABC
    c. The area and perimeter of BCD
    d. The area and perimeter of CDE

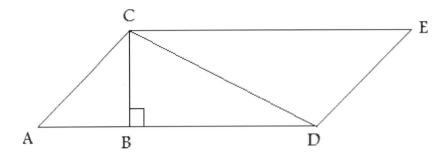

11. Given the following isosceles trapezoid. ABC is right angled. AC = 7cm, CE = 15cm and AE = 20cm (Diagram not to scale). Find:

   a. The area and perimeter of ABC and BCE
   b. The area and perimeter of the trapezoid
   c. The area and perimeter of CDE

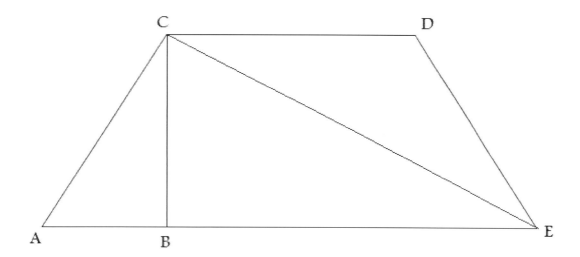

12. Given the following rhombus. BC = 6cm, AD = 18cm and find the area and perimeter the rhombus (Diagram not to scale).

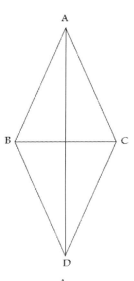

13. Given the following kite. BC = 4cm, AE = 8cm and CD = 2AC find the area and perimeter the kite (Diagram not to scale).

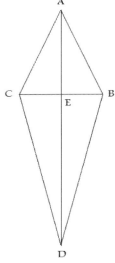

14. It is known that the perimeter of a rhombus with equal diagonals is 40cm. Find its area.

15. Find the side length of a square whose area is equal to its perimeter.

16. Find the side length of a rhombus whose area is equal to its perimeter and one of its diagonals is 5cm long.

2.6. – CIRCLES AND COMPLEX SHAPES

1. Given the following circle:

   a. Sketch a diameter.
   b. Sketch a radius.
   c. The diameter is _____ the radius
   d. Sketch a chord smaller than the diameter
   e. Sketch a chord smaller than the radius

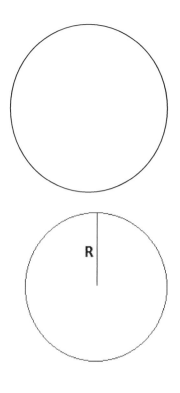

2. Given a circle with radius R, find

   The Perimeter of the circle: _____

   The Area of the circle: _____

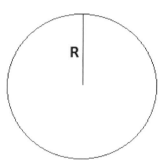

3. Given a circle with radius $\frac{4}{\pi}$ cm, find

   The Perimeter of the circle: _____

   The Area of the circle: _____

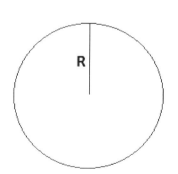

4. Given a circle with perimeter 20π cm, find

   The radius of the circle: _____

   The Area of the circle: _____

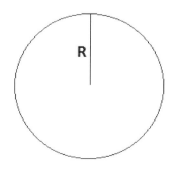

5. Given a circle with area 16π cm², find

   The radius of the circle: _____

   The perimeter of the circle: _____

139

6. The length of the perimeter of a circle with radius r is _____. The
   The area of a circle with radius r is _____.

7. Find the perimeter and area of the following shape:

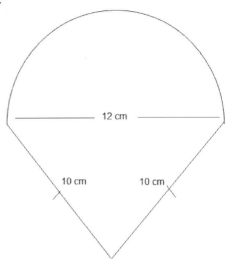

8. Given the following concentric circles with radii 4 cm and 7 cm correspondingly. Find the shaded area in terms of pi.

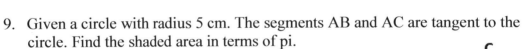

9. Given a circle with radius 5 cm. The segments AB and AC are tangent to the circle. Find the shaded area in terms of pi.

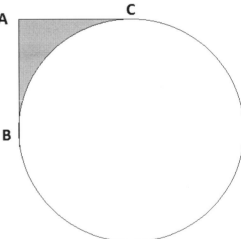

10. Given a circle with radius 10cm in which a square is circumscribed

   a. Find the length of the side of the square.
   b. Find the area of the square.
   c. Find the area of the circle
   d. Find the percentage of the area of the circle that the square occupies with 1 decimal.

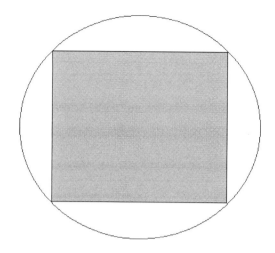

11. Given a circle with radius 10cm circumscribed in a square:

   a. Find the length of the side of the square.
   b. Find the area of the square.
   c. Find the area of the circle
   d. Find the percentage of the area of the square that the circle occupies with 1 decimal.

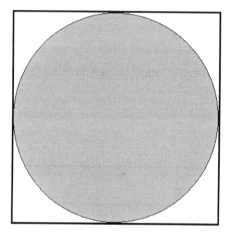

12. Find the perimeter and area of the following figure made of 3 semi circles whose radius is 3cm and a right angled triangle.

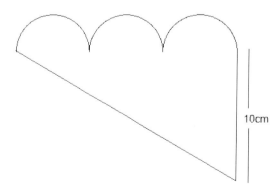

13. Find the perimeter and area of the following figure made of 4 semi circles whose radii is 1cm, 1cm, 2cm and 4 cm..

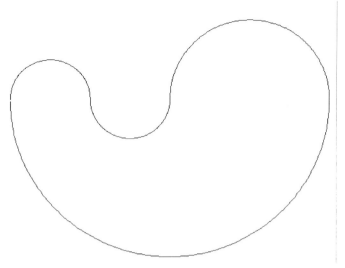

14. Find the perimeter and area of the following figure made of an isosceles right triangle rounded in its corner. The radius of the round part is 10 cm.

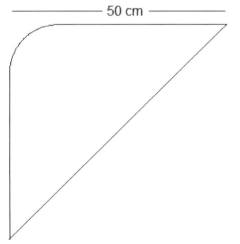

15. Find the perimeter and area of the following figure made of 2 semi circles connecting half a square whose side length is 4cm.

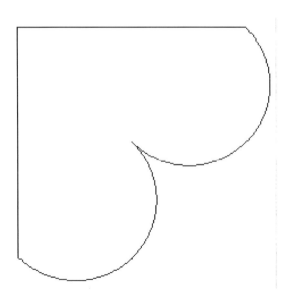

142

16. Find the perimeter and area of the following figure made identical "stairs".

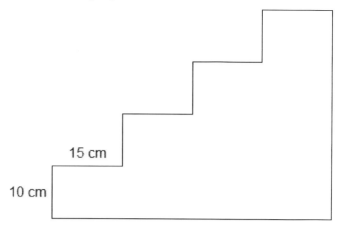

17. Find the dimensions of all the stairs in the following structure knowing that every square stair is 10cm higher and wider than the previous one and that the total area of the figure is 2044 cm^2.

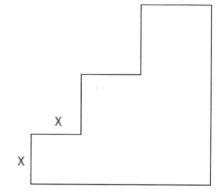

18. Find the perimeter of the following shape knowing that the area of the figure is 960 cm^2.

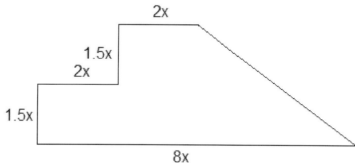

19. Find the perimeter and area of the rectangle knowing that the shaded area is π cm^2 and it occupies 50% of the rectangle.

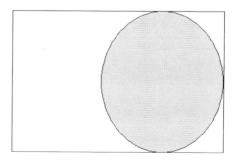

2.7. – 3D GEOMETRY, VOLUME AND SURFACE AREA

1. Volume is the amount of _____ occupied by material.

2. In international system of units we use a box of dimensions

   _____ to express a volume of 1 m³:

3. In many occasions a 1 m³ is a very big unit so a box of dimensions

   So a box of dimensions _____ is used to express a volume of 1 cm³.

4. Sometimes 1 cm³ is also called 1 ml (milliliter), there is no difference.

   In consequence 1 litre = _____ ml = _____ cm³

5. How many 1 cm³ boxes fit into 1 m³ box?

6. A smaller box that may be used is mm³. Find:

   a. 1 cm³ = _____ mm³

   b. 1 m³ = _____ mm³

   c. 6.3 cm³ = _____ mm³

   d. 0.052 m³ = _____ mm³

7. Find out about the standard volume of a milk container in your area: _____

8. A volume may be formed by "moving" or "dragging" a certain area along a path, for example by moving a circle a cylinder is formed:

   In consequence the volume of the cylinder is:

   _____

   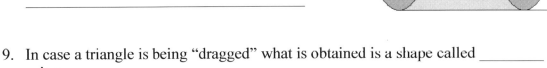

9. In case a triangle is being "dragged" what is obtained is a shape called _____ prism.

10. In case a square is being "dragged" what is obtained is a shape called _____

    prism or _____.

11. Find the volume of the following shape, made of a quadrilateral with area 20 cm² that was dragged:

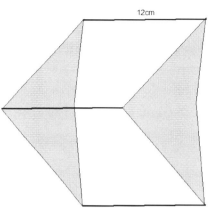

12. Surface area is equivalent to the <u>amount of paper</u> needed in order to cover all the exposed areas of a three dimensional figure (like wrapping up a present).

13. Find the surface area of the following shapes:

    a. 1 m³ cube

    b. 1 cm³ cube.

    c. 1 mm³ cube.

14. Given the following container (called cuboid or rectangular prism)

    a. Find the length of the line that connects 2 opposite corners.

    b. Find the volume of the object in m³, cm³, mm³

    c. Find the surface area of the object in m², cm², mm²

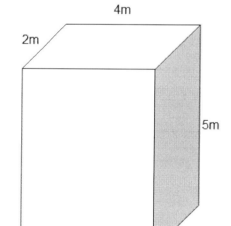

145

15. Given the following table, fill the blanks

	Shape	Surface Area	Volume
Cuboid (Rectangular Prism)			
Pyramid (Square based)			
Sphere			
Cylinder			
Cone			

16. Given the following table, fill the blanks

	Shape	Surface Area	Volume
Triangular prism			
Triangle based Pyramid (Tetrahedron)			

17. Find the volume and surface area of a sphere with radius 2 cm.

18. Find the volume and surface area of a sphere with radius 1.1 m.

19. Find the volume of a square based pyramid with base length 20 cm and height is 0.1 m.

20. Find the volume and surface area of a square based cuboid whose base length is 15 cm and height 0.2 m

21. Find the volume and surface area of a cone with radius 0.3 m and height 2 m.

22. Find the volume and surface area of a cylinder with radius 0.4 m and height 3 m.

23. Given that the volume of a square based pyramid is 10 m³ and that its height is equal to half its base length, find the perimeter of its base.

24. Given that the volume of a cuboid is 27 m³ and that the ratio between its sides is 1:2:4. Find its surface area.

25. Given that the volume of a cone is 10 m³ and that its height is 4 times the radius of the base. Find its height.

26. Given that the volume of a sphere is 9π m³. Find its surface area.

27. Find the volume and surface area of the following shape:

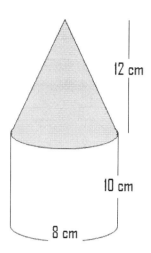

28. Find the volume and surface area of the following shape in which the cube has side length 20 cm, the cylinder has radius 5 cm and height 12 cm and the sphere has the same volume as the cylinder.

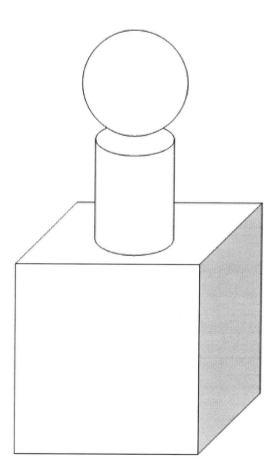

29. Find the volume and surface area of the following shape in which a square cuboid with side lengths 10 cm, 10 cm and 60 cm has 2 cylindrical openings with radius 3 cm.

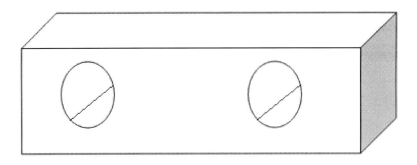

30. Find the volume and surface area of the following shape:

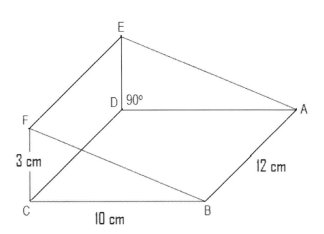

2.8. – GEOMETRIC TRANSOFRMATIONS

1. Indicate the following points on the plane: A(0,0), B(–1,6), C(4,2). Connect them to form a triangle.

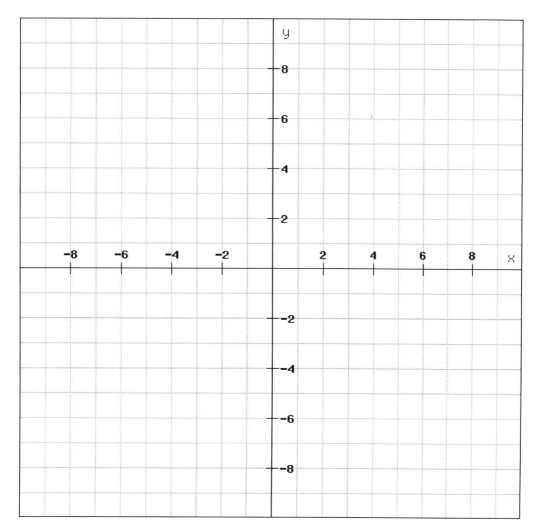

   a. Indicate the following points on the plane: A'(0,–3), B'(–1,3), C'(4,–1), Connect them to form a triangle.

   b. What can you say about the location of the 2nd triangle in comparison to the first one?

   c. This is a _____ translation.

2. Indicate the following points on the plane: A(0,0), B(–1,6), C(4,2). Connect them to form a triangle.

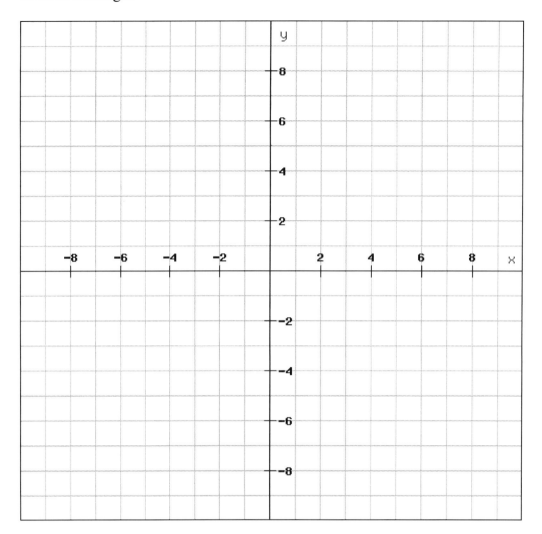

a. Indicate the following points on the plane: A'(4,0), B'(3,6), C'(8,2), Connect them to form a triangle.

b. What can you say about the location of the 2nd triangle in comparison to the first one?

c. This is a _____ translation.

152

3. Indicate the following points on the plane: A(0,0), B(–1,6), C(4,2). Connect them to form a triangle.

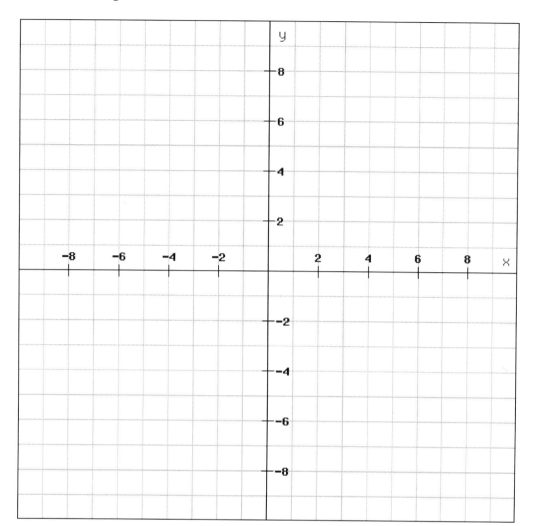

a. Indicate the following points on the plane: A'(–2,–3), B'(–3,3), C'(2,–1), Connect them to form a triangle.

b. What can you say about the location of the 2nd triangle in comparison to the first one?

c. This is a _____ and _____ translations.

4. Indicate the following points on the plane: A(1,0), B(–2,6), C(6,3). Connect them to form a triangle.

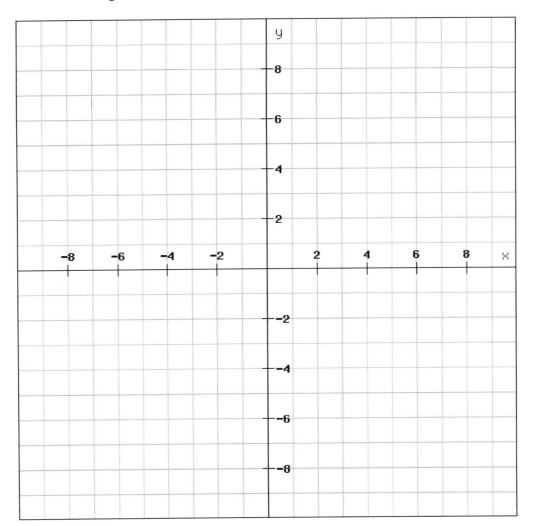

a. Indicate the following points on the plane: A'(–1,0), B'(2,6), C'(–6,3), Connect them to form a triangle.

b. What can you say about the location of the 2nd triangle in comparison to the first one?

c. This is a _____ across the y axis. The line x = 0 in this case is called the **line of** _____. When a shape is folded along a line of symmetry it will make a perfect match.

d. By changing x into ____ we are generating a _____ across the _____

5. Draw all the lines of symmetry f the following shapes:

6. Indicate the following points on the plane: A(1,1), B(–2,6), C(6,3). Connect them to form a triangle.

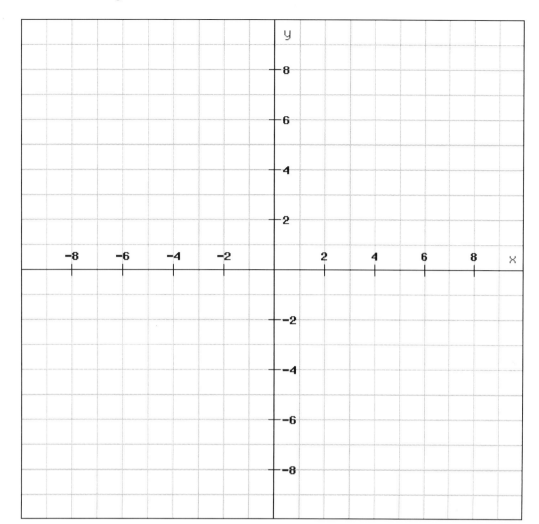

a. Indicate the following points on the plane: A'(1,–1), B'(–2,–6), C'(6,–3), Connect them to form a triangle.

b. What can you say about the location of the 2nd triangle in comparison to the first one?

c. This is a _____ across the x axis. The line _____ in this case is called the **line of** _____ When a shape is folded along a line of symmetry it will make a perfect match.

d. By changing y into ____ we are generating a _____ across the _____

7. Indicate the following points on the plane: A(–4,0), B(0,4), C(4,0), D(0, –4). Connect them to form a square.

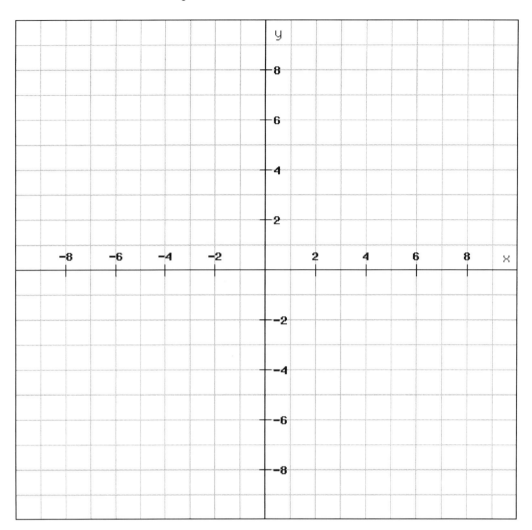

a. Indicate the following points on the plane: (Help: $\sqrt{8} \approx 2.83$)

A'($-\sqrt{8}, \sqrt{8}$), B'($\sqrt{8}, \sqrt{8}$), C'($\sqrt{8}, -\sqrt{8}$), D'($-\sqrt{8}, -\sqrt{8}$) Connect them to form a square.

b. What can you say about the location of the 2nd square in comparison to the first one?

c. This is a _____ of ____ degrees.

d. The **centre of rotation** is the point _____

e. Write down the coordinates of a square that is a rotation of 90° of the first one:

A'' = (__, __), B'' = (__, __), C'' = (__, __), D'' = (__, __)
Conclusions?

8. Indicate the following points on the plane: A(–5,0), B(5,0). Given also the point C(0,a)

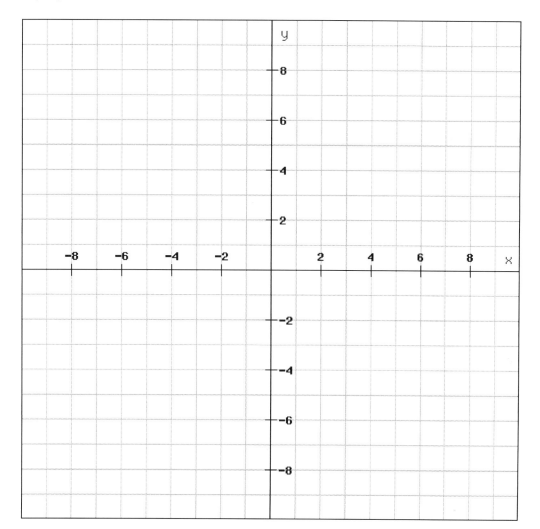

a. Show that the value of *a* in order to create an equilateral triangle is: $\sqrt{75}$
b. Write down the coordinates of the new points after translating the triangle 3 units left and 1 down.

A' = (__,__), B' = (__,__), C' = (__,__)

c. Write down the coordinates of the new points after rotation the triangle 90° clockwise. Pay attention to the question: What is the centre of the rotation?

A'' = (__,__), B'' = (__,__), C'' = (__,__)

d. Write down the coordinates of the new points after rotation the triangle 180° clockwise. Pay attention to the question: What is the centre of the rotation?

A''' = (__,__), B''' = (__,__), C''' = (__,__)

9. Indicate the following points on the plane: A(1,0), B(–2,5), C(4,3). Connect them to form a triangle.

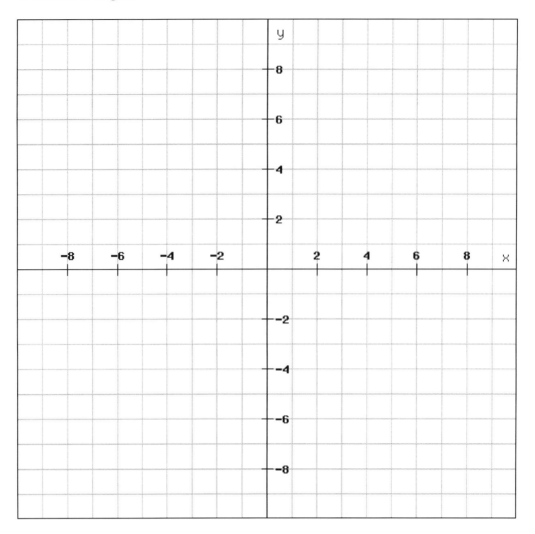

a. Indicate the following points on the plane: A'(2,0), B'(–4,10), C'(8,6), Connect them to form a triangle.

b. What can you say about the 2nd triangle in comparison to the first one?

c. This is a _____ factor ____

d. Indicate the following points on the plane: A'(0.5,0), B'(–1,2.5), C'(2,1.5), Connect them to form a triangle.

e. What can you say about the 2nd triangle in comparison to the first one?

f. This is a _____ factor ____

g. When making all sides of a shape bigger or smaller using the same factor the shape remains _____ to the original one.

10. Indicate the following points on the plane: A(0,0), B(2, 0), C(0,–3). Connect them to form a triangle.

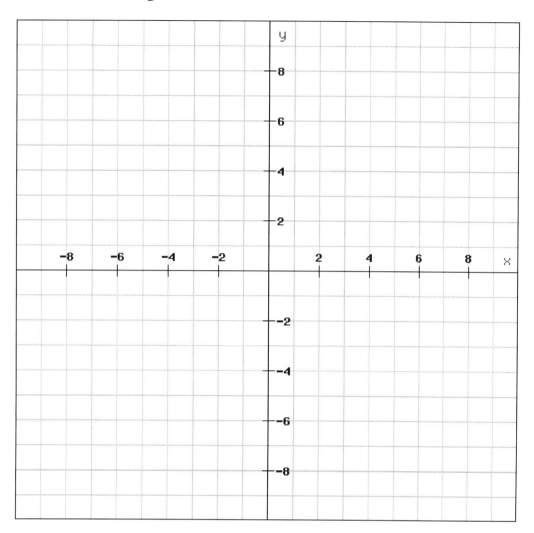

a. Indicate the points of he triangle formed if we enlarge this triangle by 3.

A' = (__, __), B' = (__, __), C' = (__, __)

b. Find the relations:

$$\frac{A'B'}{AB} = \qquad \frac{A'C'}{AC} = \qquad \frac{B'C'}{BC} =$$

11. Given a rectangle with side lengths 10 cm and 8 cm.

    a. Find its area and perimeter.

    b. Find the area and perimeter of a rectangle with sides 2 times as big.

    c. Find the area and perimeter of a rectangle with sides 3 times as big.

    d. Find the area and perimeter of a rectangle with sides n times as big.

12. Conclusion: When a certain shape with perimeter P and area A is enlarged by factor n, the perimeter of the new shape is _____ and its area is _____

13. Given a triangle ABC whose sides are 3, 4 and 5 cm long.

    a. Is his a right angled triangle?

    b. Find its area and perimeter

    c. Find the sides of another triangle whose sides are half the length of the sides of ABC. Is this triangle right angled? Find its area and perimeter.

14. Given that the area of a square is 16 times as big as the area of a different square. Find the ratio between the perimeters of the squares.

15. Explain the meaning of the operation "Zooming in/out" frequently used in digital imaging.

2.9. – CONGRUENT AND SIMILAR TRIANGLES

1. 2 triangles are similar if all of their angles are _____

2. 2 triangles are similar if <u>any</u> of the following is satisfied:

   a. 2 of their angles are _____. Sketch an example:

   b. 2 of their sides are _____ and the angles between them are _____. Sketch an example:

   c. All their sides are _____. Sketch an example:

3. All right angled triangles are similar True / False. Sketch an example to show answer:

4. Congruent triangles are similar triangles with ratio of proportionality _____

5. Similar triangles are always congruent True/False

6. Congruent triangles are always Similar True/False

7. Determine if the following pair of triangles are similar, give a reason:

8. Determine if the following pair of triangles are similar, give a reason:

161

9. Determine if the following pair of triangles are similar, give a reason:

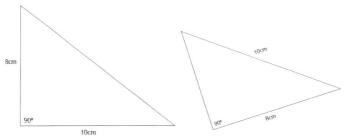

10. Determine if the following pair of triangles are similar, give a reason:

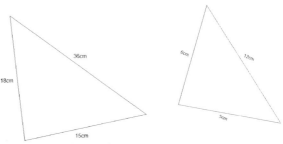

11. Determine if the following pair of triangles are similar, give a reason:

12. Determine if the following pair of triangles are similar, give a reason:

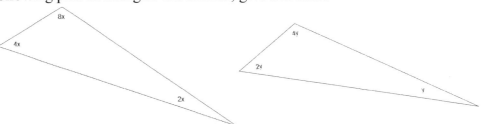

13. Given that $AB \parallel CD$, determine if the triangles ABE and CED are similar, give a reason. Given that AB = 2CD and AE = 8cm, find ED.

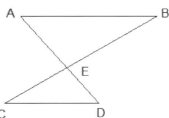

14. Given that $BC \parallel DE$, determine if the triangles ABC and ADE are similar, give a reason. Given that DE is 30% longer than BC and that AB = 20cm, find BD.

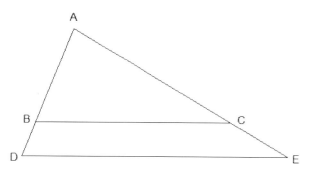

15. The shadow of a man formed by a street light on the ground is equal to twice its height. If the man is 10m away from the street light and his height is 1.90m, how high is the street light?

16. Given that $AB \parallel CD$, find ED:

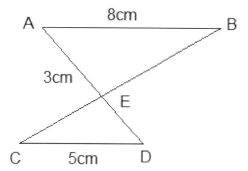

17. In the following triangle the angle BAC is a right angle. AD is an altitude from A to the BC. Show that triangles ABC, ADB and ADC are all similar. If BC = 10cm and AD = 2DC find the perimeter and area of ABD.

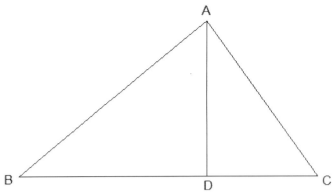

18. The following triangle AB = AC. AD is a altitude from A to the BC. Show that triangles ABD and ACD are similar. If BD = 8 cm and AB = 1.5AD, find the perimeter and area of ABC.

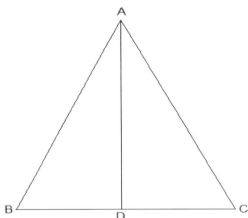

19. To measure the height of building the following operation can be performed. Jeff whose height is 180 cm puts a mirror at a distance of 20 m from a building and observed the top of the building in the mirror standing 0.4 m from it. Find the height of the building.

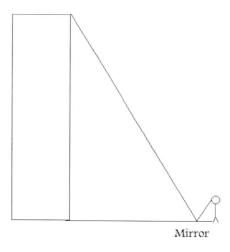
Mirror

20. Given the following diagram in which triangles FDE and ABC are similar and $\dfrac{AB}{FD} = 2$. Find:

    a. The percentage of the area that is shaded.

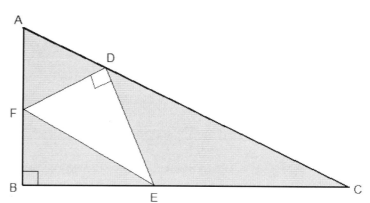

    b. The percentage by which the area of ABC is bigger than the area of FDE.

    c. The percentage by which the area of FDE is smaller than the area of ABC.

CHAPTER 3 – FUNCTIONS

3.1. – INTRODUCTION TO FUNCTIONS

1. Try to sketch an approximate graph for the <u>height</u> of an airplane <u>above sea level</u> since take off and until landing in a flight from Madrid to New York, add some reasonable numbers to the graph, pay attention that Madrid is about 600 meters above sea level:

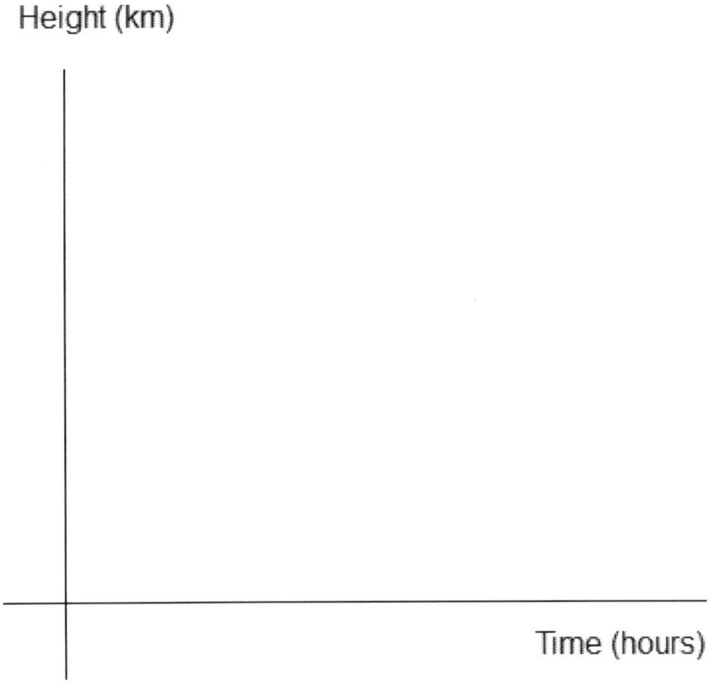

   Height (km)

   Time (hours)

   a. Height(0) = _____, it is the Height of _____

   b. Height(t) = 100cm, t = _____

   c. Write the set of possible values for the Time: _____, this is the Domain

   d. Write the set of possible values for the Height: _____, this is the Range

   e. This graph describes a function that shows how _____ depends on _____

2. Write the definition of a function in your own words:

3. Write 3 examples of relations that are functions:

4. The independent variable is usually represented in the _____

5. The dependent variable is usually represented in the _____

6. Draw a sketch of 2 functions. Can you write the mathematical expression to describe them?

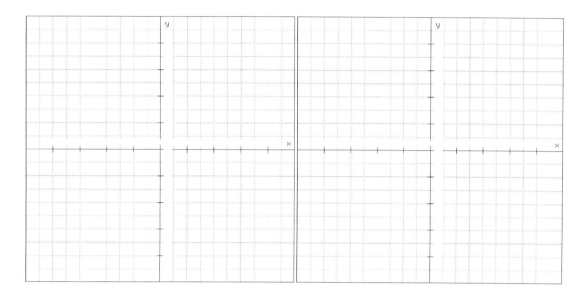

7. Write 2 examples of relations that are not functions:

8. Which one of the following graphs cannot represent function? Explain.

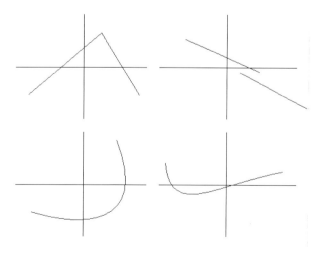

9. Draw an example of a curve that does not represent a function:

10. Draw an example of a curve that represents a function:

11. The domain of a function is the: _____

12. The Range of a function is the: _____

13. Out of the following relations circle the ones that are functions:

   a. Person's name → Person's age
   b. Person's name → Person's personal information
   c. City → Number of habitants
   d. City → Names of habitants
   e. Family → Home Address
   f. Family → Number of members
   g. Family → Members of family
   h. Satellite's name → Position of satellite
   i. Time → Position of object
   j. Time → Value of a stock
   k. Height → Shoe size
   l. Basketball player's name → Percentage of free throws scored
   m. Country → current unemployment rate
   n. Country → names of unemployed citizens
   o. Country → number of unemployed citizens
   p. Time → Maximum number of GB stored in a cubic centimeter
   q. Shoe size → eye color
   r. Football player's name → Number of goals scored in career
   s. One → One
   t. One → Many
   u. Many → One

14. Given the Shoe size – age curve for a human. Sketch an approximate graph, pay attention that a shoe size of 32.2 does not exist, think how this is seen on the graph.

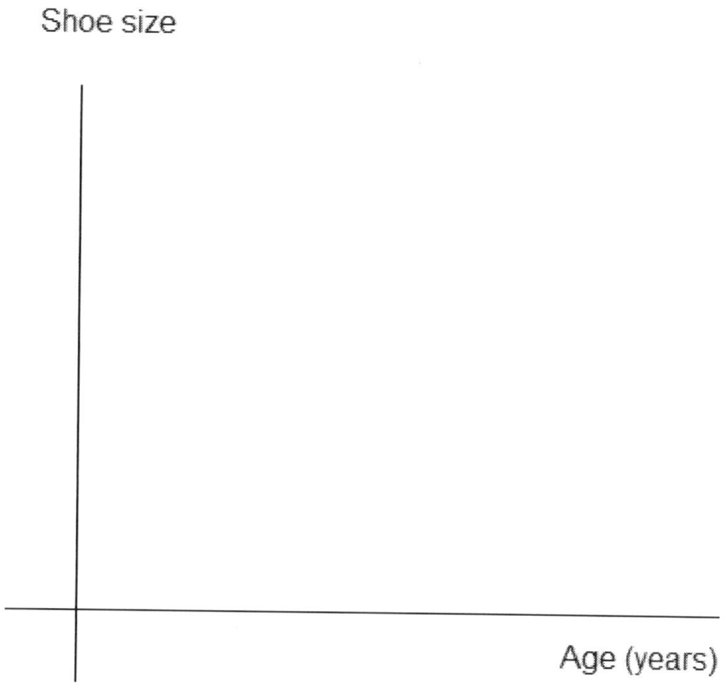

Shoe size

Age (years)

a. Shoe size(0) = _____ , it is the Shoe size of _____

b. Shoe size (t) = 30. Age = _____

c. State its domain: _____

d. State its range: _____

15. Given the following function that describes the temperature in C° as a function of time (Time = 0 corresponds to midnight):

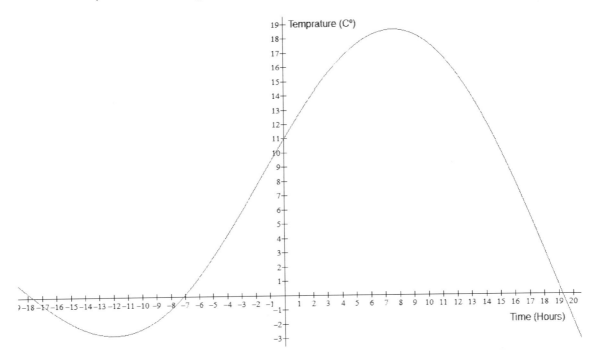

a. Temprature(4) = _____

b. Temprature (0) = _____ = Temprature (__)

c. Temprature (7) = _____

d. Temprature (t) = 3, __time = _____

e. Temprature (t) = 0, __time = _____

f. Temprature (t) = –2, __time = _____

g. State its domain: _____

h. State its range: _____

i. Function increases at: _____

j. Function decreases at: _____

k. Is this function one to one? Many to one? Explain.

16. Given the function that describes the number of rabbits in the forest (N) as a function of the number of wolves (x):

   a. Explain the tendency in your own words. Could you predict really what happens in the forest? What other kind of data you may need? Is this graph realistic?

   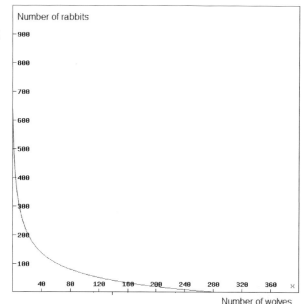

   b. N(0) = _____

   c. N(100) = _____

   d. N(x) = 400. x = _____

   e. Is N(2) < N(3) ?

   f. Is N(100) > N(101) ?

   g. State its domain: _____

   h. State its range: _____

   i. Where is the function increasing? _____

   j. Where is the function decreasing? _____

   k. Where is the function stationary? _____

   l. Is this function one to one? Many to one? Explain.

17. Given the following function:

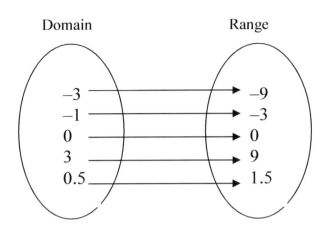
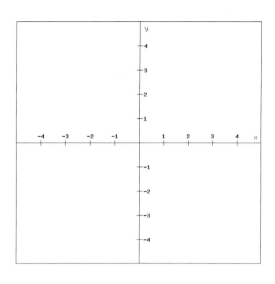

a. What are the allowed values for the independent variable (The domain)?

b. What are the allowed values for the dependent variable (The range)?

c. Sketch the function on the graph.

d. Can you write a mathematical expression to express this function?

18. Given the following function:

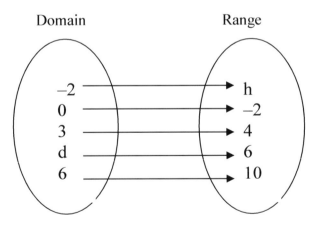

a. Can you write a mathematical expression to express this function?

b. Find h. Find d.

172

19. Use the graph of the gasoline consumption (f) as a function of speed (x) to answer:

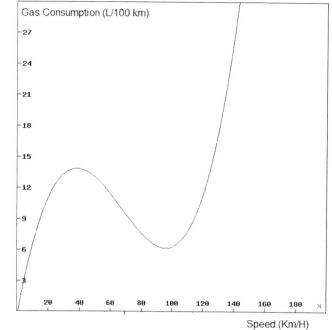

a. $f(0) = $ ____

b. $f(50) = $ ____

c. $f(5) = $ ____

d. For what values of x is $f(x) = 12$

e. Is $f(60) > f(70)$?

f. For what values of x is $f(x) > 15$?

g. For what values of x is $f(x) < 15$?

h. At what speed should the car be driven in the highway? Explain

i. Where is the function increasing? _____

j. Where is the function decreasing? _____

k. Where is the function stationary? _____

20. Functions can be represented using: _____ or _____ or _____

21. The graph below shows the unemployment rate in Spain between the years 2005 and 2014.

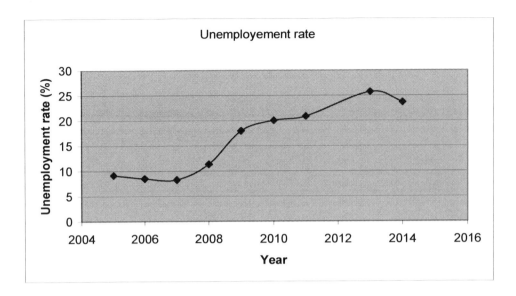

a. What was the unemployment rate at 2008?

b. When was the unemployment rate smaller than 10%?

c. When was the unemployment rate bigger than 20%?

d. When was the unemployment rate increasing?

e. When was the unemployment rate decreasing?

f. State the domain and range of the function.

22. Research the web to find functions you may be interested in, for example in the area of sports, social networks, computer science etc. You may want to search for images and try to observe the functions that appear. Try to specify in your search the term "linear functions" and observe this kind of functions as well.

3.2. – LINEAR FUNCTIONS

1. Given the function: N(x) = 60. This function represents the number of heartbeats per second (N) of a healthy man as a function of time (x). Complete the following table:

x	–5	–4	–3	–2	–1	0	1	2	3	4	5
N(x)											

- Sketch the points of the chart on a graph (use a ruler).

- State the domain of the function: _____

- State the y intercept (sketched on the graph: (____, ____)

- State the x intercept: (____, ____)

- The function is increasing on the interval: _____

- The function is decreasing on the interval: _____

- Sketch the function of the graph used for the points initially drawn

- State the range of the function: _____

- The heartbeat rate is _____

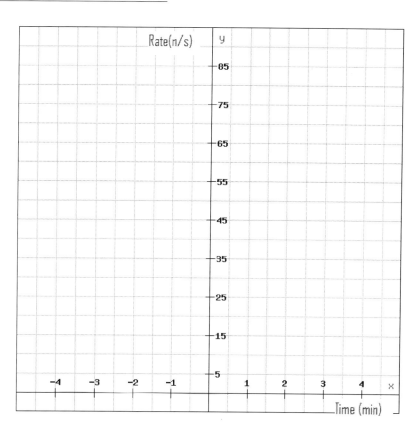

2. The distance of a John in reference to his house in his afternoon walk can be modeled by the function: $D(t) = 2t + 2$, t is the time in hours and D is the position in km.

- Complete the following table:

t	−5	−4	−3	−2	−1	0	1	2	3	4	5
D(t)											

- Sketch the points of the chart on a graph (use a ruler).

- State the domain of the function: _____

- State the *y* intercept (sketched on the graph: (____, ____)

- State the *x* intercept: (____, ____)

- The function is increasing on the interval: _____

- The function is decreasing on the interval: _____

- Sketch the function of the graph used for the points initially drawn

- What is the speed of John _____ How is that seen on the graph?

- State the range of the function: _____

- When was John at his house? _____

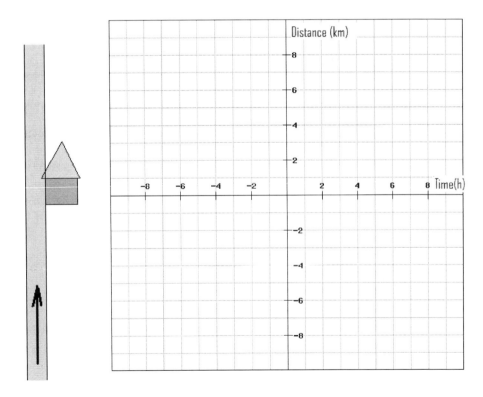

3. An elevator's behavior can be modeled by: $P(t) = -t + 3$. Where P is the floor and t is time in minutes. The building has 15 floors and 3 parking levels below ground.

- Complete the following table:

t	−5	−4	−3	−2	−1	0	1	2	3	4	5
P(t)											

- Sketch the points of the chart on a graph (use a ruler).

- State the domain of the function: _____

- State the y intercept (sketched on the graph: (____, ____)

- State the x intercept: (____, ____)

- The function is increasing on the interval: _____

- The function is decreasing on the interval: _____

- Sketch the function of the graph used for the points initially drawn

- Describe the motion of the elevator _____. How is that seen on the graph?

- State the range of the function: _____

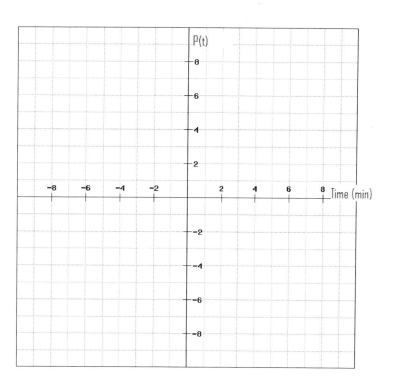

177

4. Given the function: $f(x) = \dfrac{x}{2} - 3$

- Complete the following table:

x	−2	−1	0	1	2	3	4	5	6	7	8
f(x)											

- Sketch the points of the chart on a graph (use a ruler).

- State the domain of the function: _____

- State the y intercept (sketched on the graph: (____, ____)

- State the x intercept: (____, ____)

- The function is increasing on the interval: _____

- The function is decreasing on the interval: _____

- Sketch the function of the graph used for the points initially drawn

- State the range of the function: _____

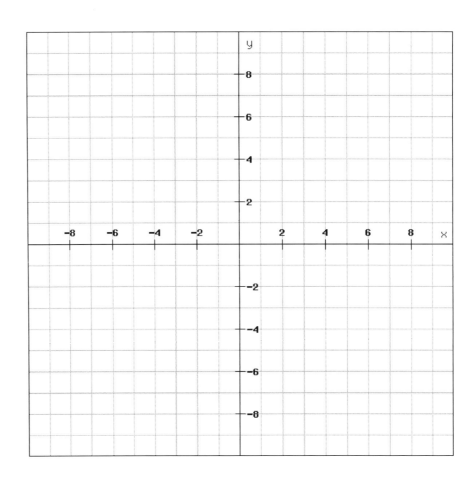

5. Given below are the equations for five different lines. Match the function with its graph.

Function	On the graph
f(x) = 20 + 2x	
g(x) = 3x + 20	
s(x) = –30 + 2x	
a(x) = 50 – x	
b(x) = – 2x + 50	

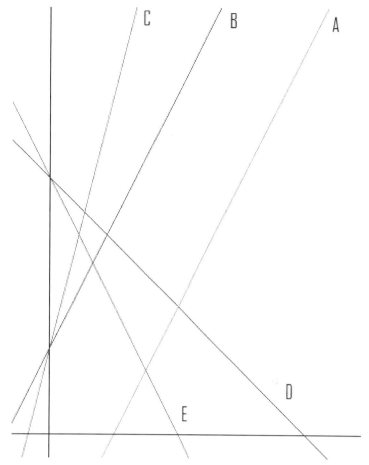

6. The general functions that describes a straight line is _____

7. We know a function is a straight line because _____

8. The y–intercept (also called vertical intercept), tells us where the line crosses the _____. The corresponding point is of the form (,).

9. The x–intercept (also called horizontal intercept), tells us where the line crosses the _____. The corresponding point is of the form (,).

10. If m > 0, the line _____ left to right. If _____ the line decreases left to right.

11. In case the line is horizontal m is _____ and the line is of the form _____.

12. The larger the value of m is, the _____ the graph of the line is.

13. Given the graph, write, the slope (m), b and the equation of the line:

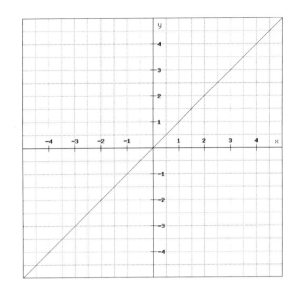

m = _____ b = _____ f(x) = _____   m = _____ b = _____ f(x) = _____

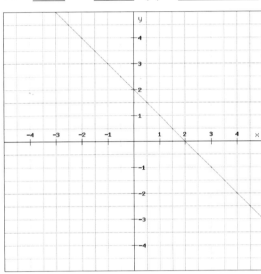
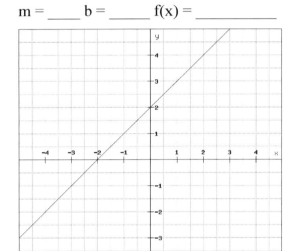

m = _____ b = _____ f(x) = _____   m = _____ b = _____ f(x) = _____

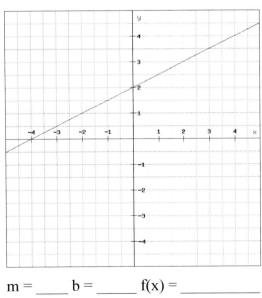
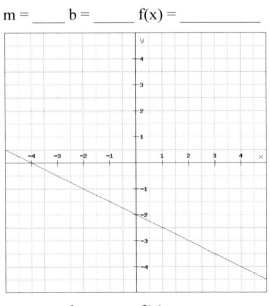

m = _____ b = _____ f(x) = _____   m = _____ b = _____ f(x) = _____

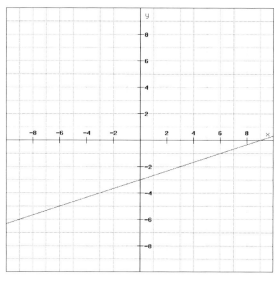

m = _____ b = _____ f(x) = _____

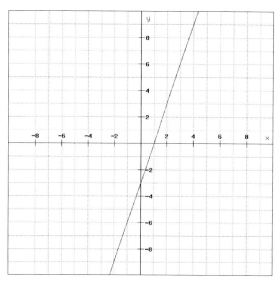

m = _____ b = _____ f(x) = _____

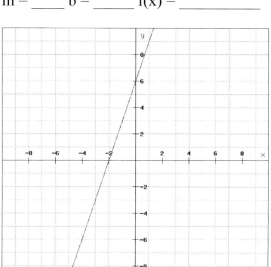

m = _____ b = _____ f(x) = _____

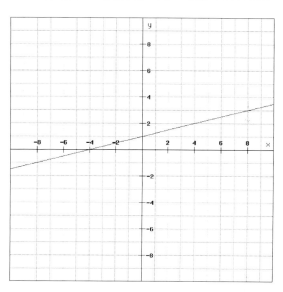

m = _____ b = _____ f(x) = _____

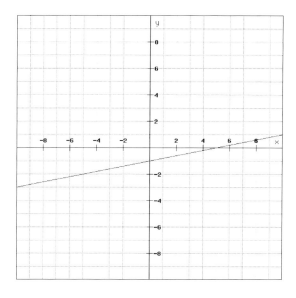

m = _____ b = _____ f(x) = _____

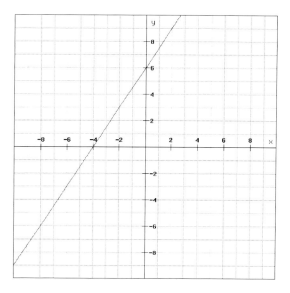

m = _____ b = _____ f(x) = _____

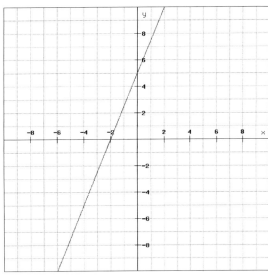
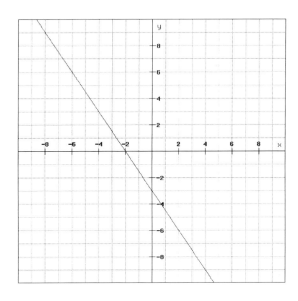

m = ____ b = _____ f(x) = _____   m = ____ b = _____ f(x) = _____

Analyze the following functions/inequalities:

1. f(x) = 1

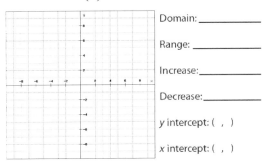

Domain: _____
Range: _____
Increase: _____
Decrease: _____
y intercept: (,)
x intercept: (,)

2. f(x) = 2

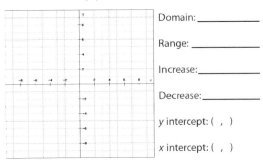

Domain: _____
Range: _____
Increase: _____
Decrease: _____
y intercept: (,)
x intercept: (,)

3. f(x) = –1

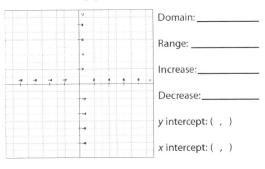

Domain: _____
Range: _____
Increase: _____
Decrease: _____
y intercept: (,)
x intercept: (,)

4. f(x) = 0

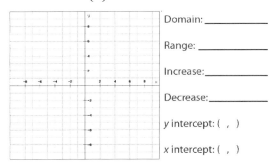

Domain: _____
Range: _____
Increase: _____
Decrease: _____
y intercept: (,)
x intercept: (,)

5. f(x) = x

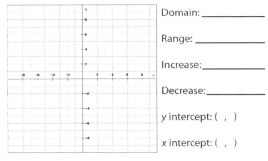

Domain: _____
Range: _____
Increase: _____
Decrease: _____
y intercept: (,)
x intercept: (,)

6. f(x) = x+1

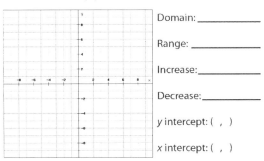

Domain: _____
Range: _____
Increase: _____
Decrease: _____
y intercept: (,)
x intercept: (,)

7. f(x) = –x

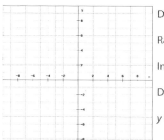

Domain: _____

Range: _____

Increase: _____

Decrease: _____

y intercept: (,)

x intercept: (,)

11. f(x) = 3 – 2x

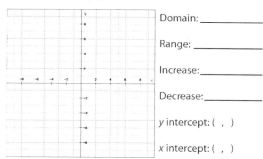

Domain: _____

Range: _____

Increase: _____

Decrease: _____

y intercept: (,)

x intercept: (,)

8. f(x) = –x–2

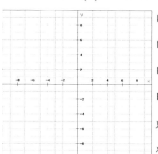

Domain: _____

Range: _____

Increase: _____

Decrease: _____

y intercept: (,)

x intercept: (,)

12. $f(x) = \dfrac{x}{3}$

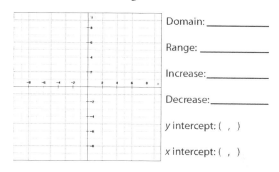

Domain: _____

Range: _____

Increase: _____

Decrease: _____

y intercept: (,)

x intercept: (,)

9. f(x) = 2x

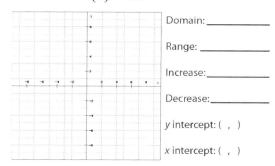

Domain: _____

Range: _____

Increase: _____

Decrease: _____

y intercept: (,)

x intercept: (,)

13. f(x) = 2x+1

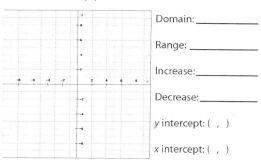

Domain: _____

Range: _____

Increase: _____

Decrease: _____

y intercept: (,)

x intercept: (,)

10. y ≤ 3x – 5

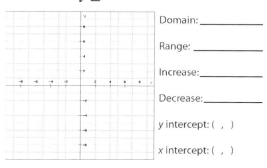

Domain: _____

Range: _____

Increase: _____

Decrease: _____

y intercept: (,)

x intercept: (,)

14. f(x) = 2x–2

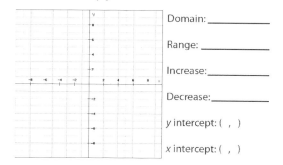

Domain: _____

Range: _____

Increase: _____

Decrease: _____

y intercept: (,)

x intercept: (,)

15. f(x) = 3x+5

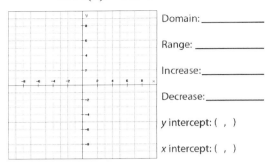

Domain: _____
Range: _____
Increase: _____
Decrease: _____
y intercept: (,)
x intercept: (,)

16. $f(x) \leq \dfrac{x}{2} - 5$

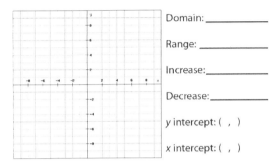

Domain: _____
Range: _____
Increase: _____
Decrease: _____
y intercept: (,)
x intercept: (,)

17. $f(x) = \dfrac{x}{4} + 6$

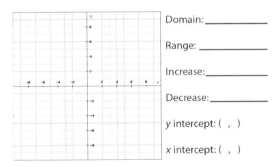

Domain: _____
Range: _____
Increase: _____
Decrease: _____
y intercept: (,)
x intercept: (,)

18. $f(x) \geq \dfrac{3x-10}{2}$

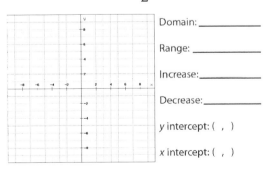

Domain: _____
Range: _____
Increase: _____
Decrease: _____
y intercept: (,)
x intercept: (,)

19. $f(x) = -\dfrac{3}{2}x - \dfrac{3}{2}$

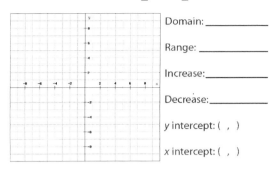

Domain: _____
Range: _____
Increase: _____
Decrease: _____
y intercept: (,)
x intercept: (,)

20. $f(x) = -\dfrac{x+3}{2}$

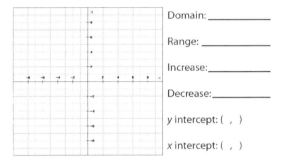

Domain: _____
Range: _____
Increase: _____
Decrease: _____
y intercept: (,)
x intercept: (,)

21. $f(x) = \dfrac{14x-1}{4}$

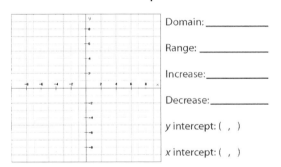

Domain: _____
Range: _____
Increase: _____
Decrease: _____
y intercept: (,)
x intercept: (,)

22. $f(x) = -\dfrac{27x-40}{15}$

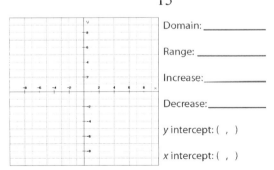

Domain: _____
Range: _____
Increase: _____
Decrease: _____
y intercept: (,)
x intercept: (,)

23. $3x + 2y = 2$

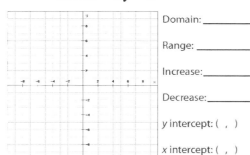

Domain: _____
Range: _____
Increase: _____
Decrease: _____
y intercept: (,)
x intercept: (,)

27. $y + 2x - 3 \geq 1$

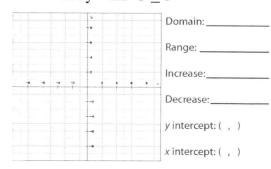

Domain: _____
Range: _____
Increase: _____
Decrease: _____
y intercept: (,)
x intercept: (,)

24. $4x - 2y - 3 = 1$

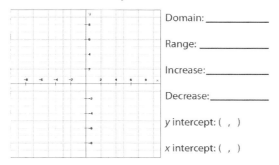

Domain: _____
Range: _____
Increase: _____
Decrease: _____
y intercept: (,)
x intercept: (,)

28. $5y + 5x = 5$

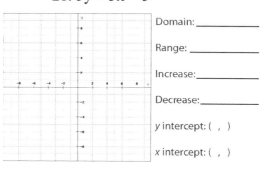

Domain: _____
Range: _____
Increase: _____
Decrease: _____
y intercept: (,)
x intercept: (,)

25. $-2y + 3x = -5$

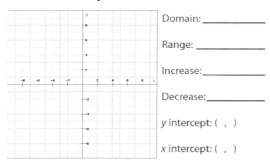

Domain: _____
Range: _____
Increase: _____
Decrease: _____
y intercept: (,)
x intercept: (,)

29. $2x - 2y - 3 = 1$

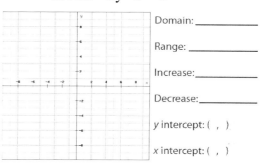

Domain: _____
Range: _____
Increase: _____
Decrease: _____
y intercept: (,)
x intercept: (,)

26. $y - x \leq 2$

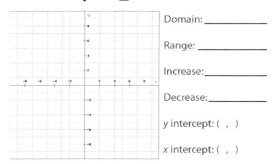

Domain: _____
Range: _____
Increase: _____
Decrease: _____
y intercept: (,)
x intercept: (,)

30. $x - 2y - 150 = 0$

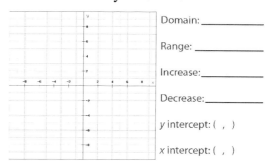

Domain: _____
Range: _____
Increase: _____
Decrease: _____
y intercept: (,)
x intercept: (,)

31. Write the equation of the line that has a slope of 2 and passes through the point (2, 4) in the forms: y = mx + b and ax + by + c = 0, (a, b ∈ Z)

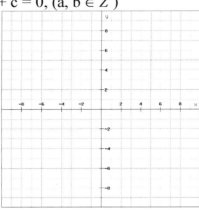

32. Write the equation of the line that has a slope of $-\dfrac{1}{2}$ and passes through the point (–2, –3) in the forms: y = mx + b and ax + by + c = 0, (a, b ∈ Z)

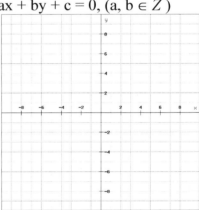

33. Write the equation of the line that has a slope of $-\dfrac{5}{2}$ and passes through the point (–1, 2) in the forms: y = mx + b and ax + by + c = 0, (a, b ∈ Z)

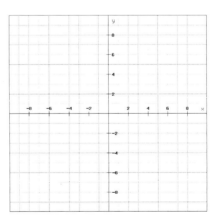

34. Find the equation of the line that passes through the points (1, 1), (2, 4), indicate its y and x intercepts and sketch it. Write its equation in the forms: y = mx + b and ax + by + c = 0, (a, b ∈ Z)

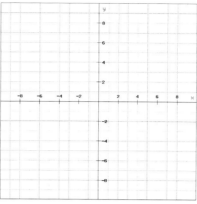

35. Find the equation of the line that passes through the points (–1, –5), (4, 3), indicate its y and x intercepts and sketch it. Write its equation in the forms: y = mx + b and ax + by + c = 0, (a, b ∈ Z)

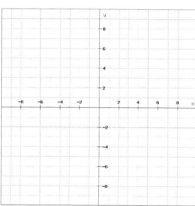

36. Find the equation of the line that passes through the points (–5, 1), (–2, 4), indicate its y and x intercepts, sketch it and write it in both formas y = mx + b and ax + by + c = 0, (a, b ∈ Z)

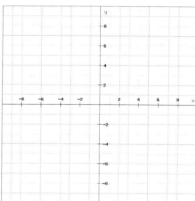

37. Write the equation of the line that is parallel to the line y = 5x – 2 and passes through the point (–2, –1). Write its equation in the forms: y = mx + b and ax + by + c = 0, (a, b ∈ Z)

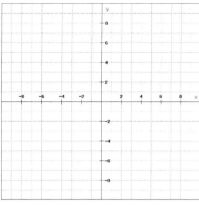

38. Write the equation of the line that is parallel to the line y = –0.5x – 1 and passes through the point (–3, 6). Write its equation in the forms: y = mx + b and ax + by + c = 0, (a, b ∈ Z)

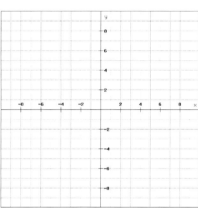

39. Sketch and write the equation of the line with a slope of $-\dfrac{1}{5}$ that passes through the point (0,2).

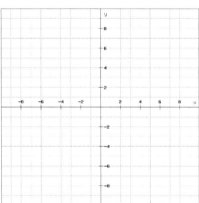

40. Sketch and write the equation of the lines with a slope: $1, 2, -3, -1, -\dfrac{1}{2}, -\dfrac{1}{3}$, that pass through the point (0,0).

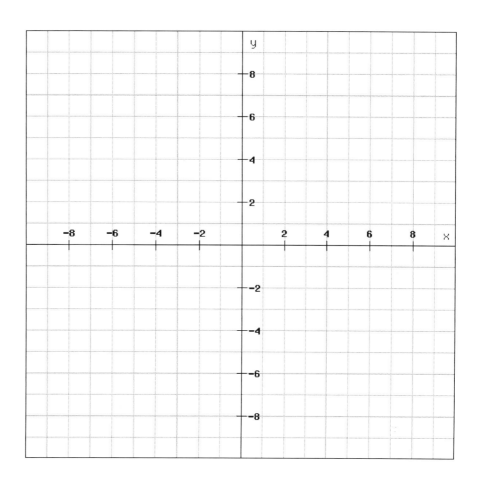

41. Sketch and write the equation of the line with a slope of -3 that passes through the point $(0,-3)$.

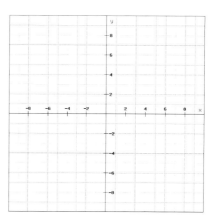

189

42. Sketch and write the equation of the line with a slope of 2 that passes through the point (2,0)

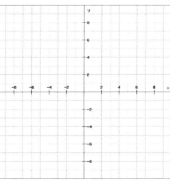

43. Sketch and write the equation of the line with a slope of $-\dfrac{1}{2}$ that passes through the point (–2,0)

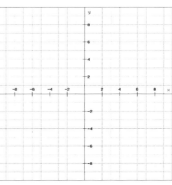

44. Sketch and write the equation of the line with a slope of 2 that passes through the point (–4,2)

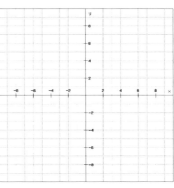

45. Find the intersection between the lines $f(x) = 2x - 3$ and $f(x) = -5x - 2$

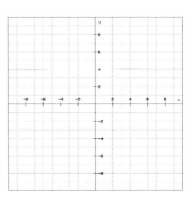

46. Find the intersection between the lines f(x) = x − 3 and f(x) = x − 4

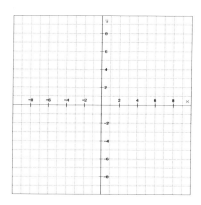

47. Find the intersection between the lines f(x) = 2x − 3 and f(x) = −2x + 7

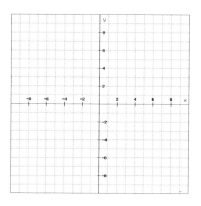

48. Find the intersection between the lines f(x) = ax − 3 and f(x) = ax + 7

49. Find the intersection between the lines f(x) = −12x − 13 and f(x) = 15x + 20.

50. Given that the lines f(x) = 2ax − 1 and f(x) = 4 − 5x + 20 do not intersect, find a.

51. Find the intersection between the lines y = 2x – 3 and 2y – 4x = – 6.

52. Given that the lines f(x) = mx – 5 and f(x) = 2x + 4 intersect at the point where x = 3, find m.

53. Given that the lines f(x) = 2x – b and f(x) = 3x + 4 intersect at the point where x = 1, find b.

54. Find the intersection between the lines 3y + 2x = 3 and 9y + 6x = 9.

55. Sketch the line $f(x) = \dfrac{-x}{2} + 3, -4 < x \leq 8$

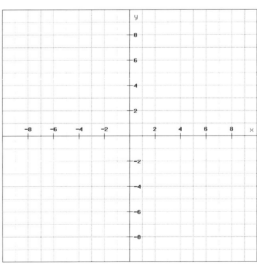

DISTANCE AND MIDPOINT BETWEEN 2 POINTS

56. Given the points (1, 2) and (5, 8). Find the distance between them. Find the midpoint. Sketch to illustrate your answer.

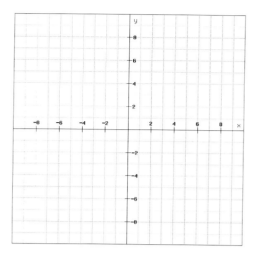

57. Given the points (–3, 2) and (5, –6). Find the distance between them. Find the midpoint. Sketch to illustrate your answer.

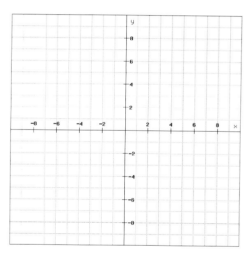

58. Given the points (–1, –6) and (–5, –1). Find the distance between them. Find the midpoint. Sketch to illustrate your answer.

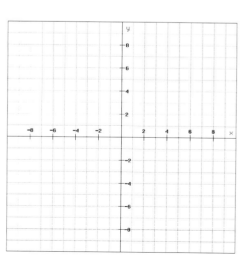

59. Given that the points $(a, -1)$ and $(5, 3)$ are 5 units away. Find a. Find the midpoint.

60. Given that the points $(1, -4)$ and $(5, c)$ are 10 units away. Find c. Find the midpoint.

61. Find the equation of all the points that are 2 units away from the origin. This equation describes a _____

62. Find the equation of all the points that are 5 units away from the point $(2, -1)$. This equation describes a _____

63. Given that the points $(1, -4)$ and $(5, c)$ are 10 units away. Find c. Find the midpoint.

64. Given the points $(-8, -7)$ and $(6, 2)$. Find the distance between them. Find the midpoint.

PERPENDICULAR LINES ($m \cdot m_\perp = -1$)

65. A slope perpendicular to 1 is _____, A slope perpendicular to 2 is _____

    A slope perpendicular to k is _____ A slope perpendicular to $\dfrac{a}{b}$ is _____

66. Find the equation of a line perpendicular to the line y = 3x – 2 that passes through the point (3, 12). Sketch to illustrate your answer.

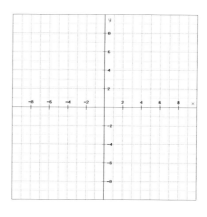

67. Find all the lines perpendicular to the line y = –3x + 4. Fin the ones that passes through the point (–3, 1). Sketch to illustrate your answer.

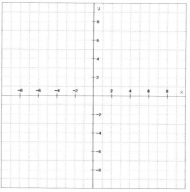

68. Find a line perpendicular to the line y = $-\dfrac{2}{5}$x + 1 that passes through the point (–1, –7). Sketch to illustrate your answer.

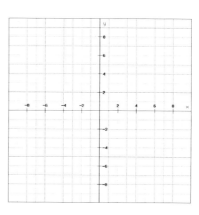

69. Given the points (–2, 5) and (4, 2).

   a. Find the equation of the line passing through them.

   b. Is the point (5, 1) on this line? Show your work.

   c. Find a perpendicular line that passes through the mid point between these points.

   d. Find all the points on the line found in c that are 0.5 units away from the point (0, 2).

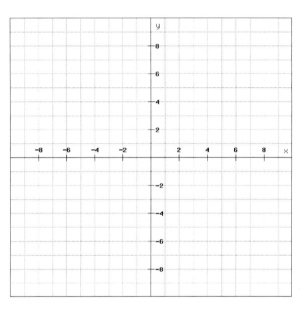

70. Find a point on the x axis that is $\sqrt{5}$ units away from the line $y = 2x + 4$

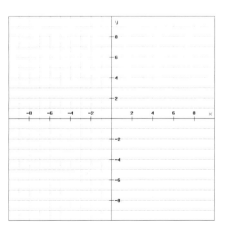

71. Find a point on the y axis that is 5 units away from the line y = 3x + 2

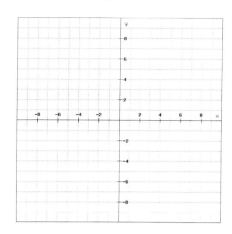

72. Given that the slope of one of the lines is 3 and that the lines are perpendicular, find the **exact** coordinates of the point of intersection of the two lines.

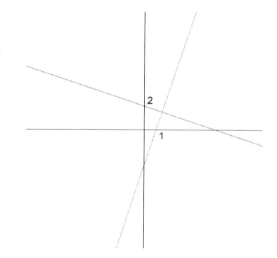

SLOPE – INTERCEPT FORM OF A LINE

73. The line $y-3=2(x+1)$ passes through the point _____ and has a slope of ____

74. The line $y+5=-3(x-51)$ passes through the point _____ and has a slope of ____

75. The line $-y+1=(x+3)$ passes through the point _____ and has a slope of ____

76. The line $2y+5=-6(x+7)$ passes through the point _____ and has a slope of ____

77. The line $y+a=m(x+b)$ passes through the point _____ and has a slope of ____

78. The line $y-a=m(x-b)$ passes through the point _____ and has a slope of ____

79. The line $y-a=m(x+b)$ passes through the point _____ and has a slope of ____

80. Write the equation $y-3=2(x+1)$ in the explicit form

81. Write the equation $y+5=2(x+6)$ in the explicit form

82. Write down the equation of a line passing through the point (5, 2) with slope 1.

83. Write down the equation of a line passing through the point (–4, –3) with slope –2.

84. Write down the equation of a line passing through the point (6, 3) with slope $\frac{2}{3}$.

85. Write down the equation of a line passing through point (–2, –5) with slope $-\frac{2}{5}$.

86. Write down the equation of the line passing through points (–2, –5), (–7, –5),

87. Write down the equation of the line passing through points (–1, –3), (6, 5),

88. Write down the equation of the line passing through points (–1, 5), (7, –2),

APPLICATION

1. The price of a new TV (in US$) is $P(t) = 500 - 20t$, t given in months.

   a. Sketch the corresponding graph.

   b. What was the initial price of the TV? _____

   c. Find the price of the TV after 10 days

   d. What is the domain of the function, reason your answer,

   e. What is the range of the function.

   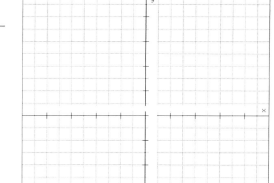

   f. What is the meaning of 20? Does it have units? What are they?

2. A certain computer has 10000 MB (Megabytes) of memory occupied by the operating system and it can store information at 200 MB per second. It is known that the Hard disk of the computer is full when 500000 MB (500 GB) is reached.

   a. Write a function to describe the amount of memory occupied as a function of time while the computer stores information and represent it on the graph. Use appropriate scale, variables and units.

   b. State its domain and range.

   c. What are the units of the slope?

   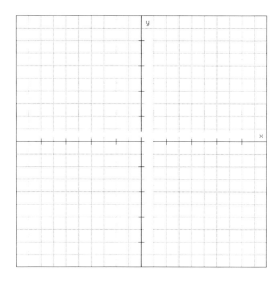

   d. How long will it take the computer to store a 700 MB file?

   e. In case it took the computer 5 seconds to store a file, find the size of the file?

199

3. In a factory there are 2 machines that produce a certain product. The operation cost (electricity, maintenance etc.) of Machine A is 250$ a month and the cost of production per product is 2$. The operation cost of Machine B is 200$ a month and the cost of production per product is 4$. The maximum number of products that both machines can make a month is 200.

   a. Write the functions to describe the cost C as a function of the number of products n for both machines. Indicate the domain and range of both functions. What are the units of the slope?

   b. Graph the functions, use appropriate scale, variables and units. Calculate the coordinates of important points on the graph.

   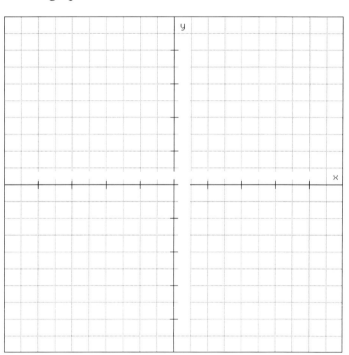

   c. Discuss in which case each machine is best.

200

4. A parking lot with 1200 parking is full after 5 hours.

   a. Write the function to describe the number of cars N as function of time t in hours. Indicate the domain and range of the function. What are the units of the slope?

   b. If the parking opens at 7, Find the number of free spots at 8:30.

   c. In case the owner needs 400 free spots after how long should he close the parking?

   d. Graph the function, use appropriate scale, variables and units.

   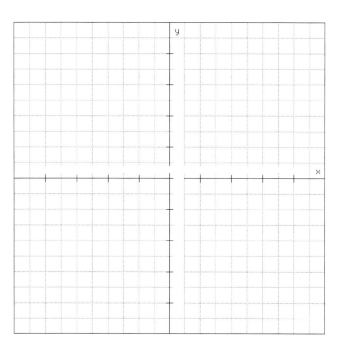

5. You need to rent a car for one day and to compare the charges of 3 different companies. Company I charges 20$ per day with additional cost of 0.20$ per mile. Company II charges 30$ per day with additional cost of 0.10$ per mile. Company III charges 60$ per day with no additional mileage charge.

   a. Write the cost function for each one of the companies.

   b. Sketch all 3 graphs on the same axes system.

   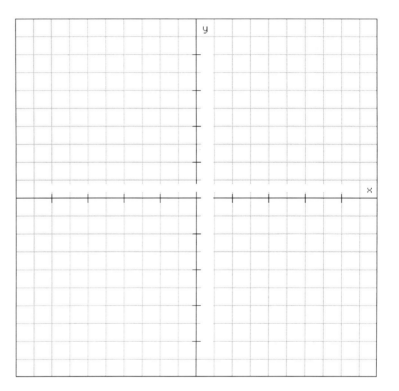

   c. Comment on the circumstances in which renting a car from each one of the companies is best.

6. A container filled with water is being emptied as can be seen in the diagram. The following graph describes the water level in the container as a function time:

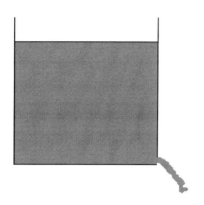
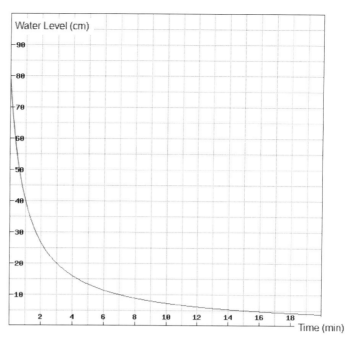

a. What was the water level in the beginning?

b. How long did it take the water level to go down by 50%?

c. How long did it take the water level to go down by 75%?

d. By what percentage did the water level go down after 7 minutes?

e. By what percentage did the water level go down after 15 minutes?

f. According to the graph, how long do you think it will take the container to be emptied completely?

g. Is this a linear function? Explain.

203

7. The height of a ball above ground as a function of time (t) in seconds is given by the following function: $Height(t) = -t(t-4)$.

   a. Fill the table:

Time(s)	0	1	2	3	4	5	6
Height(m)							

   b. Draw the corresponding points on the graph:
      Include the corresponding numbers. Is this motion linear? Explain

      |Height (m)

      Time(s)

8. The cost of making a certain product ($) is given by the function $Cost(n) = \dfrac{100}{n} + 5$ where n is the number of products made in thousands.

   a. Fill the table:

Number of products made(n)	1	2	4	5	10	20	50	100
Cost($)								

   b. Draw the corresponding points on the graph. Include the corresponding numbers. Is this graph linear? Explain

      Cost($)

      Number of products (n)

TRAVEL GRAPHS

1. Describe the motion of the train, the vertical axis represents the distance from its objective:

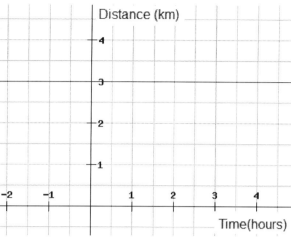

2. Describe the motion of the object, the vertical axis represents the distance from its objective:

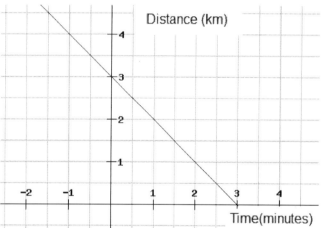

3. Describe the motion of the following object; the vertical axis describes the distance of the object from point A. Is this motion a realistic one? Explain.

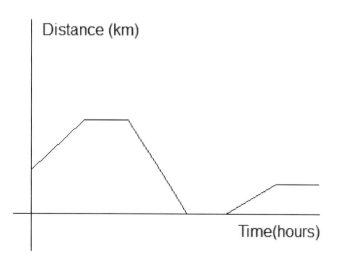

4. Determine if the following graph can describe a motion of an object, explain and describe the motion if possible.

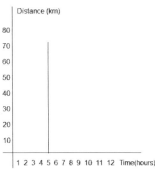

5. Determine if the following graph can describe a motion of an object, explain and describe the motion if possible.

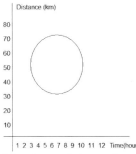

6. Determine if the following graph can describe a motion of an object, explain and describe the motion if possible.

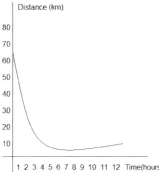

7. Given the following graph describing the motion of a certain object. Describe the motion providing the speed of the object in each part of the trip.

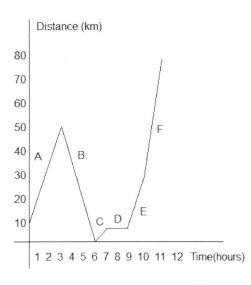

CHAPTER 4 - STATISTICS

4.1. – INTRODUCTION TO STATISTICS

In Statistics we try to obtain some conclusions by observing and/or analyzing data.

1. The set of objects that we are trying to study is called _____, the number of elements in the population can be _____ or _____.

2. Usually the _____ is too big and therefore we obtain a _____. This process is called _____.

3. We use the _____ to obtain conclusions about the _____.

Types of DATA

4. _____ data.

5. _____ data that can be divided to _____ or _____.

6. _____ can be counted while _____ data can be _____.

7. Give 3 examples of _____ data:

8. Give 3 examples of _____ _____ data:

9. Give 3 examples of _____ _____ data:

10. Given the following variables, classify them in the table:

    - Eye color
    - Shoe size
    - Height
    - Weight
    - Number of cars in a parking lot
    - Type of fruit
    - Number of apples sold a day in a store
    - Velocity of the wind
    - Temperature
    - Numbers of pages in a book
    - Name of writer
    - Number of students in a school

Categorical	Numerical Discrete	Numerical Continuous

11. In a certain class the favorite dessert of students was studies. The following results were obtained:

    Ice cream, fruit, Ice cream, coffee, cake, fruit, fruit, cake, cake, Ice cream, fruit, cake, cake

    a. How many students participated?
    b. What kind of data is this?
    c. Organize the information in a table (use technology)
    d. Represent the information in a Bar Chart (use technology)
    e. Represent the information in a Pie Chart (include the %) (use technology)

12. In a certain math class the following grades were obtained:

    70, 70, 70, 70, 70, 70, 70, 80, 80, 80, 80, 90, 90, 90

    a. How many students in the classroom?
    b. What kind of data is this?
    c. Represent this information in a table (group) (use technology)
    d. Use the table to create a bar graph (use technology)

13. In a certain math class the following grades were obtained:

    65, 72, 85, 89, 52, 71, 89, 68, 63, 76, 61, 86, 98, 79, 79, 91, 74, 89, 77, 68, 78

    a. How many students participated?
    b. What kind of data is this?
    c. Suggest a method to represent this information in a table by grouping (use technology)
    d. Use the table to create a bar graph (use technology)

14. In a certain zoo the length of a certain type of animal (in meters) was studied. The following results were obtained:

    1.77, 1.60, 1.89, 1.54, 1.77, 1.65, 1.86, 1.51, 1.67, 1.94, 1.73, 1.70, 1.66, 1.58

    a. How many animals participated?
    b. What kind of data is this?
    c. Suggest a method to represent this information in a table (use technology)
    d. Use the table to create a bar graph (use technology)

15. In a certain group shoe size was studied and the following results obtained:

    45, 36, 44, 38, 41, 42, 48, 39, 40, 42, 43, 41, 38, 45, 41, 38, 42, 44, 41, 41, 46

    a. How many students participated?
    b. What kind of data is this?
    c. Suggest a method to represent this information in a table (use technology)
    d. Use the table to create a bar graph (use technology)

16. The number of imperfections in a certain product was studies and the following results obtained in a group of products:

    0, 1, 0, 0, 1, 2, 0, 2, 0, 3, 0, 0, 2, 1, 0, 0, 0, 1, 1, 2, 0, 3, 0, 1, 1, 0, 0, 0, 1, 0

    a. How many products were tested?
    b. What kind of data is this?
    c. Suggest a method to represent this information in a table (use technology)
    d. Use the table to create a bar graph (use technology)

17. Choose a variable to collect information about in your classroom, state its kind, represent the information in a table and create a bar graph. (use technology)

4.2. – BIVARIATE DATA AND SCATTER PLOTS

1. In many occasions variables may be related to each other, for example:

    - Age – Height
    - Level of education – Average income
    - Resistance to wind – gasoline consumption

    Give 3 other examples; discuss the kind of relation that exists between the variables:

2. Given the following data about a group of students and the corresponding graph:

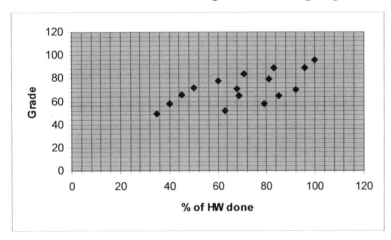

Student	% of HW done	Grade
Helena	71	84
Alexandra	68	71
Alicia	95	89
Ben	45	66
Sofia	85	65
Blanca	63	52
Anabel	35	49
Elena	40	58
Isabella	77	78
Elia	83	82
Raquel	100	96
Núria	92	70
Pablo	69	70
Martim	81	79
Iris	67	72
Carlota	79	58

   a. Sketch an approximate straight line that best fits the data.
   b. Find the equation of the line.
   c. Comment on the correlation between doing HW and obtaining grades.

3. Life expectancy of different animals was studies and the following data obtained:

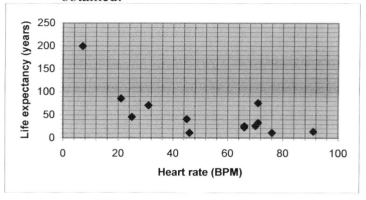

Heart rate (BPM)	Life expectancy (years)
7	200
25	46
71	76
31	71
21	86
66	26
66	23
45	41
76	11
91	14
46	11
71	33
70	26

Discuss the nature of the correlation between the heart rate and life expectancy of animals.

4. Kinetic energy of an object is given by the expression: $E = \frac{1}{2}mv^2$ where m is the mass of the object and v is the speed of the object. Given an object of 4 kg, fill the following table:

v (m/s)	0	1	2	3	4	5	6	7
E (J)								

Add the corresponding points to the graph and discuss the nature of this correlation.

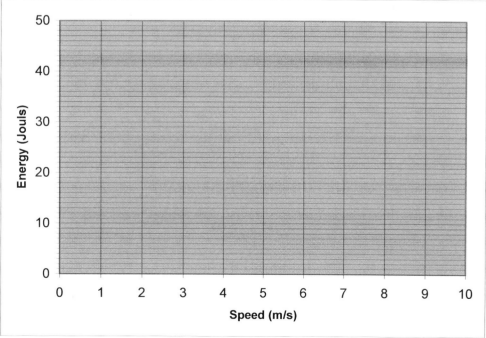

5. The relation between variables is called: _____ and if it is _____ it can be classified in the following way:

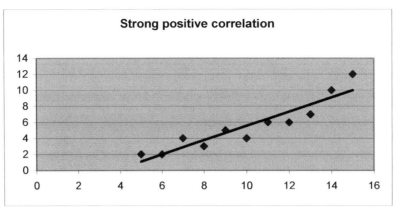

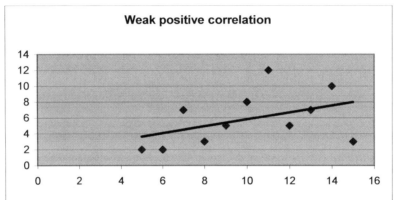

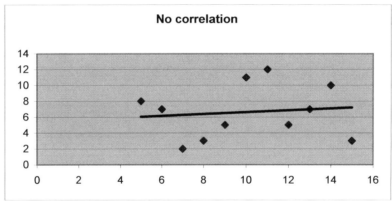

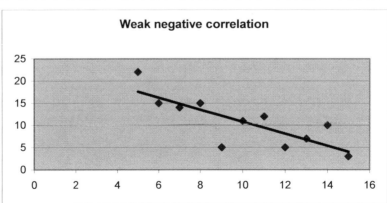

214

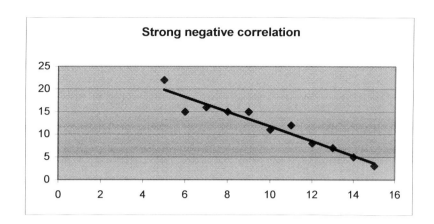

6. This correlation is characterized by a certain number called _____ coefficient (r).

7. In case of a perfect positive correlation the value of r is _____

8. In case of a perfect negative correlation the value of r is _____

9. In case of a no correlation the value of r is _____

10. Finally r is between _____ and _____

11. All of the correlations above mentioned are _____. There can be other kinds of correlation for example _____

12. In a certain math class the following data about students was found:

Name	John	Dean	Elisa	Marc	Heather	Alicia	Raquel	Kevin	Alex	Deena
HW Done (%)	58	90	75	50	40	95	100	85	75	82
Grade (%)	70	80	80	65	55	78	86	89	82	70

a. Represent the data on a graph (choose an appropriate scale)

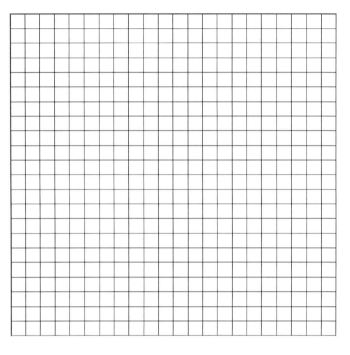

b. Is there correlation? _____ what kind? _____

c. Sketch a line that best fits the data and find its equation.

d. Use your equation to predict the grade of a student that did 72% of the HW.

e. A student obtained a grade of 77, find the percentage of the HW she did.

13. In a group of students, height and weight correlation was studies. The results are given by the table below.

    a. Represent the data on a graph (choose an appropriate scale)

Height (cm)	Weight (kg)
165	58
170	62
172	80
169	65
188	88
163	52
191	95
177	72

    b. Is there correlation? _____ what kind? _____

    c. Sketch a line that best fits the data and find its equation.

    d. Use your equation to predict the weight of a student whose height is 180 cm

    e. A student's weight is 78 kg, find his height.

217

14. In a group of students the reading speed was studied in relation to age of the student. The results are given by the table below.

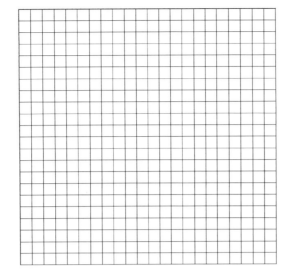

Age (years)	Spelling errors in a 1000 words
15	3
12	10
17	2
19	3
18	2
16	5
19	2
17	3
13	8
14	9
14	7
15	6

a. Represent the data on a graph (choose an appropriate scale)

b. Is there correlation? _____ what kind? _____

c. Sketch a line that best fits the data and find its equation.

d. Use your equation to predict the number of spelling errors of a student who is 13 years old.

e. Use your equation to predict the age of a student who made 4 spelling errors.

TWO WAY TABLES

1. In a certain study the following data was obtained:

   a. Fill the missing parts of the table.
   b. This type of tables is called: _____

	Smokers	None-smokers	Total
Male	27	56	
Female	35	78	
Total			

   c. Write down the number of participants in the study: _____

   d. Find the percentage of smokers in the sample: _____

   e. Find the percentage of non-smokers in the sample: _____

   f. Find the percentage of male smokers in the sample: _____

   g. Find the percentage of female smokers in the sample: _____

2. In a certain study the following data was obtained:

   a. Fill the missing parts of the table.
   b. This type of tables is called _____

	High Blood Pressure	Normal Blood Pressure	Low Blood Pressure	Total
Overweight	50	56	25	
Normal weight	35	78	44	
Total				

   c. Write down the number of participants in the study: _____

   d. Find the percentage of overweight in the sample: _____

   e. Find the percentage of normal weight in the sample: _____

   f. Find the percentage of high blood pressure in the sample: _____

   normal blood pressure in the sample: _____ low blood pressure in the

   sample: _____

3. Some students were asked about their favorite subject. The following information was obtained

   a. Fill the missing parts of the table.

	Math	History	English	Total
Male	123	86	102	
Female	x	109	100	
Total				

   b. It is known that the percentage of male in the sample is 50%, find x

   c. Find the percentage of female students who prefer math: _____

   d. Find the percentage of male students who prefer math: _____

   e. Draw a conclusion from your results

4. A new medicine called "Unbroken heart" for heart diseases is being tested and the following results obtained:

	Used "Unbroken heart"	Did not use "Unbroken heart"	Total
Cured	77	y	
Not Cured	43	45	
Total			

   a. Fill the missing parts of the table.

   b. It is known that the percentage of patients who did not use "Unbroken heart" is 40%, find y

   c. Find the percentage of cured patients who used "Unbroken heart" in the sample:

   d. Find the percentage of cured patients who did not use "Unbroken heart" in the sample:

   e. Draw a conclusion about the medicine "Unbroken heart"

4.3. – MEAN, MEDIAN, MODE AND FREQUENCY DIAGRAMS

1. The mean is _____

2. The mode is _____

3. The median is _____

   If the number of elements is _____ the median will be the element in the $\frac{n+1}{2}$ position. If the number of elements is _____ the median will be the _____ of the elements in the positions $\frac{n}{2}$ and $\frac{n}{2}+1$

4. In a certain club the number of visitors per days was studied during 1 week and the following results obtained: 50, 52, 51, 55, 55, 70, 65

   a. State the number of elements in the set: _____

   b. What kind of data is this? _____

   c. Find its mean: _____   Find its mode: _____

   d. Write the data in an increasing order:

   e. Find its Median: _____

   f. Try to obtain the answers using technology.

5. In a certain restaurant the amount of meat (kg) consumed per day was studied and the following results obtained: 11.5, 12.2, 14.6, 15.0, 23.2, 21.2, 10.1, 13.1

   a. State the number of elements in the set: _____

   b. What kind of data is this? _____

   c. Find its mean: _____   Find its mode: _____

   d. Write the data in an increasing order:

   e. Find its Median: _____

   f. Try to obtain the answers using technology.

6. In a certain math class the number of exercises per day given for HW is the following: 5, 6, 6, 6, 4, 4, 5, 5, 4, 5, 6, 6, 7, 3, 0, 3

    a. State the number of elements in the set: _____

    b. What kind of data is this? _____

    c. Find its mean: _____   Find its mode: _____

    d. Write the data in an increasing order:

    e. Find its Median: _____

    f. Try to obtain the answers using technology.

7. In the following data: 2, 2, 3, 3, 9, 9, 9 one natural number is missing. It is known that the median with the missing number is 3. Find all the possible values of the missing number.

8. In a certain math class the following grades were obtained:

    68, 79, 75, 89, 54, 81, 88, 62, 67, 75, 64, 85, 97, 77, 79, 90, 75, 89, 76, 68

    a. State the number of elements in the set: _____

    b. What kind of data is this? _____

    c. Find its mean: _____   Find its mode: _____

    d. Write the data in an increasing order:

    e. Find its Median: _____

    f. Fill the table:

Grade	Mid – Grade (Mi)	Frequency (fi)	fi x Mi	Cumulative Frequency (Fi)	Fi (%)
[51, 60]					
[61, 70]					
[71, 80]					
[81, 90]					
[91, 100]					
Total					

g. Use the table to find the mean: _____. Comment on the result compared to the previous mean obtained.

h. Discuss the advantages and disadvantages of organizing information in a table.

i. Is this the only possible choice for the left column of the table? Why? Discuss the advantages and disadvantages of organizing information in such a way.

j. Design a new table with a different _____

Grade	Mid – Grade (Mi)	Frequency (fi)	Fi x Mi

k. Use the table to find the mean: _____. Comment on the result compared to the previous mean obtained.

l. The mean of the population is denoted with the Greek letter mu: _____ and typically it is _____. The mean of the sample is denoted by _____

m. Find the modal interval in both tables:

1st: _____   2nd: _____

n. In general this method of organizing information is called _____

o. The 1st column is called _____ with upper interval boundary and _____ interval boundary.

p. The 2nd column is called _____

9. In a certain class the following heights (in m) of students were collected:

   1.77, 1.60, 1.89, 1.54, 1.77, 1.65, 1.86, 1.51, 1.67, 1.94, 1.73, 1.70, 1.66, 1.70

   a. State the number of elements in the set: _____

   b. What kind of data is this? _____

   c. Find its mean: _____   Find its mode: _____

   d. Write the data in an increasing order:

   e. Find its Median: _____

   f. Fill the table:

Grade	Mid – Grade (Mi)	Frequency (fi)	fi x Mi
[1.50 – 1.60)			
[1.60 – 1.70)			
[1.70 – 1.80)			
[1.80 – 1.90)			
[1.90 – 2.00)			
Total			

   g. Use the table to find the mean: _____. Comment on the result compared to the previous mean obtained.

   h. Discuss the advantages and disadvantages of organizing information in a table.

10. In a certain class students eye color was collected:

    Brown, Black, Brown, Blue, Brown, Blue, Green, Brown, Black, Green

    a. State the number of elements in the set: _____

    b. What kind of data is this? _____

    c. Fill the table:

Eye Color	Mid – Color (Mi)	Frequency (fi)	fi x Mi
Brown			
Blue			
Green			
Black			
Total			

    d. Obtain the mean: _____

    e. State the mode of the set: _____

    f. Find the modal interval: _____

    g. Find the Median using the original data: _____

    h. Find the median using the table, discuss your answer.

    i. Represent the data in a histogram:

STEM AND LEAF DIAGRAM

1. The following stem and leaf diagram gives the heights of a group of high school students (in cm):

Stem	Leaf
15	7 7 9
16	4 5 6 7 7 8
17	1 3 3 4 8 8
18	2 3 4 8 9 9
19	0 1 3

   a. Find the number of students in the classroom _____.

   b. Mean = _____   Median = _____   Mode = _____

   c. Min = _____   Max = _____

   d. What percentage of students is less than 165cm tall?

   e. What percentage of students is more than 182cm tall?

2. The following stem and leaf diagram gives the grades of a group of high school students in math:

Stem	Leaf
5	1 3 5 5 8
6	0 1 3 5 6 6 7
7	1 3 4 7 8
8	0 1 1 3 7 8 8
9	2 6 8

   a. Find the number of students in the classroom _____.

   b. Mean = _____   Median = _____   Mode = _____

   c. Min = _____   Max = _____

   d. 60 is the passing grade in the class room. How many students failed?

   e. What percentage of students obtained 85 or more?

4.4. – PROBABILITY

Probability is the science of chance or likelihood of an event happening

If a random experiment is repeated ____ times in such a way that each of the trials is identical and independent, where n(A) is the number of _____ event A occurred,

then: Relative frequency of event A = $P(A) = \dfrac{n(A)}{N}$ $(N \to \infty)$

Exercises

1. In an unbiased coin what is P(head) ?

   This probability is called _____.

2. Explain the difference between theoretical probability and experimental probability.

3. Throw a drawing pin and fill the table:

	Fell pointing upwards	Fell on its side	Total number of throws
Number of events			
Probability			

4. The definition of probability ("*Laplace law*") is:

   $P(A) = \dfrac{Number _____}{Total _____}$

Properties of probability

$0 \leq P(A) \leq \underline{}$

$P(U) = \underline{}$

5. Given the sentence "Good day grade eight". Find the following probabilities in case the choices are being made in a random way:

   a. P(choosing a vowel) =

   b. P(choosing a "o") =

   c. P(choosing a "e") =

   d. P(choosing a "z") =

6. In case a student is chosen randomly in your classroom. Find the probability it's a girl.

7. Find the probability of getting a prime number sum on tossing 1 dice.

8. Find the probability of getting a sum of 13 on tossing 3 dice.

9. Find the probability of being left handed in your classroom.

10. Find the probability of obtaining a sum of 4 on tossing 2 dice.

11. Find the probability of obtaining 2 tails on tossing 2 coins.

12. Find the probability that a 2 digit number divides by 10

13. Find the probability of choosing the letter b in the word probability

14. Find the probability of choosing a number that contains the digit 8 in the first hundred numbers (1 to 100).

15. Find the probability of choosing a number that contains only odd digits in the first thousand numbers (1 to 100).

16. Find the probability of choosing a palindrome number between 100 and 200. A palindrome number is one that is read the same from left to right is at is from right to left, for example 12321.

228

CHAPTER 5

5.1. – INTERNATIONAL SYSTEM OF UNITS

1. Meter(m) is a unit of _____ Other units of _____ are: _____

2. Meter square (m²) is a unit of _____ Other units of _____ are: _____

3. An area has units of _____ A length has units of _____

4. Kilo = __ Mili = __

Convert the units, use scientific notation in at least one of each type of exercises:

5. How many metres in 2.5 km?

6. How many metres in 0.5 km?

7. How many metres² in $\frac{1}{3}$ km²?

8. How many metres in 56 km?

9. How many metres in 2500 km?

10. How many km² in 26 m²?

11. How many km in 75 m?

12. How many km in 1000 m?

13. How many m in $5.2 \cdot 10^7$ km?

14. How many km² in $5.12 \cdot 10^8$ m²?

15. How many mm in 3.04 m?

16. How many mm² in 0.5 m²?

17. How many mm² in 1 m²?

18. How many mm in 2 m?

19. How many mm in 2.5 m?

20. How many mm² are 1.35 m²?

21. How many cm in $\frac{1}{3}$ m?

22. How many cm² in 56 m²?

229

23. How many cm in 3.1 km?

24. How many mm² in 0.5 cm²?

25. How many cm in in 120 m?

26. How many mm² in 5.1 cm²?

27. How many cm in 17 km?

28. How many m in 12392 km?

29. How many mm² in 5.1 m²?

30. How many m² in 2.2 mm²?

31. How many cm in 13.12 m?

32. Complete the table:

mm	cm	m	km
14			
	65		
		3	
			5
12.5			
	3.7		
		4.78	
			1.31
			0.008

mm²	cm²	m²	Km²
14			
	65		
		3	
			5
12.5			
	3.7		
		4.78	
			1.31
			0.008

5.2. – COMMON ERRORS

1. $\sqrt{A+B} = \sqrt{A} + \sqrt{B}$ True / False, Give an example to show your answer.

2. $\sqrt{A^2 + B^2} = A + B$ True / False, Give an example to show your answer.

3. $(A+B)^2 = A^2 + B^2$ True / False, if false write the correct version.

4. $(A+B)(A-B) = A^2 + B^2$ True / False, Give an example to show your answer.

5. $(A+B)(A-B) = A^2 - B^2$ True / False, if false write the correct version..

6. $(x+2)^2 = x^2 + 4x + 2$ True / False, if false write the correct version.

7. $(A-B)^2 = A^2 - B^2$ True / False, Give an example to show your answer.

8. $(2x-3)^2 = 4x^2 - 6x + 9$ True / False, if false write the correct version.

9. $(\sqrt{a} - 3)^2 = a^2 - 6a + 9$ True / False, if false write the correct version.

10. $x^2 x^3 = x^6$ True / False, if false write the correct version.

11. $(x^2)^3 = x^{(2^3)}$ True / False, if false write the correct version.

12. $\dfrac{x^{10}}{x^2} = x^5$ True / False, if false write the correct version.

13. $x^1 = 1$ True / False, if false write the correct version.

14. $x^0 = 0$ True / False, if false write the correct version.

15. $-3^2 = (-3)^2$ True / False, if false write the correct version.

16. $(4x^2) = (4x)^2$ True / False, if false write the correct version.

17. $\sqrt{7x} = 7x^{\frac{1}{2}}$ True / False, if false write the correct version.

18. $\dfrac{0}{2} = \dfrac{2}{0}$ True / False, if false write the correct version.

19. $\dfrac{14+x}{14} = x$ True / False, if false write the correct version.

20. $\dfrac{7-x}{7} = x-1$ True / False, if false write the correct version.

21. $\dfrac{a+b}{a} = 1 + \dfrac{b}{a}$ True / False, if false write the correct version.

22. $\dfrac{14+x}{14} = x + \dfrac{x}{14}$ True / False, if false write the correct version.

23. $\dfrac{1}{x+y} = \dfrac{1}{x} + \dfrac{1}{y}$ True / False, if false write the correct version.

24. An **expression** and an **equation** is the same thing.   True / False

25. $\dfrac{\left(\dfrac{a}{b}\right)}{c} = \dfrac{a}{\left(\dfrac{b}{c}\right)}$ True / False, if false write the correct version.

26. $-a^2 = (-a)^2$ True / False, if false write the correct version.

27. $a^{-2} = (-a)^2$ True / False, if false write the correct version.

28. $a^{-2} = -a^2$ True / False, if false write the correct version.

29. $a^{-2} = -\dfrac{1}{a^2}$ True / False, if false write the correct version.

30. $a^{-2} = \dfrac{1}{a^2}$ True / False, if false write the correct version.

31. $a^{-1} = -\dfrac{1}{a}$ True / False, if false write the correct version.

32. $\dfrac{1}{2} + \dfrac{1}{3} = \dfrac{1}{2+3}$ True / False, if false write the correct version.

33. $a^{-1} + a^{-1} = a^{-2}$ True / False, if false write the correct version.

34. $a^{-1} a^{-1} = a^{-2}$ True / False, if false write the correct version.

35. $a^{-2} a^{-3} = a^{-6}$ True / False, if false write the correct version.

36. $a^{-2} + a^{-3} = a^{-5}$ True / False, if false write the correct version.

ANSWER KEY
CHAPTER 1 - ALGEBRA

1.1. – ORDER OF OPERATIONS

1. The correct order of operations is:
   a. <u>Parenthesis</u>
   b. <u>Exponents</u>
   c. <u>Multiplication</u> or <u>Division</u>
   d. <u>Addition</u> or <u>Subtraction</u>

2. Given the product $3 \cdot 2$ the following is a good model: (3 times 2)

3. Given the product $4 \cdot 2$ the following is a good model: (4 times 2)

4. Given the product $3 \cdot 3$ the following is a good model: (3 times 3)

5. Given the following model, write the corresponding product sentence, is it the only possible one? $4 \cdot 5$ or $5 \cdot 4$

6. Given the following model, write the corresponding product sentence, is it the only possible one? $7 \cdot 3$ or $3 \cdot 7$

7. Calculate the following products, remember the correct order of operations

   a. $3 \cdot 8 = 24$
   b. $3 \cdot (-5) = -15$
   c. $(-9) \cdot (-3) = 27$
   d. $(-3) \cdot 7 = -21$
   e. $-(-2) \cdot (-3) = -6$
   f. $-(-11) \cdot 3 = -33$
   g. $6 \cdot (-6) =$
   h. $-(-23) \cdot (-3) =$

8. Calculate the following, , remember the correct order of operations

   a. $(-3) \cdot (-3) = 9$
   b. $-3 \cdot (-3) = 9$
   c. $3 \cdot (-3) = -9$
   d. $(-3) \cdot 3 = -9$
   e. $-3 \cdot 3 = -9$
   f. $3 \cdot 3 = 9$

9. Given the division $10 \div 2 = 5$, build a model that fits this sentence

10. Given the division $15 \div 3 = 5$, build a model that fits this sentence

11. Given the division $6 \div 6 = 1$, build a model that fits this sentence

12. Calculate the following, remember the correct order of operations

    a. $12 \div 3 = 4$
    b. $20 \div (-5) = -4$
    c. $-38 \div 2 = -17$
    d. $(-42) \div (-7) = 6$
    e. $-36 \div (-12) = 3$
    f. $-(-75) \div 5 = 15$

13. The following expression: $6 - 4/2 = 4$ which of the following is the same

    sentence: $6 - \dfrac{4}{2} = 4$ (the same) $\dfrac{6-4}{2} = 1$ (not the same)

14. The following expression: $(17-6)/6 = \dfrac{11}{6}$ which of the following is the same

    sentence: $17 - \dfrac{6}{6} = 16$ (not the same) $\dfrac{17-6}{6} = \dfrac{11}{6}$ (the same)

15. The following expression: $3 \cdot 5 + 12/3 = 19$ which of the following is the same

    sentence: $15 + \dfrac{12}{3} = 19$ (the same) $\dfrac{15-12}{3} = 1$ (not the same)

16. The following expression: $18/2 - 5 = 4$ which of the following is the same

    sentence: $\dfrac{18}{2} - 5 = 4$ (the same) $\dfrac{18}{2-5} = -6$ (not the same)

17. $-2 - 3 = 6$ True or **False**
18. $-2(-3) = 6$ **True** or False
19. $0 \cdot a = a$ True or **False**
20. $0 + a = a$ **True** or False
21. $1 + a = a$ True or **False**
22. $\dfrac{a}{a} = a \div a$ **True** or False
23. $\dfrac{a}{a} = 1$ **True** or False
24. $a \cdot a = (-a)(-a)$ **True** or False
25. $-a \cdot b = (-a)(-b)$ True or **False**
26. $-a \cdot (-b) = ab$ **True** or False
27. $a \cdot (-b) = -a - b$ True or **False**
28. $a \div b = b \div a$ True or **False**
29. $ab = ba$ **True** or False
30. $a + b = b + a$ **True** or False
31. $a - b = b - a$ True or **False**

Calculate the following; remember the correct order of operations

32. $5 + 3 \cdot 2 = 5 + 6 = 11$
33. $5 - 3 \cdot 2 = 5 - 6 = -1$
34. $3 \cdot 7 - 6 = 21 - 6 = 15$
35. $2 \cdot 3 - (-3) = 6 + 3 = 9$
36. $-(-4) \cdot 3 - (-3) = 12 + 3 = 15$
37. $-(-2) \cdot (-5) - (-6) = -10 + 6 = -4$
38. $-(-4) \cdot 3/2 - (-3)(-3) = 6 - 9 = -3$
39. $-5 \cdot 5 - (-8) \cdot 2 = -25 + 16 = -9$
40. $-2 - 5 - (-2) + 2 = -7 + 4 = -3$
41. $(-2)(-5) - (-2) \cdot 2 = 10 + 4 = 14$
42. $25 \cdot 2 - 7 = 50 - 7 = 43$
43. $15 + 4/2 = 15 + 2 = 17$
44. $14 \div 7 + 3 \cdot 6 = 2 + 18 = 20$
45. $5/5 - 30/2 \cdot 5 = 1 - 15 \cdot 5 = 1 - 75 = -74$
46. $1 + 4/2 - 8/4 \cdot 5 = 1 + 2 - 2 \cdot 5 = 3 - 10 = -7$
47. $20/4/2 + 4 = 5/2 + 4 = 13/2$
48. $12 \cdot (2+3) = 12 \cdot (5) = 60$
49. $5(3 \cdot 2/3 \cdot 2) + 2 = 5(6/3 \cdot 2) + 2 = 5(2 \cdot 2) + 2 = 22$
50. $1/2 + 3/2 = 2$
51. $6/3 - 20 \div 10 = 2 - 2 = 0$
52. $5(1 + 3 \cdot 2) + 2/2 - 8/4 = 5(7) + 1 - 2 = 34$
53. $(15 + 3) \cdot 2 - 2 = (18) \cdot 2 - 2 = 34$
54. $0/5 + 3 \cdot 2 = 0 + 6 = 6$

55. $5/0+3\cdot2-1 = Undefined$
56. $(1+1)\cdot(2-2)\cdot(4\cdot5\cdot5) = 2\cdot0\cdot100 = 0$
57. $(5+3)\cdot2 = 16$
58. $(5\cdot3)\cdot2 = 30$
59. $5\cdot(3\cdot2) = 30$
60. $5\cdot3\cdot2 = 30$
61. $100/2+21/3 = 50+7 = 57$
62. $(2+1)\div3+13 = 3\div3+13 = 14$
63. $2(-(-3)\cdot3-4/2)-1\cdot3 = 2(9-2)-1\cdot3 = 11$
64. $3(1-4/2)-15\div3 = 3(-1)-5 = -8$
65. $10(16/2-1+1)/2 = 10(8)/2 = 40$
66. $2+3(2-20/4)-(25+3)\div2 = 2+3(-3)-14 = -21$
67. $5/0 = Undefined$
68. $0/4 = 0$
69. $0/0 = Undefined$
70. $(2+4)\cdot25-2/2 = 150-1 = 149$
71. $-3\cdot5-2+(-3)(-2)(-2) = -17-12 = -29$
72. $(-2\cdot2-2\cdot3)\cdot(-2) = (-4-6)\cdot(-2) = 20$
73. $(4-5\cdot2)/2-1 = (-6)/2-1 = -4$

Fill the blank

74. $4\cdot2 = 8$
75. $16/2 = 8$
76. $6+2 = 8$
77. $10-2 = 8$
78. $\dfrac{7}{3}\cdot3 = 7$
79. $18/6 = 3$
80. $0+7 = 7$
81. $13-12 = 1$
82. $5\cdot2 = 10$
83. $-15/(-5) = 3$
84. $7+(-6) = 1$
85. $25-(-5) = 30$
86. $12/(-3) = -4$
87. $(-10)+2 = -8$
88. $(-11)\cdot(-3) = 33$
89. $(-21)/3 = -7$

Fill the blanks with 2 different options for solutions:

90. $0+2/2 = 1$ $2+2/(-2) = 1$
91. $4\cdot2/8 = 1$ $5\cdot2/5 = 1$
92. $2-2/2 = 1$ $3-2/1 = 1$
93. $1+4/2 = 3$ $2+4/4 = 3$
94. $(-9)+12\cdot1 = 3$ $(-21)+12\cdot2 = 3$
95. $12-6/6 = 11$ $14-6/2 = 11$
96. $1+3/3 = 2$ $-1+3/1 = 2$
97. $27-5/1 = 22$ $23-5/5 = 22$
98. $4\cdot2+3-5 = 6$ $4\cdot1+7-5 = 6$
99. $5/5+3 = 4$ $10/5+2 = 4$
100. $11+1/1 = 12$ $13+1/(-1) = 12$
101. $15/5+1 = 4$ $20/5+0 = 4$
102. $7-6+5 = 6$ $8-6+4 = 6$

236

1.2. – FRACTIONS

1. Given the following circle, divide it to 2 equal pieces and shade $\frac{1}{2}$

   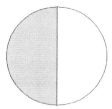

2. Given the following circle divide it to 3 equal pieces and shade $\frac{1}{3}$

   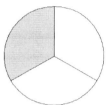

3. Given the following circle, divide it to 4 equal pieces and shade $\frac{1}{4}$

   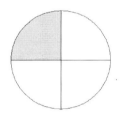

4. Given the following circle, divide it to 5 equal pieces and shade $\frac{1}{5}$

   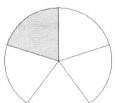

5. Given the following circle, divide it to 6 equal pieces and shade $\frac{1}{6}$

   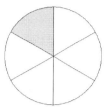

6. Given the following circle, divide it to 7 equal pieces and shade $\frac{1}{7}$

   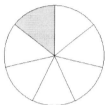

7. Given the following circle, divide it to 8 equal pieces and shade $\frac{1}{8}$

   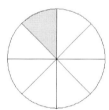

8. Given the following circle, divide it to 9 equal pieces and shade $\frac{1}{9}$

   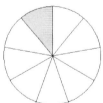

9. Given the following circle, divide it to 10 equal pieces and shade $\frac{1}{10}$

   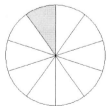

10. Given the following circle, divide it to 3 equal pieces and shade $\frac{2}{3}$

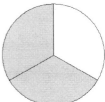

11. Given the following circle, divide it to 4 equal pieces and shade $\frac{2}{4}$

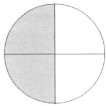

12. Given the following circle, divide it to 4 equal pieces and shade $\frac{3}{4}$

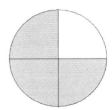

13. Given the following circle, divide it to 5 equal pieces and shade $\frac{2}{5}$

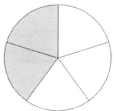

14. Given the following circle, divide it to 6 equal pieces and shade $\frac{5}{6}$

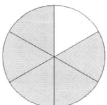

15. Given the following circle, divide it to 8 equal pieces and shade $\frac{5}{8}$

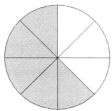

16. Given the following circle, divide it to 5 equal pieces and shade $\frac{4}{5}$

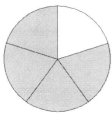

17. Given the following circle, divide it to 9 equal pieces and shade $\frac{4}{9}$

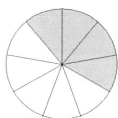

18. What fraction of the following circle is shaded: $\frac{2}{11}$

19. What fraction of the following circle is shaded: $\frac{2}{3}$

20. What fraction of the following circle is shaded: $\frac{9}{11}$

238

21. What fraction of the following circle is shaded: $\dfrac{7}{14} = \dfrac{1}{2}$

22. What fraction of the following circle is shaded: $\dfrac{5}{8}$

23. What fraction of the following circle is shaded: $\dfrac{1}{12}$

24. What fraction of the following table is shaded: $\dfrac{13}{64}$

25. What fraction of the following table is shaded: $\dfrac{9}{35}$

26. What fraction of the following table is shaded? $\dfrac{11}{24}$

27. What fraction is shaded? $\dfrac{7}{16}$

28. What fraction is shaded? $\dfrac{6}{12} = \dfrac{1}{2}$

29. What fraction is shaded? $\dfrac{13}{24}$

30. What fraction is shaded? $\dfrac{9}{24} = \dfrac{3}{8}$
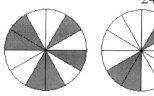

31. There were 12 cookies in the jar. John ate 7, write down the fraction of cookies john ate and the fraction that is left in the jar.
Eaten: $\dfrac{7}{12}$, Left $\dfrac{5}{12}$

32. Lia ate 3 cookies that represented $\dfrac{3}{4}$ of the cookies in the jar. Write down the number of cookies in the jar before she ate. Make a sketch to show answer.
4 cookies.

33. Rami ate $\dfrac{2}{5}$ of the cookies in the jar, Melissa ate $\dfrac{1}{4}$ of the cookies. Who ate more? Invent an imaginary jar with a number of cookies that will make the problem easy to solve.
With 20 cookies the problem is solved easily:
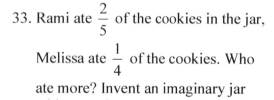

34. How much is $\dfrac{1}{2}$ of 2? Shade to show your answer: 1

35. How much is $\frac{1}{3}$ of 2? Shade to show your answer: $\frac{2}{3}$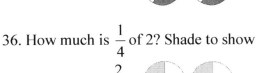

36. How much is $\frac{1}{4}$ of 2? Shade to show your answer: $\frac{2}{4}$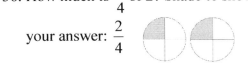

37. How much is $\frac{1}{5}$ of 2? Shade to show your answer: $\frac{2}{5}$

38. How much is $\frac{1}{3}$ of 5? 2 different ways to show your answer: $\frac{5}{3}$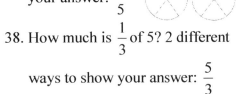

39. How much is $\frac{2}{5}$ of 4? 2 different ways to show your answer: $\frac{8}{5}$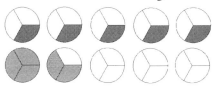

40. Sketch $\frac{3}{2}$ circles:

41. Sketch $\frac{5}{3}$ circles: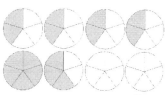

42. Sketch $\frac{7}{4}$ circles:

43. Sketch $\frac{8}{4}$ circles: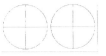

44. Sketch $\frac{7}{5}$ circles:

45. Sketch $\frac{8}{3}$ circles:

46. Nathan ate $\frac{2}{7}$ of the cookies in the jar, Melissa ate $\frac{1}{3}$ of the cookies. Who ate more? Invent an imaginary jar with a number of cookies that will make the problem easy to solve. With 21 cookies the problem is easy to solve, Melissa ate more.

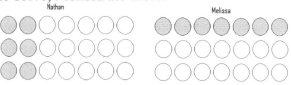

47. Write down the missing number(s) between 0 and 1: $\frac{1}{2}$

48. Write down the missing number(s) between 0 and 1: $\frac{1}{3}, \frac{2}{3}$

49. Write down the missing number(s) between 0 and 1: $\frac{1}{4}, \frac{2}{4}, \frac{3}{4}$

50. Write down the missing number(s) between 0 and 1: $\frac{1}{5}, \frac{2}{5}, \frac{3}{5}, \frac{4}{5}$

51. Write down the missing number(s) between 0 and 1: $\frac{1}{6}, \frac{2}{6}, \frac{3}{6}, \frac{4}{6}, \frac{5}{6}$

52. Write down the missing number(s) between 0 and 2: $\frac{1}{3}, \frac{2}{3}, 1, \frac{4}{3}, \frac{5}{3}$

53. Write down the missing number(s) between 0 and 2: $\dfrac{1}{4}, \dfrac{2}{4}, \dfrac{3}{4}, 1, \dfrac{5}{4}, \dfrac{6}{4}, \dfrac{7}{4}$

54. Write down the missing number(s) between 0 and 2:
$\dfrac{1}{5}, \dfrac{2}{5}, \dfrac{3}{5}, \dfrac{4}{5}, 1, \dfrac{6}{5}, \dfrac{7}{5}, \dfrac{8}{5}, \dfrac{9}{5}$
0.2, 0.4, 0.6, 0.8, 1, 1.2, 1.4, 1.6, 1.8

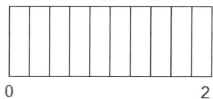

55. Write down the missing number(s) between 2 and 3:
$\dfrac{21}{10}, \dfrac{22}{10}, \dfrac{23}{10}, \dfrac{24}{10}, \dfrac{25}{10}, \dfrac{26}{10}, \dfrac{27}{10}, \dfrac{28}{10}, \dfrac{29}{10}$
2.1, 2.2, 2.3, 2.4, 2.5, 2.6, 2.7, 2.8, 2.9

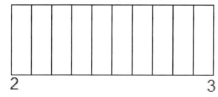

56. Write down the missing number(s) between 2 and 4:
$\dfrac{13}{6}, \dfrac{14}{6}, \dfrac{15}{6}, \dfrac{16}{6}, \dfrac{17}{6}, 3, \dfrac{19}{6}, \dfrac{20}{6}, \dfrac{21}{6}, \dfrac{22}{6}, \dfrac{23}{6}$

57. Write down the missing fractions(s): $-\dfrac{11}{5} = -2.2, \dfrac{3}{5} = 0.6$

58. Write down the missing fractions(s): $-\dfrac{6}{5} = -1.2, \dfrac{14}{5} = 2.8$

59. Write down the missing fractions(s): $-\dfrac{22}{5} = -4.4, \dfrac{17}{5} = 3.4$

60. Write down the missing fractions(s): $\dfrac{1}{10} = 0.1$

61. Write down the missing fractions(s): $\dfrac{2}{8} = 0.25, \dfrac{3}{8} = 0.375$

62. Write down the missing fractions(s): $\dfrac{7}{6}, \dfrac{8}{6} = \dfrac{4}{3}$

63. Write down the missing fractions(s): $\dfrac{15}{7}, \dfrac{16}{7}, \dfrac{17}{7}, \dfrac{18}{7}, \dfrac{19}{7}$

64. Write down the missing fractions(s): $\dfrac{28}{9}, \dfrac{29}{9}$

65. Write down the missing fractions(s): $-\dfrac{8}{9}, -\dfrac{7}{9}, -\dfrac{6}{9}, -\dfrac{5}{9}$

66. Write down the missing fractions(s): $-\dfrac{18}{5}, -\dfrac{16}{5}, -\dfrac{14}{5}, -\dfrac{12}{5}$

67. Write down the missing fraction(s): $\dfrac{15}{4}, \dfrac{18}{4}, \dfrac{21}{4}$

68. Write down the fractions in different ways:

$\dfrac{1}{2}=\dfrac{2}{4}=\dfrac{5}{10}$ $\dfrac{1}{3}=\dfrac{2}{6}=\dfrac{10}{30}$ $\dfrac{1}{4}=\dfrac{2}{8}=\dfrac{5}{20}$ $\dfrac{9}{4}=\dfrac{18}{8}=\dfrac{90}{40}$ $\dfrac{2}{3}=\dfrac{4}{6}=\dfrac{6}{9}$ $\dfrac{11}{8}=\dfrac{22}{16}=\dfrac{55}{40}$

$\dfrac{a}{b}=\dfrac{2a}{2b}=\dfrac{ka}{kb}$ $\dfrac{2a}{a}=\dfrac{2}{1}=2$ $\dfrac{x+13}{13+x}=\dfrac{1}{1}=1$ $\dfrac{x}{3x}=\dfrac{1}{3}$ $\dfrac{a-b}{b-a}=-1$

Fill the blank to make the fractions equal:

69. $\dfrac{a}{2}=\dfrac{2a}{4}$

70. $\dfrac{a-b}{4}=\dfrac{3a-3b}{12}$

71. $\dfrac{a}{b}=\dfrac{2a}{2b}$

72. $\dfrac{1}{a}=\dfrac{5}{5a}$

73. $\dfrac{1}{3}=\dfrac{a}{3a}$

74. $\dfrac{a-b}{a-b}=1$

75. $\dfrac{2-a}{-2}=\dfrac{a-2}{2}$

76. $\dfrac{2a}{b}=\dfrac{8a}{4b}$

77. $\dfrac{x^2}{2xy}=\dfrac{2xy}{4y^2}$

78. $\dfrac{2a}{7x}=\dfrac{4xa}{14x^2}$

79. The fractions that are greater than 1: $\dfrac{7}{6}, \dfrac{35}{34}, \dfrac{21}{7}, \dfrac{10001}{10000}$

80. A fraction will be greater than 1 if numerator > denominator (assuming positive)

81. Fractions that are greater than 2: $\dfrac{20}{7}, \dfrac{20001}{10000}$

82. A fraction will be greater than 2 if numerator > 2denominator (assuming positive)

83. Circle the fractions that are greater than 5: $\dfrac{47}{9}, \dfrac{100}{6}, \dfrac{28}{3}$

84. A fraction will be greater than 5 if numerator > 5denominator (assuming positive)

85. Circle the fractions that are smaller than $\dfrac{1}{2}$: $\dfrac{1}{3}, \dfrac{4}{9}, \dfrac{23}{51}$

86. A fraction will be smaller than $\dfrac{1}{2}$ if: 2numerator < denominator (assuming positive)

87. Circle the fractions that are smaller than $\dfrac{1}{3}$: $\dfrac{2}{7}, \dfrac{24}{75}, \dfrac{3}{11}$

88. A fraction will be smaller than $\dfrac{1}{3}$ if: 3numerator < denominator (assuming positive)

Fill the blank with: <,> or =, assume a, b, n are positive constants:

89. $\dfrac{1}{2} > \dfrac{1}{3}$

90. $\dfrac{1}{3} > \dfrac{1}{4}$

91. $\dfrac{2}{5} < \dfrac{3}{7}$

92. $\dfrac{5}{8} < \dfrac{7}{11}$

93. $\dfrac{12}{7} > \dfrac{13}{8}$

94. $\dfrac{21}{8} > \dfrac{13}{5}$

95. $\dfrac{35}{8} > \dfrac{17}{4}$

96. $\dfrac{a}{b} < \dfrac{a+1}{b+1}, b > a > 0$

97. $\dfrac{a}{b} < \dfrac{a+1}{b+1}, a, b > 0$

98. $\dfrac{1}{n+1} < \dfrac{1}{n}, n \geq 0$

99. $\dfrac{1}{n^2} \leq \dfrac{1}{n}, n \geq 1$

100. $\dfrac{1}{a} > \dfrac{1}{b}, b > a > 0$

101. Indicate the location of the fractions on the number line: $-\dfrac{7}{6}, -\dfrac{6}{7}, \dfrac{17}{34}, \dfrac{-1}{7}, \dfrac{10001}{5000}$

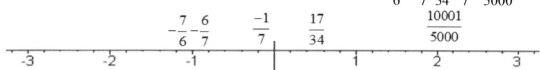

102. Indicate the location of the fractions on the number line: $-\dfrac{1}{6}, -\dfrac{8}{7}, \dfrac{20}{9}, \dfrac{-10}{20}, \dfrac{99}{50}$

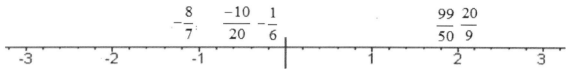

103. Indicate the location of the fractions on the number line: $-\dfrac{4}{5}, -\dfrac{3}{2}, \dfrac{5}{2}, \dfrac{9}{8}, \dfrac{100}{33}$

104. Indicate the location of the fractions on the number line: $-\dfrac{7}{5}, -\dfrac{9}{3}, \dfrac{2}{3}, \dfrac{1}{10}, -\dfrac{66}{32}$

105. Indicate the location of the fractions on the number line: $-\dfrac{7}{8}, -\dfrac{6}{13}, \dfrac{11}{21}, \dfrac{-2}{17}, \dfrac{100}{501}$

106. Indicate the location of the fractions on the number line: $-\dfrac{10}{6}, -\dfrac{8}{7}, \dfrac{181}{90}, \dfrac{-102}{200}, \dfrac{189}{60}$

107. Indicate the location of the fractions on the number line: $-\dfrac{6}{5}, -\dfrac{5}{2}, \dfrac{2}{5}, \dfrac{90}{80}, \dfrac{33}{100}$

108. Indicate the location of the fractions on the number line: $-\dfrac{12}{5}, -\dfrac{6}{3}, \dfrac{11}{6}, \dfrac{11}{10}, -\dfrac{37}{12}$

109. Indicate the location of the fractions on the number line: $-\dfrac{10}{4}, -\dfrac{2}{10}, \dfrac{64}{33}, \dfrac{21}{10}, -\dfrac{3}{1}$

ADDING AND SUBTRACTING FRACTIONS

Write the corresponding addition sentence:

1. $\dfrac{1}{2} + \dfrac{5}{6} = \dfrac{8}{6}$

2. $\dfrac{3}{5} + \dfrac{1}{6} = \dfrac{23}{30}$

3. $\dfrac{5}{12} + \dfrac{1}{3} = \dfrac{9}{12}$

4. $\dfrac{3}{4} + \dfrac{3}{11} = \dfrac{45}{44}$

5. $\dfrac{1}{2} + \dfrac{9}{10} + \dfrac{4}{5} = \dfrac{22}{10}$

6. $\dfrac{1}{4} + \dfrac{1}{6} + \dfrac{2}{5} = \dfrac{49}{60}$

7. $\dfrac{11}{12} + \dfrac{3}{3} + \dfrac{9}{10} = \dfrac{55+60+54}{60} = \dfrac{159}{60}$

8. In order to add or subtract fractions they must have <u>a common denominator</u>

9. $\dfrac{1}{2} + \dfrac{1}{2} = 1$

10. $\dfrac{1}{3} + \dfrac{1}{3} = \dfrac{2}{3}$

11. $\dfrac{2}{4} + \dfrac{3}{4} = \dfrac{5}{4}$

12. $\dfrac{2}{4} - \dfrac{5}{4} = -\dfrac{3}{4}$

13. $\dfrac{8}{7} - \dfrac{5}{7} + \dfrac{6}{7} = \dfrac{9}{7}$

14. $\dfrac{17}{11} - \dfrac{2}{11} - \dfrac{1}{11} = \dfrac{14}{11}$

15. $\dfrac{1}{2} + \dfrac{1}{2} + \dfrac{1}{2} + \dfrac{1}{2} + \dfrac{1}{2} + \dfrac{1}{2} = 3$

16. $\dfrac{1}{7} - \dfrac{20}{7} - \dfrac{3}{7} + \dfrac{5}{7} = -\dfrac{17}{7}$

17. $\dfrac{21}{17} - \dfrac{5}{17} - \dfrac{13}{17} + \dfrac{25}{17} = \dfrac{28}{17}$

18. $\dfrac{1}{3} + \dfrac{1}{2} = \dfrac{2+3}{6} = \dfrac{5}{6}$

19. $\dfrac{2}{3} - \dfrac{1}{4} = \dfrac{8-3}{12} = \dfrac{5}{12}$

244

20. $\dfrac{2}{5}+\dfrac{3}{2}=\dfrac{4+15}{10}=\dfrac{19}{10}$

21. $\dfrac{3}{4}-\dfrac{1}{2}=\dfrac{3-2}{4}=\dfrac{1}{4}$

22. $\dfrac{2}{3}+\dfrac{3}{5}=\dfrac{10+9}{15}=\dfrac{19}{15}$

23. $\dfrac{2}{3}-\dfrac{5}{6}=\dfrac{4-5}{6}=-\dfrac{1}{6}$

24. $\dfrac{3}{4}+\dfrac{3}{7}=\dfrac{21+12}{28}=\dfrac{33}{28}$

25. $\dfrac{3}{8}-\dfrac{3}{4}=\dfrac{3-6}{8}=-\dfrac{3}{8}$

26. $\dfrac{5}{8}+\dfrac{4}{5}=\dfrac{25+32}{40}=\dfrac{57}{40}$

27. $\dfrac{5}{7}+\dfrac{4}{14}=\dfrac{10+4}{14}=1$

28. $\dfrac{1}{2}+\dfrac{1}{3}+\dfrac{1}{4}=\dfrac{6+4+3}{12}=\dfrac{13}{12}$

29. $\dfrac{1}{2}+\dfrac{3}{4}-\dfrac{2}{5}=\dfrac{10+15-8}{20}=\dfrac{17}{20}$

30. $\dfrac{2}{3}-\dfrac{3}{4}+\dfrac{3}{5}=\dfrac{40-45+36}{60}=\dfrac{31}{60}$

31. $\dfrac{1}{2}+\dfrac{3}{4}+\dfrac{5}{6}=\dfrac{6+9+10}{12}=\dfrac{25}{12}$

32. $\dfrac{3}{2}-\dfrac{2}{3}-\dfrac{4}{5}=\dfrac{45-20-24}{30}=\dfrac{1}{30}$

33. $\dfrac{4}{5}+\dfrac{1}{6}+\dfrac{5}{7}=\dfrac{168+35+150}{210}=\dfrac{353}{210}$

34. $\dfrac{7}{4}-\dfrac{7}{8}-\left(-\dfrac{7}{12}\right)=\dfrac{42-21+14}{24}=\dfrac{35}{24}$

35. $\dfrac{1}{2}-\left(-\dfrac{5}{8}\right)-\dfrac{9}{10}=\dfrac{20+25-36}{40}=\dfrac{9}{40}$

36. $-\dfrac{3}{2}-\dfrac{3}{4}-\dfrac{9}{16}=\dfrac{-24-12-9}{16}=-\dfrac{45}{16}$

37. $\dfrac{2}{3}+\dfrac{5}{6}+\dfrac{-11}{12}=\dfrac{8+10-11}{12}=\dfrac{7}{12}$

38. $\dfrac{7}{8}-\dfrac{-5}{6}+\dfrac{7}{10}=\dfrac{105+100+84}{120}=\dfrac{289}{120}$

39. $\dfrac{3}{8}+\dfrac{3}{16}-\dfrac{7}{32}=\dfrac{12+6-7}{32}=\dfrac{11}{32}$

40. $\dfrac{1}{a}+\dfrac{1}{a}=\dfrac{2}{a}$

41. $\dfrac{2}{a}-\dfrac{7}{a}=-\dfrac{5}{a}$

42. $\dfrac{5}{a}-\dfrac{b}{a}=\dfrac{5-b}{a}$

43. $\dfrac{c}{a}+\dfrac{b}{a}=\dfrac{c+b}{a}$

44. $\dfrac{5}{a}-\dfrac{b}{a}+\dfrac{c}{a}=\dfrac{5-b+c}{a}$

45. $\dfrac{2b}{a}-\dfrac{3c}{a}+\dfrac{c}{a}=\dfrac{2b-2c}{a}$

46. $\dfrac{1}{a}+\dfrac{1}{b}=\dfrac{b+a}{ab}$

47. $\dfrac{2}{a}-\dfrac{1}{b}=\dfrac{2b-a}{ab}$

48. $\dfrac{c}{a}-\dfrac{d}{b}=\dfrac{cb-ad}{ab}$

49. $\dfrac{c}{a}-\dfrac{d}{b}+\dfrac{5}{b}=\dfrac{cb-da+5a}{ab}$

50. $\dfrac{c}{a}-1+\dfrac{5}{b}=\dfrac{c-ab+5a}{ab}$

51. $\dfrac{1}{ab}+\dfrac{1}{a}+\dfrac{1}{b}=\dfrac{1+b+a}{ab}$

52. $\dfrac{1}{ab}+\dfrac{1}{ab}+\dfrac{1}{b}=\dfrac{2+a}{ab}$

53. $\dfrac{1}{ab}+\dfrac{1}{ab}+\dfrac{1}{ab}=\dfrac{3}{ab}$

54. $\dfrac{c}{ab}+\dfrac{1}{b}+\dfrac{1}{a}=\dfrac{c+a+b}{ab}$

55. $\dfrac{c}{ab}-\dfrac{1}{b}+\dfrac{2}{a}=\dfrac{c-a+2b}{ab}$

56. $2+\dfrac{1}{x}=\dfrac{2x+1}{x}$

57. $\dfrac{5}{2x}-\dfrac{1}{x}=\dfrac{5-2}{2x}=\dfrac{3}{2x}$

58. $2-\dfrac{3}{x}=\dfrac{2x-3}{x}$

59. $\dfrac{x}{3}-2=\dfrac{x-6}{3}$

60. $\dfrac{2}{5}-\dfrac{7}{2x}=\dfrac{4x-35}{10x}$

61. $\dfrac{3}{5x}-\dfrac{1}{2x}=\dfrac{6-5}{10x}=\dfrac{1}{10x}$

62. $a-\dfrac{1}{2}=\dfrac{2a-1}{2}$

63. $\dfrac{1}{1+x}-1=\dfrac{1-(1+x)}{1+x}=\dfrac{-x}{1+x}$

64. $2 - \dfrac{4}{2+x} = \dfrac{2(2+x)-4}{2+x} = \dfrac{2x}{2+x}$

66. $\dfrac{2x}{3} - \dfrac{x+1}{4} - \dfrac{3x}{8} = \dfrac{16x - 6(x+1) - 9x}{24} = \dfrac{x-6}{24}$

65. $\dfrac{2x}{3} - \dfrac{x}{2} - \dfrac{x}{6} = \dfrac{4x - 3x - x}{6} = 0$

67. Jeff spent $\dfrac{1}{5}$ of his savings and later spent $\dfrac{1}{4}$ of his savings, what fraction of his savings did he spend in total? What fraction of his savings is left?
Spent: $\dfrac{1}{4} + \dfrac{1}{5} = \dfrac{9}{20}$ Left $1 - \dfrac{9}{20} = \dfrac{11}{20}$

68. Lia walked $\dfrac{2}{3}$ of the distance home and stopped to rest. Later she walked a $\dfrac{1}{4}$ more. What fraction of the distance did she walk in total? What part she still needs to walk?
Walked: $\dfrac{2}{3} + \dfrac{1}{4} = \dfrac{11}{12}$ Left $1 - \dfrac{11}{12} = \dfrac{1}{12}$

69. Dina ate $\dfrac{1}{9}$ of the cookies in the jar, Dan ate a $\dfrac{1}{6}$ and Ben $\dfrac{2}{11}$. What fraction of the cookies is left in the jar? Which one of the 3 ate more cookies?
Left $1 - \left(\dfrac{1}{9} + \dfrac{1}{6} + \dfrac{2}{11}\right) = 1 - \left(\dfrac{22 + 33 + 36}{198}\right) = 1 - \left(\dfrac{91}{198}\right) = \dfrac{107}{198}$, Ben ate more $\dfrac{36}{198}$

70. Robyn did $\dfrac{5}{6}$ of her HW. Later she did $\dfrac{1}{13}$ of the HW. What part of her HW she still needs to do.
Left $1 - \left(\dfrac{5}{6} + \dfrac{1}{13}\right) = 1 - \left(\dfrac{65+6}{78}\right) = 1 - \left(\dfrac{71}{78}\right) = \dfrac{7}{78}$

True or False:

71. $\dfrac{a+b}{c} = \dfrac{a}{c} + \dfrac{b}{c}$ **True**

72. $\dfrac{a+b}{c+d} = \dfrac{a}{c} + \dfrac{b}{d}$ **False**

73. $\dfrac{a+b}{a} = 1 + \dfrac{b}{a}$ **True**

74. $\dfrac{a-b}{b-a} = -1$ **True**

75. $\dfrac{a}{c+d} = \dfrac{a}{c} + \dfrac{a}{d}$ **False**

76. $\dfrac{c-d}{d} = c$ **False**

77. $\dfrac{c-d}{d} = -1 + c$ **False**

78. $\dfrac{ab}{ad} = \dfrac{b}{d}$ **True**

79. $\dfrac{a(c-d)}{a} = c - d$ **True**

80. $\dfrac{ac-d}{c-d} = a$ **False**

81. $\dfrac{2a+d}{d-2a} = -1$ **False**

MULTIPLYING FRACTIONS

1. $\dfrac{1}{1} \cdot \dfrac{1}{2} = \dfrac{1}{2}$

2. $\dfrac{2}{1} \cdot \dfrac{1}{2} = 1$

3. $\dfrac{a}{1} \cdot \dfrac{1}{a} = 1$

4. $\dfrac{3}{1} \cdot \dfrac{1}{1} = 3$

5. $(-4) \cdot \dfrac{1}{2} = -2$

6. $6 \cdot \dfrac{1}{3} = 2$

7. $20 \cdot \dfrac{1}{5} = 4$

8. $\dfrac{1}{2} \cdot \dfrac{1}{2} = \dfrac{1}{4}$

9. $\dfrac{1}{2} \cdot \left(-\dfrac{1}{3}\right) = -\dfrac{1}{6}$

10. $\dfrac{1}{2} \cdot \dfrac{1}{4} = \dfrac{1}{8}$

11. $\dfrac{1}{2} \cdot \dfrac{1}{5} = \dfrac{1}{10}$

12. $\dfrac{1}{3} \cdot \dfrac{1}{10} = \dfrac{1}{30}$

13. $\dfrac{2}{3} \cdot \dfrac{6}{1} = 4$

14. $\left(-\dfrac{4}{5}\right) \cdot \dfrac{7}{-8} = \dfrac{1}{5} \cdot \dfrac{7}{2} = \dfrac{7}{10}$

15. $\dfrac{2}{5} \cdot \dfrac{3}{4} = \dfrac{1}{5} \cdot \dfrac{3}{2} = \dfrac{3}{10}$

16. $\dfrac{8}{5} \cdot \dfrac{17}{-2} = \dfrac{4}{5} \cdot \dfrac{17}{-1} = -\dfrac{68}{5}$

17. $\dfrac{9}{5} \cdot \dfrac{4}{9} = \dfrac{4}{5}$

18. $\dfrac{12}{15} \cdot \dfrac{15}{9} = \dfrac{12}{9}$

19. $-\dfrac{8}{a} \cdot \dfrac{a}{7} = -\dfrac{8}{7}$

20. $\dfrac{12}{a} \cdot \dfrac{a}{27} = \dfrac{12}{27}$

21. $\dfrac{-x}{a} \cdot \dfrac{-a}{x} = 1$

22. $\dfrac{y}{b} \cdot \dfrac{b}{x} = \dfrac{y}{x}$

23. $\dfrac{1}{2}$ of 50 is $\dfrac{1}{2} \cdot 50 = 25$

24. $\dfrac{1}{3}$ of 66 is $\dfrac{1}{3} \cdot 66 = 22$

25. $\dfrac{1}{4}$ of 48 is $\dfrac{1}{4} \cdot 48 = 12$

26. $\dfrac{2}{5}$ of 20 is $\dfrac{2}{5} \cdot 20 = 8$

27. $\dfrac{7}{9}$ of 81 is $\dfrac{1}{9} \cdot 81 = 9$

28. $\dfrac{1}{2}$ of $\dfrac{3}{-2}$ is $\dfrac{1}{2} \cdot \left(-\dfrac{3}{2}\right) = -\dfrac{3}{4}$

29. $\dfrac{1}{2}$ of $\dfrac{3}{4}$ is $\dfrac{1}{2} \cdot \dfrac{3}{4} = \dfrac{3}{8}$

30. $\dfrac{2}{7}$ of $\dfrac{6}{5}$ is $\dfrac{2}{7} \cdot \dfrac{6}{5} = \dfrac{12}{35}$

31. $\dfrac{4}{3}$ of $\dfrac{2}{3}$ is $\dfrac{4}{3} \cdot \dfrac{2}{3} = \dfrac{8}{9}$

32. $\dfrac{10}{3}$ of $-\dfrac{2}{5}$ is $\dfrac{10}{3} \cdot \left(-\dfrac{2}{5}\right) = -\dfrac{20}{15} = -\dfrac{4}{3}$

33. $\dfrac{8}{7}$ of $\dfrac{13}{4}$ is $\dfrac{8}{7} \cdot \dfrac{13}{4} = \dfrac{2}{7} \cdot \dfrac{13}{1} = \dfrac{26}{7}$

34. $\dfrac{11}{2}$ of $\dfrac{12}{7}$ is $\dfrac{11}{2} \cdot \dfrac{12}{7} = \dfrac{132}{14}$

35. $\dfrac{1}{2}$ of $\dfrac{1}{2}$ of $\dfrac{1}{2}$ is $\dfrac{1}{2} \cdot \dfrac{1}{2} \cdot \dfrac{1}{2} = \dfrac{1}{8}$

36. $\dfrac{1}{3}$ of $\dfrac{3}{4}$ of $\dfrac{3}{4}$ is $\dfrac{1}{3} \cdot \dfrac{3}{4} \cdot \dfrac{3}{4} = \dfrac{9}{48}$

37. $\dfrac{2}{3}$ of $\dfrac{3}{4}$ of $-\dfrac{4}{5}$ is $\dfrac{2}{3} \cdot \dfrac{3}{4} \cdot \left(-\dfrac{4}{5}\right) = \dfrac{2}{1} \cdot \dfrac{1}{1} \cdot \left(-\dfrac{1}{5}\right) = -\dfrac{2}{5}$

38. $\dfrac{4}{3}$ of $\dfrac{3}{4}$ of 6 is $\dfrac{4}{3} \cdot \dfrac{3}{4} \cdot 6 = 6$

39. $\dfrac{5}{6}$ of $\dfrac{7}{4}$ of $\dfrac{12}{7}$ is $\dfrac{5}{6} \cdot \dfrac{7}{4} \cdot \dfrac{12}{7} = \dfrac{5}{1} \cdot \dfrac{1}{2} \cdot \dfrac{1}{1} = \dfrac{5}{2}$

40. $\dfrac{8}{3}$ of $\dfrac{5}{3}$ of 10 is $\dfrac{8}{3} \cdot \dfrac{5}{3} \cdot 10 = \dfrac{400}{9}$

41. $\dfrac{5}{3}$ of $\dfrac{8}{3}$ of 10 is $\dfrac{5}{3} \cdot \dfrac{8}{3} \cdot 10 = \dfrac{400}{9}$

42. $\dfrac{a}{b}$ of $\dfrac{b}{3}$ of $\dfrac{2}{a}$ is $\dfrac{a}{b} \cdot \dfrac{b}{3} \cdot \dfrac{2}{a} = \dfrac{2}{3}$

43. Jim ate 220 grams of pasta. Lily ate $\frac{2}{3}$ of Jim, find the amount of pasta Lily ate.

$\frac{2}{3} \cdot 220 = \frac{440}{3}$ grams

44. Jessica walks $2\frac{2}{3}$ miles every morning. Marc walks $\frac{4}{5}$ of Jessica, find the distance Marc walks every morning. $\frac{4}{5} \cdot \frac{8}{3} = \frac{32}{15}$ miles $= 2\frac{2}{15}$ miles

45. Michael ate $\frac{1}{3}$ of the 66 cookies in the jar, how many cookies did he eat?

$\frac{1}{3} \cdot 66 = 22$ cookies

46. Lisa climbed 130 meters. Mervin climbed $\frac{2}{5}$ more than Lisa. Find the distance Mervin climbed. $130 + \frac{2}{5} \cdot 130 = 130 \cdot (1 + \frac{2}{5}) = 130 \cdot (\frac{7}{5}) = 182$ meters

47. Juan ate $\frac{2}{3}$ of $\frac{2}{5}$ the 50 cookies in the jar, how many cookies did he eat?

$\frac{2}{3} \cdot \frac{2}{5} \cdot 50 = \frac{200}{15} \approx 13$ cookies

48. Paul bought 5 Kg of fruit. He ate $\frac{3}{8}$ of the fruit. Ruth ate $\frac{2}{7}$ of Paul.

   a. How many Kg of fruit did Paul eat? $\frac{3}{8} \cdot 5 = \frac{15}{8}$ Kg

   b. How many Kg of fruit did Ruth eat? $\frac{2}{7} \cdot \frac{15}{8} = \frac{30}{56}$ Kg

   c. How many Kg of fruit is left? $5 - \left(\frac{15}{8} + \frac{30}{56}\right) = 5 - \left(\frac{135}{56}\right) = \frac{145}{56}$ Kg

49. Raquel walked 10 miles on Monday and $\frac{1}{6}$ more on Tuesday. How many km did she walk on Tuesday? $10 + \frac{1}{6} \cdot 10 = 10 \cdot (1 + \frac{1}{6}) = 10 \cdot (\frac{7}{6}) = \frac{70}{6}$ miles

50. Liam's height is 186 cm. Daphne's height is $\frac{1}{12}$ less. Find Daphne's height.

$186 - \frac{1}{12} \cdot 186 = 186 \cdot (1 - \frac{1}{12}) = 186 \cdot (\frac{11}{12}) = 170.5$ cm

51. Ben's weight is 66 kg. Lana's weight is $\frac{2}{11}$ more. Find Lana's weight.

$66 + \frac{2}{11} \cdot 66 = 66 \cdot (1 + \frac{2}{11}) = 66 \cdot (\frac{13}{11}) = 78$ Kg

52. Rafa drove 500 km his 3 day trip. $\frac{2}{5}$ of the trip in day 1 and $\frac{5}{12}$ in day 2.

   a. How many km did he drive in day 1? $\frac{2}{5} \cdot 500 = 200 km$

   b. How many km did he drive in day 2? $\frac{5}{12} \cdot 500 \approx 208 km$

   c. How many km did he drive in day 3? $500 - (208 + 200) = 92 km$

   d. What fraction of the way was driven in day 3? $\frac{92}{500}$

53. To <u>increase</u> an amount x by a fraction $\frac{a}{b}$ we can operate in the following ways:

   a. Find first $\frac{a}{b} \cdot x$ and than using addition: $x + \frac{a}{b} \cdot x$

   b. Using multiplication directly: $x \cdot \left(1 + \frac{a}{b}\right)$

54. To <u>decrease</u> an amount x by a fraction $\frac{a}{b}$ we can operate in the following ways:

   a. Find first $\frac{a}{b} \cdot x$ and than using subtraction: $x - \frac{a}{b} \cdot x$

   b. Using multiplication directly: $x \cdot \left(1 - \frac{a}{b}\right)$

DIVIDING FRACTIONS

1. How many halves fit into 1? <u>2</u> in consequence $1 \div \frac{1}{2} = 2$

2. How many thirds fit into 1? <u>3</u> in consequence $1 \div \frac{1}{3} = 3$

3. How many halves fit into 2? <u>4</u> in consequence $2 \div \frac{1}{2} = 4$

4. How many thirds fit into 2? <u>6</u> in consequence $2 \div \frac{1}{3} = 6$

5. How many quarters fit into 2? <u>8</u> in consequence $2 \div \frac{1}{4} = 8$

6. How many fifths fit into 4? <u>20</u> in consequence $4 \div \frac{1}{5} = 20$

7. How many quarters fit into half? <u>2</u> in consequence $\frac{1}{2} \div \frac{1}{4} = 2$

8. How many quarters fit into three halves? <u>6</u> in consequence $\frac{3}{2} \div \frac{1}{4} = 6$

9. How many sixths fit into two thirds? <u>4</u> in consequence $\frac{2}{3} \div \frac{1}{6} = 4$

10. In general $\dfrac{a}{b} \div \dfrac{c}{d} = \dfrac{\left(\dfrac{a}{b}\right)}{\left(\dfrac{c}{d}\right)} = \dfrac{\left(\dfrac{a}{b}\right)\left(\dfrac{d}{c}\right)}{\left(\dfrac{c}{d}\right)\left(\dfrac{d}{c}\right)} = \dfrac{a}{b} \cdot \dfrac{d}{c} = \dfrac{ad}{bc}$

11. $\dfrac{7}{9} \div \dfrac{2}{5} = \dfrac{7}{9} \cdot \dfrac{5}{2} = \dfrac{35}{18}$

12. $12 \div \dfrac{3}{5} = 12 \cdot \dfrac{5}{3} = 20$

13. $\dfrac{12}{7} \div \dfrac{5}{6} = \dfrac{12}{7} \cdot \dfrac{6}{5} = \dfrac{72}{35}$

14. $\dfrac{2}{3} \div 7 = \dfrac{2}{3} \cdot \dfrac{1}{7} = \dfrac{2}{21}$

15. $\dfrac{11}{3} \div \dfrac{12}{5} = \dfrac{11}{3} \cdot \dfrac{5}{12} = \dfrac{55}{36}$

16. $\dfrac{2}{7} \div \dfrac{3}{8} = \dfrac{2}{7} \cdot \dfrac{8}{3} = \dfrac{16}{21}$

17. $11 \div \dfrac{3}{7} = 11 \cdot \dfrac{7}{3} = \dfrac{77}{33}$

18. $\dfrac{9}{7} \div 11 = \dfrac{9}{7} \cdot \dfrac{1}{11} = \dfrac{9}{77}$

19. $\dfrac{\left(\dfrac{7}{12}\right)}{\left(\dfrac{9}{5}\right)} = \left(\dfrac{7}{12}\right) \cdot \left(\dfrac{5}{9}\right) = \dfrac{35}{108}$

20. $\dfrac{\left(\dfrac{2}{11}\right)}{\left(\dfrac{3}{5}\right)} = \left(\dfrac{2}{11}\right)\left(\dfrac{5}{3}\right) = \dfrac{10}{33}$

21. $\dfrac{4}{\left(\dfrac{3}{5}\right)} = 4 \cdot \left(\dfrac{5}{3}\right) = \dfrac{20}{3}$

22. $\dfrac{2}{\left(\dfrac{2}{7}\right)} = 2 \cdot \left(\dfrac{7}{2}\right) = 7$

23. $\dfrac{\left(\dfrac{7}{12}\right)}{2} = \left(\dfrac{7}{12}\right) \cdot \dfrac{1}{2} = \dfrac{7}{24}$

24. $\dfrac{\left(\dfrac{2}{3}\right)}{4} = \left(\dfrac{2}{3}\right) \cdot \dfrac{1}{4} = \dfrac{1}{6}$

25. $\dfrac{\left(\dfrac{a}{2}\right)}{\left(\dfrac{a}{3}\right)} = \left(\dfrac{a}{2}\right) \cdot \left(\dfrac{3}{a}\right) = \dfrac{3}{2}$

26. $\dfrac{a}{\left(\dfrac{a}{5}\right)} = a \cdot \left(\dfrac{5}{a}\right) = 5$

27. $\dfrac{2}{\left(\dfrac{2}{b}\right)} = 2 \cdot \left(\dfrac{b}{2}\right) = b$

28. $\dfrac{\left(\dfrac{4}{a}\right)}{\left(\dfrac{5}{a}\right)} = \left(\dfrac{4}{a}\right) \cdot \left(\dfrac{a}{5}\right) = \dfrac{4}{5}$

29. $\dfrac{\left(\dfrac{2}{3}\right)}{2} = \left(\dfrac{2}{3}\right) \cdot \dfrac{1}{2} = \dfrac{1}{3}$

30. $\dfrac{\left(\dfrac{a}{b}\right)}{a} = \left(\dfrac{a}{b}\right) \dfrac{1}{a} = \dfrac{1}{b}$

31. $\dfrac{\left(\dfrac{2x}{5}\right)}{(4x)} = \left(\dfrac{2x}{5}\right) \cdot \left(\dfrac{1}{4x}\right) = \dfrac{1}{10}$

32. $\dfrac{(x)}{\left(\dfrac{4x}{5}\right)} = x \cdot \left(\dfrac{5}{4x}\right) = \dfrac{5}{4}$

33. $\dfrac{\left(\dfrac{3x}{7}\right)}{\left(\dfrac{4x}{11}\right)} = \left(\dfrac{3x}{7}\right)\left(\dfrac{11}{4x}\right) = \dfrac{33}{28}$

34. $\dfrac{\left(\dfrac{x}{12}\right)}{(3x)} = \left(\dfrac{x}{12}\right)\left(\dfrac{1}{3x}\right) = \dfrac{1}{36}$

35. $1 + \dfrac{2}{3} = \dfrac{3}{3} + \dfrac{2}{3} = \dfrac{5}{3}$

36. $\dfrac{5}{6} + \dfrac{2}{3} = \dfrac{5}{6} + \dfrac{4}{6} = \dfrac{9}{6} = \dfrac{3}{2}$

37. $\dfrac{2}{7}-\dfrac{1}{6}=\dfrac{12}{42}-\dfrac{7}{42}=\dfrac{5}{42}$

38. $5\cdot\dfrac{3}{8}-\dfrac{2}{12}=\dfrac{45}{24}-\dfrac{4}{24}=\dfrac{41}{24}$

39. $\left(\dfrac{2}{14}-\dfrac{3}{7}\right)\cdot\dfrac{2}{9}=\left(\dfrac{2}{14}-\dfrac{6}{14}\right)\cdot\dfrac{2}{9}=-\dfrac{4}{14}\cdot\dfrac{2}{9}=-\dfrac{4}{63}$

40. $\left(\dfrac{7}{2}-\dfrac{4}{3}\right)\cdot\dfrac{1}{5}=\left(\dfrac{21}{6}-\dfrac{8}{6}\right)\cdot\dfrac{1}{5}=\dfrac{13}{6}\cdot\dfrac{1}{5}=\dfrac{13}{60}$

41. $\dfrac{5}{6}+\dfrac{2}{3}-6=\dfrac{5}{6}+\dfrac{4}{6}-\dfrac{36}{6}=-\dfrac{27}{6}$

42. $\dfrac{1}{a}+\dfrac{1}{a}=\dfrac{2}{a}$

43. $\dfrac{1}{d}+d=\dfrac{1}{d}+\dfrac{d^2}{d}=\dfrac{1+d^2}{d}$

44. $\dfrac{1}{a}+\dfrac{a}{1}=\dfrac{1}{a}+\dfrac{a^2}{a}=\dfrac{1+a^2}{a}$

45. $\dfrac{1}{b+1}+b=\dfrac{1}{b+1}+\dfrac{b(b+1)}{b+1}=\dfrac{1+b(b+1)}{b+1}$

46. $\dfrac{a}{b}+\dfrac{1}{b}=\dfrac{a+1}{b}$

47. $\dfrac{a}{b}+\dfrac{d}{b}=\dfrac{a+d}{b}$

48. $\dfrac{a}{c}+\dfrac{d}{b}=\dfrac{ab}{cb}+\dfrac{cd}{cb}=\dfrac{ab+cd}{cb}$

49. $\dfrac{a+b}{b}+\dfrac{d}{b}+2=\dfrac{a+b+d}{b}$

50. $\dfrac{\left(\dfrac{a}{b}\right)}{b}=\dfrac{\left(\dfrac{a}{b}\right)\left(\dfrac{1}{b}\right)}{b\left(\dfrac{1}{b}\right)}=\dfrac{a}{b^2}$

51. $\dfrac{a\left(\dfrac{b}{a}\right)}{\left(\dfrac{a}{b}\right)\left(\dfrac{b}{a}\right)}=b$

52. $\dfrac{\left(\dfrac{b}{a}\right)\left(\dfrac{1}{b}\right)}{b\left(\dfrac{1}{b}\right)}=\dfrac{1}{a}$

53. $\dfrac{\left(\dfrac{b}{a}\right)}{1}=\dfrac{b}{a}$

54. $\dfrac{\left(\dfrac{1}{a}\right)}{b}=\dfrac{1}{ab}$

55. $\dfrac{\left(\dfrac{b}{1}\right)}{b}=1$

56. $\dfrac{1}{\left(\dfrac{a}{b}\right)}=\dfrac{b}{a}$

57. $\dfrac{\left(\dfrac{a}{b}\right)}{\left(\dfrac{a}{b}\right)}=1$

58. $\dfrac{\left(\dfrac{b}{a}\right)}{\left(\dfrac{a}{b}\right)}=\dfrac{b^2}{a^2}$

59. $\dfrac{\left(\dfrac{a}{1}\right)}{\left(\dfrac{a}{b}\right)}=b$

60. $\dfrac{\left(\dfrac{a}{b}\right)}{\left(\dfrac{1}{b}\right)}=a$

61. $\dfrac{\left(\dfrac{c+1}{d}\right)}{\left(\dfrac{1}{d}+d\right)}=\dfrac{\left(\dfrac{c+1}{d}\right)}{\left(\dfrac{1+d^2}{d}\right)}=\left(\dfrac{c+1}{1+d^2}\right)$

62. $\dfrac{1}{d}+\dfrac{2}{d^2}+\dfrac{1}{d^3}=\dfrac{d^2+2d+1}{d^3}$

63. $\dfrac{2}{3}+\dfrac{3a}{c}-\dfrac{b}{2}=\dfrac{4c+18a-3cb}{6c}$

64. $\dfrac{\left(\dfrac{4}{b}-\dfrac{a}{7}\right)}{2}=\dfrac{\left(\dfrac{28-ab}{7b}\right)}{2}=\dfrac{28-ab}{14b}$

65. $\dfrac{a}{c(c+1)} + \dfrac{d}{c+1} = \dfrac{a+dc}{c(c+1)}$

66. $\dfrac{\left(2x+\dfrac{1}{x}\right)}{\left(1+\dfrac{1}{x}\right)} = \dfrac{\left(\dfrac{2x^2+1}{x}\right)}{\left(\dfrac{x+1}{x}\right)} = \left(\dfrac{2x^2+1}{x+1}\right)$

67. $\dfrac{12}{2a} \times \dfrac{a+1}{6} = \dfrac{(a+1)}{a}$

68. $\dfrac{12}{2a} \div \dfrac{a}{6} = \dfrac{36}{2a^2}$

69. $3 \times \dfrac{4}{3} = 4$

70. $3 \div \dfrac{4}{3} = \dfrac{9}{4}$

71. $12 - \dfrac{4}{3} = \dfrac{32}{3}$

72. $a \times \dfrac{b}{3c} = \dfrac{ab}{3c}$

73. $\dfrac{b}{3a} \div 3a = \dfrac{b}{3a^2}$

74. $\dfrac{b}{3a} \times 3a = b$

75. $\dfrac{\left(\dfrac{1}{3}+\dfrac{2}{5}\right)}{\left(\dfrac{5}{3}-\dfrac{1}{3}\right)} = \dfrac{\left(\dfrac{11}{15}\right)}{\left(\dfrac{4}{3}\right)} = \dfrac{33}{60} = \dfrac{11}{20}$

76. $\dfrac{\left(\dfrac{b}{3c}\right)}{2} = \dfrac{b}{6c}$

77. $\dfrac{\left(\dfrac{1}{2}\right)}{2\left(\dfrac{2}{3c}\right)} = \dfrac{3c}{8}$

78. $\dfrac{\left(\dfrac{1}{2}\right)}{2} = \dfrac{1}{4}$

79. $\dfrac{\left(\dfrac{2}{7}\right)}{3} = \dfrac{2}{21}$

80. $\dfrac{2}{\left(\dfrac{2}{7}\right)} = \dfrac{1}{7}$

81. $\dfrac{3}{\left(\dfrac{a}{7}\right)} = \dfrac{21}{a}$

82. $\dfrac{6}{\left(\dfrac{8}{3}\right)} = \dfrac{9}{4}$

83. $\dfrac{\left(\dfrac{4}{3}\right)}{\left(\dfrac{3}{4}\right)} = \dfrac{16}{9}$

84. $\dfrac{\left(\dfrac{2}{3}\right)}{\left(\dfrac{4}{5}\right)} = \dfrac{6}{5}$

85. $\dfrac{\left(\dfrac{2}{3}\right)}{\left(\dfrac{2}{3}\right)} = 1$

86. $\left(\dfrac{a}{b}\right) \cdot \left(\dfrac{c}{a}\right) = \dfrac{c}{b}$

87. $\left(\dfrac{2}{c}\right) \cdot \left(\dfrac{c}{7}\right) = \dfrac{2}{7}$

88. $\left(\dfrac{b+1}{3}\right) \cdot \left(\dfrac{2}{b}\right) = \dfrac{2(b+1)}{3b}$

89. $\left(\dfrac{z+1}{z-2}\right) \cdot \left(\dfrac{4}{z+1}\right) = \dfrac{4}{z-2}$

90. $\left(\dfrac{3a+6}{5}\right) \cdot \left(\dfrac{1}{a+2}\right) = \dfrac{3}{5}$

91. $\left(\dfrac{2c-4}{c}\right) \cdot \left(\dfrac{2c}{4c-8}\right) = 1$

92. $\dfrac{1}{\left(\dfrac{2}{4}\right)} \cdot \left(\dfrac{2}{3}\right) = \dfrac{4}{3}$

93. $\dfrac{\left(\dfrac{3}{4}\right)}{\left(\dfrac{a}{2}\right)} \cdot \left(\dfrac{2}{3}\right) = \dfrac{1}{a}$

94. $\dfrac{\left(\dfrac{1}{a}\right)}{\left(\dfrac{2}{a}\right)} + 2 = \dfrac{5}{2}$

95. $\dfrac{\left(x+\dfrac{1}{x}\right)}{\left(1-\dfrac{1}{x}\right)} = \dfrac{x^2+1}{x-1}$

96. $\dfrac{\left(\dfrac{1}{1+x}+1\right)}{\left(x-\dfrac{2}{x}\right)} = \dfrac{x(2+x)}{(x^2-2)(1+x)}$

97. Juan has 40 cookies. He wants to share the cookies with his classmates. There are 25 students in hiss classroom, how should Juan split the cookies?
$\dfrac{40}{25} = \dfrac{8}{5} = 1+\dfrac{3}{5}$ $1+\dfrac{3}{5}$ cookies each.

98. Gina has an 120 m² field. She wants to grow carrots on a third of the field, potatoes on a fifth and use the rest as a playground. How many square meters should she use in each case?
$Carrots: \dfrac{1}{3} \cdot 120 = 40 m^2$ $Potatoes: \dfrac{1}{5} \cdot 120 = 24 m^2$ $Playground := 120-64 = 56 m^2$

99. Lia has needs two fifths cup of sugar to bake a cake. If she has three cups of sugar how many cakes can she bake? $\dfrac{(3)}{\left(\dfrac{2}{5}\right)} = \dfrac{15}{2} = 7.5$ She can bake 7 cakes.

100. In the construction of a new road twenty five kilometers long a sign should be put every 100 m (1km = 1000m). Find the number of signs that should be put along the road. If the cost of each sign is 50$, find the total cost.
$\dfrac{25000}{100} = 250\,signs$ $Cost: 250 \cdot 50 = 12500\$$

101. A quarter of a kilogram of fruit costs 2$. Find the cost of three and a half Kg of fruit. $\dfrac{\left(\dfrac{7}{2}\right)}{\left(\dfrac{1}{4}\right)} \cdot 2 = \left(\dfrac{7}{2}\right) \cdot 8 = 28\$$

102. A can of drink contains 400ml (1 Liter = 1000ml). Find the number of cans that can be filled with 500 liters of drink. $\dfrac{(500)}{\left(\dfrac{400}{1000}\right)} = 500\left(\dfrac{10}{4}\right) = 1250\,cans$

103. How many $\dfrac{2}{5}$ kg of meat are needed to feed a certain animal that needs to eat 8 kg of meat a day? $\dfrac{(8)}{\left(\dfrac{2}{5}\right)} = 8\left(\dfrac{5}{2}\right) = 20$

1.3. – DECIMALS AND FRACTIONS

Write the fractions as decimals:

1. $\frac{1}{10} = \underline{0.1}$
2. $\frac{1}{100} = \underline{0.01}$
3. $\frac{1}{1000} = \underline{0.001}$
4. $\frac{1}{10000} = \underline{0.0001}$
5. $\frac{2}{10} = \underline{0.2}$
6. $\frac{7}{100} = \underline{0.07}$
7. $\frac{-29}{1000} = \underline{-0.029}$
8. $\frac{966}{10000} = \underline{0.0966}$
9. $\frac{75}{10} = \underline{7.5}$
10. $\frac{101}{100} = \underline{1.01}$
11. $\frac{-135}{1000} = \underline{0.135}$
12. $\frac{30000}{10000} = \underline{3}$
13. $\frac{1}{2} = \underline{0.5}$
14. $\frac{1}{5} = \underline{0.2}$
15. $\frac{1}{4} = \underline{0.25}$
16. $\frac{1}{3} = \underline{0.333\ldots}$
17. $\frac{1}{8} = \underline{0.125}$
18. $\frac{1}{9} = \underline{0.111\ldots}$
19. $\frac{2}{5} = \underline{0.4}$
20. $\frac{2}{4} = \underline{0.5}$
21. $\frac{3}{5} = \underline{0.6}$
22. $\frac{4}{5} = \underline{0.8}$
23. $\frac{3}{4} = \underline{0.75}$
24. $\frac{7}{5} = \underline{1.4}$
25. $\frac{5}{4} = \underline{1.25}$
26. $\frac{9}{5} = \underline{1.6}$
27. $\frac{2}{9} = \underline{0.222\ldots}$
28. $\frac{1}{20} = \underline{0.02}$
29. $\frac{3}{20} = \underline{0.06}$
30. $\frac{8}{5} = \underline{1.6}$
31. $\frac{18}{10} = \underline{1.8}$

Write the decimals as fractions:

32. $0.3 = \underline{\frac{3}{10}}$
33. $0.2 = \underline{\frac{2}{10}}$
34. $0.1 = \underline{\frac{1}{10}}$
35. $0.01 = \underline{\frac{1}{100}}$
36. $0.02 = \underline{\frac{2}{100}}$
37. $0.11 = \underline{\frac{11}{100}}$
38. $0.24 = \underline{\frac{24}{100}}$
39. $1.3 = \underline{\frac{13}{10}}$
40. $1.57 = \underline{\frac{157}{10}}$
41. $0.011 = \underline{\frac{11}{1000}}$
42. $0.418 = \underline{\frac{418}{1000}}$
43. $0.17 = \underline{\frac{17}{100}}$
44. $1.4 = \underline{\frac{14}{10}}$
45. $2.043 = \underline{\frac{2043}{1000}}$
46. $75.2 = \underline{\frac{752}{10}}$
47. $4.12 = \underline{\frac{412}{100}}$
48. $1.307 = \underline{\frac{1307}{1000}}$
49. $1.111 = \underline{\frac{1111}{1000}}$
50. $132.87 = \underline{\frac{13287}{100}}$
51. $6.234 = \underline{\frac{6234}{1000}}$

Perform the operations <u>using fractions only</u>; give the answer as a decimal and fraction:

52. $40 \cdot 0.1 = \underline{4}$
53. $95 \cdot 0.01 = \underline{0.95}$
54. $46 \cdot 0.001 = \underline{0.046}$
55. $7 \cdot 0.0001 = \underline{0.0007}$
56. $8345 \cdot 0.001 = \underline{8.345}$
57. $962 \cdot 0.01 = \underline{9.62}$
58. $14 \cdot 0.001 = \underline{0.014}$
59. $-6423 \cdot 0.0001 = \underline{-0.6423}$
60. $3117 \cdot 0.1 = \underline{311.7}$
61. $1053 \cdot 0.01 = \underline{10.53}$
62. $3500 \cdot 0.001 = \underline{3.5}$
63. $0.17 \cdot 0.0001 = \underline{0.000017}$
64. $13 \cdot 1.2 = \frac{13}{1} \cdot \frac{12}{10} = \frac{156}{10} = 1.56$

65. $24 \cdot 0.22 = \dfrac{24}{1} \cdot \dfrac{22}{100} = \dfrac{528}{100} = 5.28$

66. $2.5 \cdot 1.7 = \dfrac{25}{10} \cdot \dfrac{17}{10} = \dfrac{425}{100} = 4.25$

67. $7.1 \cdot 8.8 = \dfrac{71}{10} \cdot \dfrac{88}{10} = \dfrac{6248}{100} = 62.48$

68. $0.14 \cdot 2.01 = \dfrac{14}{100} \cdot \dfrac{201}{100} = \dfrac{2814}{10000} = 0.2814$

69. $87.4 \cdot 0.2 = \dfrac{874}{10} \cdot \dfrac{2}{10} = \dfrac{1748}{100} = 17.48$

70. $30.5 \cdot 0.3 = \dfrac{305}{10} \cdot \dfrac{3}{10} = \dfrac{915}{100} = 9.15$

71. $0.211 \cdot 1.38 = \dfrac{211}{1000} \cdot \dfrac{138}{100} = \dfrac{29118}{100000} = 0.29118$

72. $0.4 \cdot 1.23 = \dfrac{4}{10} \cdot \dfrac{123}{100} = \dfrac{492}{1000} = 0.492$

73. $1.03 \cdot 2.5 = \dfrac{103}{100} \cdot \dfrac{25}{10} = \dfrac{2575}{1000} = 2.575$

74. $31.7 \cdot 0.19 = \dfrac{317}{10} \cdot \dfrac{19}{100} = \dfrac{6023}{1000} = 6.023$

75. $21.1 \cdot 1.13 = \dfrac{211}{10} \cdot \dfrac{113}{100} = \dfrac{23843}{1000} = 23.843$

76. $0.41 \cdot 5.56 = \dfrac{41}{100} \cdot \dfrac{556}{100} = \dfrac{22796}{10000} = 2.2796$

77. $3.1 \cdot 0.641 = \dfrac{31}{10} \cdot \dfrac{641}{1000} = \dfrac{19871}{10000} = 1.9871$

78. $13.6 \cdot 8.9 = \dfrac{136}{10} \cdot \dfrac{89}{10} = \dfrac{12104}{100} = 12.104$

79. $1.08 \cdot 0.03 = \dfrac{108}{100} \cdot \dfrac{3}{100} = \dfrac{324}{10000} = 0.0324$

Perform the operations <u>using fractions only</u>; give the answer as a decimal and fraction:

80. $\dfrac{1}{0.1} = \underline{10}$

81. $\dfrac{4}{0.01} = \underline{400}$

82. $\dfrac{-57}{0.001} = \underline{-57000}$

83. $\dfrac{-2.4}{0.01} = \underline{-240}$

84. $\dfrac{7}{0.1} = \underline{70}$

85. $\dfrac{0.51}{0.01} = \underline{51}$

86. $\dfrac{-31.7}{0.001} = \underline{-31700}$

87. $\dfrac{0.024}{0.01} = \underline{2.4}$

88. $\dfrac{15}{0.01} = \underline{1500}$

89. $\dfrac{-216}{0.01} = \underline{-21600}$

90. $\dfrac{-45.7}{0.001} = \underline{-45700}$

91. $\dfrac{-12.4}{0.01} = \underline{-1240}$

92. $\dfrac{1}{0.02} = \dfrac{1}{\left(\dfrac{2}{100}\right)} = \left(\dfrac{100}{2}\right) = 50$

93. $\dfrac{-2}{0.03} = \dfrac{-2}{\left(\dfrac{3}{100}\right)} = \left(-\dfrac{200}{2}\right) = -100$

94. $\dfrac{-4.7}{0.05} = \dfrac{-4.7}{\left(\dfrac{5}{100}\right)} = \left(-\dfrac{470}{2}\right) = -235$

95. $\dfrac{-1.2}{0.06} = \dfrac{-1.2}{\left(\dfrac{6}{100}\right)} = \left(\dfrac{-120}{6}\right) = -20$

96. $\dfrac{1}{0.25} = \dfrac{1}{\left(\dfrac{25}{100}\right)} = \left(\dfrac{100}{25}\right) = 4$

97. $\dfrac{-2}{0.9} = \dfrac{-2}{\left(\dfrac{9}{100}\right)} = \left(\dfrac{-200}{9}\right)$

98. $\dfrac{-5.1}{0.2} = \dfrac{-5.1}{\left(\dfrac{2}{10}\right)} = \left(\dfrac{-51}{2}\right)$

99. $\dfrac{-1.3}{0.05} = \dfrac{-1.3}{\left(\dfrac{5}{100}\right)} = \left(\dfrac{-130}{5}\right) = -26$

100. $\dfrac{1}{0.015} = \dfrac{1}{\left(\dfrac{15}{1000}\right)} = \left(\dfrac{1000}{15}\right) = \dfrac{200}{3}$

101. $\dfrac{-12}{0.6} = \dfrac{-12}{\left(\dfrac{6}{10}\right)} = \left(\dfrac{-120}{6}\right) = -20$

102. $\dfrac{-14}{0.003} = \dfrac{-14}{\left(\dfrac{3}{1000}\right)} = \left(\dfrac{-1400}{3}\right)$

103. $\dfrac{-0.3}{0.02} = \dfrac{\left(-\dfrac{3}{10}\right)}{\left(\dfrac{2}{100}\right)} = \left(-\dfrac{3}{10}\right)\left(\dfrac{100}{2}\right) = -15$

104. 0.2 units on the left of −1: −1.2
105. 0.5 units on the left of −3: −3.5
106. 0.3 units on the right of −1: −0.7
107. 0.4 units on the right of −2: −1.6
108. 0.8 units on the left of −9: −9.8
109. 0.2 units on the left of 0: −0.2
110. 0.9 units on the right of −9: −8.1
111. 0.2 units on the right of −4: −3.8
112. 0.21 units on the left of −1: −1.21
113. 0.51 units on the left of −2: −1.51
114. 0.32 units on the right of −1: −0.68
115. 0.06 units on the right of −10: −9.94
116. 0.11 units on the right of −1: −0.89
117. 0.01 units on the right of −2: −1.99
118. 0.36 units on the right of 9: 9.36
119. 0.06 units on the right of 10: 10.06
120. 0.17 units on the right of −9: −8.83
121. 0.53 units on the left of −3: −3.53

122. 0.01 units on the left of −7: −7.01
123. 0.02 units on the right of −1: −0.98
124. 0.002 units on the right of −10: −9.998
125. 0.111 units on the right of −1: −0.889
126. 0.021 units on the right of −2: −1.979
127. 0.4 units on the right of 9: 9.4
128. 0.04 units on the right of 10: 10.04
129. 0.202 units on the right of −9: −8.798
130. Close to 2 on its left: 1.999 right: 2.001
131. Close to 1 on its left: 0.999 right: 1.001
132. Close to 0 on its left: −0.001 right: 0.001
133. Close to −1 on its left: −1.001 right: −0.999
134. Close to −7 on its left: −7.001 right: −6.999
135. Close to −12 on its left: −12.001 right: −11.999
136. Close to −2 on its left: −2.001 right: −1.999
137. Close to −10 on its left: −10.001 right: −9.999
138. Close to 9 on its left: 8.999 right: 9.001
139. Close to 100 on its left: 99.999 right: 100.001

140. The numbers between 3 and 3.1: 3.01, 3.06. Fractions: $\left(\dfrac{301}{100}\right), \left(\dfrac{306}{100}\right)$

141. The numbers between 6.2 and 6.3: 6.21, 6.25. Fractions: $\left(\dfrac{621}{100}\right), \left(\dfrac{625}{100}\right)$

142. The numbers between 6.2 and 6.21: 6.201, 6.202. Fractions: $\left(\dfrac{6201}{1000}\right), \left(\dfrac{6202}{1000}\right)$

143. The numbers between −5.2 and −5.3: −5.21, −5.22. Fractions: $\left(-\dfrac{521}{100}\right), \left(-\dfrac{522}{100}\right)$

144. The numbers between 0.25 and 0.251: 0.2501, 0.2502. Fractions: $\left(\dfrac{2501}{10000}\right), \left(\dfrac{2502}{10000}\right)$

145. The numbers between 1.11 and 1.111: 1.1101, 1.1102. Fractions: $\left(\dfrac{11101}{10000}\right), \left(\dfrac{11102}{10000}\right)$

146. The numbers between 0.21 and 0.22: 0.211, 0.212. Fractions: $\left(\dfrac{211}{1000}\right), \left(\dfrac{212}{1000}\right)$

147. The numbers between 5.99 and 5.999: 5.991, 5.992. Fractions: $\left(\dfrac{5991}{1000}\right), \left(\dfrac{5992}{1000}\right)$

148. The numbers between 6 and 6.01: 6.001, 6.002. Fractions: $\left(\dfrac{6001}{1000}\right), \left(\dfrac{6002}{1000}\right)$

149. The values are: 11.2, 12, 12.4

150. The values are: 4.72, 4.77, 4.86

151. The values are: -0.62, -0.57, -0.5

152. 2 fractions: $\dfrac{22}{60}, \dfrac{23}{60}$

153. 2 fractions: $\dfrac{105}{1100}, \dfrac{106}{1100}$

154. 2 fractions: $\dfrac{25}{70}, \dfrac{26}{70}$

155. 2 fractions: $-\dfrac{35}{220}, -\dfrac{36}{220}$

156. 2 fractions: $\dfrac{155}{90}, \dfrac{156}{90}$

1.4. – TYPES OF NUMBERS

Natural Numbers (N): $N = \{1, 2, 3, 4...\}$
Integers (Z): $Z = \{...-4, -3, -2, -1, 0, 1, 2, 3, 4...\}$
Rational Numbers (Q): $Q = \{\dfrac{a}{b}, a, b \in Z\}$

Numbers that **can** be written as <u>fractions</u> being both the numerator and the denominator <u>integers</u>.

Examples: $\dfrac{1}{1}, \dfrac{2}{3}, \dfrac{-7}{3}, \dfrac{4}{-1}, \dfrac{0}{2}, 0.55, 0.121212...$

Irrational Numbers (Q'): $Q' \neq \{\dfrac{a}{b}, a, b \in Z\}$ Numbers that <u>cannot</u> be written as fractions, being both the <u>numerator</u> and the <u>denominator</u> integers.

Examples: $\pi, \sqrt{2}, e ...$

Real Numbers (R): $R = Q + Q'$ (Rationals and Irrationals)

Exercises:
1. Natural numbers are contained in the <u>Integer</u> numbers.
2. Integer numbers are contained in the <u>Rational</u> numbers
3. Rational numbers are contained in the <u>Real</u> numbers.
4. Irrational numbers are located <u>in the outermost ring</u>.
5. Shade the area in which the irrational numbers are located:
6. True or False:
    a. Some Integers are also Natural: <u>True</u>
    b. All Real numbers are Integers: <u>False</u>
    c. All Rational numbers are Real: <u>True</u>
    d. Some Real numbers are Rational: <u>True</u>
    e. All Integer numbers are Rational: <u>True</u>
    f. All Real numbers are Irrational: <u>False</u>
    g. Some Irrational numbers are Real and some are not: <u>False</u>
    h. Some Irrational numbers can be written as fractions using Integers: <u>False</u>
    i. Some integers are negative: <u>True</u>
    j. Some Irrationals are negative: <u>True</u>
    k. Some Natural numbers are negative: <u>False</u>
7. Write the value of the numbers with 10 decimal numbers (use a calculator)

    $\sqrt{2} = 1.4142135624...$ $\sqrt{3} = 1.7320508076...$
    $\sqrt{4} = 2.0000000000$ $\sqrt{5} = 2.2360679775...$
    $\dfrac{5}{6} = 0.8333333333...$ $\dfrac{43}{27} = 1.5925925925...$
    $\dfrac{122}{90} = 1.3555555555...$ $\dfrac{158}{990} = 0.15959595959...$

    Write a conclusion: <u>Fractions can be written as decimals with repetitive pattern, there are numbers such as root of 2 in which the decimals follow no pattern or the pattern is not repetitive, these numbers are called irrational numbers.</u>
8. Write down all the Natural number smaller than 3.01: <u>1, 2, 3</u>
9. Write down all the Integer numbers between $-\dfrac{5}{2}$ and $\dfrac{3}{2}$: <u>–2, –1, 0, 1</u>

10. Write down a Rational number between $\frac{1}{100}$ and $\frac{1}{10}$: $\frac{1}{20}$

11. Write down a positive Rational number smaller than $\frac{1}{137}$: $\frac{1}{138}$

12. Write down an Integer that is not a Natural : -2

13. Write down a Natural that is not an Integer: Not possible

14. Write down a Rational that is not an Integer: $\frac{1}{2}$

15. Circle the irrational numbers:
    0. 56734 **0.121231234...**
    0.1212212221... 0. 8719
    0.333… 0. 226666…
    $\pi^2 =$ $\sqrt{\pi} =$

16. Estimate the following numbers with 1 decimal, follow the example:
    $\sqrt{3} \approx 1.75$ $\sqrt{1}<\sqrt{3}<\sqrt{4} \Rightarrow 1<\sqrt{3}<2; 1.6\cdot 1.6=2.56; 1.7\cdot 1.7=2.89; 1.8\cdot 1.8=3.24 \Rightarrow 1.7<\sqrt{3}<1.8$
    $\sqrt{5} \approx 2.25$ $\sqrt{4}<\sqrt{5}<\sqrt{9} \Rightarrow 2<\sqrt{5}<3; 2.2\cdot 2.2=4.84; 2.3\cdot 2.3=5.29 \Rightarrow 2.2<\sqrt{5}<2.3$
    $\sqrt{6} \approx 2.45$ $\sqrt{4}<\sqrt{6}<\sqrt{9} \Rightarrow 2<\sqrt{6}<3; 2.4\cdot 2.4=5.76; 2.5\cdot 2.5=6.25 \Rightarrow 2.4<\sqrt{6}<2.5$
    $\sqrt{7} \approx 2.65$ $\sqrt{4}<\sqrt{7}<\sqrt{9} \Rightarrow 2<\sqrt{7}<3; 2.6\cdot 2.6=6.76; 2.7\cdot 2.7=7.29 \Rightarrow 2.6<\sqrt{7}<2.7$
    $\sqrt{8} \approx 2.85$ $\sqrt{4}<\sqrt{8}<\sqrt{9} \Rightarrow 2<\sqrt{7}<3; 2.8\cdot 2.8=7.84; 2.9\cdot 2.9=8.41 \Rightarrow 2.8<\sqrt{8}<2.9$
    $\sqrt{10} \approx 3.15$ $\sqrt{9}<\sqrt{10}<\sqrt{16} \Rightarrow 3<\sqrt{10}<4; 3.1\cdot 3.1=9.61; 3.2\cdot 3.2=10.24 \Rightarrow 3.1<\sqrt{10}<3.2$
    $\sqrt{55} \approx 7.5$ $\sqrt{49}<\sqrt{55}<\sqrt{64} \Rightarrow 7<\sqrt{55}<8$
    $\sqrt{245} \approx 15.5$ $\sqrt{225}<\sqrt{245}<\sqrt{256} \Rightarrow 15<\sqrt{245}<16$

17. Locate the following numbers on the number line without finding their exact value:

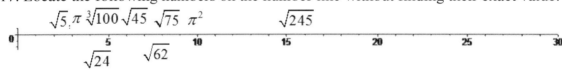

18. Locate the following numbers on the number line without finding their exact value:

19. Fill the table with yes or no (follow the example):

Number	Natural	Integer	Rational	Real
-3	no	yes	yes	yes
π	no	no	no	yes
$-3.66776677...$	no	no	yes	yes
-25.56	no	no	yes	yes
$\sqrt{31}$	no	no	no	yes
$-5\frac{2}{3}$	no	no	yes	yes
$\sqrt[3]{8}$	yes	yes	yes	yes

20. Fill the numbers column with appropriate numbers and yes or no.

Number	Natural	Integer	Rational	Real
−5	no	yes	yes	yes
0.15		no	yes	yes
Does not exist	yes	yes	yes	
$\sqrt{5}$	no	no	no	yes
$\dfrac{5}{7}$	No	no	yes	yes
0	no	Yes	yes	yes
0.333…	no	no	yes	yes
Does not exist		yes	no	

21. If possible, convert the following numbers into the form: $\dfrac{n}{m}$

a. $0.333\ldots = \dfrac{1}{3}$

b. $1.050050005\ldots =$ Irrational

c. $2.4\ldots = \dfrac{24}{10}$

d. $1.1818\ldots = \dfrac{117}{99}$

e. $-2.4545\ldots = \dfrac{297}{99}$

f. $37.29 = \dfrac{3729}{100}$

g. $12.377377\ldots = \dfrac{12365}{999}$

h. $-30.32 = \dfrac{-3032}{100}$

i. $0.325325\ldots = \dfrac{325}{99}$

j. $3.12331233\ldots = \dfrac{31230}{9999}$

k. $7774.21 = \dfrac{777421}{100}$

l. $78.253 = \dfrac{78253}{1000}$

m. $1.654654\ldots = \dfrac{1653}{999}$

n. $1.2131313\ldots = \dfrac{1201}{990}$

o. $1.55747474\ldots = \dfrac{15419}{9900}$

p. $5.333123123\ldots = \dfrac{532779}{99900}$

22. Given the following diagram:

Write the following numbers in the appropriate location in the diagram:

a. 3.2
b. 0.1234...
c. −2
d. 13
e. $\dfrac{1}{2}$
f. 2π
g. 1
h. −7.3
i. 1.222...
j. $\dfrac{1}{\sqrt{5}}$
k. $\sqrt{2}+1$
l. $\dfrac{8}{2}$

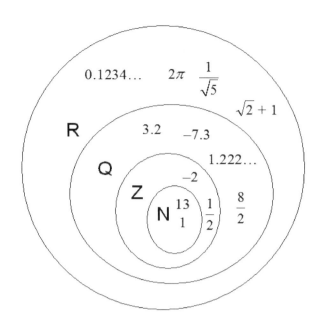

Circle the right option

23. The number −2 is:

    a. Integer and Natural.
    b. Positive
    c. Integer and Rational
    d. Natural and Real
    e. Natural and Rational
    f. None of the above

24. The number 3.41414141..... is:

    a. Integer and Natural.
    b. Natural
    c. Integer and Real
    d. Rational and Integer
    e. Rational
    f. None of the above

25. The number 3.41 is:

    a. Integer and Natural.
    b. Integer
    c. Rational and Real
    d. Integer and Real
    e. Rational and negative
    f. None of the above

26. The number $\sqrt{31}$ is:

    a. Integer and Natural.
    b. Integer
    c. Decimal
    d. Integer and Real
    e. Rational
    f. Irrational

27. The number 5 is:

    a. Natural.
    b. Integer
    c. Real
    d. Integer and Natural
    e. Rational and Natural
    f. All of the above

1.5. – EXPONENTS

Product:
$a^0 = 1$
$a^1 = a$
$a^2 = a \times a$
$a^3 = a \times a \times a$
...
$a^3 a^2 = a \cdot a \cdot a \cdot a \cdot a = a^5$

$$a^m a^n = a^{m+n}$$

Division:
$$\frac{a^5}{a^3} = \frac{a \cdot a \cdot a \cdot a \cdot a}{a \cdot a \cdot a} = \frac{a \cdot a}{1} = a^2$$

$$\frac{a^2}{a^5} = \frac{a \cdot a}{a \cdot a \cdot a \cdot a \cdot a} = \frac{1}{a \cdot a \cdot a} = \frac{1}{a^3} = a^{-3}$$

$$\frac{a^m}{a^n} = a^{m-n}$$

Power:
$(a^2)^3 = (a^2)(a^2)(a^2) = a^6$

$\left(\frac{a^2}{b}\right)^3 = \left(\frac{a^2}{b}\right)\left(\frac{a^2}{b}\right)\left(\frac{a^2}{b}\right) = \left(\frac{a^6}{b^3}\right)$

$$(a^m)^n = a^{mn}$$

$$\left(\frac{a^m}{b^k}\right)^n = \left(\frac{a^{mn}}{b^{kn}}\right)$$

Radicals:
$(a^3)^{\frac{1}{2}} = a^{\frac{3}{2}} = \sqrt[2]{a^3} = \sqrt{a^3}$

$(a^4)^{\frac{1}{7}} = a^{\frac{4}{7}} = \sqrt[7]{a^4}$

$$(a^m)^{\frac{1}{n}} = a^{\frac{m}{n}} = \sqrt[n]{a^m}$$

Exercises

Write in all possible forms and evaluate without using a calculator (follow example):

1. $4^{-1} = \frac{1}{4} = 0.25$
2. $10^0 = \underline{1}$
3. $10^1 = \underline{10}$
4. $10^3 = \underline{1000}$
5. $10^{-1} = \underline{\frac{1}{10} = 0.1}$
6. $10^{-2} = \underline{\frac{1}{100} = 0.01}$
7. $10^{-3} = \underline{\frac{1}{1000} = 0.001}$
8. $10^{-4} \underline{\frac{1}{10000} = 0.0001}$
9. $2^0 = 1$
10. $2^1 = 2$
11. $2^{-1} = \underline{\frac{1}{2} = 0.5}$
12. $2^{-2} = \underline{\frac{1}{2^2} = \frac{1}{4} = 0.25}$
13. $2^{-3} = \underline{\frac{1}{2^3} = \frac{1}{8} = 0.125}$
14. $2^{-4} = \underline{\frac{1}{2^4} = \frac{1}{16} = 0.0625}$
15. $(-1)^0 = \underline{1}$
16. $-1^0 = -1$
17. $(-1)^1 = -1$
18. $-1^1 = -1$

19. $(-1)^{-1} = \dfrac{1}{-1} = -1$

20. $-1^2 = -1$

21. $(-1)^2 = 1$

22. $-1^2 = -1$

23. $(-1)^{-2} = \dfrac{1}{(-1)^2} = \dfrac{1}{1} = 1$

24. $-1^{-2} = -\dfrac{1}{1^2} = -\dfrac{1}{1} = -1$

25. $(-3)^0 = 1$

26. $(-3)^1 = -3$

27. $-3^1 = -3$

28. $(-3)^2 = 9$

29. $-3^2 = -9$

30. $(-3)^{-1} = \dfrac{1}{(-3)^1} = \dfrac{1}{-3} = -\dfrac{1}{3}$

31. $-3^{-1} = -\dfrac{1}{3^1} = -\dfrac{1}{3}$

32. $(-3)^{-2} = \dfrac{1}{(-3)^2} = \dfrac{1}{9}$

33. $-3^{-2} = -\dfrac{1}{3^2} = -\dfrac{1}{9}$

34. $9^{\frac{1}{2}} = \sqrt{9} = \pm 3$

35. $16^{\frac{3}{4}} = \left(2^4\right)^{\frac{3}{4}} = 2^3 = 8$

36. $(3^{-1})^2 = 3^{-2} = \dfrac{1}{3^2} = \dfrac{1}{9}$

37. $(-8^{-3})^{\frac{2}{3}}$

$(-1)^{\frac{2}{3}}\left(2^{-9}\right)^{\frac{2}{3}} = \sqrt[3]{(-1)^2}\left(2^{-6}\right) = \dfrac{1}{64}$

38. $27^{-\frac{4}{3}} = 3^{-4} = \dfrac{1}{81} =$

39. $125^{-\frac{1}{3}} = 5^{-1} = \dfrac{1}{5} =$

40. $16^{\frac{3}{4}} = 2^3 = 8 =$

41. $(2^{-1})^2 = 2^{-2} = \dfrac{1}{4} =$

42. $(-8^{-3})^{\frac{2}{3}} = (-1)^{\frac{2}{3}} \cdot (8^{-3})^{\frac{2}{3}} = 1 \cdot 8^{-2} = \dfrac{1}{64}$

43. $(-27^{-1})^{\frac{2}{3}} = (-1)^{\frac{2}{3}} \cdot (27^{-1})^{\frac{2}{3}} = 1 \cdot 3^{-2} = \dfrac{1}{9}$

44. $(16^{-1})^{-\frac{3}{2}} = (2^{-4})^{-\frac{3}{2}} = 2^6 = 64$

45. $\left(\dfrac{1}{2}\right)^0 = 1$

46. $\left(\dfrac{1}{2}\right)^1 = \dfrac{1}{2}$

47. $\left(\dfrac{1}{2}\right)^{-1} = \dfrac{1}{\left(\dfrac{1}{2}\right)} = 2$

48. $\left(\dfrac{1}{2}\right)^2 = \dfrac{1}{4}$

49. $\left(-\dfrac{1}{2}\right)^{-\frac{5}{3}} = \dfrac{1}{\left(-\dfrac{1}{2}\right)^{\frac{5}{3}}} = \dfrac{1}{(-1)^{\frac{5}{3}}(2^{-1})^{\frac{5}{3}}} = \dfrac{2^{\frac{5}{3}}}{\sqrt[3]{(-1)^5}} = -\sqrt[3]{32}$

50. $\left(-\dfrac{2}{3}\right)^{-2} = \dfrac{9}{4}$

51. $\left(\dfrac{2}{5}\right)^1 = \dfrac{2}{5}$

52. $\left(\dfrac{100}{9}\right)^{-\frac{3}{2}} = \left(\dfrac{10^2}{3^2}\right)^{-\frac{3}{2}} = \left(\dfrac{10}{3}\right)^{-3} = \dfrac{27}{1000}$

53. $\left(\dfrac{6}{7}\right)^2 = \dfrac{36}{49}$

54. $\left(\dfrac{a}{b}\right)^{-1} = \dfrac{1}{\left(\dfrac{a}{b}\right)} = \dfrac{b}{a}$

55. $\left(\dfrac{1}{b}\right)^{-1} = \dfrac{1}{\left(\dfrac{1}{b}\right)} = b$

56. $b^{-1} = \dfrac{1}{b}$

57. $\left(\dfrac{-7}{2}\right)^{-2} = \dfrac{4}{49}$

58. $\left(\dfrac{3}{-2}\right)^{1} = -\dfrac{3}{2}$

59. $\left(\dfrac{-1}{\sqrt{2}}\right)^{-2} = \dfrac{2}{1} = 2$

60. $\left(\dfrac{5\sqrt{6}}{2}\right)^{2} = \dfrac{150}{4} = \dfrac{75}{2}$

61. $\left(\dfrac{-\sqrt{3}}{2}\right)^{-2} = \dfrac{4}{3}$

62. $\left(\dfrac{1+3\sqrt{2}}{-2}\right)^{2} = \dfrac{19+6\sqrt{2}}{4}$

63. $\left(\dfrac{-5}{3-\sqrt{2}}\right)^{-2} = \dfrac{11-6\sqrt{2}}{25}$

64. $\left(\dfrac{3+\sqrt{3}}{3}\right)^{2} = \dfrac{12+2\sqrt{2}}{9}$

65. $\left(\dfrac{-2-\sqrt{5}}{2+\sqrt{2}}\right)^{-2} = \dfrac{9+4\sqrt{5}}{6+4\sqrt{2}}$

66. $\left(\dfrac{-27}{8}\right)^{\frac{2}{3}} = \dfrac{9}{4}$

67. $\left(\dfrac{16}{9}\right)^{\frac{3}{4}} = \left(\dfrac{2^4}{3^2}\right)^{\frac{3}{4}} = \dfrac{2^3}{3^{\frac{3}{2}}} = \dfrac{8}{\sqrt{27}}$

68. $\left(\dfrac{1}{2}\right)^{\frac{3}{2}} = \dfrac{1}{\sqrt{8}}$

69. $\left(\dfrac{9}{16}\right)^{\frac{1}{2}} = \dfrac{3}{4}$

70. $\left(\dfrac{8}{27}\right)^{-\frac{1}{3}} = \dfrac{3}{2}$

71. $a^{-2} = \dfrac{1}{a^2}$

72. $a^{-\frac{1}{2}} = \dfrac{1}{\sqrt{a}}$

73. $a^{-\frac{2}{7}} = \dfrac{1}{\sqrt[7]{a^2}}$

74. $5^2 5^{-11} = 5^{-9}$

75. $4^{34} \cdot 2^{-70} = 2^{68-70} = 2^{-2} = \dfrac{1}{4}$

76. $9^{-3} \cdot 3^{-9} = 3^{-6-9} = 3^{-15}$

77. $a^b a^{-b} = 1$

78. $(-125)^{\frac{2}{3}} =$

$(-1)^{\frac{2}{3}}(5^3)^{\frac{2}{3}} = \sqrt[3]{(-1)^2} \cdot 5^2 = \sqrt[3]{1} \cdot 5^2 = 25$

79. $\dfrac{5^7}{5^4} = 5^3 = 125$

80. $\dfrac{3^8}{9^2}3^{-2} = 3^{8-2-4} = 9$

81. $\dfrac{3^1}{9^{\frac{1}{2}}}3^{-\frac{1}{2}} = 3^{1-\frac{1}{2}-\frac{1}{2}} = 3^0 = 1$

82. $\dfrac{\sqrt{2} \cdot 4^2}{2^{\frac{3}{2}}}2^{-\frac{1}{2}} = 2^{\frac{1}{2}+4-\frac{1}{2}-\frac{3}{2}} = 2^{\frac{5}{2}} = \sqrt{32}$

83. $\dfrac{a^{-1}}{a^{-2}} = a$

84. $\sqrt{\dfrac{a^{-8}}{a^{-10}}} = a$

85. $\sqrt{\sqrt{a}} = a^{\frac{1}{4}}$

34

86. $a\sqrt{a} = a^{\frac{1}{2}+1} = a^{\frac{3}{2}}$

87. $\sqrt{\sqrt[3]{a}} = a^{\frac{1}{3}\cdot\frac{1}{2}} = a^{\frac{1}{6}}$

88. $\dfrac{1}{\sqrt[4]{\sqrt{\sqrt{a}}}} = a^{-\frac{1}{2}\cdot\frac{1}{2}\cdot\frac{1}{4}} = a^{-\frac{1}{16}}$

89. $\sqrt{\sqrt[7]{\sqrt{a^2}}} = a^{\frac{2}{7}\cdot\frac{1}{2}\cdot\frac{1}{2}} = a^{\frac{1}{14}}$

90. $\sqrt{a\sqrt{a^2}} = \sqrt{a\cdot a} = \sqrt{a^2} = a$

91. $\dfrac{2\sqrt{a}}{\sqrt{2a}} = \dfrac{2}{\sqrt{2}} = \sqrt{2}$

92. $\dfrac{\sqrt{a}}{\sqrt[3]{\sqrt{a}}} = a^{\frac{1}{2}-\frac{1}{6}} = a^{\frac{1}{3}}$

93. $\dfrac{a\sqrt{a}}{\sqrt[5]{\sqrt{a}}} = a^{\frac{3}{2}-\frac{1}{10}} = a^{\frac{7}{5}}$

94. $\dfrac{\sqrt{8}\sqrt{a}}{\sqrt{2a}} = 2a^{-\frac{1}{2}}$

95. $\sqrt{\dfrac{\sqrt{aa^{-1}}}{a\sqrt{a^{-2}}}} = a^{-\frac{1}{4}}$

96. $\dfrac{a}{\sqrt{2a^{-1}}} = \dfrac{a^{\frac{3}{2}}}{\sqrt{2}}$

97. $\dfrac{\sqrt{\frac{1}{a}}}{\sqrt{aa^{-2}}} = a^0 = 1$

98. $\left(\dfrac{2}{5}\right)^3 \times \left(\dfrac{5}{3}\right)^4 = \dfrac{2^3 5^4}{5^3 3^4} = \dfrac{40}{81}$

99. $\left(\dfrac{4}{7}\right)^2 \div \left(\dfrac{9}{7}\right) = \dfrac{2^4 7^1}{7^2 3^2} = \dfrac{16}{63}$

100. $\sqrt{\left(\dfrac{7}{5}\right)^6 \div \left(\dfrac{49}{125}\right)^3} = \sqrt{\dfrac{7^6 5^9}{7^6 5^6}} = 5^{\frac{3}{2}}$

101. $\left(\dfrac{2}{5}\right)^3 \cdot \left(\dfrac{3}{5}\right)^{-2} = \dfrac{2^3 3^{-2}}{5^3 5^{-2}} = \dfrac{8}{45}$

102. $\left(\dfrac{4^2}{5^{-1}}\right)^2 \cdot \left(\dfrac{25^{-1}}{64}\right)^2 = \dfrac{2^8 5^{-4}}{5^{-2} 2^{12}} = \dfrac{1}{400}$

103. $\left(\dfrac{3^{-5}}{4^2}\right)^2 \div \left(\dfrac{9^{-1}}{2^3}\right)^3 = \dfrac{3^{-10} 2^9}{2^8 3^{-6}} = \dfrac{2}{81}$

104. $\left(\dfrac{3}{4}\right)^5 \div \left(\dfrac{9}{64}\right)^2 = \dfrac{3^5 \cdot 2^{12}}{2^{10} 3^4} = 3 \cdot 2^2 = 12$

105. $\sqrt[3]{\left(\dfrac{3}{4}\right)^5 \div \left(\dfrac{9}{64}\right)^2} = \sqrt[3]{\dfrac{3^5 2^{12}}{2^{10} 3^4}} = \sqrt[3]{12}$

106. $\left(\dfrac{2^{-3}}{3^{-2}}\right)^3 \cdot \left(\dfrac{4}{27}\right)^2 = \dfrac{2^{-9} \cdot 2^4}{3^{-6} 3^6} =$

$= 2^{-5} = \dfrac{1}{32}$

107. $2^{-1} + 1 = \dfrac{1}{2} + 1 = \dfrac{3}{2}$

108. $3^{-1} - 3^{-2} = \dfrac{1}{3} - \dfrac{1}{9} = -\dfrac{2}{9}$

109. $5^{-1} - 5^{-2} = \dfrac{1}{5} - \dfrac{1}{25} = \dfrac{4}{25}$

110. $3^{-2} + 2^{-2} = \dfrac{1}{9} + \dfrac{1}{4} = \dfrac{13}{36}$

111. $3^{-1} + 4^{-2} = \dfrac{1}{3} + \dfrac{1}{4} = \dfrac{7}{12}$

112. $7^{-1} + 2^{-2} = \dfrac{1}{7} + \dfrac{1}{4} = \dfrac{11}{28}$

113. $8^{-2} - 3^{-1} = \dfrac{1}{64} - \dfrac{1}{3} = -\dfrac{61}{192}$

114. $7^{-2} - 2^{-3} = \dfrac{1}{49} - \dfrac{1}{8} = -\dfrac{41}{392}$

115. $a^{-1} + a^{-1} = \dfrac{1}{a} + \dfrac{1}{a} = \dfrac{2}{a}$

116. $ba^{-1} + a^{-1} = \dfrac{b}{a} + \dfrac{1}{a} = \dfrac{b+1}{a}$

117. $2x^{-1} + x^{-2} = \dfrac{2}{x} + \dfrac{1}{x^2} = \dfrac{2x+1}{x^2}$

Write in Standard notation:

1. $7 \cdot 10^2 = 700$
2. $6.3 \cdot 10^{-2} = 0.063$
3. $2 \cdot 10^{-1} = 0.2$
4. $3 \cdot 10^3 = 3000$
5. $12 \cdot 10^{-3} = 0.012$
6. $156 \cdot 10^4 = 1560000$
7. $91.43 \cdot 10^7 = 914300000$
8. $78.0101 \cdot 10^{-5} = 0.000780101$
9. $78818.112 \cdot 10^5 = 7881811200$
10. $782 \cdot 10^{-9} = 0.000000782$

Write in scientific notation:

11. $0.135 = 1.35 \cdot 10^{-1}$
12. $0.071 = 7.1 \cdot 10^{-2}$
13. $0.0000001 = 1 \cdot 10^{-7}$
14. $91.2 = 9.12 \cdot 10^1$
15. $12.02 = 1.202 \cdot 10^1$
16. $10000 = 1 \cdot 10^4$
17. $0.0000114 = 1.14 \cdot 10^{-5}$
18. $0.006023 = 6.023 \cdot 10^{-3}$
19. $0.0155 = 1.55 \cdot 10^{-2}$
20. $0.000204 = 2.04 \cdot 10^{-4}$
21. $101000 = 1.01 \cdot 10^5$
22. $11.01 = 11.01 \cdot 10^1$
23. $2022 = 2.022 \cdot 10^3$
24. $251 = 2.51 \cdot 10^2$
25. $101.102 = 1.01102 \cdot 10^2$
26. $9.200 = 9.2 \cdot 10^0$
27. $230.80 = 2.3080 \cdot 10^2$
28. $209.1 = 2.091 \cdot 10^2$
29. $24.18 = 2.418 \cdot 10^1$
30. $5500 = 5.5 \cdot 10^3$
31. $65000 = 6.5 \cdot 10^4$
32. $0.00545 = 5.45 \cdot 10^{-3}$
33. $0.000015 = 1.5 \cdot 10^{-5}$
34. $0.0505 = 5.05 \cdot 10^{-2}$
35. $0.005045 = 5.045 \cdot 10^{-3}$

Calculate

36. $5 \cdot 10^7 \cdot 7 \cdot 10^3 = 35 \cdot 10^{10} = 3.5 \cdot 10^{11}$
37. $6 \cdot 10^{-7} \cdot 12 \cdot 10^3 = 72 \cdot 10^{-4} = 7.2 \cdot 10^{-3}$
38. $\dfrac{10 \cdot 10^{-3}}{5 \cdot 10^{-6}} = 2 \cdot 10^3 = 2000$
39. $15 \cdot 10^{-6} \cdot 2 \cdot 10^{-3} = 30 \cdot 10^{-9} = 3 \cdot 10^{-8}$
40. $1.5 \cdot 10^{-16} \cdot 20 \cdot 10^{13} = 30 \cdot 10^{-3} = 3 \cdot 10^{-2} = 0.03$
41. $5 \cdot 10^{-12} - 8 \cdot 10^{-12} = -3 \cdot 10^{-12}$
42. $\dfrac{6 \cdot 10^{-7}}{12 \cdot 10^3} = 0.5 \cdot 10^{-10} = 5 \cdot 10^{-11}$
43. $12 \cdot 10^{-10} + 18 \cdot 10^{-10} = 30 \cdot 10^{-10} = 3 \cdot 10^{-9}$

44. $2 \cdot 10^{-19} - 80 \cdot 10^{-20} =$
    $= 2 \cdot 10^{-19} - 8 \cdot 10^{-19} = -6 \cdot 10^{-19}$

45. $7.1 \cdot 10^{-7} - 20 \cdot 10^{-9} =$
    $= 71 \cdot 10^{-8} - 2 \cdot 10^{-8} = 69 \cdot 10^{-8} =$
    $= 6.9 \cdot 10^{-7}$

46. $12 \cdot 10^{13} \cdot 2.5 \cdot 10^{13} = 18 \cdot 10^{26} = 1.8 \cdot 10^{27}$
47. $15 \cdot 10^{-6} \cdot 21 \cdot 10^6 = 315$
48. $\dfrac{120 \cdot 10^{-22}}{1.1 \cdot 10^{-19}} \approx 109 \cdot 10^{-3} = 1.09 \cdot 10^{-1} = 0.109$

49. In a chemical experiment there are 30 million reactions. In a later experiment there are 6 million reactions. Find, using scientific notation how many more reactions take place in the first experiment.
$30 \cdot 10^6 - 6 \cdot 10^6 = 24 \cdot 10^6 = 2.4 \cdot 10^7$ more reactions

50. The number of US citizens is approximately 300 million. The number of Chinese citizens is approximately 5 times bigger.
   a. Write the number of US and Chinese citizens in scientific notation.
      $US: 300 \cdot 10^6 = 3 \cdot 10^8$ $China: 1500 \cdot 10^6 = 1.5 \cdot 10^9$
   b. How many citizens in both countries together.
      $300 \cdot 10^6 + 1500 \cdot 10^6 = 1800 \cdot 10^6 = 1.8 \cdot 10^9$

51. The number of molecules in 1 gram of water is approximately $1.08 \cdot 10^{25}$. Find the number of molecules in 1 litre of water.
    $1000 \cdot 1.08 \cdot 10^{25} = 1080 \cdot 10^{25} = 1.08 \cdot 10^{28}$ molecules

52. The speed of light is approximately 300 million meters per second. The speed of sound is approximately 300 meters per second.

   a. Write the speed of light and sound in scientific notation.
      $Light: 300 \cdot 10^6 = 3 \cdot 10^8 \, m/s$ $Sound: 3 \cdot 10^2 \, m/s$
   b. By what factor is the speed of light faster than the speed of sound?
      $\dfrac{3 \cdot 10^8}{3 \cdot 10^2} = 10^6 = 1000000$ (one million times faster)
   c. The sun is 150 million km away from earth, how long does it take the light to travel from the earth to the sun. Write your answer in scientific notation.
      $\dfrac{150 \cdot 10^9}{3 \cdot 10^8} = 50 \cdot 10 = 500 \, s = 5 \cdot 10^2 \, s \approx 8 \min$
   d. What distance can sound reach in one minute? Write your answer in scientific notation.
      $300 \cdot 60 = 18000 \, m = 1.8 \cdot 10^4 \, m = 18 km$

1.6. – ROOTS AND RATIONALIZATION

Simplify as much as possible:

1. $\sqrt{0} = \underline{0}$
2. $\sqrt{1} = \underline{\pm 1}$
3. $\sqrt{4} = \underline{\pm 2}$
4. $\sqrt[3]{8} = 2$
5. $\sqrt{16} \cdot \sqrt{25} = 4 \cdot 5 = \pm 20$
6. $\sqrt[4]{2} \cdot \sqrt[4]{8} = \sqrt[4]{16} = \pm 2$
7. $\sqrt{-1} = i$ Not a real number
8. $\left(\sqrt{4}\right)^2 = 4$
9. $\left(\sqrt{-6}\right)^2 = -6$
10. $\left(-\sqrt{5}\right)^2 \cdot \left(\sqrt[3]{3}\right)^3 = 5 \cdot 3 = 15$
11. $\left(\sqrt{532}\right)^2 = 532$
12. $\left(\sqrt{a}\right)^2 \left(\sqrt[n]{a}\right)^n = a^2$
13. $\sqrt{\dfrac{a^2}{9}} = \pm \dfrac{a}{3}$
14. $\sqrt{\dfrac{8}{200}} = \sqrt{\dfrac{4}{100}} = \dfrac{2}{10} = \dfrac{1}{5}$
15. $\sqrt{3} + \sqrt{3} = 2\sqrt{3}$
16. $\sqrt{2} + \sqrt{2} + \sqrt{2} = \underline{3\sqrt{2}}$

17. $\sqrt{0.01} = \sqrt{\dfrac{1}{100}} = \dfrac{1}{10}$
18. $\sqrt{0.25} = \sqrt{\dfrac{25}{100}} = \dfrac{5}{10} = \dfrac{1}{2}$
19. $\sqrt{2.25} = \sqrt{\dfrac{225}{100}} = \dfrac{15}{10} = \dfrac{3}{2}$
20. $\sqrt{0.16} = \sqrt{\dfrac{16}{100}} = \dfrac{4}{10} = 0.4$
21. $\sqrt{0.36} = \sqrt{\dfrac{36}{100}} = \dfrac{6}{10} = 0.6$
22. $\sqrt{0.0081} = \sqrt{\dfrac{81}{10000}} = \dfrac{9}{100} = 0.09$
23. $\sqrt{6.25} = \sqrt{\dfrac{625}{100}} = \dfrac{25}{10} = 2.5$
24. $\sqrt{20.25} = \sqrt{\dfrac{2025}{100}} = \dfrac{45}{10} = 4.5$

25. $\sqrt{2} + \sqrt{8} + \sqrt{2} = \underline{4\sqrt{2}}$
26. $\sqrt{4} + \sqrt{2} + \sqrt{8} = \underline{3\sqrt{2} + 2}$
27. $\sqrt{9} + \sqrt{12} + \sqrt{27} = \underline{6\sqrt{3} + 3}$
28. $\sqrt{50} + \sqrt{75} + \sqrt{12} = \underline{5\sqrt{2} + 7\sqrt{3}}$
29. $\sqrt[3]{16} + \sqrt[3]{54} = 2\sqrt[3]{2} + 3\sqrt[3]{2} = 5\sqrt[3]{2}$
30. $\sqrt[4]{32} - \sqrt[4]{162} = 2\sqrt[4]{2} - 3\sqrt[4]{2} = -\sqrt[4]{2}$
31. $\sqrt{27} + \sqrt{81} + \sqrt{48} = \underline{7\sqrt{3} + 9}$
32. $\sqrt{200} + \sqrt{50} - \sqrt{18} = \underline{12\sqrt{2}}$
33. $\sqrt{20} + \sqrt{80} - \sqrt{125} = \underline{-\sqrt{5}}$
34. $\sqrt{10}\sqrt{10} = \underline{10}$
35. $\sqrt[3]{a} \cdot \sqrt[3]{a} \cdot \sqrt[3]{a} = a$
36. $\sqrt{3}\sqrt{9}\sqrt{3} = \underline{9}$
37. $\dfrac{\sqrt{50}}{\sqrt{2}} = \underline{5}$
38. $\dfrac{\sqrt{72}}{\sqrt{2}} = \underline{6}$
39. $\sqrt{15}\dfrac{\sqrt{75}}{\sqrt{5}} = \underline{15}$
40. $\sqrt{3}\dfrac{\sqrt{24}}{\sqrt{2}} = \underline{6}$
41. $\sqrt{x}\sqrt{x} = x$
42. $\sqrt{x} + \sqrt{x} = 2\sqrt{x}$

Rationalize the denominator:

43. $\dfrac{1}{\sqrt{23}} = \left(\dfrac{1}{\sqrt{23}}\right)\cdot\left(\dfrac{\sqrt{23}}{\sqrt{23}}\right) = \dfrac{\sqrt{23}}{23}$

44. $\left(\dfrac{3}{\sqrt{2}+1}\right)\cdot\left(\dfrac{\sqrt{2}-1}{\sqrt{2}-1}\right) = \dfrac{3(\sqrt{2}-1)}{4}$

45. $\left(\dfrac{-7}{\sqrt{3}-2}\right)\cdot\left(\dfrac{\sqrt{3}+2}{\sqrt{3}+2}\right) = \dfrac{7(\sqrt{3}+2)}{-1} = -7(\sqrt{5}+2)$

46. $\dfrac{\sqrt{2}+3}{-5}$, Denominator already rational

47. $\left(\dfrac{\sqrt{2}+3}{\sqrt{5}-5}\right)\cdot\left(\dfrac{\sqrt{5}+5}{\sqrt{5}+5}\right) = \dfrac{(\sqrt{2}+3)(\sqrt{5}+5)}{-20}$

48. $\left(\dfrac{\sqrt{2}}{\sqrt{6}+\sqrt{7}}\right)\cdot\left(\dfrac{\sqrt{6}-\sqrt{7}}{\sqrt{6}-\sqrt{7}}\right) = \dfrac{\sqrt{2}(\sqrt{6}-\sqrt{3})}{-1}$

49. $\left(\dfrac{\sqrt{2}-1}{2\sqrt{6}-\sqrt{3}}\right)\cdot\left(\dfrac{2\sqrt{6}+\sqrt{3}}{2\sqrt{6}+\sqrt{3}}\right) = \dfrac{(\sqrt{2}-1)(2\sqrt{5}+\sqrt{3})}{21}$

50. $\left(\dfrac{-1}{2\sqrt{a}+b}\right)\cdot\left(\dfrac{2\sqrt{a}-b}{2\sqrt{a}-b}\right) = \left(\dfrac{-2\sqrt{a}+b}{4a-b^2}\right)$

51. $\left(\dfrac{3\sqrt{a}-b}{2\sqrt{a}+\sqrt{b}}\right)\left(\dfrac{3\sqrt{a}-b}{2\sqrt{a}-\sqrt{b}}\right) = \left(\dfrac{(3\sqrt{a}-b)^2}{4a-b}\right)$

Rationalize the numerator:

52. $\dfrac{\sqrt{16}}{\sqrt{5}} = \dfrac{4}{\sqrt{5}}$

53. $\left(\dfrac{3-\sqrt{5}}{\sqrt{5}+1}\right)\cdot\left(\dfrac{3+\sqrt{5}}{3+\sqrt{5}}\right) = \dfrac{4}{(\sqrt{5}+1)(3+\sqrt{2})}$

54. $\left(\dfrac{-7}{\sqrt{5}-2}\right)$, Numerator already rational

55. $\left(\dfrac{\sqrt{2}+3}{\sqrt{6}-5}\right)\left(\dfrac{\sqrt{2}-3}{\sqrt{2}-3}\right) = \dfrac{-7}{(\sqrt{6}-5)(\sqrt{2}-3)}$

56. $\left(\dfrac{\sqrt{2}}{\sqrt{2x}+\sqrt{3}}\right)\cdot\left(\dfrac{\sqrt{2}}{\sqrt{2}}\right) = \dfrac{2}{\sqrt{2}(\sqrt{2x}+\sqrt{3})}$

57. $\left(\dfrac{\sqrt{b}-a}{\sqrt{a}-\sqrt{3}}\right)\cdot\left(\dfrac{\sqrt{b}+a}{\sqrt{b}+a}\right) = \dfrac{b-a^2}{(\sqrt{a}-\sqrt{3})(\sqrt{b}+a)}$

58. $\left(\dfrac{-3\sqrt{7}+4}{2\sqrt{5}+7}\right)\left(\dfrac{-3\sqrt{7}-4}{-3\sqrt{7}-4}\right) = \dfrac{47}{(2\sqrt{5}+7)(-3\sqrt{7}-8)}$

59. $\left(\dfrac{\sqrt{a}-2\sqrt{b}}{2\sqrt{a}+\sqrt{b}}\right)\cdot\left(\dfrac{\sqrt{a}+2\sqrt{b}}{2\sqrt{a}+\sqrt{b}}\right) = \left(\dfrac{a-4b}{4a+4\sqrt{ab}+b}\right)$

1.7. – PERCENTAGES

1. A percentage is a way to represent <u>a part of a whole</u> we sometimes use <u>fractions</u> or <u>decimals</u> for that purpose.

2. Write as a fraction and as a decimal:

   a. $1\% = \dfrac{1}{100} = 0.01$

   b. $10\% = \dfrac{10}{100} = 0.1$

   c. $79\% = \dfrac{79}{100} = 0.79$

   d. $100\% = \dfrac{100}{100} = 1$

   e. $101\% = \dfrac{101}{100} = 1.01$

   f. $110\% = \dfrac{110}{100} = 1.1$

   g. $200\% = \dfrac{200}{100} = 2$

   h. $0.1\% = \dfrac{1}{1000} = 0.001$

   i. $0.14\% = \dfrac{14}{10000} = 0.0014$

   j. $0.06\% = \dfrac{6}{10000} = 0.0006$

   k. $0.072\% = \dfrac{72}{100000} = 0.00072$

   l. $1.02\% = \dfrac{102}{10000} = 0.0102$

   m. $7.056\% = \dfrac{7056}{100000} = 0.07056$

   n. $5356\% = \dfrac{5356}{100} = 53.56$

A PERCENTAGE OF AN AMOUNT (same as a fraction of an amount)

3. Find (write the expression and simplify it to get a final answer):

   a. 1% of 800 = <u>8</u>
   b. 2% of 800 = <u>16</u>
   c. 3% of 800 = <u>23</u>
   d. 10% of 800 = <u>80</u>
   e. 15% of 800 = <u>120</u>
   f. 20% of 800 = <u>160</u>
   g. 25% of 800 = <u>200</u>
   h. 35% of 800 = <u>280</u>
   i. 100% of 600 = <u>600</u>
   j. 101% of 600 = <u>606</u>
   k. 110% of 600 = <u>660</u>
   l. 120% of 600 = <u>720</u>
   m. 125% of 600 = <u>750</u>
   n. 140% of 600 = <u>840</u>
   o. 200% of 600 = <u>1200</u>
   p. 300% of 600 = <u>1800</u>

4. Find (write the expression and simplify it to get a final answer):

   a. 1% of 60 = <u>0.6</u>
   b. 2% of 60 = <u>1.2</u>
   c. 10% of 110 = <u>11</u>
   d. 15% of 7 = <u>10.5</u>
   e. 20% of 130 = <u>26</u>
   f. 25% of 450 = <u>112.5</u>
   g. 35% of 2100 = <u>685</u>
   h. 100% of 1356 = <u>1356</u>
   i. 101% of 530 = <u>535.3</u>
   j. 110% of 160 = <u>176</u>
   k. 120% of 122 = <u>146.4</u>
   l. 125% of 250 = <u>312.5</u>
   m. 140% of 910 = <u>1274</u>
   n. 200% of 2400 = <u>4800</u>
   o. 300% of 110 = <u>330</u>
   p. $A\%$ of $M = \dfrac{AM}{100}$

5. $\dfrac{170}{200} = \dfrac{85}{100} = 85\%$

6. $\dfrac{18}{20} = 0.9 = 90\%$

7. $\dfrac{75}{80} \approx 0.94 = 94\%$

8. $P_{shaded} = \dfrac{\left(\dfrac{80}{100}x\right)\cdot\left(\dfrac{80}{100}x\right)}{x^2} = \dfrac{64}{100} = 64\%$

   $P_{NotShaded} = 100 - 64 = 36\%$

9. In a certain box of cookies there are 80 cookies of 3 colours: white, brown and black. 15% of the cookies are white, 15 cookies are brown and the rest are black.

   a. The percentage and the number of cookies.

   $P_{Brown} = \dfrac{15}{90} = 0.166.. \approx 17\%$

   $White = \dfrac{20}{100} \cdot 90 = 18 \; cookies$

   $P_{Black} = \dfrac{90-18-15}{90} = \dfrac{57}{90} = 0.633.. \approx 63\%$

   (57 cookies)

   b. Dani ate 2 cookies of each colour; find the new percentages of each kind.

   $P_{Brown} = \dfrac{13}{84} \approx 0.15 = 15\%$

   $P_{White} = \dfrac{16}{84} \approx 0.19 = 19\%$

   $P_{Black} = \dfrac{55}{84} \approx 0.65 = 65\%$

10. His benefit $\dfrac{750}{5000} = 0.15 = 15\%$

11. Her lost $\dfrac{400}{3400} \approx 0.12 = 12\%$

12. The percentage of it that is shaded : $\dfrac{50}{100} = 50\%$

13. The percentage of it that is shaded: $\dfrac{1}{8} = \dfrac{12.5}{100} = 12.5\%$

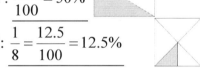

14. It is known that the area shaded is 20% of 70% of the circle.

    Shaded: $\dfrac{20}{100} \cdot \dfrac{70}{100} = \dfrac{14}{100} = 14\%$ Not Shaded: 86%

15. It is known that 10% of 75% of a population of 5000 students usually do sports. How many students usually do sports?

    $\dfrac{10}{100} \cdot \dfrac{75}{100} \cdot 5000 = 75 \; Students$

16. The amount. $\dfrac{5}{100} \cdot \dfrac{40}{100} x = 30 \;\;; x = 1500$

17. $\dfrac{60}{100} \cdot \dfrac{30}{100} x = 10 \;\;; x = \dfrac{1000}{18} \; euros$

18. 10% of 20% of 30% of 500. $\dfrac{10}{100} \cdot \dfrac{20}{100} \cdot \dfrac{30}{100} \cdot 500 = 3$

19. 20% of 30% of 30% of 300. $\dfrac{10}{100}\cdot\dfrac{30}{100}\cdot\dfrac{30}{100}\cdot 200 = 1.8$

20. Find 80% of 120% of 400. $\dfrac{70}{100}\cdot\dfrac{130}{100}\cdot 4000 = 3640$

21. Find 90% of 130% of 70% 500. $\dfrac{90}{100}\cdot\dfrac{130}{100}\cdot\dfrac{70}{100}\cdot 600 = 491.4$

22. The amount. $\dfrac{30}{100}\cdot\dfrac{30}{100}x = 63\ ; x = 700\ euros$

23. The amount. $\dfrac{10}{100}\cdot\dfrac{30}{100}\cdot\dfrac{5}{100}x = 45\ ; x = 30000\ euros$

INCREASE OR DECREASE BY A PERCENTAGE

24. The price of a Car is A $. In case the price increases by:

   a. 1.01A   f. 1.1A   k. 1.9A   p. 3A
   b. 1.02A   g. 1.18A   l. 2A   q. 3.28A
   c. 1.03A   h. 1.3A   m. 2.01A   r. 4A
   d. 1.05A   i. 1.5A   n. 2.08A
   e. 1.08A   j. 1.58A   o. 2.1A

25. The price of a Stock is A $.

   a. 0.99A   d. 0.95A   g. 0.82A   j. 0.42A
   b. 0.98A   e. 0.92A   h. 0.7A   k. 0.1A
   c. 0.97A   f. 0.90A   i. 0.5A   l. 0

   m. Can't be it means negative price
   n. Can't be it means negative price

26.
   a. 1.1   f. 0.949   j. $1+\dfrac{M}{100}=\dfrac{100+M}{100}$
   b. 1.25   g. 0
   c. 1.072   h. 2
   d. 0.88   i. 3   k. $1-\dfrac{S}{100}=\dfrac{100-S}{100}$
   e. 0.65

27. The new price $50\left(1+\dfrac{14}{100}\right) = 50\left(\dfrac{114}{100}\right) = 57\$$

28. The new price $40\left(1-\dfrac{8}{100}\right) = 40\left(\dfrac{92}{100}\right) = 36.8\$$

29. His height. $150\left(1+\dfrac{16}{100}\right) = 150\left(\dfrac{116}{100}\right) = 174\ cm$

30. His brother kicks the ball: $60\left(1-\dfrac{18}{100}\right) = 60\left(\dfrac{82}{100}\right) = 49.2\ m$

31. The price before discount:
$$P\left(1-\frac{5}{100}\right)=38 \quad P\left(\frac{95}{100}\right)=38 \quad P=\frac{38}{\left(\frac{95}{100}\right)}=\frac{3800}{95}=40 \; euros$$

32. The price of a TV after it increased by 15% was 437$ find the price before the increase.
$$P\left(1+\frac{15}{100}\right)=437 \quad P=\frac{437}{\left(\frac{115}{100}\right)}=\frac{43700}{115}=380 \; euros$$

33. Xavier's height
$$100\left(1+\frac{10}{100}\right)\left(1+\frac{5}{100}\right)=100\left(\frac{110}{100}\right)\left(\frac{105}{100}\right)=\left(\frac{11\cdot 105}{10}\right)=115.5 cm$$

34. The price of a bike after a 4% discount was 120$ find the price before discount.
$$P\left(1-\frac{4}{100}\right)=120 \quad P\left(\frac{96}{100}\right)=120 \quad P=\frac{120}{\left(\frac{96}{100}\right)}=\frac{12000}{96}=125\$$$

35. $B\frac{110}{100}\cdot\frac{90}{100}=\frac{99}{100}B$, so overall change is 1% decrease.

36. $C\frac{120}{100}\cdot\frac{70}{100}=\frac{84}{100}C$, so overall change is 16% decrease.

37. $D\frac{80}{100}\cdot\frac{40}{100}=\frac{32}{100}D$, so overall change is 68% decrease

38. $E\frac{170}{100}\cdot\frac{160}{100}=\frac{272}{100}E$, so the overall change is 172% increase.

39. $E\left(\frac{103}{100}\right)^{48}=E(1.03)^{48}$

40. $M\left(\frac{89}{100}\right)^{12}=M(0.89)^{12}$

41. $M\left(\frac{92.8}{100}\right)^{16}=M(0.928)^{16}$

42. $M\left(\frac{100+x}{100}\right)^n=M\left(1+\frac{x}{100}\right)^n$

BIGGER OR SMALLER BY A PERCENTAGE

43. Find the percentage by which:
    a. 5 is bigger than 4:
    $$\frac{5-4}{4}=\frac{1}{4}=0.25=25\%$$
    b. 4 is smaller than 5:
    $$\frac{5-4}{5}=\frac{1}{5}=0.2=20\%$$
    c. 11 is bigger than 10:
    $$\frac{11-10}{10}=\frac{1}{10}=0.1=10\%$$
    d. 10 is smaller than 11:
    $$\frac{11-10}{11}=\frac{1}{11}\approx 0.091=9.1\%$$

e. 51 is bigger than 50:
$$\frac{51-50}{50} = \frac{1}{50} = 0.02 = 2\%$$

f. 40 is smaller than 45:
$$\frac{45-40}{45} = \frac{5}{45} \approx 0.0889 = 8.89\%$$

g. 2 is bigger than 1:
$$\frac{2-1}{1} = 1 = 100\%$$

h. 1 is smaller than 2:
$$\frac{2-1}{2} = 0.5 = 50\%$$

i. 3 is bigger than 1:
$$\frac{3-1}{1} = 2 = 200\%$$

j. 1 is smaller than 3:
$$\frac{3-1}{3} = 0.66... = 66.66...\%$$

k. 10 is bigger than 1:
$$\frac{10-1}{1} = 9 = 900\%$$

l. 1 is smaller than 10:
$$\frac{10-1}{10} = 0.9 = 90\%$$

m. 1000 is bigger than 200:
$$\frac{1000-200}{200} = 4 = 400\%$$

n. 200 is smaller than 1000:
$$\frac{1000-200}{1000} = 0.8 = 80\%$$

o. A is bigger than B:
$$\frac{A-B}{B} = \frac{A}{B} - 1 = \left(\frac{A}{B} - 1\right) \cdot 100\%$$

p. x is smaller than y:
$$\frac{y-x}{y} = 1 - \frac{y}{x} = \left(1 - \frac{y}{x}\right) \cdot 100\%$$

44. Alexandra runs more than David by $\frac{12-6}{6} = 1 = 100\%$

David runs less than Alexandra $\frac{12-6}{12} = 0.5 = 50\%$

45. Yael dedicates more time than Alex by $\frac{90-80}{80} = 0.125 = 12.5\%$

Alex dedicates less time than Yael by $\frac{90-80}{90} = 0.11... = 11.1...\%$

46. Ricardo drives to work 40% less than Rhona. Rhona drives to work 10% more than Alex who drives 500 km per week.

   a. Rhona drive to work per week $500\left(1 + \frac{10}{100}\right) = 550 km$

   b. Ricardo drive to work per week $550\left(1 - \frac{40}{100}\right) = 330 km$

   c. By what percentage does Ricardo drive more or less than Alex? Ricardo drives less than Alex by $\frac{500-330}{500} = 0.34 = 34\%$

47. Toni dedicates more time than Michael by $\frac{2.5-1}{1} = 1.5 = 150\%$

Michael dedicates less time than Toni by $\frac{2.5-1}{2.5} = 0.6 = 60\%$

1.8. – EVALUATING EXPRESSIONS

Evaluate the expression given the value of x:

1. $x = 2$, $x^2 + x = 6$
2. $x = -4$, $x^2 + x = 12$
3. $x = -2$, $5x^2 + 3x = 14$
4. $x = -4$, $x^{-1} = -\dfrac{1}{4}$
5. $x = -2$, $x^3 = -8$
6. $x = -3$, $x^{-3} = \dfrac{1}{(-3)^3} = \dfrac{1}{-27}$
7. $x = -9$, $2x^{-2} = \dfrac{2}{(-9)^2} = \dfrac{2}{81}$
8. $x = 4$, $x^{-2} + x = \dfrac{1}{16} + 4 = \dfrac{65}{16}$
9. $x = -4$, $2x^2 + \dfrac{x}{2} = 32 - 2 = 30$
10. $x = -2$, $\dfrac{1}{x} + \dfrac{x}{2} = -\dfrac{1}{2} - 1 = -\dfrac{3}{2}$
11. $x = 4$, $\dfrac{1}{x-3} + \dfrac{x}{2} = 1 + 2 = 3$
12. $x = 8$, $\dfrac{8}{x-4} + \dfrac{x-2}{2} = 2 + 3 = 5$
13. $x = -1$, $7x^{-3} + 2x^{-1} + 1 = \dfrac{7}{(-1)^3} + \dfrac{2}{(-1)} + 1 = -8$
14. $x = 3$, $x^{-2} + x + x^2 = \dfrac{1}{9} + 3 + 9 = \dfrac{109}{9}$
15. $x = 2$, $x^{-3} + x^{-2} + x^{-1} + x^0 =$
    $= \dfrac{1}{8} + \dfrac{1}{4} + \dfrac{1}{2} + 1 = \dfrac{15}{8}$

16. $x = 2$, $2x^{-2} \cdot x^{-1} = \dfrac{2}{4} \cdot \dfrac{1}{2} = \dfrac{1}{4}$
17. $x = -1$, $x^{-200} - 2x^{501} =$
    $= \dfrac{1}{(-1)^{200}} - \dfrac{2}{(-1)^{501}} = 1 - 2 = -1$
18. $x = -5$, $5x^{-2} - x^2 =$
    $= \dfrac{5}{(-5)^2} - (-5)^2 = \dfrac{5}{25} - 25 = -\dfrac{120}{5}$
19. $x = -2$, $2^x = 2^{-2} = \dfrac{1}{4}$
20. $x = -2$, $3^x = 3^{-2} = \dfrac{1}{9}$
21. $x = -2$, $2^{2x+1} = 2^{-4+1} = 2^{-3} = \dfrac{1}{8}$
22. $x = -1$, $2^{3x-1} = 2^{-3-1} = 2^{-4} = \dfrac{1}{16}$
23. $x = 2$, $2^{\frac{3}{x}} = 2^{\frac{3}{2}} = \sqrt{8}$
24. $x = -\dfrac{1}{2}$, $4^x = 4^{-\frac{1}{2}} = \dfrac{1}{4^{\frac{1}{2}}} = \dfrac{1}{\sqrt{4}} = \dfrac{1}{2}$
25. $x = -\dfrac{2}{3}$, $8^x = 8^{-\frac{2}{3}} = (2^3)^{-\frac{2}{3}} = 2^{-2} = \dfrac{1}{4}$
26. $x = -\dfrac{2}{3}$, $27^{-x} = 27^{\frac{2}{3}} = 3^{3\frac{2}{3}} = 9$

1.09. – EXPANDING AND FACTORING

Expand:

1. $(x+1)^2 = x^2 + 2x + 1$
2. $(x-1)^2 = x^2 - 2x + 1$
3. $(x+2)^2 = x^2 + 4x + 4$
4. $(x-2)^2 = x^2 - 4x + 4$
5. $(a+b)^2 = a^2 + 2ab + b^2$
6. $(a-b)^2 = a^2 - 2ab + b^2$
7. $(2a+b)^2 = 4a^2 + 4ab + b^2$
8. $(a-3b)^2 = a^2 - 6ab + 9b^2$
9. $(2x+3)^2 = 4x^2 + 6x + 9$
10. $(4-x)^2 = 16 - 8x + x^2$
11. $(x+2)(x-3) = x^2 - x - 3$
12. $(x-2)(x+2) = x^2 - 4$
13. $(3+x)(x-7) = x^2 - 4x - 21$
14. $(x+3)(x-3) = x^2 - 9$
15. $(2x+2)(x-5) = 2x^2 - 8x - 10$
16. $(2x+4)(2x-4) = 4x^2 - 16$
17. $(3x-1)(x+2) = 3x^2 + 5x - 2$
18. $(x+4)(x^2 - 4x + 3) = x^3 - 13x + 12$
19. $(5x+6)(5x-6) = 25x^2 - 36$
20. $(x+6)(x^5 - 6x^2 - 3x + 1) =$
    $x^6 + 6x^5 - 6x^3 - 39x^2 - 17x + 6$
21. $(x-a+2)(x+2a+b) =$
    $x^2 + x(b+a+2) - ab + 4a + 2b - 2a^2$
22. $(\sqrt{a} - \sqrt{b})(\sqrt{a} + \sqrt{b}) = a - b$
23. $(2x-3c)(2x+3c-1) =$
    $4x^2 - 9c^2 - 2x + 3c$
24. $x(x+8)^2 = x^3 + 16x^2 + 64x$
25. $(x-6)^2 3x = x^3 - 36x^2 + 108x$
26. $2 - (x+1)^2 = 1 - 2x - x^2$
27. $(x+3)^2 - (x+2)^2 = 2x + 5$
28. $(x-2)^2 + (x+2)^2 = 2x^2 + 8$
29. $(x-\sqrt{2})^2 = x^2 - 2\sqrt{2}x + 2$
30. $(x-\sqrt{2})(x+\sqrt{2}) = x^2 - 2$
31. $5(x-\sqrt{a})(x+\sqrt{a}) = 5x^2 - 5a$
32. $(\sqrt{a} - \sqrt{b})^2 = a - 2\sqrt{a}\sqrt{b} + b$
33. $2(x-\sqrt{10})(x+\sqrt{10}) = 2x^2 - 20$
34. $(x - \frac{2}{x})^2 = x^2 - 4 + \frac{4}{x^2}$
35. $(x - \frac{2}{\sqrt{x}})^2 = x^2 - 4\sqrt{x} + \frac{4}{x}$
36. $(3x - \frac{2}{3\sqrt{x}})^2 = 9x^2 - 4\sqrt{x} + \frac{4}{9x}$
37. $2(\sqrt{a} - \frac{1}{\sqrt{a}})^2 = 2a - 4 + \frac{2}{a}$
38. $(\sqrt{a} - \frac{1}{\sqrt{a}})(-\sqrt{a} - \frac{1}{\sqrt{a}}) = -a + \frac{1}{a}$
39. $(x^2 - y^2)^2 = x^4 - 2x^2 y^2 + y^4$
40. $(2x^3 - 3y^4)^2 = 4x^6 - 12x^3 y^4 + 9y^8$
41. $(2^x + 2^{-x})^2 = 2^{2x} + 2 + 2^{-2x}$
42. $(4^{2x} + 2^{-x})^2 = 2^{8x} + 2^{3x+1} + 2^{-2x}$
43. $(3^{2x} + 3^{-2x})^2 = 3^{4x} + 2 + 3^{-4x}$
44. $(7^x - 7)^2 = 7^{2x} - 2 \cdot 7^{x+1} + 49 j$
45. $(a^{nx} - b^{nx})^2 = a^{2nx} - 2a^{nx} b^{nx} + b^{2nx}$
46. $(x^2 - y^2)(x^2 + y^2) = x^4 - y^4$
47. $(x^3 - y^3)(x^3 + y^3) = x^6 - y^6$
48. $(x^n - y^n)(x^n + y^n) = x^{2n} - y^{2n}$
49. $(a^x - b^x)^2 = a^{2x} - 2a^x b^x + b^{2x}$
50. $(a^{mx} - a^{-mx})^2 = a^{2mx} - 2 + b^{-2mx}$
51. $(a^{mx} - a^{-mx})(a^{mx} + a^{-mx}) = a^{2mx} - a^{-2mx}$

Given the following polynomials, obtain the maximum possible common factor:

1. $x - ax = x(1 - a)$
2. $3x - x - ax = x(2 - a)$
3. $-x + ax = x(a - 1)$
4. $xy + 2x = x(y + 2)$
5. $8xy - 2y = 2x(4y - 1)$
6. $-6x + 12xy = 6x(2y - 1)$
7. $12xyz + 2xy = 2xy(6z - 1)$
8. $14xy - 2yz = 2y(7x - z)$
9. $12xz + 14xyz = 2xz(6 + 7y)$
10. $xy + 4y^2 + 5y = y(x + 4y + 5)$

11. $z - 4z^2 + 8zy = z(1 - 4z + 8y)$
12. $-8x^3 - 4xyz = -4x(x^2 + yz)$
13. $-6x^4 + x^2y^2 + x^2 = x^2(-6x^2 + y^2 + 1)$
14. $-9x^7y^3 + 3x^3y = 3yx^2(-3y^2x^5 + x)$
15. $-90x^{10}y^5 - 3x^3y^4 =$
    $-3x^3y^4(-30x^7y + 1)$
16. $-80x^4y^6z^8 + 8x^{12}y^4z^6 =$
    $8x^4y^4z^6(-10x^8y^2z^2 + x^8)$
17. $xyz + 2x^2y^2z^2 + 3x^3y^3z^3 =$
    $xyz(1 + 2xyz + x^2y^2z^2)$
18. $10x^3y^2z^4 + 2x^2y^6z^4 - 5x^2y^4z^2 =$
    $x^2y^2z^2(10xz^2 + 2z^2y^4 + 5y^2)$
19. $20x^{30}y^{20}z^{40} - 2x^{20}y^{60}z^{40} - 2x^{20}y^{40}z^{20} =$
    $2x^{20}y^{20}z^{20}(10x^{2}z^{20} - z^{20}y^{40} - y^{20})$
20. $ax^m + x^m = x^m(a + 1)$
21. $ax^{m+1} + x^m = x^m(ax + 1)$
22. $ax^m + x^{m-1} = x^m(a + x^{-1})$
23. $ax^m - x = x(ax^{m-1} - 1)$
24. $-ax^m - x^{2m} = -x^m(a + x^m)$
25. $z^{n+1} - z^{n+2} = z^n(z - z^2)$
26. $ax^{m+2} + x^{m-1} = x^{m-1}(ax^3 + 1)$

Given the following polynomials factor, if possible.

1. $x^2 - 6x + 9 = (x - 3)^2$
2. $x^2 - 5x + 6 = (x - 3)(x - 2)$
3. $x^2 + 4x + 10 = Not\ possible$
4. $-x^2 - x + 6 = -(x + 3)(x - 2)$
5. $x^2 + x - 6 = (x + 3)(x - 2)$
6. $x^2 + 5x + 6 = (x + 3)(x + 2)$
7. $-x^2 + 7x - 10 = -(x - 2)(x - 5)$
8. $x^2 - 6x + 12 = Not\ possible$
9. $x^2 + 3x + 2 = (x + 2)(x + 1)$
10. $x^2 - x - 2 = (x - 2)(x + 1)$
11. $-x^2 + 4x = -x(x - 4)$
12. $-x^2 + 4x - 10 = Not\ possible$
13. $x^2 + x - 2 = (x + 2)(x - 1)$
14. $x^2 + 3x + 7 = Not\ possible$
15. $x^2 - 3x + 2 = (x - 2)(x - 1)$
16. $x^2 - x + 7 = Not\ possible$
17. $x^2 + 5x + 9 = Not\ possible$
18. $-x^2 - 5x + 6 = Not\ possible$
19. $x^2 - 2xa + a^2 = (x - a)^2$
20. $x^2 - a^2 = (x - a)(x + a)$
21. $c^2 - a^2 = (c - a)(c + a)$
22. $x^2 - x = x(x - 1)$
23. $2x^2 - x = x(2x - 1)$
24. $2x^2 + 3x = x(2x + 3)$
25. $x^2 + 5x = x(x + 5)$
26. $x^2 - 7x + 12 = (x - 3)(x - 4)$
27. $2x^2 - 4x = 2x(x - 2)$
28. $x^2 - 7x + 10 = (x - 2)(x - 5)$
29. $x^2 - 7x + 6 = (x - 1)(x - 6)$
30. $x^2 - x - 12 = (x - 4)(x + 3)$
31. $x^2 + x - 12 = (x + 4)(x - 3)$
32. $x^2 - 3x - 10 = (x - 5)(x + 2)$
33. $x^2 - 8x - 9 = (x - 9)(x + 1)$
34. $x^2 - 1 = (x - 1)(x + 1)$
35. $x^2 + 1 = Not\ possible$
36. $x^2 - 2 = (x - \sqrt{2})(x + \sqrt{2})$
37. $x^2 - 3 = (x - \sqrt{3})(x + \sqrt{3})$
38. $x^2 - 4 = (x - 2)(x + 2)$
39. $-x^2 + 1 = -(x + 1)(x - 1)$
40. $-x^2 + 2 = -(x + \sqrt{2})(x - \sqrt{2})$
41. $-x^2 + 3 = -(x + \sqrt{3})(x - \sqrt{3})$
42. $-x^2 + 4 = -(x + 2)(x - 2)$
43. $-x^2 + 13 = -(x + \sqrt{13})(x - \sqrt{13})$
44. $-x^2 + 49 = -(x + 7)(x - 7)$
45. $2x^2 - 72 = 2(x + 6)(x - 6)$
46. $-x^2 - 2 = Not\ possible$
47. $5x^2 - 125 = 5(x - 5)(x + 5)$
48. $-x^2 + 81 = -(x + 9)(x - 9)$
49. $-3x^2 + 27 = -3(x + 3)(x - 3)$
50. $2x^2 - 6 = 2(x + \sqrt{3})(x - \sqrt{3})$
51. $3x^2 - 1 = 3(x + \sqrt{\frac{1}{3}})(x - \sqrt{\frac{1}{3}})$
52. $-2x^2 - 3 = -2(x^2 + \frac{3}{2})$
53. $5x^2 - 6 = 5(x - \sqrt{\frac{6}{5}})(x + \sqrt{\frac{6}{5}})$
54. $4x^2 - 2 = 4(x - \sqrt{\frac{1}{2}})(x + \sqrt{\frac{1}{2}})$

55. $-8x^2 - 1 = -8(x^2 + \frac{1}{8})$

56. $x^2 - b = (x + \sqrt{b})(x - \sqrt{b})$

57. $ax^2 - b = a(x + \sqrt{\frac{b}{a}})(x - \sqrt{\frac{b}{a}})$

58. $-ax^2 + b = -a(x + \sqrt{\frac{b}{a}})(x - \sqrt{\frac{b}{a}})$

59. $2x^2 - 4x + 2 = 2(x-1)^2$

60. $3x^2 - 3x - 18 = 3(x-3)(x+2)$

61. $-4x^2 + 20x + 24 = -4(x-6)(x+1)$

62. $7x^2 + 7x - 630 = 7(x+10)(x-9)$

63. $-5x^2 + 10x + 75 = -5(x-5)(x+3)$

64. $3x^2 - 12x - 63 = 3(x-7)(x+3)$

65. $2x^2 + 2x - 112 = 2(x+8)(x-7)$

66. $2x^2 - 12x - 14 = 2(x-7)(x+1)$

67. $-5x^2 + 15x + 90 = -5(x-6)(x+3)$

68. $-3x^2 - 12x - 12 = -3(x+2)^2$

69. $-2x^2 - 26x - 84 = -2(x+6)(x+7)$

70. $6x^2 + 48x + 72 = 6(x+6)(x+2)$

Factor and simplify:

1. $\dfrac{x^2 - 6x + 9}{x^2 - 7x + 12} = \dfrac{(x-3)}{(x-4)}$

2. $\dfrac{x^2 - 5x + 6}{x^2 + x - 6} = \dfrac{(x-3)}{(x+3)}$

3. $\dfrac{x^2 - 9}{x^2 - 7x + 12} = \dfrac{(x+3)}{(x-4)}$

4. $\dfrac{x^2 - 1}{x^2 - 2x + 1} = \dfrac{(x+1)}{(x-1)}$

5. $\dfrac{x^2 - 6x + 8}{x^2 - 4x + 4} = \dfrac{(x-4)}{(x-2)}$

6. $\dfrac{x^2 - 16}{x^2 + 5x + 4} = \dfrac{(x-4)}{(x+1)}$

7. $\dfrac{x^2 - x - 2}{x^2 + 6x + 5} = \dfrac{(x-2)}{(x+5)}$

8. $\dfrac{3x + 9}{x^2 - 9} = \dfrac{3}{(x-3)}$

9. $\dfrac{x^2 - 6x}{x^2 - 7x + 6} = \dfrac{x}{(x-1)}$

10. $\dfrac{x^2 - x}{x^2 + x - 2} = \dfrac{x}{(x+2)}$

11. $\dfrac{x^2 - 4}{x^2 + x - 2} = \dfrac{(x-2)}{(x-1)}$

12. $\dfrac{4 - x}{x - 4} = -1$

13. $\dfrac{x^2 - x}{1 - x} = -x$

14. $\dfrac{2x - 1}{4x^2 - 4x + 1} = \dfrac{1}{(2x-1)}$

15. $\dfrac{x^2 - 2x}{x^2 - 4} = \dfrac{x}{(x+2)}$

16. $\dfrac{4x^2 + 4x + 1}{2x^2 + 5x + 2} = \dfrac{(2x+1)}{(x+2)}$

17. $\dfrac{3x^2 + 4x + 1}{9x^2 - 1} = \dfrac{(3x+1)}{(3x-1)}$

18. $\dfrac{4x^2 + 4x - 3}{2x^2 - 13x + 15} = \dfrac{(2x-1)(2x+3)}{(x-5)(2x-3)}$

19. $\dfrac{4x^2 + 4x - 3}{2x^2 + 13x + 15} = \dfrac{(2x-1)}{(x+5)}$

20. $\dfrac{5x^2 - 12x + 4}{10x^2 + 16x - 8} = \dfrac{(x-2)}{(2x+4)}$

277

1.10. – RATIO AND PROPORTION

1. The ratio between 2 and 12 is the same as between <u>20</u> and a 120.
2. The ratio between 1 and 7 is the same as between <u>5</u> and 35.
3. The ratio between 2 and 24 is the same as between 6 and <u>72</u>
4. The ratio 2:3:7 is the same as <u>4:6:14</u>
5. Divide 180 in the ratio 2:3 $\frac{180}{5}=36;\quad \frac{2}{3}=\frac{2\cdot 36}{3\cdot 36}=\frac{72}{108}$
6. Divide 2800 in the ratio 3:4 $\frac{2800}{7}=400;\quad \frac{3}{4}=\frac{3\cdot 400}{4\cdot 400}=\frac{1200}{1600}$
7. Divide 180 in the ratio 2:3:4 $\frac{180}{9}=20;\quad 2:3:4=2\cdot 20:3\cdot 20:4\cdot 20=40:60:80$
8. Divide 720 in the ratio 2:5:8 $\frac{720}{15}=48;\quad 2:5:8=2\cdot 48:5\cdot 48:8\cdot 48=96:240:384$
9. Divide 30 in the ratio 1:2:3 $\frac{30}{6}=5;\quad 1:2:3=1\cdot 5:2\cdot 5:3\cdot 5=5:10:15$
10. The dimensions, perimeter and area of the bedroom.
    Dimensions: $7:8=7\cdot 60:8\cdot 60=420:480$ *Area*: $420\cdot 480=201600cm^2=20.16m^2$
    Perimeter: $2(420+480)=1800cm=18m$

The ingredients needed to make:

a. A cake half as big: $2:1:3=2\cdot \frac{1}{2}:1\cdot \frac{1}{2}:3\cdot \frac{1}{2}=1:\frac{1}{2}:\frac{3}{2}$ (eggs, sugar, flower)

b. A cake 2.5 times as big: $2:1:3=2\cdot \frac{5}{2}:1\cdot \frac{5}{2}:3\cdot \frac{5}{2}=5:\frac{5}{2}:\frac{15}{2}$ (eggs, sugar, flower)

11. The amount of pasta each one of the family members will eat: <u>Parents 300g children 150g.</u>
    $1:1:2:2 \quad \frac{900}{6}=150 \quad 1\cdot 150:1\cdot 150:2\cdot 150:2\cdot 150=150:150:300:300$

12. The scale of a map is 1:800000. Find the real distance represented by:
    a. 1 cm $1:600000cm=6km$
    b. 9 cm $1:600000=9:9\cdot 600000=9:5400000=9:54km$
    c. Distance in the map that represent 10km $\frac{1000000cm}{600000}=\frac{10}{6}cm$
    d. Distance in the map that represent 50km $\frac{5000000cm}{600000}=\frac{50}{6}cm$

13. The scale of a map is 1:1000000. Find the real distance represented by:
    a. 1.5 cm $1:1000000cm=10km$
    b. 10 cm $10:10000000cm=100km$
    c. The distance in the map that represent 20km $\frac{2000000cm}{1000000}=2cm$
    d. The distance in the map that represent 120km $\frac{12000000cm}{1000000}=12cm$

14. Math: 600, Science: 500, English: 450
    $\frac{1550}{31}=50 \qquad 600:500:450$

1.11. – EQUATIONS OF THE 1ST DEGREE

1. In real life we sometimes use equations to solve a <u>problem</u>. For example: We want to use tiles to pave our garden. We know that the size of the garden is 20 m^2 and that every tile is 100 cm^2, how many tiles should we buy? (Ignoring the shape of the garden)
2. When solving any equation the central idea is to <u>operate equally</u> on both sides of the equation.
3. A linear equation, sometimes called an equation of the 1st degree is an equation in which the variable is <u>to the power of 1</u>
4. An equation may have a <u>solution</u> but not always. For example the equation
   x + 1 = x   <u>does not have a solution</u> and the equation
   x + 1 = x + 1 <u>has infinite solutions</u>

1st Degree Equations

1. $x + 1 = 2 \quad x = 1$
2. $x + 2 = x \quad$ No solution
3. $x - 1 = -1 \quad x = 0$
4. $x - 1 = -x \quad x = \frac{1}{2}$
5. $x - 2 = 2 - x \quad x = 2$
6. $-x - 2 = 1 - x \quad$ No solution
7. $-x - 2 = -2 - x \quad$ Infinite solutions
8. $-5x - 12 = (3 - 3x)2$
   $-5x - 12 = 6 - 6x \quad x = 18$
9. $5x - 3 = -3x + 2 \quad x = \frac{5}{8}$
10. $2 - 4x - 22 = 2(4 + 3x)$
    $-4x - 20 = 8 + 6x \quad x = \frac{-28}{10}$
11. $x - 1 = 4 - x \quad x = \frac{5}{2}$
12. $7 - (12x - 2) = -7x + 2$
    $9 - 12x = -7x + 2 \quad x = \frac{7}{5}$
13. $\frac{1}{x} = 5 \quad x = \frac{1}{5}$
14. $\frac{4}{x} = 12 \quad x = \frac{1}{3}$
15. $\frac{2}{x} = \frac{1}{2} \quad x = 4$
16. $\frac{5}{x} = 1 \quad x = 5$
17. $\frac{x}{12} = 5 \quad x = 60$
18. $\frac{x}{7} + 2 = 52 \quad x = 21$
19. $\frac{2x}{7} + 2 = 5 - 3x$
    $2x + 14 = 35 - 21x \quad x = \frac{21}{23}$
20. $\frac{2x}{7} + \frac{2}{5} = -2x + 1$
    $10x + 14 = -70x + 35 \quad x = \frac{21}{80}$
21. $\frac{x}{2} + \frac{3}{4} = 1 \quad 2x + 3 = 4 \quad x = \frac{1}{2}$

22. $\dfrac{2x+1}{7}+\dfrac{2}{5}=\dfrac{x-2}{5}+1$
$10x+5+14=7x-14+35 \qquad x=\dfrac{2}{3}$

23. $\dfrac{2-x}{6}+\dfrac{x+4}{12}=x-8$
$4-2x+x+4=12x-96 \qquad x=8$

24. $\dfrac{3x-5}{20}=\dfrac{x}{10} \qquad 3x-5=2x \qquad x=5$

25. $\dfrac{x}{7}-\dfrac{1-x}{6}=2$
$6x-7+7x=84 \qquad x=\dfrac{91}{13}=7$

26. $\dfrac{2x-2}{6}-\dfrac{6-3x}{24}=x-6$
$8x-8-6+3x=24x-144 \qquad x=10$

27. $\dfrac{9-x}{5}-\dfrac{5x-2}{3}=-x-1$
$27-3x-25x+10=-15x-15 \qquad x=4$

28. $\dfrac{2x-1}{x}=3 \qquad 2x-1=3x \qquad x=-1$

29. $\dfrac{x+2}{2x}=5 \qquad x+2=10x \qquad x=\dfrac{2}{9}$

30. $\dfrac{x-2}{2x-1}=6 \qquad x-2=12x-6 \qquad x=\dfrac{4}{11}$

31. $\dfrac{2x-2}{x+1}=-2 \qquad 2x-2=-2x-2 \qquad x=0$

32. $\dfrac{2x}{7}+1=\dfrac{-5x}{7} \qquad 2x+7=-5x \qquad x=-1$

33. $\dfrac{2x}{7}+4=\dfrac{3x}{2} \qquad 4x+56=21x \qquad x=\dfrac{56}{17}$

34. $\dfrac{2}{x}-3=\dfrac{3}{2x} \qquad 4-6x=3 \qquad x=\dfrac{1}{6}$

35. $\dfrac{2}{x-2}-3=\dfrac{3}{x-2} \qquad 2-3x+6=3 \qquad x=\dfrac{5}{3}$

36. $\dfrac{-2}{x}=\dfrac{3}{x-2} \qquad -2x+4=3x \qquad x=\dfrac{4}{5}$

37. $\dfrac{4}{x+1}=\dfrac{4}{x+2} \qquad No\ Solution$

38. $\dfrac{2}{x+1}=\dfrac{4}{x+2} \qquad 2x+4=4x+4 \qquad x=0$

39. $\dfrac{2}{2x+1}-2=\dfrac{4}{2x+1} \qquad -2-4x-2=4 \qquad x=-2$

40. $\dfrac{x}{2}-\dfrac{x}{5}=3 \qquad 5x-2x=30 \qquad x=10$

41. $\dfrac{2}{x}+\dfrac{3}{5}=3 \qquad 10+3x=15x \qquad x=\dfrac{5}{6}$

42. $\dfrac{2x-7}{2}-\dfrac{3x}{5}=x \qquad 10x-35-6x=10x \qquad x=-\dfrac{35}{6}$

43. $1-\dfrac{1}{x}=7-\dfrac{3x+1}{x}$
$-1=6x-3x-1 \qquad x=0(Not Valid)$

44. $3-\dfrac{2x}{x-2}=7-\dfrac{2x+1}{x-2}$
$3x-6-2x=7x-14-2x-1 \qquad x=\dfrac{9}{4}$

45. $\dfrac{2-x}{x-2}=1 \qquad 2-x=x-2 \qquad x=2(Not Valid)$

46. $\dfrac{2-x}{x-2}=-1$
$2-x=-x+2 \qquad Infinite Solutions$

47. $\dfrac{5-7x}{3x-2}=-1+\dfrac{5}{3x-2}$
$5-7x=-3x+2+5 \qquad x=-\dfrac{1}{2}$

48. $\dfrac{15-x}{3-x}=7-\dfrac{5x}{3-x} \qquad 15-x=21-3x-5x \qquad x=\dfrac{6}{7}$

49. An equation whose solution is 1: $\dfrac{ax}{5}=1$ $\dfrac{a}{5}=1$ $a=5 \Rightarrow \dfrac{5x}{5}=1$

50. An equation whose solution is 4: $\dfrac{x+k}{6}=2$ $\dfrac{4+k}{6}=2$ $k=8 \Rightarrow \dfrac{x+8}{6}=2$

51. An equation whose solution is 3:

$\dfrac{ax+k}{5}=10$ $\dfrac{3a+k}{5}=10$ $k=50-3a \Rightarrow \dfrac{ax+50-3a}{5}=10$

52. An equation whose solution is -1

$\dfrac{ax+k}{8}=4$ $\dfrac{-a+k}{8}=4$ $k=a+32 \Rightarrow \dfrac{ax+a+32}{8}=4$

Solve for x

1. $\dfrac{4}{x}=\dfrac{a}{x+6}$
   $x=\dfrac{24}{a-4}$

2. $\dfrac{14}{x+2}=\dfrac{a}{x+2}-a$
   $x=-\dfrac{14+a}{a}$

3. $\dfrac{2}{x+3}-a=\dfrac{a+b}{x+3}$
   $x=\dfrac{2-b-4a}{a}$

4. $\dfrac{5}{2x+1}-3a=\dfrac{b}{2x+1}$
   $x=\dfrac{5-b-3a}{6a}$

5. $\dfrac{-2x}{a+3}=\dfrac{x+2}{2a-1}$
   $x=-\dfrac{2a+6}{5a+5}$

6. $\dfrac{-5x+1}{2a}=\dfrac{bx}{3a+2}$
   $x=\dfrac{3a+2}{15a+2ab+10}$

7. $\dfrac{a}{x+2}=\dfrac{b}{x+2}-b+1$
   $x=-\dfrac{a+b+2}{b+1}$

8. $\dfrac{b}{2x-4}-3=\dfrac{b}{2x-4}-b+1$
   No Solution

9. $\dfrac{1}{ax+2}=\dfrac{b}{x+a}$
   $x=\dfrac{a-2b}{ba-1}$

10. $\dfrac{1}{ax+2}=\dfrac{b}{ax+2}-3$
    $x=\dfrac{b-7}{3a}$

11. $3\dfrac{x}{ax+2}=3$
    $x=\dfrac{6}{1-3a}$

12. $-3\dfrac{2x}{ax+3}=b$
    $x=-\dfrac{3b}{ab+6}$

13. $\dfrac{2x-3}{2ax+5} = -3b$
    $x = \dfrac{3-15b}{6ab+2}$

14. $\dfrac{x}{ax+2} = \dfrac{2}{a} - 3$
    $x = -\dfrac{4-6a}{3a^2 - a}$

15. $\dfrac{bx}{x+2} = 3 - b$
    $x = \dfrac{6-2b}{2b-3}$

16. $\dfrac{b+x}{x-3} = \dfrac{b}{x-3} + a$
    $x = \dfrac{-3a}{1-a}$

17. $\dfrac{bx}{a} = 2x + 8$
    $x = \dfrac{8a}{b-2a}$

18. $\dfrac{ax+b}{dx+2} = c - g$
    $x = \dfrac{2g - 2c + b}{dc - gd - a}$

19. $\dfrac{1}{x+2} + \dfrac{1}{b} = 2$
    $x = \dfrac{3b-2}{1-2b}$

20. $\dfrac{1-a}{x} + \dfrac{2a}{x} = 2b$
    $x = \dfrac{1+a}{2b}$

21. $\dfrac{2+x}{\left(\dfrac{1}{x}\right)} = 3x \quad 2+x=3 \quad x=1$

22. $\dfrac{7-2x}{\left(\dfrac{2}{x}+2\right)} = \dfrac{x}{2} \quad 7-2x = 1+x \quad x=3$

23. $\dfrac{\left(1-\dfrac{x}{2}\right)}{\left(\dfrac{x}{4}\right)} = -\dfrac{4}{x} \quad 1-\dfrac{x}{2} = -1 \quad x=4$

24. $\dfrac{2}{\left(1-\dfrac{x}{a}\right)} = a \quad 2 = a-x \quad x=2-a$

25. $\dfrac{\left(\dfrac{3}{2x}-a\right)}{a} = b \quad \dfrac{3}{2x} - a = ab$
    $3 - 2xa = 2xab \quad 3 = x(2a + 2ab)$
    $x = \dfrac{3}{2a(1+b)}$

26. Complete RHS of the equation so solution is a

    $xa + 1 = a^2 + 1$ (plug a into x)

27. Complete RHS of the equation, solution is $a - 1$

    $\dfrac{1}{xa} - a = \dfrac{1}{(a-1)a} - a$

    (plug $a - 1$ into x)

28. Complete RHS of the equation so solution is $2a$

    (plug $2a$ into x)

    $x - \dfrac{1}{xa} = 2a - \dfrac{1}{2a^2}$

29. Complete RHS of the equation so solution is $4a+1$ (plug $4a+1$ into x)

    $\dfrac{x+1}{xa} - 1 = \dfrac{4a+2}{(4a+1)a} - 1$

1.12. – SYSTEMS OF EQUATIONS OF THE 1ST DEGREE

1. One equation with 1 variable may have <u>one</u> or <u>infinite</u> or <u>zero</u> solutions.

   Examples:
   $x+1=2 \quad x=1 \quad OneSolution$
   $x+1=x \quad NoSolution$
   $x+1=x+1 \quad InfiniteSolutions$

2. One equation with 2 two variables may have <u>infinite</u> or <u>zero</u> solutions.

   Examples:
   $x+y+1=x+y \quad NoSolution$
   $x+y=1 \quad InfiniteSolutions$

3. Equations of the first degree are equations in which the <u>variables are the power of one</u>. Examples with 1,2 and 3 variables:
   $2x+2=1 \quad 1\_Var$
   $5x+2y=6 \quad 2\_Var$
   $5x+2y-2z=21 \quad 3\_Var$

4. Equations of the 2nd degree are equations in which <u>at least one variable is to the power of two</u>. Give examples with 1 and 2 variables:
   $2x^2+2=1 \quad 1\_Var \quad 5x+2y^2=6 \quad 2\_Var \quad 5x+2y^2-2z^2=21 \quad 3\_Var$

5. The solution to one equation of the first degree with 2 variables from a graphical point of view, is a <u>point</u> The collection of points will form a <u>line</u>

6. A system whose only solution is x = 1, y = 2. Is this a unique system? Explain
   $x+y=3$
   $x-y=-1$ This is not the only system whose solution is (1, 2) there are infinite since infinite lines intersect at that point

7. A system whose only solution is x = 0, y = –2
   $2x+y=-2$
   $3x-y=2$

8. A system whose only solution is x = –3, y = $\frac{1}{2}$.
   $x+2y=-2$
   $2x-2y=-7$

9. A system whose only solution is x = 15, y = –6.
   $x+y=9$
   $2x-y=36$

10. A system of equations that has no solution
    $2x+y=5$
    $2x+y=6$

11. A system of equations that has infinite solutions
    $2x+y=5$
    $4x+2y=10$

12. Given the equations I) x + y = 2, II) y – x = 2
    a. Write a few solutions to the equations
       I) (0, 2), (1, 1), (3, -1), (-1, 3)
       II) (0, 2), (2, 4), (-2, 0), (0, 2)
    b. Show the solutions on the graph.
    c. Draw a conclusion:

    In each one of the cases the points lie on a straight line. The lines intersect.

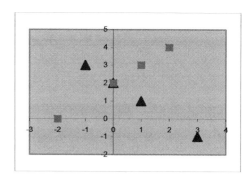

13. Given the equations I) 2x + y = 3, II) y + 2x = 5
    a. Write a few solutions to the equations
       I) (0, 3), (1, 1), (2, -1), (-1, 5)
       II) (0, 5), (1, 3), (-1, 7), (2, 1)
    b. Show the solutions on the graph.
    c. Draw a conclusion:

    In each one of the cases the points lie on a straight line. The lines are parallel.

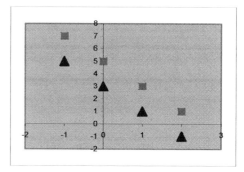

14. Given the equations I) x – 2y = 2, II) 4y – 2x = –4
    a. Write a few solutions to the equations
       I) (0, -1), (2, 0), (4, 1), (6, 2)
       II) (-2, -2), (2, 0), (8, 3), (0, -1)
    b. Show the solutions on the graph.
    c. Draw a conclusion: The 2 lines are identical

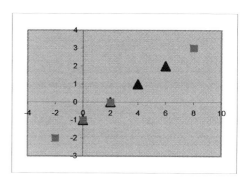

15. $x + y = 2$
    $2x - y = 1$
    $x = 1, y = 1$

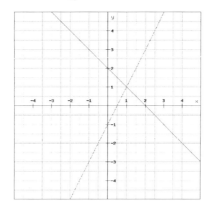

16. $x + y = 2$
    $2x + 2y = 1$
    No solution Parallel lines

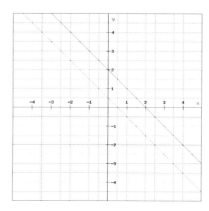

17. $4x+2y=6$
$6x+3y=9$

Infinite Solutions Identical Lines

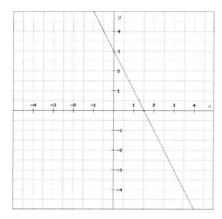

18. $x-y=1$
$3x-2y=4 \qquad x=2, y=1$

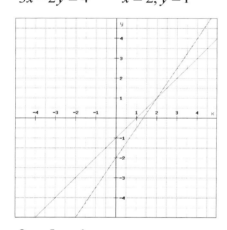

19. $2x-5y=1$
$3x-7y=2 \qquad x=3, y=1$

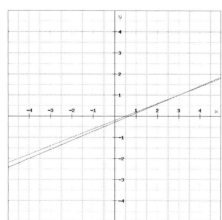

20. $2x-5y=-8$
$3x-2y=-1 \qquad x=1, y=2$

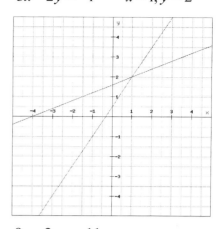

21. $9x-2y=-11$
$8x-3y=-22 \qquad x=1, y=10$

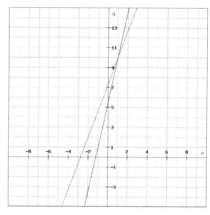

22. $5x+1=2y$
$4y+x-3=0 \qquad x=\dfrac{1}{11}, y=\dfrac{8}{11}$

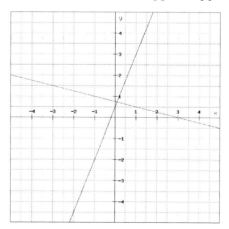

23. $\begin{aligned} 5x+3y &= 2-2y \\ -y+2x-5 &= 0 \end{aligned}$ $x=\dfrac{9}{5}, y=-\dfrac{7}{5}$

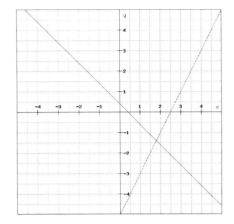

24. $\begin{aligned} 5x &= 2y \\ -y+2x &= 0 \end{aligned}$ $x=0, y=0$

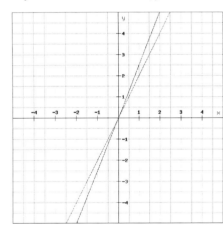

25. $\begin{aligned} x &= 2y-7 \\ 4y-2x &= 0 \end{aligned}$

No solution   Parallel   lines

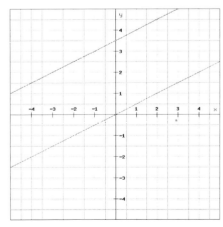

26. $\begin{aligned} -5x+1 &= 2y \\ -4y+x-3 &= x \end{aligned}$ $x=\dfrac{1}{2}, y=-\dfrac{3}{4}$

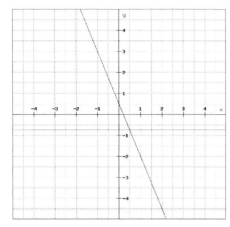

27. $\begin{aligned} 5x+1 &= 2y \\ 10y-25x &= 10 \end{aligned}$

No solution   Parallel   lines

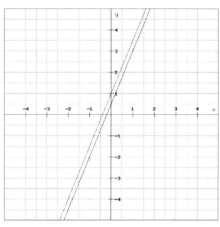

28. $\begin{aligned} 2x+1 &= 2y \\ -4y+4x+2 &= 0 \end{aligned}$

Infinite Solutions   Identical   Lines

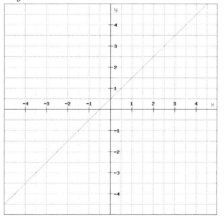

29. $\begin{array}{l} x+1=2y \\ 4y-2x-3=0 \end{array}$

   No solution   Parallel lines

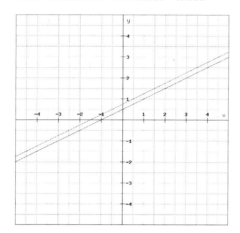

30. $\begin{array}{l} 4x=y \\ 3y-12x=0 \end{array}$

   Infinite Solutions   Identical Lines

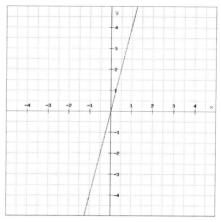

31. $\begin{array}{l} 2x+7y=4 \\ 3y-5x-3=0 \end{array}$ $x=-\dfrac{9}{41}, y=\dfrac{26}{41}$

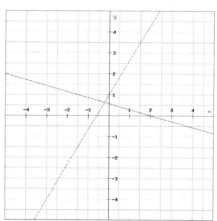

32. $\begin{array}{l} \dfrac{x}{5}+1=2y \\ \dfrac{y}{3}+\dfrac{x}{2}-3=0 \end{array}$ $x=\dfrac{85}{16}, y=\dfrac{33}{32}$

33. $\begin{array}{l} \dfrac{x}{5}+2=6y \\ -3y+\dfrac{x}{10}+1=0 \end{array}$ $x=30, y=-10$

34. $\begin{array}{l} \dfrac{x}{2}+1=\dfrac{y}{3} \\ -2y+3x+6=0 \end{array}$ $x=-\dfrac{4}{3}, y=-1$

35. $\begin{array}{l} \dfrac{2x}{3}-2=-y \\ \dfrac{y}{2}+\dfrac{x}{3}-3=0 \end{array}$ *No Solution*

36. $\dfrac{x}{5} = 1 + \dfrac{y}{10}$
    $\dfrac{-y}{2} - \dfrac{x}{2} = -10 \qquad x = 10, y = 10$

37. $\dfrac{x}{4} = \dfrac{y-1}{2} + 2$
    $\dfrac{x+2}{2} = 5 - \dfrac{y-1}{2} \qquad x = 8, y = 1$

38. $1 - \dfrac{3x}{2} = \dfrac{y-1}{3}$
    $3x - 2 = \dfrac{2-2y}{3} \qquad x = \dfrac{2}{3}, y = 1$

39. $\dfrac{2x}{7} = \dfrac{2y-5}{14} - 2$
    $8x = 4y - 1 \qquad$ No Solution

40. Write 2 equations representing this information. Find the number of cars and motorbikes in the parking lot.

    $4x + 2y = 88$
    $x + y = 25 \qquad x = 19, y = 6$

    19 cars, 6 motorbikes

41. How many bars of each type were sold?

    $1.2x + 1.4y = 3960$
    $x + y = 3000 \qquad x = 1200, y = 1800$

    1200 Dark, 1800 White

42. Find the numbers. $\dfrac{x}{3} + \dfrac{y}{4} = 65$
    $x + y = 100 \qquad x = 480, y = -380$

43. Find the dimensions of the field and show how it was divided. The diagram is not to scale. As can be seen from the results x > y

    $2x + 2y = 80$
    $2x + 2\dfrac{y}{2} = 70 \qquad x = 30, y = 10$

44. Jeff played soccer for 0.5 hours and later basketball for 1 hour. He burned 500 calories in total. Dina played soccer for 1 hour and later basketball for 0.5 hour. She burned 550 calories in total. Find the number of calories burned in 1 hour of a soccer game and 1 hour of basketball game.

    $\dfrac{x}{2} + y = 500$
    $x + \dfrac{y}{2} = 550 \qquad x = 400, y = 300$

    Soccer: 400 cal/h   Basketball 300 cal/h

1.13 – INTERVAL NOTATION AND INEQULITIES

1. Represent the following Intervals on the real line:
   a. $x \in (1, 4]$
   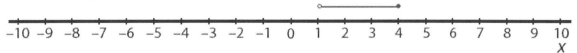
   b. $x \in (4,7)$
   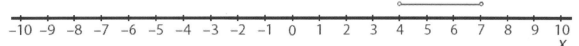
   c. $x \in [-6,8]$

   d. $x \in [-7,0)$
   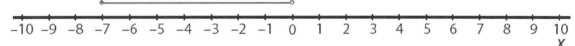
   e. $x \in [-\infty,-2)$
   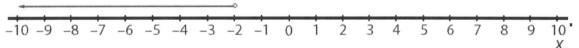
   f. $x \in [-\infty,3]$
   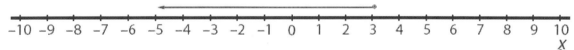
   g. $x \in (5, \infty)$

   h. $\{x \mid 8 < x < 10\}$
   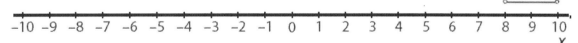
   i. $\{x \mid -8 < x < -3\}$

   j. $\{x \mid 0 < x < 1\}$
   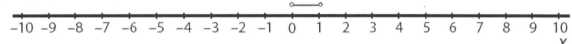
   k. $\{x \mid \infty < x < 2\}$ Not Possible
   l. $\{x \mid 2 < x < \infty\}$
   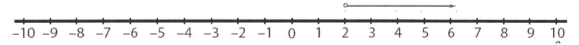

289

2. Write each one of the Intervals using all types of notations:

   a. $x \in (5, 6) = 5 \leq x \leq 6$

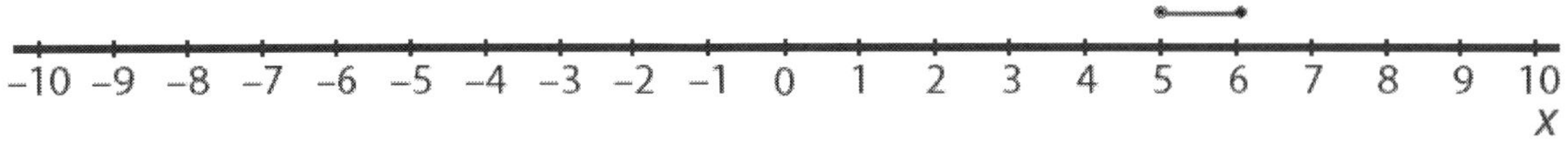

   b. $x \in (-\infty, 4) = x < 4$

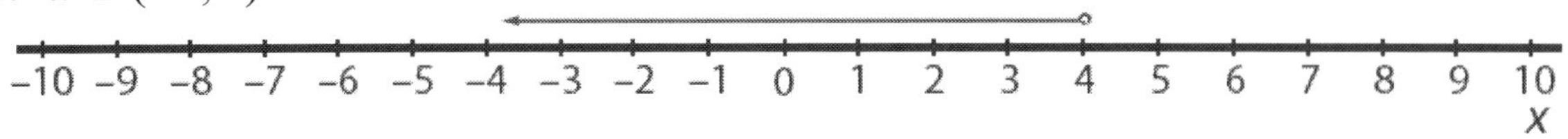

   c. $x \in (2, 3) = 2 < x < 3$

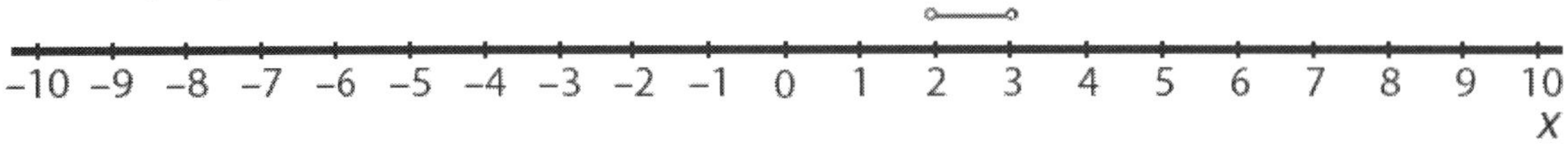

   d. $x \in (5, \infty) = 5 < x$

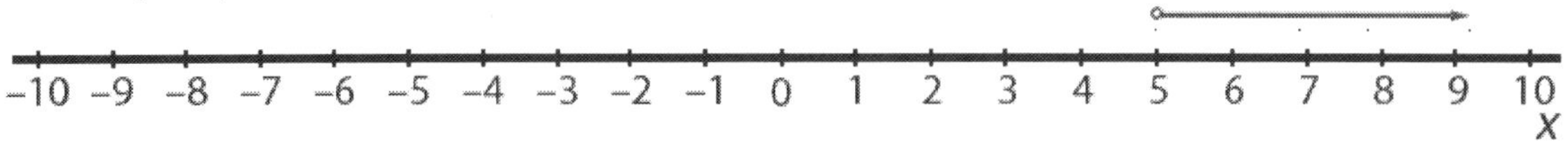

   e. $x \in \,]-4, 10] = -4 < x \leq 10$

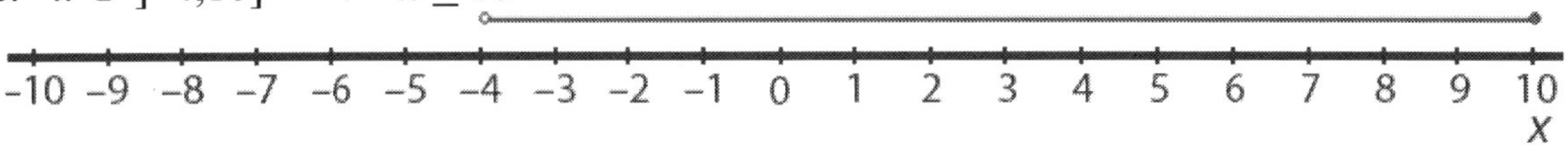

   f. $x \in [-9, -2[\,= -9 \leq x < -2$

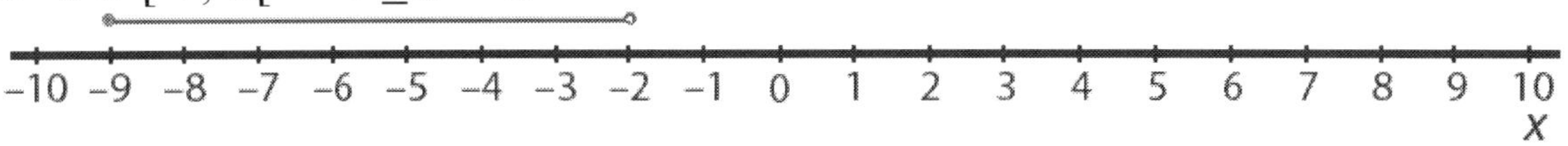

   g. $\{x \mid 6 < x < 8\} = x \in (6, 8)$

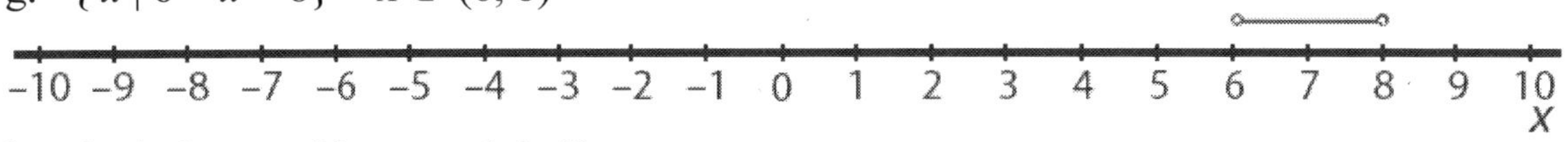

   h. $\{x \mid -3 < x < 2\} = x \in (-3, 2)$

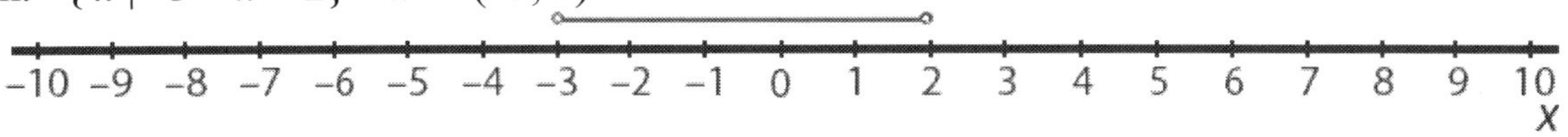

3. Solve the following inequalities and shade the solution on the given diagram:

   a. $-x \leq 2$
      $x \geq -2$

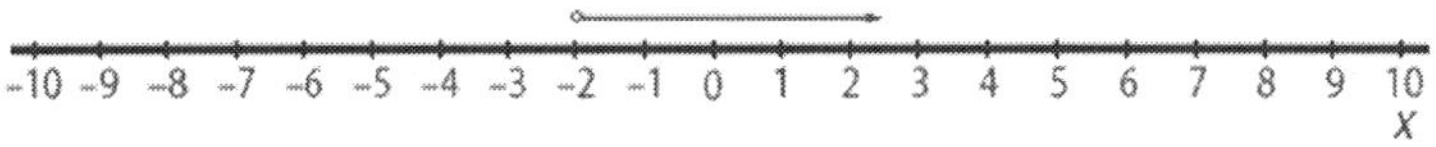

   b. $5 - x \leq 0$
      $x \geq 5$

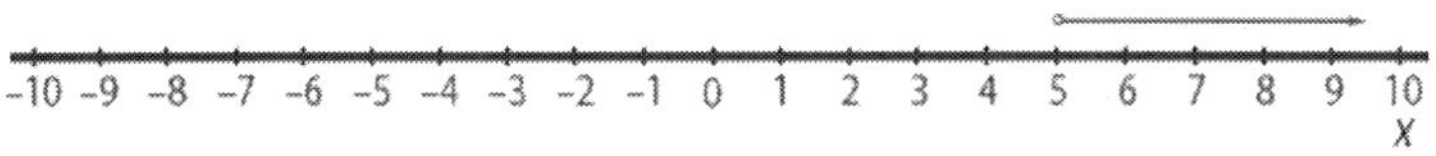

   c. $8 - 2x \leq 2$
      $x \geq 3$

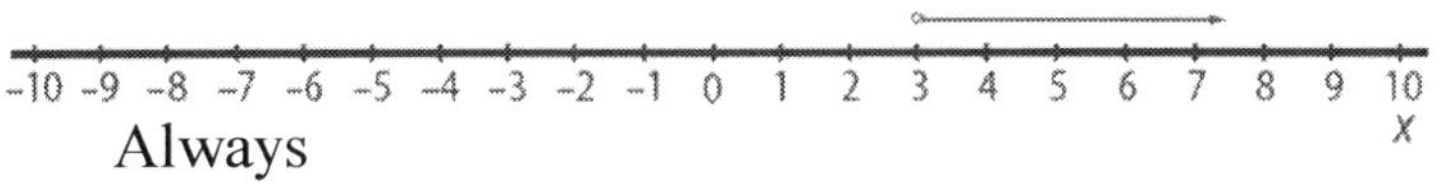

   d. $-2x \leq 3 - 2x$
      Always
      $3 \geq 0$

   e. $7 + x \leq x + 1$
      Never
      $7 \leq 1$

f. $-2x \leq 2x+4 \qquad x \geq -1$

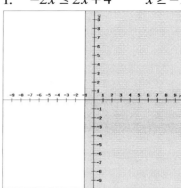

g. $-3x \leq 2x \qquad x \geq 0$

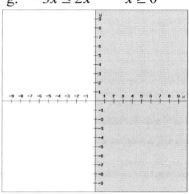

h. $-5x+1 \leq 2x-6 \qquad x \geq 1$

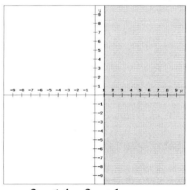

i. $3x \leq 4+3x+1$
$0 \leq 5, \forall x \in \mathbb{R}$

j. $\dfrac{x}{2} \leq x+4 \qquad x \geq -8$

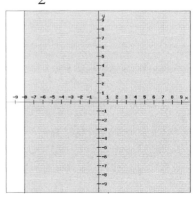

k. $\dfrac{x}{3} \leq \dfrac{x}{12}+2 \qquad x \leq 8$

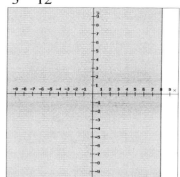

l. $\dfrac{2x-4}{6} \leq x-4 \qquad x \geq 5$

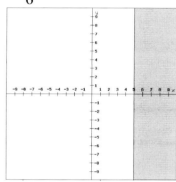

m. $\dfrac{2-x}{5} \geq \dfrac{x-2}{5}-2 \qquad x \leq 7$

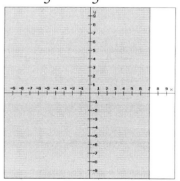

n. $\dfrac{11-2x}{5} \geq \dfrac{2x}{3}-\dfrac{x-1}{2}$

$x \leq 3$

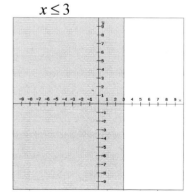

o. $\dfrac{-x}{5} + \dfrac{1}{4} \leq \dfrac{x-2}{4} - \dfrac{x-1}{2}$ $x \geq -5$

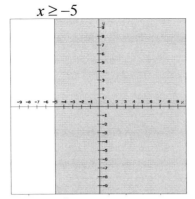

p. $\dfrac{y+8}{6} \leq -y - 1$ $y \leq -2$

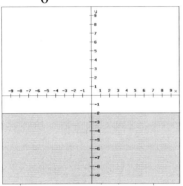

q. $\dfrac{2-2y}{2} \leq \dfrac{2y}{4} - 2$ $2 \leq y$

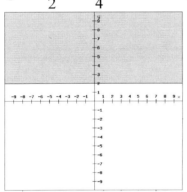

r. $\dfrac{4-y}{5} \leq \dfrac{2y}{2} - 2y$ $y \leq -1$

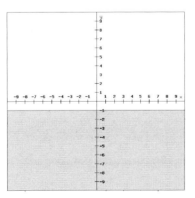

s. $\dfrac{1+y}{5} - 1 \leq y - \dfrac{2y-2}{2}$ $y \leq 9$

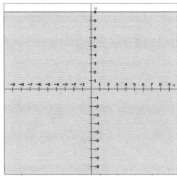

t. $-2 \leq 2x \leq 4$ $-1 \leq x \leq 2$

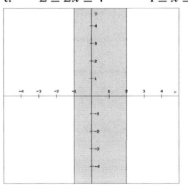

u. $-8 \leq \dfrac{-6x+3}{4} \leq 7$ $\dfrac{35}{6} \geq x \geq -\dfrac{25}{6}$

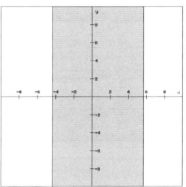

v. $-10 \leq 4y + 2 \leq 9$ $-3 \leq y \leq \dfrac{7}{4}$

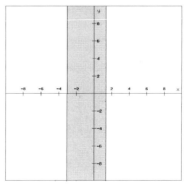

w. $0 \leq \dfrac{y+2}{3} \leq 2$ $-2 \leq y \leq 4$

4.
- a. Solve the inequality $2x \leq 4$ $x \leq 2$
- b. Solve the inequality $-x < 3$. $x > -3$
- c. Represent both solutions on the real number line:

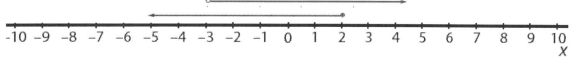

- d. State their intersection: $x \in (-3, 2]$

5.
- a. Solve the inequality $2x - 2 \leq 4$ $x \leq 3$
- b. Solve the inequality $-3x + 4 > -2$. $x < 2$
- c. Represent both solutions on the real line:

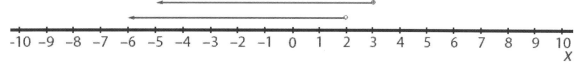

- d. State their intersection: $x \in (-\infty, 2)$

6.
- a. Solve the inequality $x - 2 \leq -7$ $x \leq -5$
- b. Solve the inequality $-2x + 10 \leq -2$. $x \geq 6$
- c. Represent both solutions on the real line:

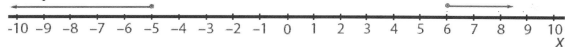

- d. State their intersection: None

7.
- a. Solve the inequality $3x - 10 \leq 2$ $x \leq 4$
- b. Solve the inequality $-x < -3$. $x > 3$
- c. Represent both solutions on the real line:

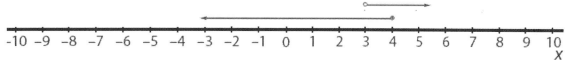

- d. State their intersection: $x \in (3, 4]$

8.
- a. Solve the inequality $5x - 3 \leq 2$ $x \leq 1$
- b. Solve the inequality $-2x + 2 > -2$. $x < 2$
- c. Represent both solutions on the real line:

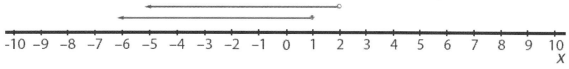

- d. State their intersection: $x \in (-\infty, 1]$

9.
- a. Solve the inequality $2x - 2 \leq -12$ $x \leq -5$
- b. Solve the inequality $-2x - 8 \leq -2$. $x \geq -3$
- c. Represent both solutions on the real line: d. State their intersection: None

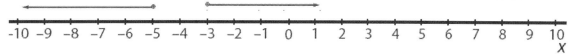

293

1.14. – EQUATIONS OF THE 2ND DEGREE

1. The solution of the equation $A \cdot B \cdot C \cdot ... = 0$ is $\underline{A = 0}$ or $\underline{B = 0}$ or $\underline{C = 0}$ etc.
2. Write an equation whose solutions are 1 and 2: $(x-1)(x-2) = 0$
3. Write an equation whose solutions are -3 and 7: $(x+3)(x-7) = 0$
4. Write an equation whose solutions are $\frac{1}{2}$ and b: $(x-\frac{1}{2})(x-b) = 0$
5. Write an equation whose solutions are a and b: $(x-a)(x-b) = 0$

Solve:

6. $(x-5)(x+8) = 0$
   $x = 5, -8$

7. $2(x-15)(x+58) = 0$
   $x = 15, -58$

8. $(x-\frac{1}{2})(x+22.3) = 0$
   $x = \frac{1}{2}, -22.3$

9. $3(x-\sqrt{5})(x+\sqrt[5]{8}) = 0$
   $x = \sqrt{5}, -\sqrt[5]{8}$

10. $c(x-a)(x+b) = 0$
    $x = a, -b$

11. $x(2x-4)(3x+\frac{7}{3}) = 0$
    $x = 0, 2, -\frac{7}{9}$

12. $(5x-1)(\frac{x}{13}+22)x = 0$
    $x = 0, \frac{1}{5}, -286$

13. $x(3x+7) = 0$
    $x = 0, -\frac{7}{3}$

14. $(2x-5)x = 0$
    $x = 0, \frac{5}{2}$

15. $3(2x-1)(3x+1)(2x-3) = 0$
    $x = \frac{1}{2}, -\frac{1}{3}, \frac{3}{2}$

16. $(2x-4)x(5x-\frac{1}{2}) = 0$
    $x = 0, 2, \frac{1}{10}$

17. $(\frac{2}{x}-4)x = 0$
    $x = 0, \frac{1}{2}$

18. $6(\frac{1}{2x}-3)(\frac{x}{2}+1)(\frac{2}{x}-1)x = 0$
    $x = 0, \frac{1}{6}, -2, 2$

19. $-5(\frac{3}{2x}-1)(\frac{ax}{b}+c)(\frac{1}{x}+1)x = 0$
    $x = \frac{3}{2}, -\frac{bc}{a}, -1, 0$

20. $-5(\frac{2}{x}+2)(\frac{a}{x}+c)(\frac{5}{x}+10)x = 0$
    $x = -1, -\frac{a}{c}, -\frac{1}{2}, 0$

21. $-50(x+2)^{10}(\frac{1}{x}+7)^{120}=0$
$x=-2,-\frac{1}{7}$

22. $16(2x-0.2)^{10}(\frac{3}{2x}+5)^{10}=0$
$x=\frac{1}{10},-\frac{3}{10}$

23. $x(x-a)^{10}(a+x)^{10}=0$
$x=0,a,-a$

Factor and Solve:

24. $x^2-6x+9=0$
$(x-3)(x-3)=0 \quad x=3$

25. $x^2-5x+6=0$
$(x-2)(x-3)=0 \quad x=2,3$

26. $-x^2-x+6=0$
$-(x+3)(x-2)=0 \quad x=2,-3$

27. $x^2+x=6$
$(x+3)(x-2)=0 \quad x=2,-3$

28. $x^2+5x+6=0$
$(x+2)(x+3)=0 \quad x=-2,-3$

29. $-x^2+7x-10=0$
$-(x-2)(x-5)=0 \quad x=2,5$

30. $x^2+3x+2=0$
$(x+2)(x+1)=0 \quad x=-1,-2$

31. $x^2-x-2=0$
$(x-2)(x+1)=0 \quad x=2,-1$

32. $-x^2=-4x$
$-x(x-4)=0 \quad x=0,4$

33. $x^2+x-2=0$
$(x+2)(x-1)=0 \quad x=-2,1$

34. $x^2-3x=-2$
$(x-2)(x-1)=0 \quad x=2,1$

35. $-x^2-5x+6=0$
$-(x+6)(x-1)=0 \quad x=1,-6$

36. $x^2-2xa+a^2=0$
$(x-a)(x-a)=0 \quad x=a$

37. $x^2=a^2$
$(x-a)(x+a)=0 \quad x=a,-a$

38. $x^2-x=0$
$x(x-1)=0 \quad x=0,1$

39. $2x^2-x=0$
$x(2x-1)=0 \quad x=0,\frac{1}{2}$

40. $2x^2+3x=0$
$x(2x+3)=0 \quad x=0,-\frac{3}{2}$

41. $x^2+5x+2=2$
$x(x+5)=0 \quad x=0,-5$

42. $x^2-7x=-12$
$(x-3)(x-4)=0 \quad x=3,4$

43. $2x^2-4x=0$
$2x(x-2)=0 \quad x=0,2$

44. $x^2-6x=-10+x$
$(x-2)(x-5)=0 \quad x=2,5$

45. $x^2-7x+6=0$
$(x-1)(x-6)=0 \quad x=1,6$

46. $x^2 - x - 12 = 0$
    $(x-4)(x+3) = 0 \quad x = 4, -3$

47. $x^2 + 3x - 1 = 2x + 11$
    $(x+4)(x-3) = 0 \quad x = 3, -4$

48. $x^2 - 3x - 10 = 0$
    $(x-5)(x+2) = 0 \quad x = -2, 5$

49. $x^2 - 6x = 9 + 2x$
    $(x+1)(x-9) = 0 \quad x = -1, 9$

50. $x^2 - 1 + x = x$
    $(x-1)(x+1) = 0 \quad x = 1, -1$

51. $x^2 - 2 = 0$
    $(x-\sqrt{2})(x+\sqrt{2}) = 0 \quad x = \sqrt{2}, -\sqrt{2}$

52. $x^2 - 3 = 0$
    $(x-\sqrt{3})(x+\sqrt{3}) = 0 \quad x = \sqrt{3}, -\sqrt{3}$

53. $x^2 - 4 = 0$
    $(x-2)(x+2) = 0 \quad x = 2, -2$

54. $-x^2 + 1 = 0$
    $-(x-1)(x+1) = 0 \quad x = 1, -1$

55. $-x^2 + 2 = 0$
    $-(x-\sqrt{2})(x+\sqrt{2}) = 0 \quad x = \sqrt{2}, -\sqrt{2}$

56. $-x^2 + 3 = 0$
    $-(x-\sqrt{3})(x+\sqrt{3}) = 0 \quad x = \sqrt{3}, -\sqrt{3}$

57. $-x^2 + 4 = 0$
    $-(x-2)(x+2) = 0 \quad x = 2, -2$

58. $-x^2 + 13 = 0$
    $-(x-\sqrt{13})(x+\sqrt{13}) = 0 \quad x = \sqrt{13}, -\sqrt{13}$

59. $-x^2 + 49 = 0$
    $(x-7)(x+7) = 0 \quad x = 7, -7$

60. $2x^2 - 72 = 0$
    $2(x-6)(x+6) = 0 \quad x = 6, -6$

61. $-x^2 - 2 = 0$
    Cannot be factorized, no solutions

62. $5x^2 - 125 = 0$
    $5(x-5)(x+5) = 0 \quad x = 5, -5$

63. $-x^2 + 81 = 0$
    $-(x-9)(x+9) = 0 \quad x = 9, -9$

64. $-3x^2 + 27 = 0$
    $-3(x-3)(x+3) = 0 \quad x = 3, -3$

65. $2x^2 - 6 = 0$
    $2(x-\sqrt{3})(x+\sqrt{3}) = 0 \quad x = \sqrt{3}, -\sqrt{3}$

66. $3x^2 - 1 = 0$
    $3(x-\sqrt{\tfrac{1}{3}})(x+\sqrt{\tfrac{1}{3}}) = 0 \quad x = \sqrt{\tfrac{1}{3}}, -\sqrt{\tfrac{1}{3}}$

67. $5x^2 - 6 = 0$
    $5(x-\sqrt{\tfrac{6}{5}})(x+\sqrt{\tfrac{6}{5}}) = 0 \quad x = \sqrt{\tfrac{6}{5}}, -\sqrt{\tfrac{6}{5}}$

68. $4x^2 - 2 = 0$
    $4(x-\sqrt{\tfrac{1}{2}})(x+\sqrt{\tfrac{1}{2}}) = 0 \quad x = \sqrt{\tfrac{1}{2}}, -\sqrt{\tfrac{1}{2}}$

69. $x^2 - b = 0$
    $(x-\sqrt{b})(x+\sqrt{b}) = 0 \quad x = \sqrt{b}, -\sqrt{b}$

70. $ax^2 - b = 0$
    $a(x-\sqrt{\tfrac{b}{a}})(x+\sqrt{\tfrac{b}{a}}) = 0 \quad x = \sqrt{\tfrac{b}{a}}, -\sqrt{\tfrac{b}{a}}$

71. $-ax^2 + b = 0$
    $-a(x-\sqrt{b})(x+\sqrt{b}) = 0 \quad x = \sqrt{b}, -\sqrt{b}$

72. $2x^2 - 4x + 2 = 0$
    $2(x-1)(x-1) = 0 \quad x = 1$

73. $3x^2 - 3x - 18 = 0$
    $3(x-3)(x+2) = 0 \quad x = 3, -2$

74. $-5x^2 + 10x + 75 = 0$
    $-5(x-5)(x+3) = 0 \quad x = 5, -3$

75. $3x^2 - 12x - 63 = 0$
    $3(x-7)(x+3) = 0 \quad x = 7, -3$

76. $2x^2 + 2x - 112 = 0$
    $2(x-8)(x+7) = 0 \quad x = 8, -7$

77. $2x^2 - 12x = 14$
    $2(x+1)(x-7) = 0 \quad x = 7, -1$

78. $-5x^2 + 15x + 90 = 0$
    $-5(x+3)(x-6) = 0 \quad x = 6, -3$

79. $-3x^2 - 12x - 12 = 0$
    $-3(x+2)(x+2) = 0 \quad x = -2$

80. $-2x^2 - 26x - 84 = 0$
    $-2(x+6)(x+7) = 0 \quad x = -6, -7$

81. $6x^2 + 48x + 72 = 0$
    $6(x+6)(x+2) = 0 \quad x = -2, -6$

Solve by taking the square, cubic or other root, factor if possible:

82. $x^2 = 2$
    $x = \pm\sqrt{2}$

83. $x^4 - 8 = 28$
    $x = \pm\sqrt[4]{36} = \pm\sqrt{6}$

84. $2x^3 = -2$
    $x = \sqrt[3]{-1} = -1$

85. $x^2 = 9$
    $x = \pm 3$

86. $x^2 - 8 = 1$
    $x = \pm 3$

87. $2x^5 - 5 = 1$
    $x = \sqrt[5]{3}$

88. $2 - x^{11} + 4 = 1$
    $x^{11} = 5$
    $x = \sqrt[11]{5}$

    $20 - 3x^2 - 227 = 1$

89. $x^2 = -\dfrac{208}{3}$
    No Solution

90. Draw a conclusion about equations of the form $x^n = c$ (same as $x^n - c = 0$)

	c > 0	c = 0	c < 0
n is even	2 real solutions $x = \pm\sqrt[n]{c}$	1 solution (x = 0)	0 real solutions
n is odd	1 real solution $x = \sqrt[n]{c}$	1 solution (x = 0)	1 real solution $x = -\sqrt[n]{c}$

91. Draw a conclusion about equations of the form $x^2 = bx$ (same as $x^2 - bx = 0$)

    Can always be factored: $x(x-b) = 0 \quad x_1 = 0 \quad x_2 = b$

92. Given the equations $x^2 = -1$, $x^2 = 1$

    a. Explain why one of them cannot be solved by taking the square root while the other can. The equation $x^2 = -1$ cannot be solved since negative numbers do not have even roots, that is due to the fact that any number raised to an even power will be positive or zero but never negative.

297

b. Can that equation be solved by factoring? Explain <u>No, it does not have solutions therefore no associated factors.</u>

93. Given the equation $(x-1)^2 = 0$

   a. Solve it by taking the square root. $(x-1)(x-1) = 0$ $x = 1$

   b. Can the equation be solved by factoring? It is already factored

94. Draw a conclusion about the number of solutions of quadratic equations.

   Quadratic equations may have 2 solutions (2 different factors), 1 solution (2 identical factors) or no solution.

95. Given the equation $(x-\pi)(x+\sqrt{2}) = 0$

   a. Its solutions are π and $\sqrt{2}$

   b. In case the equation is expanded the following equation is obtained:

   $x^2 - x(\pi - \sqrt{2}) - \pi\sqrt{2} = 0$ The solutions of this equation are <u>π</u> and <u>$\sqrt{2}$</u> (It is the same equation therefore the same solutions, no need to solve again)

   c. Conclusion: In general <u>factored</u> equations are easier to solve. When an equation is not factorised it may be difficult to find its solutions.

96. Write a quadratic equation that represents the numbers. Solve the equation by factoring to obtain all the possible solutions.

   $x(x+1) = 56$ $x^2 + x - 56 = 0$ $(x+8)(x-7) = 0$
   $x = -8$ $x = 7$

   So the numbers are –8 and –7 or 7 and 8.

97. Write a quadratic equation that represents the information. Solve the equation by factoring and find the perimeter of the field.

   $x^2 = 4$ $(x-2)(x+2) = 0$ $x = 2$ $P = 8km$

98. Write a quadratic equation that represents the information. Solve the equation and find the perimeter of the square.

   $(x+2)^2 = x^2 + 40$ $4x + 4 = 40$ $x = 9$ $P = 36cm$

99. One side of a rectangular field is 2 m longer than the other. It is known that the area of the field is 360 m². Write a quadratic equation that represents the information. Solve the equation by factoring and find the perimeter of the field.

   $x(x+2) = 360$ $x^2 + 2x - 360 = 0$ $(x+20)(x-18) = 0$ $x = 18$ $P = 36 + 40 = 76m$

CHAPTER 2 - GEOMETRY

2.1. – INTRODUCTION TO GEOMETRY

POINTS

1. Indicate the following points on the plane: A(1,5), B(–1, 4), C(–3, –7), D(6,–5), E(–1, –1), F(2, 0), G(0,–4), H(–4, 0)

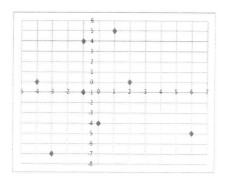

LINES

2. Indicate the following points on the plane: A(0,0), B(1, 1), C(–2, –2), D(6,6)

    a. What do these points have in common? $y = x$ in all of them
    b. Could you describe all the points that satisfy this property? How? $y = x$

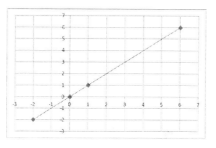

3. The points on the plane: A(0,0), B(1, 2), C(–2, –4), D(4,8)

    a. What do these points have in common? $y = 2x$ in all of them
    b. Could you describe all the points that satisfy this property? How $y = 2x$ in all of them
    c. The following points E(0,1), F(1, 3), G(–2, –3), H(4,9)
    d. What do these points have in common? What is the relation between this line and the previous line? In this line $y = 2x + 1$. It is identical to the previous line only shifted 1 unit up.

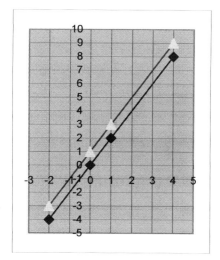

4. The points on the plane: A(0, –2), B(1, 1), C(2, 4), D(–2,–8)
    a. What do these points have in common? $y = 3x – 2$ in all of them
    b. Could you describe all the points that satisfy this property? How? $y = 3x – 2$ in all of them
    c. On the same graph sketch the following points E(0,1), F(1, 4), G(–2, –5), H(2, 7)
    d. What do these points have in common? What is the relation between this line and the previous line? $y = 3x + 1$ in all of them, this line is the same as the other, shifted 3 units up so lines are parallel.

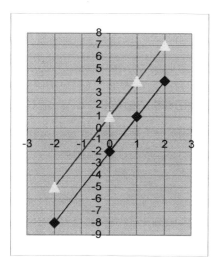

299

2.2. – ANGLES

1. An angle is the figure formed by <u>two</u> lines called <u>rays</u> that start at a common point.

    For example:
2. A straight angle is: <u>such that the 2 lines are aligned, we say this angle is 180°</u>
3. An acute angle is: <u>smaller than 90°</u>
4. A right angle is: <u>equal to 90°</u>
5. An obtuse angle is: <u>bigger than 90°</u>
6. A reflex angle is: <u>between 180° and 360°</u>
7. Given the following diagram:
    a. CA and CB are <u>rays</u>
    b. The shaded angle can be called <u>acute</u> or <u>less than 90°</u>

8. We say that the following angle has a size of <u>90</u> degrees or <u>90°</u>
9. Use the following square to sketch an angle of 45° degrees:
10. Two angles are complementary if their sum is <u>90°</u>
11. Two angles are supplementary if their sum is <u>180°</u>
12. The complementary of 20° is <u>70°</u> The complementary of x° is <u>90 – x°</u>
13. The supplementary of 20° is <u>160°</u> The supplementary of x° is <u>180 – x°</u>
14. The complementary of 42° is <u>48°</u> The complementary of x° is <u>90 – x°</u>
15. The supplementary of 126° is <u>54°</u> The supplementary of x° is <u>180 – x°</u>
16. The complementary of 81° is <u>9°</u> The complementary of x° is <u>90 – x°</u>
17. The supplementary of 0° is <u>180°</u> The supplementary of x° is <u>180 – x°</u>
18. Find all the unknown angles:
    $6x = 180; x = 30°$
    Angles are 30°, 60°, 90°

19. Find all the unknown angles:
    $2x = 50; x = 25$
    Angles are 25°, 50°, y = 65°

    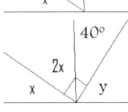

20. Straight lines are <u>parallel</u> or   <u>intersecting</u>
21. Given the following diagram:
    a. The angles x and y are <u>supplementary</u>
    b. The angles x and a are <u>equal</u> (opposite)
    c. The angles y and b are <u>equal</u> (opposite)

    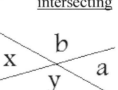

22. Given the following diagram:
    a. The angles a and e are <u>corresponding angles</u>
    b. The angles b and e are <u>interior angles</u>
    c. The angles b and f are <u>corresponding angles</u>
    d. The angles c and e are <u>alternating interior angles</u>
    e. The angles h and b are <u>alternating interior angles</u>
    f. The angles e and g are <u>equal</u> (opposite)
    g. The angles c and h are <u>interior angles</u>
    h. The angles g and h are <u>supplementary</u>
    i. The angles b and d are <u>equal</u> (opposite)
    j. Which angle is a corresponding angle pair with g? <u>c</u>
    k. Which angle is an alternate angle pair with g? <u>a</u>
    l. Which angle is a co-interior angle pair with e? <u>b</u>

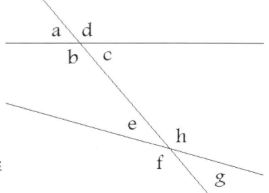

23. Given the following diagram in which the transversal intersects 2 parallel lines: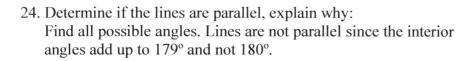
    a. The angles a and e are equal (corresponding angles)
    b. The angles b and e are supplementary (interior angles)
    c. The angles b and f are equal (corresponding angles)
    d. The angles c and e are equal (alternating angles)
    e. The angles h and b are equal (alternating angles)
    f. The angles e and g are equal (opposite angles)
    g. The angles c and h are supplementary (interior angles)

24. Determine if the lines are parallel, explain why:
    Find all possible angles. Lines are not parallel since the interior angles add up to 179° and not 180°.

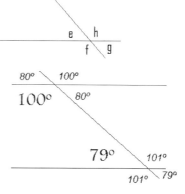

25. Determine if the lines are parallel, explain why:
    Find all possible angles. Lines are parallel since the interior angles add up to 180°.

26. Determine if the lines are parallel, explain why. Find all possible angles. Lines are parallel since the corresponding angles are equal

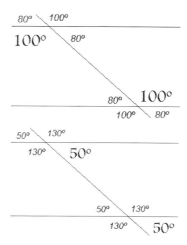

27. Sketch corresponding angle:

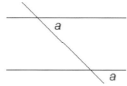

28. Sketch alternate interior angles: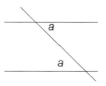

29. Sketch alternate exterior angles: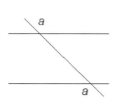

30. Given the AB is parallel to CD, find the angles a, b, c, d, e.

    a = 48°, b = 132°, c = 132°, d = 42°, e = 48°

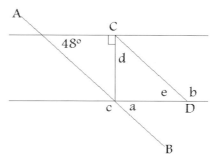

301

31. The sum of the angles in a triangle is 180°
32. The sum of the angles in a square is 360°
33. The sum of the angles in a rectangle is 360°
34. The sum of the angles in a quadrilateral is 360°
35. The sum of the angles in a pentagon is 540°
36. The sum of the angles in an hexagon is 720°
37. The sum of the angles in an heptagon is 900°
38. The sum of the angles in an octagon is 1080°
39. The sum of the angles in a shape with n sides is $180(n-2)$

    the reason is that for each side added another triangle is created and therefore 180° added.
40. Find the regular polygons with which you can fill the floor with tiles. Explain why does this happen.

    We can only do it using equilateral triangles, squares or hexagons.
    The reason is that the angle of a regular polygon with n sides is given by:

    $$\alpha = \frac{180(n-2)}{n}, \text{ for example:}$$

    Equilateral triangle n = 3, $\alpha = \frac{180(3-2)}{3} = 60°$

    Square n = 4, $\alpha = \frac{180(4-2)}{4} = 90°$

    Pentagon n = 5, $\alpha = \frac{180(5-2)}{5} = 108°$

    Hexagon n = 6, $\alpha = \frac{180(6-2)}{6} = 120°$

    Heptagon n = 7 $\alpha = \frac{180(7-2)}{7} \approx 129°$

    Octagon n = 8 $\alpha = \frac{180(8-2)}{8} = 135°$

    ...

    All the rest are between 135° and 180°.

    The tile's angle must be a divisor of 360° to complete the circle at each point. The divisors of 360 are: 1,2,3,4,5,6,8,10,12,15, 18, 20, 24, 30, 36, 40, 45, **60**, 72, **90**, **120**, 180. The only ones that appear on both lists are 60, 90, 120.

41. Find all the unknown angles:

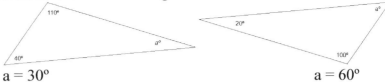

a = 30° a = 60°

42. Find all the unknown angles:

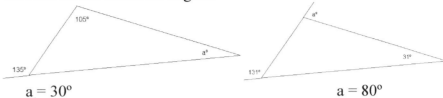

a = 30° a = 80°

43. Find all the unknown angles:

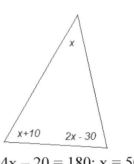 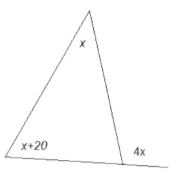

4x − 20 = 180; x = 50° 200 − 2x = 180; x = 10°
Angles: 50°, 60°, 70° Angles: 10°, 30°, 140°

44. Find all the unknown angles:

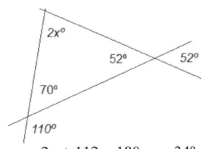 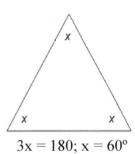

2x + 112 = 180; x = 34° 3x = 180; x = 60°
Angle: 68°

45. Find all the unknown angles:

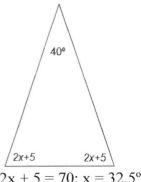 

2x + 5 = 70; x = 32.5° 5x = 180; x = 36°
Angles: 70° Angles: 72°, 36°, 72°

2.3. – SQUARES, RECTANGLES AND TRIANGLES

1. The following points on the plane: A(0, 6), B(6, 0), C(0, 0)

   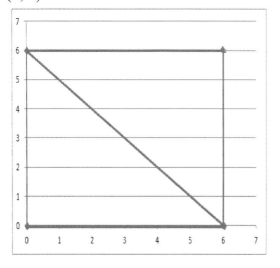

   b. Find all the angles of the triangles you can 45°, 45°, 90°.
   c. This kind of triangle is called right angled and isosceles
   d. Write down the lengths of the 2 equal sides: 6
   e. Write down the Pythagorean Theorem: $H^2 = a^2 + b^2$ This theorem is only true in right triangles.
   f. Use P. Theorem to find the length of the third side of the triangle. $H = \sqrt{72}$
   g. Add the point D(6, 6) to the graph. The form ABCD is a Rectangle. The area of this shape is A = 36
   h. Use the area of the square to find the area of the triangle. Half of it so 18.

2. Indicate the following points on the plane: A(–4, 0), B(2, 6), C(8, 0)

   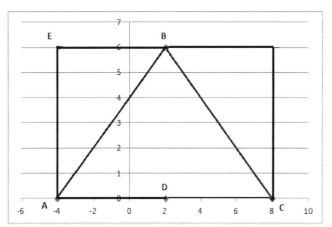

   b. This kind of triangle is called isosceles
   c. Write down the Pythagorean Theorem: $H^2 = a^2 + b^2$ This theorem is only true in right angled triangles.
   d. Add the point D (2, 0) to the graph. The triangle ABD is right angled
   e. The length of AD is 6 The Length of BD is 6 Use P. Theorem to find the length of AB. $AB = \sqrt{72}$
   f. In consequence state the length of BC: $BC = \sqrt{72}$
   g. The perimeter of the triangle ABC is $12 + 2\sqrt{72}$
   h. Add the point E (–4, 6) to the graph. The shape AEBD is square. The area of this shape is 36. Use this area to find the area of the triangle ABD and ABC. Area ABD is half so 18, ABC is twice ABD so 36

3. Indicate the following points on the plane: A(–6, 0), B(3, 6), C(5, 0)

b. Is this triangle isosceles or right angled? <u>No</u>

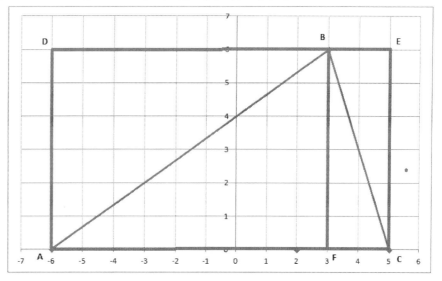

c. The shape ADEC is a <u>rectangle.</u> The area of this shape is <u>66</u>.
d. The llength of AB: $AB = \sqrt{36+81} = \sqrt{117}$ and BC $BC = \sqrt{4+36} = \sqrt{40}$
e. The perimeter of the triangle ABC is $Perimeter = \sqrt{40} + \sqrt{117} + 11$
f. The line BF is called the <u>Height</u> of the triangle.
g. Every triangle has <u>3</u> heights. . A height is a lines that starts at a <u>vertex</u> and ends at <u>the opposite side</u> forming an angle of <u>90°</u> with it.
h. Find the area of the triangles ABF, FBC and ABC.

$Area_{ABF} = \dfrac{54}{2} = 27$ $Area_{FBC} = \dfrac{12}{2} = 6$ $Area_{ABC} = \dfrac{66}{2} = 33$

4. Indicate the following points on the plane: A (–5, 0), B (5, 0), C (0, $\sqrt{75}$)

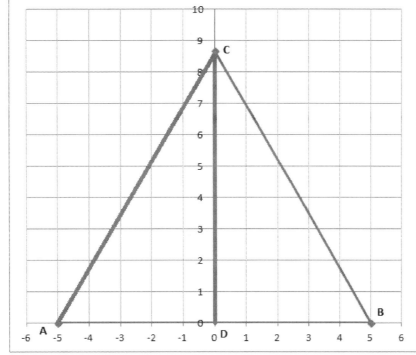

a. Done
b. Length of AB: $AB = 10 \qquad BC = \sqrt{25 + 75} = 10$
c. What kind of triangle is this? <u>Equilateral, all sides are equal and have a length of 10</u>
d. What can you say about the angles of this triangle?<u> All angles are equal and all are 60°</u>
e. The perimeter of the triangle ABC is <i>Perimeter = 30</i>
f. Find the area of the triangle ABC. $Area_{ABF} = \dfrac{base \cdot height}{2} = \dfrac{10 \cdot \sqrt{75}}{2} = 5\sqrt{75}$

The area of the triangle is half of the rectangle that can be built around it as seen in previous exercises. That is the origin of the formula provided for the area.

5. Define and sketch an example, include all the known angles and lengths of sides in your example.

   a. Equilateral triangle:
      <u>3 equal sides, 3 equal angles of 60°</u>

   c. Right angled triangle: <u>One 90° angle</u>

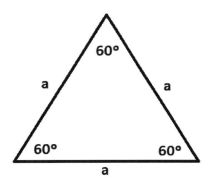
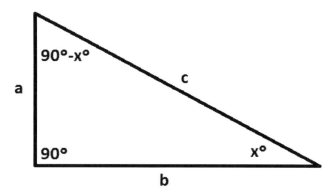

   b. Isosceles triangle:
      <u>2 equal sides with corresponding 2 equal angles.</u>
      <u>Altitude bisects apex and base</u>

   d. Right angled and isosceles triangle:

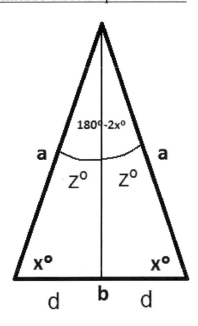
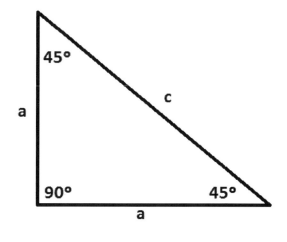

6. Given the following right angled triangle, find the missing side, perimeter and area of the triangle.

   $x = \sqrt{100-64} = 6$

   $A = \dfrac{48}{2} = 24 cm^2 \quad P = 24 cm$

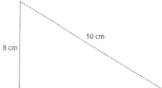

7. Given the following right angled triangle, find the missing side, perimeter and area of the triangle.

   $Hyp = \sqrt{25+144} = 13$

   $A = \dfrac{60}{2} = 30 cm^2 \quad P = 30 cm$

8. Given the following right angled triangle, find the missing side, perimeter and area of the triangle.

   $x = \sqrt{16-4} = \sqrt{12}$

   $A = \dfrac{2\sqrt{12}}{2} = \sqrt{12} cm^2 \quad P = 6 + \sqrt{12} cm$

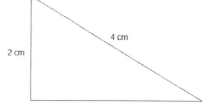

9. Given the following right angled triangles, find the missing sides, perimeter and area of the triangle.

   $100 = x^2 + 4x^2 \quad x = \sqrt{20}$

   $A = \dfrac{2\sqrt{20} \cdot \sqrt{20}}{2} = 20 cm^2 \quad P = 10 + 3\sqrt{20} cm$

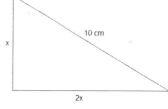

10. The vertex angle of an isosceles triangle is 42°, find the size of its base angle.
    BaseAngle = (180 – 42) / 2 = 69°

11. The vertex angle of an isosceles triangle is 110°, find the size of its base angle.
    BaseAngle = (180 – 110) / 2 = 35°

12. The base angle of an isosceles triangle is 50°, find the size of its vertex angle.
    VertexAngle = 180 – 100 = 80°

13. The base angle of an isosceles triangle is 33°, find the size of its vertex angle.
    VertexAngle = 180 – 66 = 114°

14. Given the isosceles triangle:

    y = 7cm   a = 72° b = 36°

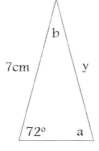

15. Given the diagram, find:

    x = 60° y = 8cm a = 50° b = 80°

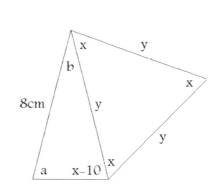

307

16. The base of an isosceles triangle is 10 cm, its side is 12 cm. Find its perimeter and area. $Perimeter = 10 + 24 = 34 cm$

$$height = \sqrt{144 - 25} = \sqrt{119} \qquad Area = \frac{10\sqrt{119}}{2} = 5\sqrt{119} cm^2$$

17. The base angle of an isosceles triangle is 5x + 7, the vertex angle is 2x − 2; find the size of the angles.
$Perimeter = 2(5x + 7) + 2x - 2 = 180; x = 14$
$BaseAngle = 77°, VertexAngle = 26°$

18. The base angle of an isosceles triangle is 9x − 10, the vertex angle is 12x − 10; find the size of the angles.
$Perimeter = 2(9x - 10) + 12x - 10 = 180; x = 7$
$BaseAngle = 53°, VertexAngle = 74°$

19. Given the following triangle, it is known that AB = 10cm, AD = 7cm and DC = 4cm. Angle CDB = 90°. Find:

    a. DB = 3cm, $BC = \sqrt{9 + 16} = 5cm$, $AC = \sqrt{16 + 49} = \sqrt{65} cm$
    b. $A_{ABC} = \frac{10 \cdot 4}{2} = 20 cm^2$
    c. $Perimeter_{ABC} = 15 + \sqrt{65} = cm$

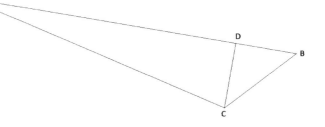

20. Given the following triangle, it is known that AC = 13cm, DB = 4cm and DC = 5cm. Angle CDB = 90°. Find:

    a. $AD = \sqrt{169 - 25} = 12cm$ $BC = \sqrt{16 + 25} = \sqrt{41} cm$
    b. $A_{DCB} = \frac{4 \cdot 5}{2} = 10 cm^2$
    c. $Perimeter_{ABC} = 13 + 12 + 4 + \sqrt{41} = 29 + \sqrt{41} cm$

21. Given the following triangle, it is known that AC = 20cm, DB = 10cm and DC = 11 cm. Angle CDB = 90° and angle CEA = 90°. Find:

    a. $BC = \sqrt{100 + 121} = \sqrt{221} cm$
       $AB = \sqrt{81 + 100} = \sqrt{181} cm$
    b. $A_{ABC} = \frac{20 \cdot 10}{2} = 100 cm^2$
    c. $Perimeter_{ABC} = 20 + \sqrt{181} + \sqrt{221} cm$
    d. What do EC and BD have in common?
       Both are heights of the triangle ABC.

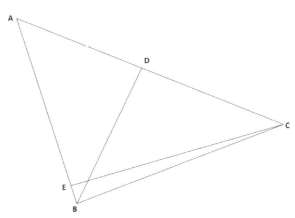

e. The lengths of EC, EB and $Area_{ABC} = \dfrac{EC \cdot AB}{2} = \dfrac{EC \cdot \sqrt{181}}{2} = 100$

$EC = \dfrac{200}{\sqrt{181}} cm \quad EB = \sqrt{221 - \dfrac{40000}{181}} \approx 0.0743 cm$

$AE = AB - EB = \sqrt{181} - \sqrt{221 - \dfrac{40000}{181}} cm$

22. Find the perimeter and area of an isosceles right angled triangle whose <u>leg</u> is 10cm.
$10^2 + 10^2 = z^2; z = \sqrt{200} cm \qquad P = 20 + \sqrt{200} cm \qquad A = \dfrac{100}{2} = 50 cm^2$

23. Find the perimeter and area of a right angled triangle whose sides are $6, x, 10$
$6^2 + x^2 = 10^2; x = 8cm \qquad P = 24cm \qquad A = \dfrac{48}{2} = 24cm^2$

24. Find the perimeter and area of a right angled triangle whose sides are $\sqrt{x}, \sqrt{x}, \dfrac{x}{2}$
$x + x = \dfrac{x^2}{4}; x = 8cm \qquad P = 2\sqrt{8} + 4 cm \qquad A = \dfrac{8}{2} = 4cm^2$

25. Find the area of an isosceles right angled triangle whose <u>perimeter</u> is 20cm.
Taking x is the legs and y as the hypotenuse:
$x^2 + x^2 = y^2, y = \sqrt{2} \cdot x; 2x + \sqrt{2} \cdot x = 20; x = \dfrac{20}{2+\sqrt{2}} \qquad A = \dfrac{1}{2}\left(\dfrac{20}{2+\sqrt{2}}\right)^2 cm^2$

26. Find the area of an equilateral triangle whose perimeter is 30cm.
$3x = 30; x = 10cm \qquad h^2 + 5^2 = 10^2; h = \sqrt{75} \qquad A = \dfrac{10\sqrt{75}}{2} = 5\sqrt{75} cm^2$

27. Given a right angled isosceles triangle whose longest side is 10 cm long.
    a. Sketch the triangle.
    b. Find the perimeter of the triangle.
    c. Find the area of the triangle.

$x^2 + x^2 = 100 \qquad x = \sqrt{50} \qquad Perimeter = 10 + 2\sqrt{50}$

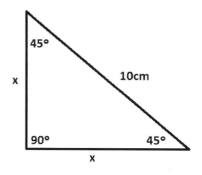

$Area = \dfrac{\sqrt{50} \cdot \sqrt{50}}{2} = 25 cm^2$

28. Given a right angled isosceles triangle whose smallest side is X cm long.
    a. Sketch the triangle.
    b. Find the perimeter of the triangle in terms of X.
    c. Find the area of the triangle in terms of X.

$X^2 + X^2 = c^2 \qquad c = \sqrt{2}X \qquad Perimeter = X(2+\sqrt{2})$

$Area = \dfrac{X^2}{2} cm^2$

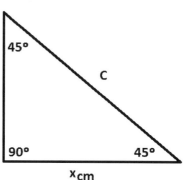

29. Given an equilateral triangle whose side is 10 cm long.

   a. Sketch the triangle.
   b. Find the perimeter of the triangle.
   c. Find the area of the triangle.

   $h^2 + 5^2 = 10^2; h = \sqrt{75}$ $P = 30 cm$ $A = \dfrac{10\sqrt{75}}{2} = 5\sqrt{75} cm^2$

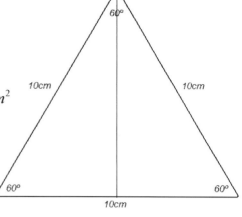

30. Given an equilateral triangle whose side is X cm long.

   a. Sketch the triangle.
   b. Find the perimeter of the triangle in terms of X.
   c. Find the area of the triangle in terms of X.

   $h^2 + \left(\dfrac{x}{2}\right)^2 = x^2; h = \dfrac{\sqrt{3} \cdot x}{2}$ $P = 3x\, cm$ $A = \dfrac{\sqrt{3} \cdot x^2}{4} cm^2$

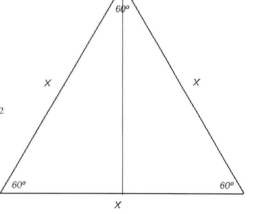

31. Find the perimeter of an isosceles triangle whose base is half of its side and its area is 20 cm².

   $h^2 + \left(\dfrac{x}{2}\right)^2 = 4x^2;\quad h = \dfrac{\sqrt{15}}{2}x \quad A = \dfrac{\sqrt{15}x^2}{4} = 20 \quad x = \sqrt{\dfrac{80}{\sqrt{15}}} \quad P = 5\sqrt{\dfrac{80}{\sqrt{15}}}$

32. Find the perimeter of an isosceles triangle whose base is six fifths of its side and its area is 12 cm².

   $h^2 + \left(\dfrac{3x}{5}\right)^2 = x^2;\quad h = \dfrac{4}{5}x \quad A = \dfrac{24x^2}{50} = 12 \quad x = \sqrt{25} = 5 \quad P = 5+5+6 = 16 cm$

33. Find the perimeter of a right angled triangle in which 1 leg is 10% longer than the other and whose area is 55 cm².

   $x^2 + \left(\dfrac{11x}{10}\right)^2 = y^2;\quad y = \dfrac{\sqrt{221}}{10}x \quad A = \dfrac{11x^2}{20} = 55 \quad x = 10 cm \quad P = 21+\sqrt{221}\, cm$

34. Find the area of a right angled triangle in which 1 leg is 25% shorter than the other and whose perimeter is 24cm

   $x^2 + \left(\dfrac{3x}{4}\right)^2 = y^2;\quad y = \dfrac{5}{4}x \quad P = x + \dfrac{3x}{4} + \dfrac{5x}{4} = 24 \quad x = 8$

   $A = 8 \cdot 6 \cdot \dfrac{1}{2} = 24 cm^2$

35. Given the following diagram (not to scale), BD = 8 cm, AD = 17, DC = 104 cm,

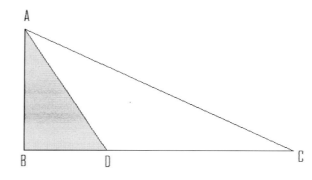

a. Find the perimeter and area of ABC
$$AB^2 + 8^2 = 17^2 \qquad AB = 15cm$$
$$15^2 + 112^2 = AC^2 \qquad AC = 113cm$$
$$P_{ABC} = 15 + 112 + 113 = 240cm$$
$$A_{ABC} = \frac{112 \cdot 15}{2} = 840cm^2$$

b. Find the perimeter and area of ABD.
$$AB^2 + 8^2 = 17^2 \qquad AB = 15cm$$
$$P_{ABD} = 39cm$$
$$A_{ABD} = \frac{8 \cdot 15}{2} = 60cm^2$$

c. Find the perimeter and area of ADC.
$$P_{ADC} = 17 + 104 + 113 = 234cm$$
$$A_{ADC} = \frac{104 \cdot 15}{2} = 780cm^2$$

d. Determine the percentage of the area that is shaded.
$$\frac{60}{840} \approx 0.071 = 7.1\%$$

e. Determine the percentage by which the area of ABC is bigger than ABD
$$\frac{840 - 60}{60} = 13 = 1300\%$$

f. Determine the percentage by which the area of ABD is smaller than ABC
$$\frac{840 - 60}{840} \approx 0.93 = 93\%$$

g. Determine the percentage by which the perimeter of ABC is bigger than ABD
$$\frac{240 - 39}{39} \approx 5.2 = 520\%$$

h. Determine the percentage by which the perimeter of ABD is smaller than ABC
$$\frac{240 - 39}{240} \approx 0.84 = 84\%$$

2.4. – DISTANCE AND MIDPOINT

1. Indicate the following points on the plane: A(2,3), B(6, 9), C(–3, –7), D(6,–5)

   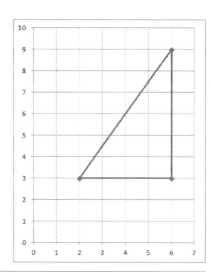

   a. Add the point (6, 3) and use Pythagorean Theorem to find the distance between the points A and B.
   $AB = \sqrt{16+36} = \sqrt{52}$

   b. The distance between the points C and D.
   $CD = \sqrt{81+4} = \sqrt{85}$

   c. Distance AC
   $AC = \sqrt{25+100} = \sqrt{125}$

   d. Midpoint between AB
   $Mid_{AB} = \left(\dfrac{2+6}{2}, \dfrac{3+9}{2}\right) = (4,6)$

   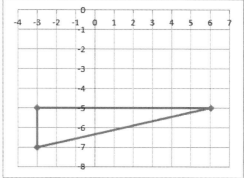

   e. Find the midpoint between CD
   $Mid_{CD} = \left(\dfrac{-3+6}{2}, \dfrac{-7-5}{2}\right) = \left(\dfrac{3}{2}, -6\right)$

   f. Find the midpoint between AC
   $Mid_{AC} = \left(\dfrac{2-3}{2}, \dfrac{3-7}{2}\right) = \left(-\dfrac{1}{2}, -2\right)$

2. Find the distance between (1, 3) and (7, –3), find the mid point.
   $Midpoint = \left(\dfrac{1+7}{2}, \dfrac{3-3}{2}\right) = (4,0)$ $Distance = \sqrt{(7-1)^2 + (-3-3)^2} = \sqrt{72}$

3. Find the distance between (a, b) and (c, d), find the mid point.
   $Midpoint = \left(\dfrac{a+b}{2}, \dfrac{c+d}{2}\right)$ $Distance = \sqrt{(c-a)^2 + (d-b)^2}$

4. Find a point whose distance to the point (2, 1) is 7. <u>There are infinite, many solutions, for example: (a, b) is the point.</u>
   $Distance = \sqrt{(a-2)^2 + (b-1)^2} = 7$, <u>if we choose b = 1, we obtain a = 9 so the point is (9, 1)</u>

5. Find a point whose distance to the point (–4, 2) is 3, can you draw a conclusion about such points in general? <u>There are infinite, the equation that describes them must be the equation of a circle. For example: (a, b) is the point.</u>
   $Distance = \sqrt{(a+4)^2 + (b-2)^2} = 3$, <u>if we choose b = 2, we obtain a = –1 so the point is (–1, 2)</u>
   $Midpoint = \left(\dfrac{a-2}{2}, \dfrac{5+b}{2}\right) = (0,0); a = 2; b = -5$

6. The midpoint between the points (a, 5) and (–2, b) is (0, 0) find a and b.
   $Midpoint = \left(\dfrac{a-2}{2}, \dfrac{5+b}{2}\right) = (0,0); a = 2; b = -5$

7. The distance between the points $(c, 4)$ and $(0, 0)$ is 5 find c.

   $Distance = \sqrt{(c-0)^2 + (4-0)^2} = 5 \qquad c^2 + 16 = 25 \qquad c = \pm 3$

8. The distance between the points $(1, -2)$ and $(6, b)$ is 13 find b.

   $Distance = \sqrt{(1-6)^2 + (-2-b)^2} = 13 \qquad \sqrt{25 + 4 + 4b + b^2} = 13$

   $b^2 + 4b - 140 = 0 \qquad (b+14)(b-10) = 0 \qquad b = 10, -14$

9. The distance between the points $A(0, a)$ and $B(2a, 0)$ is 10 find points A and B.

   $Distance = \sqrt{(0-2a)^2 + (a-0)^2} = 10 \qquad \sqrt{5}a = 10 \qquad a = \pm\dfrac{10}{\sqrt{5}}$

10. Given points $A(3, -2)$, $B(6, 1)$ and $C(0, a)$. It is known that $AC = BC$, find a. Show on diagram.

    $Distance = \sqrt{(3-0)^2 + (-2-a)^2} = \sqrt{(6-0)^2 + (1-a)^2}$

    $7 + 4a + a^2 = 37 + 2a + a^2 \qquad 2a = 30 \qquad a = 15$

11. Given points $A(-12, -8)$, $B(-4, 7)$ and $C(a, 0)$. It is known that $AC = BC$, find a.

    $Distance = \sqrt{(-12-a)^2 + (-8-0)^2} = \sqrt{(-4-a)^2 + (7-0)^2}$

    $208 + 24a + a^2 = 65 + 8a + a^2 \qquad 16a = -143 \qquad a = -\dfrac{143}{16}$

2.5. – QUADRILATERAS

1. Given the following table, fill the blank using *a, b, c, d, h, r*

	Shape	Area	Perimeter
Square		$A = a^2$	$P = 4a$
Rectangle		$A = ab$	$P = 2(a+b)$
Parallelogram		$A = ah$	$P = 2(a+b)$
Isosceles Trapezoid		$A = \dfrac{h}{2}(a+c)$	$P = a + 2b + c$
Trapezpezoid		$A = \dfrac{h}{2}(a+b)$	$P = a+b+c+d$
Rhombus		$A = \dfrac{dr}{2}$	$P = 4a$
Kite		$A = \dfrac{dr}{2}$	$P = 2(a+b)$

2. Given the following quadrilaterals. Write the name of each one of them:

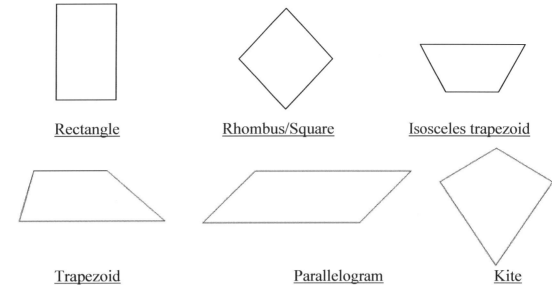

Rectangle   Rhombus/Square   Isosceles trapezoid

Trapezoid   Parallelogram   Kite

3. Given the following table, fill the blanks with yes or no.

	Shape (sketch)	Only 1 pair of parallel sides	2 pairs of parallel sides	1 pair of equal sides	2 pairs of equal sides	4 equal sides
Square		No	Yes	No	No	Yes
Rectangle		No	Yes	No	Yes	No
Parallelogram		No	Yes	No	Yes	No
Isosceles Trapezoid		Yes	No	Yes	No	No
Trapezoid		Yes	No	No	No	No
Rhombus		No	Yes	No	No	Yes
Kite		No	No	No	No	No

4. True or False
   a. A square is also a parallelogram   **True** / False
   b. A square is also a rectangle   **True** / False
   c. A square is also a trapezoid   **True** / False
   d. A parallelogram is also a square   True / **False**
   e. A rectangle is also a square   True / **False**
   f. A rhombus is always a parallelogram **True** / False
   g. A parallelogram is always r rhombus True / **False**
   h. A parallelogram is sometimes a rhombus **True** / False
   i. A rhombus is always a kite   **True** / False
   j. All the shapes above mentioned are quadrilaterals **True** / False

5. Given the following table, fill the blanks with yes or no.

	Shape (Sketch diagonals as well)	Diagonals are perpendicular	Diagonals are equal	Diagonals bisect angle	Diagonals bisect each other
Square		Yes	Yes	Yes	Yes
Rectangle		No	Yes	No	Yes
Paralleogram		No	Yes	No	Yes
Isosceles Trapezoid		No	Yes	No	No
Trapezpezoid		No	No	No	No
Rhombus		Yes	Yes	Yes	Yes
Kite		Yes	No	No	No

6. Given a square with diagonal of 4 cm, find its area and perimeter.
$x^2 + x^2 = 16; x = \sqrt{8}; Area = 8cm^2 \quad Perimeter = 4\sqrt{8} cm$

7. Given a square with diagonal of a cm, find its area and perimeter.
$x^2 + x^2 = a^2; x = \frac{\sqrt{a}}{2}; Area = \frac{a}{4} cm^2 \quad Perimeter = 2\sqrt{a} cm$

8. Given a rectangle with diagonal of 7m and one side is twice as large as the other, find its area and perimeter.
$x^2 + (2x)^2 = 7^2; x = \frac{7}{\sqrt{5}}; Area = \frac{49}{5} cm^2 \quad Perimeter = \frac{28}{\sqrt{5}} cm$

9. Given a rectangle with diagonal of 20m and one side is twice as large as the other, find its area and perimeter.
$x^2 + (2x)^2 = 20^2; x = \frac{20}{\sqrt{5}}; Area = \frac{400}{5} cm^2 \quad Perimeter = \frac{80}{\sqrt{5}} cm$

10. Given the following parallelogram. ABC is isosceles and right angled. AB = 2cm, CD = 5cm (Diagram not to scale). Find:

a. The area and perimeter of the parallelogram
$2^2 + BD^2 = 5^2; BD = \sqrt{21}; Area = 2(2+\sqrt{21})cm^2$
$2^2 + 2^2 = AC^2; AC = \sqrt{8}; Perimeter = 2(2+\sqrt{21}+\sqrt{8})cm$

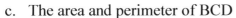

b. The area and perimeter of ABC
$Area = \dfrac{2\cdot 2}{2} = 2cm^2 \quad Perimeter = 4+\sqrt{8}cm$

c. The area and perimeter of BCD
$Area = \dfrac{\sqrt{21}\cdot 2}{2} = \sqrt{21}cm^2 \quad Perimeter = 7+\sqrt{21}cm$

d. The area and perimeter of CDE
$Area = 2(2+\sqrt{21})-2-\sqrt{21} = 2+\sqrt{21}cm^2 \quad Perimeter = 7+\sqrt{21}+\sqrt{8}cm$

11. Given the following isosceles trapezoid. ABC is right angled. AC = 7cm, CE = 15cm and AE = 20cm (Diagram not to scale). Find:

a. The area and perimeter of ABC and BCE
$CB = h; AB = x; BE = 20-x$
$x^2 + h^2 = 7^2; \quad (20-x)^2 + h^2 = 15^2$
$x = \dfrac{28}{5} = 5.6cm; \quad h = \dfrac{21}{5} = 4.1cm$
$Area_{ABC} = \dfrac{1}{2}\cdot\dfrac{28}{5}\cdot\dfrac{21}{5} = \dfrac{294}{25} = 11.76cm^2; Perimeter_{ABC} = 7+\dfrac{28}{5}+\dfrac{21}{5} = \dfrac{84}{5} = 16.8cm$
$Area_{BCE} = \dfrac{1}{2}\cdot\dfrac{82}{5}\cdot\dfrac{21}{5} = \dfrac{861}{25} = 34.44cm^2; Perimeter_{BCE} = 15+\dfrac{82}{5}+\dfrac{21}{5} = \dfrac{853}{50} = 17.06cm$

b. The area and perimeter of the trapezoid
$Area_{ACDE} = \dfrac{21}{5}\cdot\dfrac{(20+11.8)}{2} = 66.78cm^2; Perimeter_{ACDE} = 20+11.8+14 = 45.8cm$

c. The area and perimeter of CDE
$Area_{CDE} = 66.78-16.8-17.06 = 32.94cm^2; Perimeter_{CDE} = 15+11.8+7 = 33.8cm$

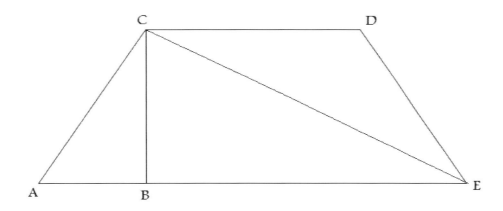

12. Given the following rhombus. BC = 6cm, AD = 18cm and find the area and perimeter the rhombus (Diagram not to scale).

$$Area_{ABC} = \frac{6 \cdot 18}{2} = 54 cm^2$$

$$3^2 + 9^2 = AB^2; AB = \sqrt{90}$$

$$Perimeter = 4\sqrt{90} cm$$

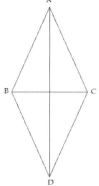

13. Given the following kite. BC = 4cm, AE = 8cm and CD = 2AC find the area and perimeter the kite (Diagram not to scale).

$$2^2 + 8^2 = AC^2; AC = \sqrt{68}; CD = 2\sqrt{68}$$

$$Perimeter = 6\sqrt{68} cm$$

$$2^2 + ED^2 = \left(2\sqrt{68}\right)^2; ED = \sqrt{268}$$

$$Area_{ABC} = \frac{4 \cdot (8+\sqrt{268})}{2} = 2 \cdot (8+\sqrt{268}) cm^2$$

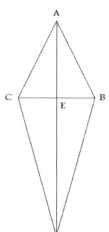

14. It is known that the perimeter of a rhombus with equal diagonals is 40cm. Find its area. <u>Rhombus with equal diagonals is a square.</u>

$$x = \frac{40}{4} = 10 cm; \quad Area = 100 cm^2$$

15. Find the side length of a square whose area is equal to its perimeter.

$$x^2 = 4x \quad x = 0 cm \quad or \quad x = 4 cm$$

16. Find the side length of a rhombus whose area is equal to its perimeter and one of its diagonals is 5cm long.

$$\frac{5d}{2} = 4\sqrt{\left(\frac{5}{2}\right)^2 + \left(\frac{d}{2}\right)^2} \qquad \frac{25d^2}{4} = 16\left(\left(\frac{5}{2}\right)^2 + \left(\frac{d}{2}\right)^2\right)$$

$$\frac{25d^2}{4} = \frac{400}{4} + \frac{16d^2}{4} \qquad 9d^2 = 400 \qquad d = \frac{20}{3}$$

The diagonals are 5 and $\frac{20}{3}$

$$Side = \sqrt{\left(\frac{5}{2}\right)^2 + \left(\frac{20}{6}\right)^2} = \sqrt{\left(\frac{25}{4}\right) + \left(\frac{400}{36}\right)} = \sqrt{\left(\frac{625}{36}\right)} = \frac{25}{6} cm$$

2.6. – CIRCLES AND COMPLEX SHAPES

1. Given the following circle:
   a. Sketch a diameter.
   b. Sketch a radius.
   c. The diameter is 2 times the radius
   d. Sketch a chord smaller than the diameter
   e. Sketch a chord smaller than the radius

   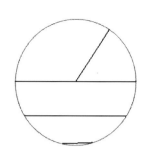

2. Given a circle with radius R, find
   The Perimeter of the circle: $2\pi R$ The Area of the circle: πR^2

3. Given a circle with radius $\frac{4}{\pi}$ cm, find

   The Perimeter of the circle: $2\pi \frac{4}{\pi} = 8cm$ The Area of the circle: $\pi\left(\frac{4}{\pi}\right)^2 = \frac{16}{\pi} cm^2$

4. Given a circle with perimeter 20π cm, find
   The radius of the circle: $2\pi R = 20\pi$ $R = 10cm$
   The Area of the circle: $\pi 10^2 = 100\pi \ cm^2$

5. Given a circle with area $16\pi \ cm^2$, find
   The radius of the circle: $\pi R^2 = 16\pi \ cm^2$ $R = 4cm$
   The perimeter of the circle: $2\pi 4 = 8\pi \ cm$

6. The length of the perimeter of a circle with radius r is $2\pi r$. The
   The area of a circle with radius r is πr^2

7. Find the perimeter and area of the following shape:

   $P = 10 + 10 + 6\pi = 20 + 6\pi \ cm$

   $A = 36\pi + A_{triangle}$ $A_{triangle} = \frac{1}{2} \cdot 12 \cdot \sqrt{100 - 36} = 48 \ cm^2$

   $A = 36\pi + 48 \ cm^2$

8. Given the following concentric circles with radii 4 cm and 7 cm correspondingly.
   Find the shaded area in terms of pi.
   $A_{shaded} = \pi(49 - 16) = 33\pi \ cm^2$

   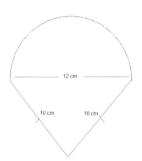

9. Given a circle with radius 5 cm. The segments AB and AC are tangent to the circle.
   Find the shaded area in terms of pi.

   $A_{shaded} = A_{sector} - A_{shaded} = \frac{A_{square} - A_{circle}}{4} = \frac{100 - 25\pi}{4} \approx 5.37 \ cm^2$

10. Given a circle with radius 10cm in which a square is circumscribed
    Since CD = 2R = 10cm and EC = ED = x
    Using Pythagorean theorem: $2x^2 = 400; \ x = \sqrt{200} = EC = ED$

    a. Find the area of the square: $Area_{square} = \sqrt{200}\sqrt{200} = 200 cm^2$
    b. Find the area of the circle: $Area_{circle} = 100\pi \ cm^2$
    c. Find the percentage of the area of the circle that the square occupies.
    $\frac{Area_{square}}{Area_{circle}} = \frac{200}{100\pi} = \frac{2}{\pi} \approx 0.637 \approx 64\%$

    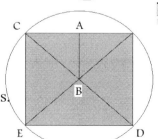

11. Given a circle with radius 10cm circumscribed in a square:

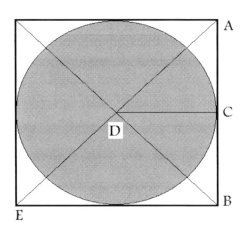

  a. Find the length of the side of the square.
     2R = 20 cm
     Find the area of the square.
     Area = 400 cm²
  b. Find the area of the circle
     $Area_{circle} = 100\pi \ cm^2$
  c. Find the percentage of the area of the square that the circle occupies.
     $\dfrac{Area_{circle}}{Area_{square}} = \dfrac{100\pi}{400} = \dfrac{\pi}{4} \approx 0.785 \approx 79\%$

12. Find the perimeter and area of the following figure made of 3 semi circles whose radius is 3cm and a right angled triangle.

   $P = 9\pi + \sqrt{100+324} = 9\pi + \sqrt{424}$

   $A = \dfrac{1}{2}\cdot 10 \cdot 18 + \dfrac{3}{2}\pi 3^2 = 90 + \dfrac{27}{2}\pi \ cm^2$

13. Find the perimeter and area of the following figure made of 4 semi circles whose radii is 1cm, 1cm, 2cm and 4 cm.

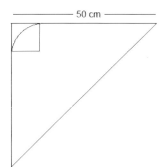

   $P = 2\pi(\dfrac{1}{2}+\dfrac{1}{2}+1+2) = 8\pi \ cm$

   $A = \dfrac{1}{2}\pi(1-1+2+4) = 3\pi \ cm^2$

14. Find the perimeter and area of the following figure made of an isosceles right triangle rounded in its corner. The radius of the round part is 10 cm.

   $P = \sqrt{2500+2500} + 40 + 40 + \dfrac{1}{4}2\pi 10 = \sqrt{5000} + 80 + 5\pi \ cm$

   $A = \dfrac{2500}{2} - (100 - \dfrac{1}{4}\pi 100) = 1150 + 25\pi \ cm^2$

15. Find the perimeter and area of the following figure made of 2 semi circles connecting half a square whose side length is 4cm.

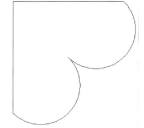

   $R_{circles} = \dfrac{1}{4}\sqrt{16+16} = \sqrt{2}$

   $P = 4 + 4 + 2\pi\sqrt{2} = 8 + \pi 2\sqrt{2} \ cm$

   $A = \dfrac{1}{2}\cdot 16 + \pi\left(\sqrt{2}\right)^2 = 8 + 2\pi \ cm^2$

16. Find the perimeter and area of the following figure made identical "stairs".

$P = 2(10 \cdot 4 + 15 \cdot 4) = 200$ cm

$A = 10 \cdot 150 = 1500$ cm^2

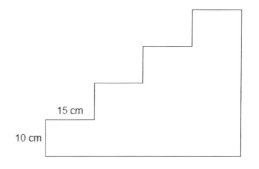

15 cm

10 cm

17. Find the dimensions of all the stairs in the following structure knowing that every stair is 10cm higher than the previous one and that the total area of the figure is 2044 cm^2.

$A = x(x + x + 10 + x + 20) + (x + 10)(x + 10 + x + 20) + (x + 20)^2 = 2044$

$3x^2 + 30x + 2x^2 + 30x + 20x + 300 + x^2 + 40x + 400 = 2044$

$6x^2 + 120x - 1344 = 0 \qquad x^2 + 20x - 224 = 0$

$x = 8, -28 (x = 8cm)$

$P = 4(x + x + 10 + x + 20) = 4(3x + 30) = 12x + 120 = 216$ cm

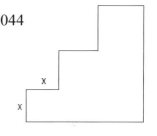

18. Find the perimeter of the following shape knowing that the area of the figure is 960 cm^2.

$A = \dfrac{3}{2}x \cdot 2x + 2x \cdot 3x + \dfrac{1}{2} 4x \cdot 3x = 960$

$3x^2 + 6x^2 + 6x^2 = 960 \qquad 15x^2 = 64 \qquad x = 8cm$

$P = 4x + 3x + 8x + \sqrt{16x^2 + 9x^2} = 15x + 5x = 20x = 160cm$

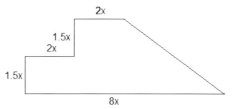

19. Find the perimeter and area of the rectangle knowing that the shaded area is π cm^2 and occupies 50% of the rectangle.

$\pi R^2 = \pi \qquad R = 1$ cm

$Width = 2cm$

$A_{rec} = 2 \cdot A_{circle} = 2\pi = 2L \qquad L = \pi$ cm

$P_{rec} = 4 + 2\pi$ cm

2.7. – 3D GEOMETRY, VOLUME AND SURFACE AREA

1. Volume is the amount of <u>space</u> occupied by material.
2. In international system of units we use a box of dimensions <u>1 meter by 1 meter by 1</u> meter to express a volume of 1 m³:
3. In many occasions a 1 m³ is a very big unit so a box of dimensions So a box of dimensions <u>1 cm by 1 cm by 1 cm</u> is used to express a volume of 1 cm³.
4. Sometimes 1 cm³ is also called 1 ml (milliliter), there is no difference. In consequence <u>1 litre = 1000 ml = 1000 cm³</u>

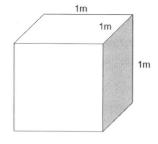

5. How many 1 cm³ boxes fit into 1 m³ box?

   $1m = 100cm$ so $1m^3 = 1m \times 1m \times 1m = 100cm \times 100cm \times 100cm = 1000000 cm^3 = 10^6 cm^3$

6. A smaller box that may be used is mm³. Find:

   a. 1 cm³ = <u>1000</u> mm³ (since 1cm = 10mm)
   b. 1 m³ = <u>10^9</u> mm³
   c. 6.3 cm³ = <u>6300</u> mm³
   d. 0.052 m³ = <u>$5.2 \cdot 10^7$</u> mm³

7. The standard volume of a milk container in your area: 1L = 1000ml
8. A volume may be formed by "moving" or "dragging" a certain area along a path, for example by moving a circle a cylinder is formed: In consequence the volume of the cylinder is:

   $V_{Cylinder} = Area_{circle} \cdot d_{distance\_dragged} = \pi R^2 d$

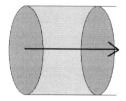

9. In case a triangle is being "dragged" what is obtained is a shape called <u>a triangular</u> prism.
10. In case a square is being "dragged" what is obtained is a shape called <u>square</u> prism or <u>cuboid</u>
11. Find the volume of the following shape, made of a quadrilateral with area 20 cm² that was dragged: $V_{Prism} = Area_{quadrilateral} \cdot d_{distance\_dragged} = 20 \cdot 12 = 240 cm^3$
12. Surface area is equivalent to the <u>amount of paper</u> needed in order to cover all the exposed areas of a three dimensional figure (like wrapping up a present).
13. Find the surface area of the following shapes:

   a. 1 m³ cube. $S_{Cube} = Area_{square} \cdot 6_{sides} = 1 \cdot 6 = 6m^3 = 6000000 cm^3 = 6000000000 mm^3$
   b. 1 cm³ cube. $S_{Cube} = Area_{square} \cdot 6_{sides} = 1 \cdot 6 = 6cm^3 = 0.000006 m^3 = 6000 mm^3$
   c. 1 mm³ cube. $S_{Cube} = Area_{square} \cdot 6_{sides} = 1 \cdot 6 = 6mm^3 = 0.006 cm^3 = 0.000000006 m^3$

14. Given the following container (called cuboid or rectangular prism)
    a. Find the length of the line that connects 2 opposite corners.
       $d = \sqrt{4+16+25} = \sqrt{45} m$
    b. Find the volume of the object in m³, cm³, mm³
       $V_{Prism} = 2 \cdot 4 \cdot 5 = 40 m^3 = 40 \cdot 10^6 cm^3 = 40 \cdot 10^9 mm^3$
    c. Find the surface area of the object in m², cm², mm²
       $S_{Cube} = 2 \cdot (2 \cdot 4) + 2 \cdot (2 \cdot 5) + 2 \cdot (4 \cdot 5) = 76 m^2 = 760000 cm^2 = 76000000 mm^2$

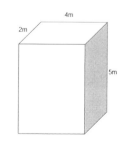

15. Given the following table, fill the blanks

	Shape	Surface Area	Volume
Cuboid (Rectangular Prism)		$S = 2(ab+bc+ac)$	$V = abc$
Pyramid (Square based)		$S = a^2 + 4A$ A = Area Side	$V = \dfrac{a^2 h}{3}$
Sphere		$S = 4\pi r^2$	$V = \dfrac{4}{3}\pi r^3$
Cylinder		$S = 2\pi r h$	$V = \pi r^2 h$
Cone		$S = \pi r L + \pi r^2$	$V = \dfrac{\pi r^2 h}{3}$

16. Given the following table, fill the blanks

	Shape	Surface Area	Volume
Triangular prism		$A = 2ac + ab + 2S$	$V = Sa$
Triangle based Pyramid (Tetrahedron)		$S = A_{base} + A_{triangles}$	$S = \dfrac{A_{base} \cdot h}{3}$

17. Find the volume and surface area of a sphere with radius 2 cm.
$$A = 4\pi 2^2 = 16\pi \ cm^2 \qquad V = \frac{4}{3}\pi 2^3 = \frac{32}{3}\pi \ cm^3$$

18. Find the volume and surface area of a sphere with radius 1.1 m.
$$A = 4\pi \cdot \left(\frac{11}{10}\right)^2 = \pi \cdot \frac{484}{10} = 48.4\pi \ m^2 \qquad V = \frac{4}{3}\pi \left(\frac{11}{10}\right)^3 = \frac{5324}{3000}\pi \ m^3$$

19. Find the volume of a square based pyramid with base length 20 cm and height is 0.1 m. $V = \frac{1}{2} \cdot 20^2 \cdot 10 = 2000 \ cm^3$

20. Find the volume and surface area of a square based cuboid whose base length is 15 cm and height 0.2 m
$$V = 15^2 \cdot 20 = 4500 \ cm^3 \qquad A = 2 \cdot 15^2 + 4 \cdot 15 \cdot 20 = 450 + 1200 = 1650 \ cm^2$$

21. Find the volume and surface area of a cone with radius 0.3 m and height 2 m.
$$V = \frac{\pi \cdot 30^2 \cdot 200}{3} = \frac{180000\pi}{3} = 60000\pi \ cm^3$$
$$L = \sqrt{30^2 + 200^2} = \sqrt{40900} \qquad A = \pi \cdot 30^2 + \pi \cdot 30\sqrt{40900} \ cm^2$$

22. Find the volume and surface area of a cylinder with radius 0.4 m and height 3 m.
$$V = \pi \cdot (0.4)^2 \cdot 3 = 0.48\pi \ m^3 \quad A = 2\pi \cdot (0.4)^2 + 2\pi \cdot 0.4 \cdot 3 = 2.72\pi \ m^2$$

23. Given that the volume of a square based pyramid is 10 m³ and that its height is equal to half its base length, find the perimeter of its base.
$$V = \frac{x^2 \left(\frac{x}{2}\right)}{3} = \frac{x^3}{6} = 10m^3; x = \sqrt[3]{60}; P = 4\sqrt[3]{60}m$$

24. Given that the volume of a cuboid is 27 m³ and that the ratio between its sides is 1:2:4. Find its surface area.
$$V = x \cdot 2x \cdot 4x = 27 \ m^3; x = \sqrt[3]{\frac{27}{8}} = \frac{3}{2}; A = 2\left(\frac{3}{2} \cdot 3 + \frac{3}{2} \cdot 6 + 3 \cdot 6\right) = 63 \ cm^2$$

25. Given that the volume of a cone is 10 m³ and that its height is 4 times the radius of the base. Find its height.
$$V = \frac{\pi \cdot R^2 \cdot 4R}{3} = 10m^3; R = \sqrt[3]{\frac{30}{4\pi}} = \sqrt[3]{\frac{15}{2\pi}}; height = 4\sqrt[3]{\frac{15}{2\pi}} \ m$$

26. Given that the volume of a sphere is 9π m³. Find its surface area.
$$V = \frac{4\pi R^3}{3} = 9\pi; R = \sqrt[3]{\frac{27}{4}} = \frac{3}{\sqrt[3]{4}}; A = 4\pi \frac{9}{\sqrt[3]{16}} = \frac{36\pi}{\sqrt[3]{16}} \ m^2$$

27. Find the volume and surface area of the following shape:

$$V = \frac{4\pi \left(\frac{5}{2}\right)^3}{3} + \pi 5^2 \cdot 15 = \frac{125\pi}{6} + 375\pi \ cm^3$$

$$A = 4\pi \left(\frac{5}{2}\right)^2 + 2\pi 5^2 + 2\pi \cdot 5 \cdot 15 = 25\pi + 50\pi + 150\pi = 225\pi \ cm^2$$

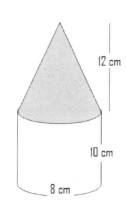

28. Find the volume and surface area of the following shape in which the cube has side length 20 cm, the cylinder has radius 5 cm and height 12 cm and the sphere has the same volume as the cylinder.

$$V = 20^3 + 2 \cdot \pi 5^2 \cdot 12 = 8000 + 600\pi \quad cm^3$$

$$V_{cylinder} = V_{sphere} = \frac{4}{3}\pi R^3 = 300\pi; R = \sqrt[3]{\frac{900}{4\pi}}$$

$$A = 6 \cdot 20^2 + 2\pi 5 \cdot 12 + 4\pi \left(\sqrt[3]{\frac{900}{4\pi}}\right)^2$$

$$A = 2400 + 120\pi + 4\pi \left(\sqrt[3]{\frac{450}{2\pi}}\right)^2 \quad cm^2$$

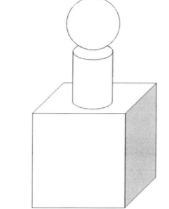

29. Find the volume and surface area of the following shape in which a square cuboid with side lengths 10 cm, 10 cm and 60 cm has 2 cylindrical openings with radius 3 cm.

$$V = 10^2 \cdot 60 - 2 \cdot \pi 3^2 \cdot 10 = 6000 - 180\pi \quad cm^3$$

$$A = 10^2 + 4 \cdot 600 - 4 \cdot \pi 3^2 + 2 \cdot 2\pi 3 \cdot 10 =$$

$$A = 100 + 2400 - 36\pi + 120\pi = 2500 + 84\pi \quad cm^2$$

30. Find the volume and surface area of the following shape:

$$V = \frac{3 \cdot 10}{2} \cdot 12 = 180 cm^3$$

$$L = \sqrt{10^2 + 3^2} = \sqrt{109}$$

$$A = \frac{3 \cdot 10}{2} \cdot 2 + 12 \cdot \sqrt{109} + 10 \cdot 12 + 3 \cdot 12 = 186 + 12 \cdot \sqrt{109} cm^2$$

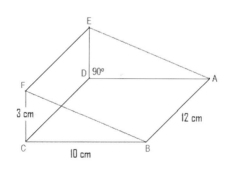

2.8. – GEOMETRIC TRANSOFRMATIONS

1. The points on the plane: A(0,0), B(–1,6), C(4,2). Connect them to form a triangle.

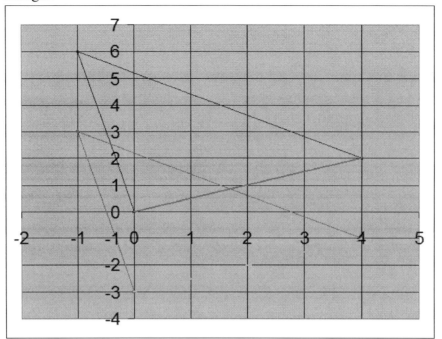

   b. What can you say about the location of the 2nd triangle in comparison to the first one? It is shifted 3 units down
   c. This is a vertical translation.

2. The points on the plane: A(0,0), B(–1,6), C(4,2). Connect them to form a triangle.

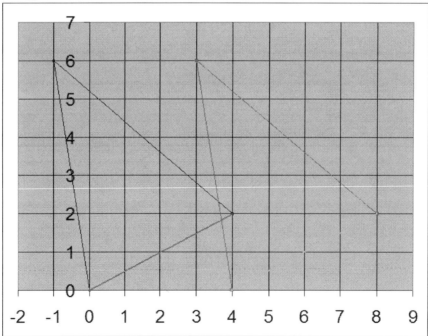

   b. What can you say about the location of the 2nd triangle in comparison to the first one? It is shifted 4 units to the right
   c. This is a horizontal translation.

3. Indicate the following points on the plane: A(0,0), B(–1,6), C(4,2). Connect them to form a triangle.

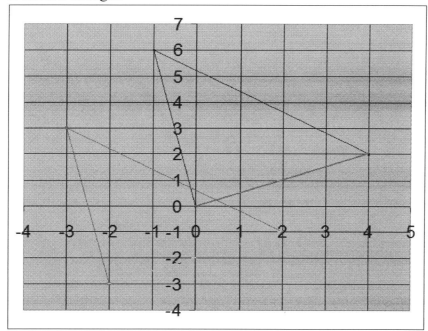

  b. What can you say about the location of the 2nd triangle in comparison to the first one? It is shifted 2 units to the left and 3 down
  c. This is a horizontal and vertical translations.

4. Indicate the following points on the plane: A(1,0), B(–2,6), C(6,3). Connect them to form a triangle.

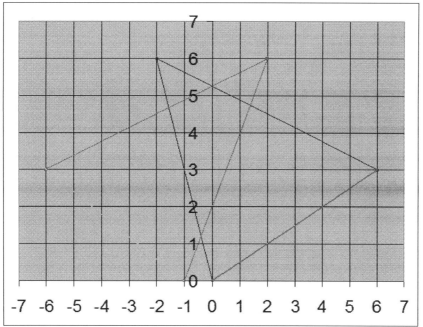

  a. What can you say about the location of the 2nd triangle in comparison to the first one? It is reflected.
  b. This is a Reflection across the y axis. The line x = 0 in this case is called the **line of** symmetry
  c. On changing x into –x we are generating a Reflection across the y axis

5. Draw all the lines of symmetry f the following shapes: The circle has <u>infinite</u> lines of symmetry, <u>any line passing through the centre.</u>

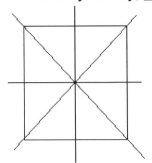 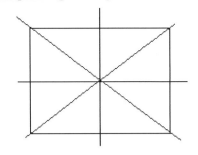 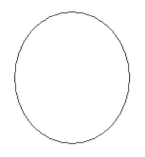

6. Indicate the following points on the plane: A(1,1), B(–2,6),C(6,3). Connect them to form a triangle.
    a. What can you say about the location of the 2nd triangle in comparison to the first one?
    b. This is a <u>Reflection</u> about the x axis. The line <u>y = 0</u> in this case is called the **line of** symmetry
    c. On changing y into <u>–y</u> we are generating a <u>Reflection</u> across the <u>x axis</u>

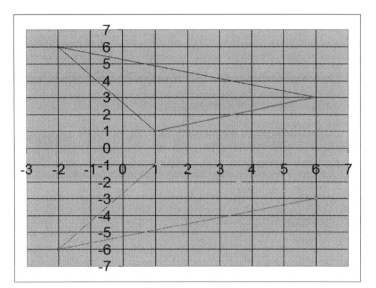

7. Indicate the following points on the plane: A(–4,0), B(0,4),C(4,0), D(0, –4). Connect them to form a square.
    a. What can you say about the location of the 2nd square in comparison to the first one? <u>It is rotated 45° clockwise</u>
    b. This is a <u>Rotation</u> of <u>45° clockwise</u> degrees.
    a. The **centre of rotation** is the point (0, 0)
    c. Write down the coordinates of a square that is a rotation of 90° of the first one:
       A'' = (4,0), B'' = (0, –4), C'' = (–4, 0), D'' = (0, 4)
       Conclusions? <u>Same coordinates, Squares remain invariant under 90° rotation, they have rotational symmetry of 90°</u>

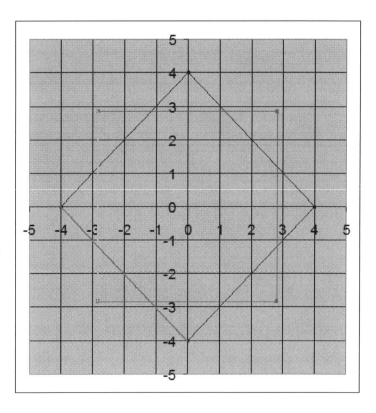

328

8. Indicate the following points on the plane: A(–5,0), B(5,0). Given also the point C(0,a)

   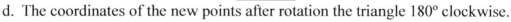

   a. The value of a in order to create an equilateral triangle is: $\sqrt{75}$
      Side of triangle is 10. Using Pythagorean T.
      $a = \sqrt{100 - 25} = \sqrt{75}$
   b. The coordinates of the new points after translating the triangle 3 units left and 1 down. A' = (–8, –1), B' = (2,–1), C' = (–3, $\sqrt{75}$ –1)
   c. The coordinates of the points after rotation the triangle 90° clockwise. Centre of rotation is the point (0, 0)
      A'' = (0,5), B'' = (0,–5), C'' = ($\sqrt{75}$,0)
   d. The coordinates of the new points after rotation the triangle 180° clockwise.
      A'' = (5,0), B'' = (–5,0), C'' = (0,–$\sqrt{75}$)

9. Indicate the following points on the plane: A(1,0), B(–2,5), C(4,3). Connect them to form a triangle.

   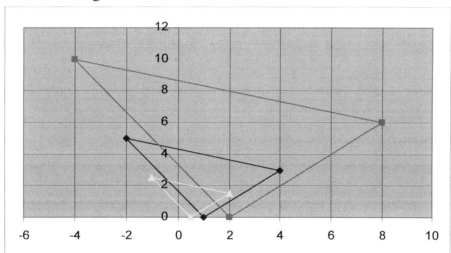

   a. Indicate the following points on the plane: A'(2,0), B'(–4,10), C'(8,6), Connect them to form a triangle.
   b. The 2nd triangle in comparison to the first one? Similar, just bigger
   c. This is a dilation factor 2
   d. Indicate the following points on the plane: A'(0.5,0), B'(–1,2.5), C'(2,1.5), Connect them to form a triangle.
   e. The 3rd triangle in comparison to the first one? Similar, just smaller
   f. This is a dilation factor 1/2
   g. When making all sides of a shape bigger or smaller using the same factor the shape remains similar to the original one.

10. Indicate the following points on the plane: A(0,0), B(2, 0), C(0,–3). Connect them to form a triangle.

   a. The points are: A' = (0,0), B' = (6, 0), C' = (0, –9)
   b. The relations:
   $\dfrac{A'B'}{AB} = 3$
   $\dfrac{A'C'}{AC} = 3$
   $\dfrac{B'C'}{BC} = 3$

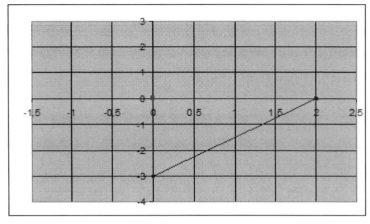

11. Given a rectangle with side lengths 10 cm and 8 cm.

   a. Find its area and perimeter. $A = 80 \ cm^2$ $P = 20 + 16 = 36 \ cm$
   b. Find the area and perimeter of a rectangle with sides 2 times as big.
   $A = 20 \cdot 16 = 320 \ cm^2$ $P = 40 + 32 = 72 \ cm$
   c. Find the area and perimeter of a rectangle with sides 3 times as big.
   $A = 30 \cdot 24 = 720 \ cm^2$ $P = 60 + 48 = 108 \ cm$
   d. Find the area and perimeter of a rectangle with sides n times as big.
   $A = 10n \cdot 8n = 80n^2 \ cm^2$ $P = 20n + 16n = 36n \ cm$

12. Conclusion: When a certain shape with perimeter P and area A is enlarged by factor n, the perimeter of the new shape is nP and its area is $n^2 A$

13. Given a triangle ABC whose sides are 3, 4 and 5 cm long.
   a. Is his a right angled triangle? Yes: 25 = 16 + 9
   a. Find its area and perimeter $A = \dfrac{12}{2} = 6 \ cm^2$ $P = 3 + 4 + 5 = 12 \ cm$
   b. The sides of another triangle whose sides are half the length of the sides of ABC are: 2.5, 2, 1.5. Is this triangle right angled? Yes 6.25 = 4 + 2.25 Find its area and perimeter.
   $A = \dfrac{3}{2} = 1.5 \ cm^2$ $P = 2.5 + 2 + 1.5 = 6 \ cm$

14. Given that the area of a square is 16 times as big as the area of a different square. Find the ratio between the sides of the squares.
$\dfrac{A_2}{A_1} = 16 = \left(\dfrac{a_1}{a_2}\right)^2 ; \dfrac{a_1}{a_2} = 4$

15. Explain the meaning of the operation "Zooming in/out" frequently used in digital imaging. Zoom means create a similar image by multiplying the distance between any 2 points by a constant. If the constant is great than 1 than we "zoom in", if the constant is between 0 and 1, we "zoom out".

2.9. – CONGRUENT AND SIMILAR TRIANGLES

1. 2 triangles are similar if all of their angles are <u>equal</u>
2. 2 triangles are similar if <u>any</u> of the following is satisfied:
   a. 2 of their angles are <u>equal (AA)</u>. Sketch an example:

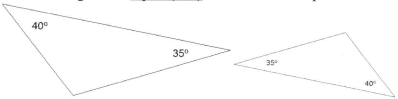

   b. 2 of their sides are <u>proportional</u> and the angles between them are <u>equal (SAS)</u>. Sketch an example:

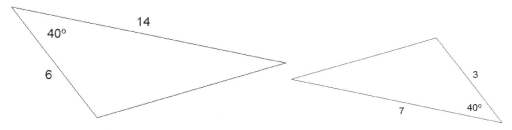

   c. All the sides are <u>proportional (SSS)</u>. Sketch an example:

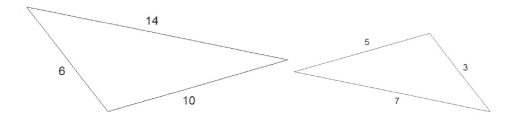

3. All right angled triangles are similar True / **False**. Sketch an example to show answer:

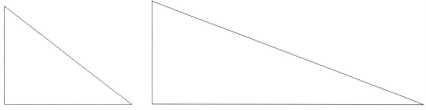

4. Congruent triangles are similar triangles with ratio of proportionality <u>1</u>
5. Similar triangles are always congruent True/**False**
6. congruent triangles are always Similar **True**/False
7. Determine if the following pair of triangles are similar, give a reason: <u>Similar, all angles are identical (AA)</u>
8. Determine if the following pair of triangles are similar, give a reason: <u>Not similar, no condition is satisfied</u>

331

9. Determine if the following pair of triangles are similar, give a reason: Not similar, no condition is satisfied
10. Determine if the following pair of triangles are similar, give a reason: Similar (SSS)
11. Determine if the following pair of triangles are similar, give a reason: Not similar, no condition is satisfied (in general for any x, y)
12. Determine if the following pair of triangles are similar, give a reason: Similar, AAA (angles are 180°/7, 360°/7, 720°/7 in both)
13. Given that $AB \parallel CD$, determine if the triangles ABE and CED are similar, give a reason: Similar, AA, ED = 4cm
14. Given that $BC \parallel DE$, determine if the triangles ABC and ADE are similar, give a reason: Similar, AA. AD = 20(1 + 0.3) = 26cm. BD = 26 – 20 = 6cm
15. The shadow of a man formed by a street light on the ground is equal to twice its height. If the man is 10m away from the street light and his height is 1.80m, how high is the street light?

    Since : $\triangle ABC \sim \triangle ADE\,(AA)$

    $$\frac{3.80}{3.80+10} = \frac{1.90}{h}$$

    $h = 6.9 m$

16. Given that $AB \parallel CD$, find ED:

    Since : $\triangle ABE \sim \triangle DCE\,(AA)$

    $$\frac{8}{5} = \frac{3}{ED}$$

    $ED = \frac{15}{8}$ cm

17. In the following triangle the angle BAC is a right angle. AD is an altitude from A to the BC. Show that triangles ABC, ADB and ADC are all similar. If BC = 10cm and AD = 2DC find the perimeter and area of ABD. All are similar as can be seen all 3 have the same angles: 90, x and 90-x.

    Since : $\triangle ABD \sim \triangle CAD\,(AA)$

    $DC = a \quad AD = 2a$

    $AC = \sqrt{5}a;\quad \dfrac{10}{\sqrt{5}a} = \dfrac{\sqrt{5}a}{a}$

    $a = 2\ cm = DC \quad AD = 4\ cm$

    $AC = 2\sqrt{5}\ cm \quad AB = 2AC = 4\sqrt{5}\ cm$

    $Perimeter_{ABD} = 12 + 4\sqrt{5}\ cm$

    $Area_{ABD} = 16\ cm^2$

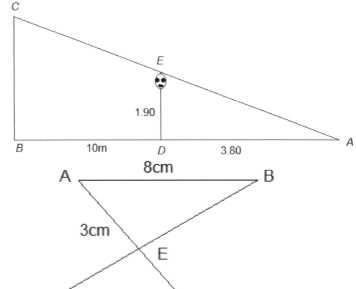

18. The following triangle AB = AC. AD is a altitude from A to the BC. Show that triangles ABD and ACD are similar. If BD = 8 cm and AB = 1.5AD, find the perimeter and area of ABC. Triangles are similar by AA (90° and y)

$$9z^2 = 4z^2 + 8^2$$

$$z = \frac{8}{\sqrt{5}}$$

$$AD = \frac{16}{\sqrt{5}} \text{ cm}; AB = \frac{24}{\sqrt{5}} \text{ cm}$$

$$Perimeter_{ABC} = 8(2 + \frac{6}{\sqrt{5}}) \text{ cm}$$

$$Area_{ABC} = \frac{128}{\sqrt{5}} \text{ cm}^2$$

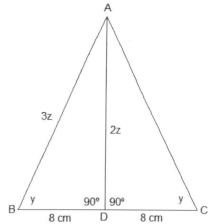

19. To measure the height of building the following operation can be performed. Jeff whose height is 180 cm puts a mirror at a distance of 20 m from a building and observed the top of the building in the mirror standing 0.4 m from it. Find the height of the building.

$$Since: \Delta ABC \sim \Delta EDC \, (AA)$$

$$\frac{1.8}{h} = \frac{0.4}{20} \quad h = 90m$$

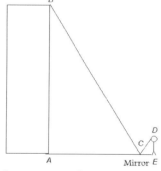

20. Given the following diagram in which triangles FDE and ABC are similar and $\frac{AB}{FD} = 2$. Find:

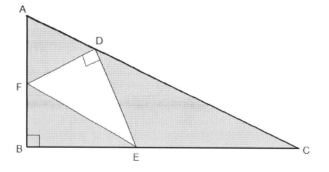

a. The percentage of the area that is shaded.
   Since triangles are similar

$$\frac{AB}{FD} = \frac{BC}{DE} = 2 \quad A_{FDE} = \frac{FD \cdot DE}{2}$$

$$A_{ABC} = \frac{AB \cdot BC}{2} = \frac{2FD \cdot 2DE}{2} = 4A_{FDE}$$

$$\frac{A_{FDE}}{A_{ABC}} = \frac{1}{4} = 0.25 = 25\% \text{ Shaded}$$

b. The percentage by which the area of ABC is bigger than the area of FDE.

$$A_{ABC} = 4A_{FDE} \quad \frac{A_{ABC} - A_{FDE}}{A_{FDE}} = \frac{3}{1} = 300\%$$

c. The percentage by which the area of FDE is smaller than the area of ABC.

$$A_{ABC} = 4A_{FDE} \quad \frac{A_{ABC} - A_{FDE}}{A_{ABC}} = \frac{3}{4} = 0.75 = 75\%$$

CHAPTER 3 – FUNCTIONS

3.1. – INTRODUCTION TO FUNCTIONS

1. Try to sketch an approximate graph for the height of a human, add some reasonable numbers to the graph:

   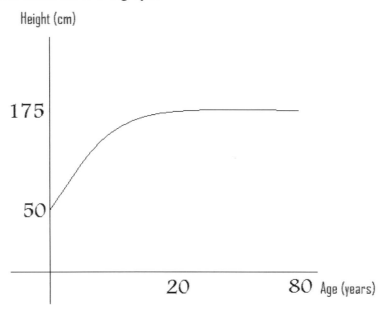

   a. Height(0) = <u>50cm</u> it is the Height of <u>a new born baby</u>
   b. Height(t) = 100cm, t = <u>2 years</u>
   c. Write the set of possible values for the Age: $Age \in [0, 80]$ this is the Domain
   d. Write the set of possible values for the Height: $Height \in [50, 175]$ this is the Range:
   e. This graph describes a function that shows how <u>height</u> depends on <u>age</u>

2. Write the definition of a function in your own words:
   <u>A one to one or many to one relation between "things" (variables),</u>

3. Write 3 examples of relations that <u>are</u> functions:
   <u>Day of the week</u> → <u>color of my shirt</u>
   <u>Word</u> → <u>First letter of word</u>
   <u>Time</u> → <u>Temperature</u>

4. The independent variable is usually represented in the <u>horizontal axis</u>

5. The dependent variable is usually represented in the <u>vertical axis</u>

6. Draw a sketch of 2 functions. Can you write the mathematical expression to describe them?

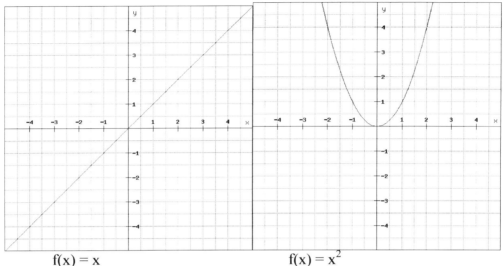

$f(x) = x$ $f(x) = x^2$

7. Write 2 examples of relations that <u>are not</u> functions:
   <u>Name of person → Personal information   (one to many)</u>
   <u>Name of City → Names of habitants   (one to many)</u>

8. Which one of the following graphs cannot represent function? Explain.

   2 y values for a certain x value.

   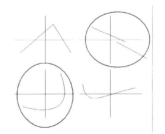

9. Draw an example of a curve that does not represent a function:

10. Draw an example of a curve that represents a function:

11. The domain of a function is the: <u>The set of allowed values of the independent variable ("what x can be")</u>

12. The Range of a function is the: <u>The set of allowed values of the dependent variable ("what y can be")</u>

13. Out of the following relations circle the ones that are functions:

    a. **Person's name → Person's age**
    b. Person's name → Person's personal information
    c. **City → Number of habitants**
    d. City → Names of habitants
    e. Family → Home Address
    f. **Family → Number of members**
    g. Family → Members of family
    h. **Satellite's name → Position of satellite**
    i. **Time → Position of object**
    j. **Time → Value of a stock**
    k. **Height → Shoe size**
    l. **Basketball player's name → Percentage of free throws scored**
    m. **Country → current unemployment rate**
    n. Country → names of unemployed citizens
    o. **Country → number of unemployed citizens**
    p. **Time → Maximum number of GB stored in a cubic centimeter**
    q. Shoe size → eye color
    r. **Football player's name → Number of goals scored in career**
    s. **One → One**
    t. One → Many
    u. **Many → One**

14. Given the Shoe size – age curve for a human. Sketch an approximate graph, pay attention that a shoe size of 32.2 does not exist, think how this is seen on the graph.

    a. Shoe size(0) = <u>17</u>, it is the Shoe size of <u>a new born</u>
    b. Shoe size (t) = 30. Age = <u>7</u>
    c. State its domain:
       $Age \in [0, 80]$
    d. State its range:
       $Shoe\ Size \in \{0,1,2,3...80\}$

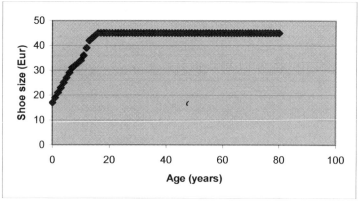

336

15. Given the following function that describes the temperature in C° as a function of time (Time = 0 corresponds to midnight):
    a. Temprature(4) = 16°
    b. Temprature (0) = 11° = Temprature (15)
    c. Temprature (7) = 18°
    d. Temprature (t) = 3, time = −5
    e. Temprature (t) = 0, time = −17.5, −7.1, 19.1
    f. Temprature (t) = −2 , time = −9, −16
    g. State its domain: $Time \in [-19, 20]$
    h. State its range: $Temp \in [-3, 19]$
    i. Function increases at: $Time \in (-12, 8)$
    j. Function decreases at: $Time \in (-19, -12) \cup (8, 20)$
    k. Is this function one to one? Many to one? Explain. Many to one, for example for instants −17.5, −7.1, 19.1 the tempratue is 0.

16. Given the function that describes the number of rabbits in the forest (N) as a function of the number of wolves (x):

    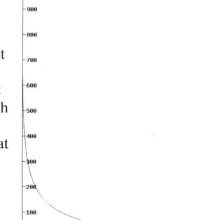

    a. Explain the tendency in your own words. Could you predict really what happens in the forest? What other kind of data you may need? Is this graph realistic? This graph is not realistic since as the number of wolves increases the number of rabbits decreases but at some point the wolves will not have enough food so their number will never grow to a point where the rabbits disappear. Beyond that of course the numerical values are not realistic.
    b. N(0) = 600 rabbits
    c. N(100) = 80 rabbits
    d. N(x) = 400. x = 10 wolves
    e. Is N(2) < N(3) ? No
    f. Is N(100) > N(101) ? yes
    g. State its domain: $Number\ of\ wolves \in \{0, 1, 2..., 280\}$
    h. State its range: $Number\ of\ rabbits \in \{0, 1, 2..., 600\}$
    i. Where is the function increasing? never
    j. Where is the function decreasing? always
    k. Where is the function stationary? never
    l. Is this function one to one? Many to one? Explain. One to one, for every "x" there is a unique "y"

17. Given the following function:

Domain   Range

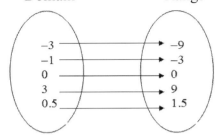
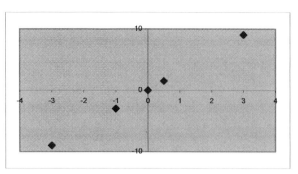

a. Allowed values for independent variable: $\{-3,-1,0,0.5,3\}$

b. Allowed values for dependent variable: $\{-9,-3,0,9,1.5\}$

c. Sketch the function on the graph.

d. A mathematical expression to express function: f(x) = 3x

18. Given the following function:

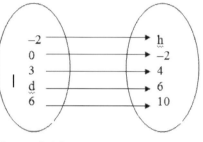

a. A mathematical expression to express this function: f(x) = 2x − 2

b. Find h. Find d. h = −6, d = 4

19. Use the graph of the gasoline consumption (f) as a function of speed (x) to answer:

a. $f(0) = $ 0L

b. $f(50) = $ 12L

c. $f(5) = $ 3L

d. For what values of x is $f(x) = 12$

    $x = 20, 60, 120$ km/h

e. Is $f(60) > f(70)$? yes

f. For what values of x is $f(x) > 12$?

    $x \in (20,60) \cup (120,140]$ km/h

g. For what values of x is $f(x) < 15$?

    $x \in [0,130]$ km/h

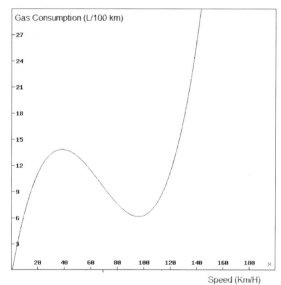

h. At what speed should the car be driven in the highway? Explain

    Approximately 100 km/h where the consumption of gasoline is minimum.

i. Where is the function increasing? $x \in (0,40) \cup (100,140)$ km/h

j. Where is the function decreasing? $x \in (40,100)$ km/h

k. Where is the function stationary? $x \in \{40,100\}$ km/h

20. Functions can be represented using: <u>graphs</u> or <u>expressions</u> or <u>lists/tables</u>

21. The graph below shows the unemployment rate in Spain between the years 2005 and 2014.

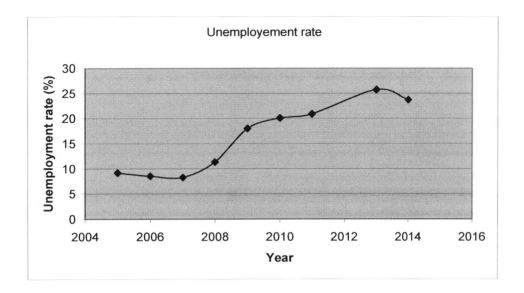

   a. What was the unemployment rate at 2008? <u>11%</u>
   b. When was the unemployment rate smaller than 10%? $Year \in [1/2005, 8/2007]$
   c. When was the unemployment rate bigger than 20%? $Year \in [1/2010, 12/2014]$
   d. When was the unemployment rate increasing? $Year \in [1/2007, 1/2013]$
   e. When was the unemployment rate decreasing?
      $Year \in (1/2005, 1/2017) \cup (4/2013, 12/2014)$
   f. State the domain and range of the function.
      $Domain: Year \in [2005, 2014]$
      $Range: Unemployement \ Rate \in [8, 26]$

22. Research the web to find functions you may be interested in, for example in the area of sports, social networks, computer science etc. You may want to search for images and try to observe the functions that appear. Try to specify in your search the term "linear functions" and observe this kind of functions as well.

3.2. – LINEAR FUNCTIONS

1. Given the function: N(x) = 60. This function represents the number of heartbeats per second of a healthy man. Complete the following table:

x	–5	–4	–3	–2	–1	0	1	2	3	4	5
N(x)	60	60	60	60	60	60	60	60	60	60	60

- The domain of the function: $x \in \mathbb{R}$
- The y intercept : (0, 60)v
- State the x intercept: None
- The function is increasing on the interval: Never
- The function is decreasing on the interval: Never
- The range of the function: $f(x) \in \{60\}$
- The heartbeat rate is 60 beats per minute

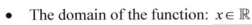

2. The distance of a John in reference to his house in his afternoon walk can be modeled by the function: D(t) = 2t + 2, t is the time in hours and D is the position in km.

t	–5	–4	–3	–2	–1	0	1	2	3	4	5
D(t)	–8	–6	–4	–2	0	2	4	6	8	10	12

- The domain of the function: $t \in \mathbb{R}$
- The y intercept: (0, 2)
- The x intercept: (–1, 0)
- The function is increasing on the interval: $t \in \mathbb{R}$
- The function is decreasing on the interval: Never
- What is the speed of John 2 km/h. How is that seen on the graph? It is the slope of the line
- State the range of the function: $f(t) \in \mathbb{R}$
- When was John at his house? At instant –1 h

3. An elevator's behavior can be modeled by: P(t) = –t + 3. Where P is the floor and t is time in minutes. The building has 15 floors and 3 parking levels below ground.

t	–5	–4	–3	–2	–1	0	1	2	3	4	5
P(t)	8	7	6	5	4	3	2	1	0	–1	–2

- State the domain of the function: $t \in [-12, 6]$
- The y intercept : (0, 3), The x intercept: (3, 0)
- The function is increasing on the interval: Never
- The function is decreasing on the interval: $t \in [-12, 6]$
- Describe the motion of the elevator The elevator is descending How is that seen on the graph? The negative slope of the line, y values are decreasing with time
- State the range of the function: $f(t) \in [-3, 15]$

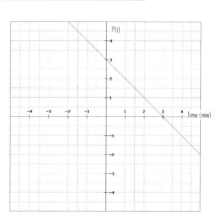

4. Given the function: $f(x) = \dfrac{x}{2} - 3$

x	−2	−1	0	1	2	3	4	5	6	7	8
f(x)	−4	−3.5	−3	−2.5	−2	−1.5	−1	−0.5	0	0.5	1

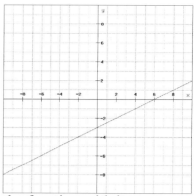

- Sketch the points of the chart on a graph
- The domain of the function: $x \in R$
- The y intercept: $(0, -3)$
- The x intercept: $(6, 0)$
- The function is increasing on the interval: $x \in R$
- The function is decreasing on the interval: Never
- State the range of the function: $f(x) \in R$

5. Given below are the equations for five different lines. Match the function with its graph.

Function	On the graph
f(x) = 20 + 2x	**B**
g(x) = 3x + 20	**C**
s(x) = −30 + 2x	**A**
a(x) = 50 − x	**D**
b(x) = − 2x + 50	**E**

6. The general functions that describes a straight line is $\underline{f(x) = mx + b}$
7. We know a function is a straight line because <u>x is to the power of 1 only</u>
8. The y–intercept (also called vertical intercept), tells us where the line crosses the <u>y axis</u>. The corresponding point is of the form <u>(0 , b)</u>.
9. The x–intercept (also called horizontal intercept), tells us where the line crosses the <u>x axis</u>. The corresponding point is of the form (p , 0).
10. If m > 0, the line <u>increases</u> left to right. If <u>m < 0</u> the line decreases left to right.
11. In case the line is horizontal m is <u>zero</u> and the line is of the form <u>f(x) = b</u>
12. The larger the value of m is, the <u>steeper</u> the graph of the line is.
13. Given the graph, write, the slope (m), b and the equation of the line:

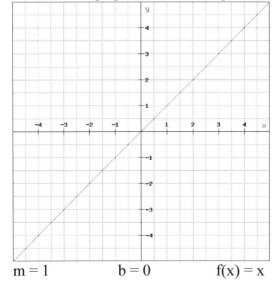

m = 1   b = 0   f(x) = x

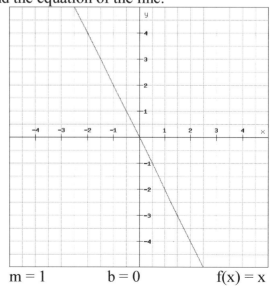

m = 1   b = 0   f(x) = x

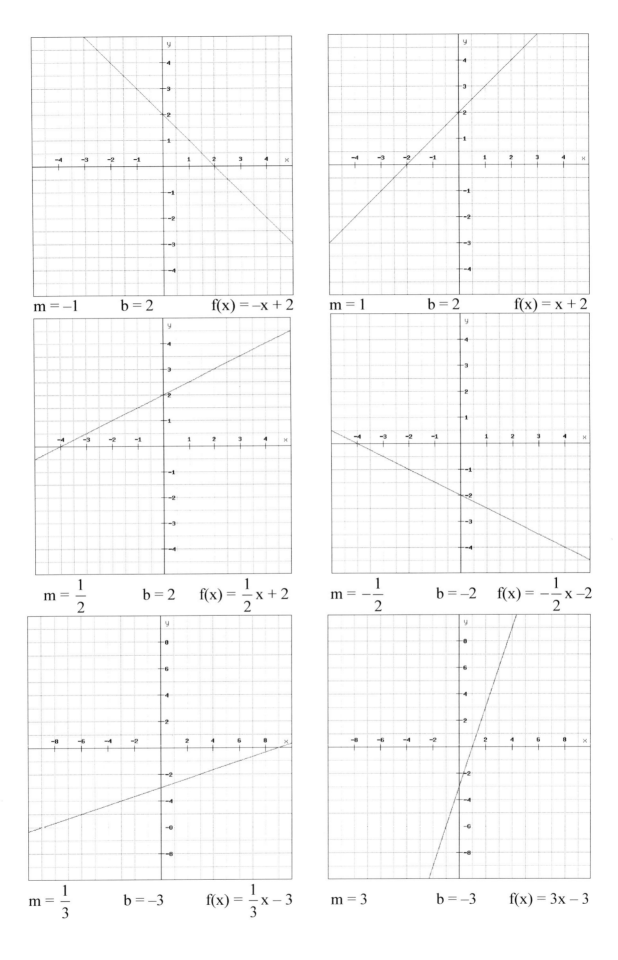

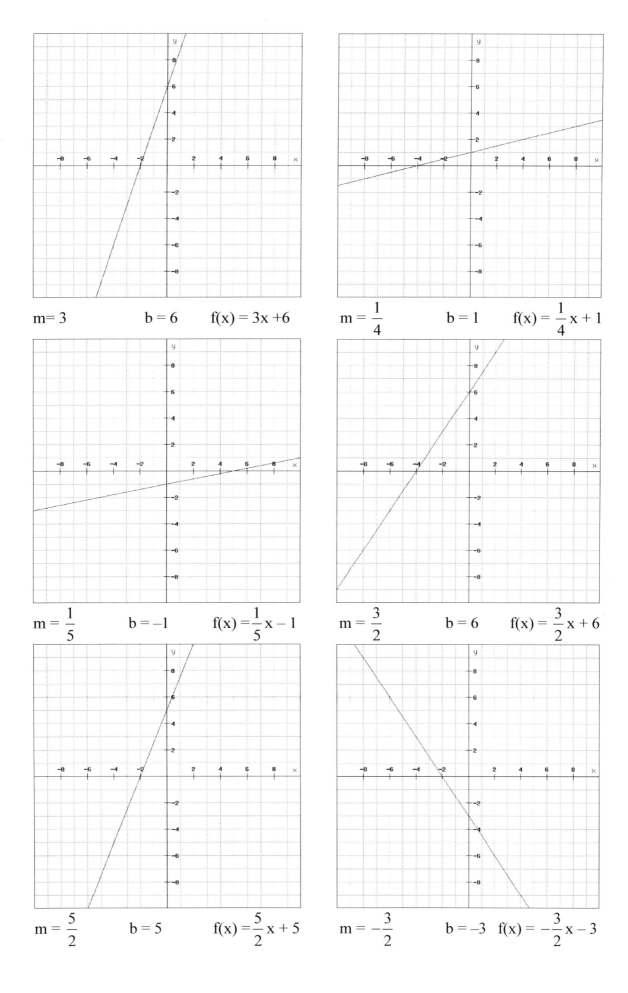

m = 3   b = 6 $f(x) = 3x + 6$

$m = \dfrac{1}{4}$ b = 1 $f(x) = \dfrac{1}{4}x + 1$

$m = \dfrac{1}{5}$ b = −1 $f(x) = \dfrac{1}{5}x - 1$

$m = \dfrac{3}{2}$ b = 6 $f(x) = \dfrac{3}{2}x + 6$

$m = \dfrac{5}{2}$ b = 5 $f(x) = \dfrac{5}{2}x + 5$

$m = -\dfrac{3}{2}$ b = −3 $f(x) = -\dfrac{3}{2}x - 3$

Analyze the following functions/inequlities:

1. f(x) = 1

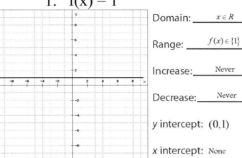

Domain: $x \in R$
Range: $f(x) \in \{1\}$
Increase: Never
Decrease: Never
y intercept: (0, 1)
x intercept: None

2. f(x) = 2

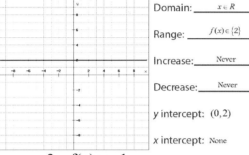

Domain: $x \in R$
Range: $f(x) \in \{2\}$
Increase: Never
Decrease: Never
y intercept: (0, 2)
x intercept: None

3. f(x) = –1

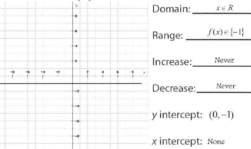

Domain: $x \in R$
Range: $f(x) \in \{-1\}$
Increase: Never
Decrease: Never
y intercept: (0, –1)
x intercept: None

4. f(x) = 0

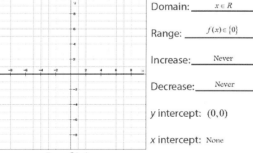

Domain: $x \in R$
Range: $f(x) \in \{0\}$
Increase: Never
Decrease: Never
y intercept: (0, 0)
x intercept: None

5. f(x) = x

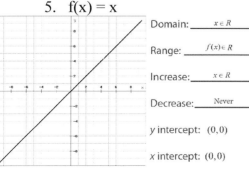

Domain: $x \in R$
Range: $f(x) \in R$
Increase: $x \in R$
Decrease: Never
y intercept: (0, 0)
x intercept: (0, 0)

6. f(x) = x+1

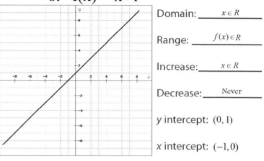

Domain: $x \in R$
Range: $f(x) \in R$
Increase: $x \in R$
Decrease: Never
y intercept: (0, 1)
x intercept: (–1, 0)

7. f(x) = –x

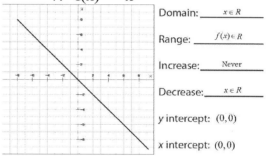

Domain: $x \in R$
Range: $f(x) \in R$
Increase: Never
Decrease: $x \in R$
y intercept: (0, 0)
x intercept: (0, 0)

8. f(x) = – x – 2

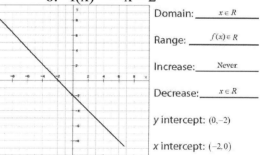

Domain: $x \in R$
Range: $f(x) \in R$
Increase: Never
Decrease: $x \in R$
y intercept: (0, –2)
x intercept: (–2, 0)

9. f(x) = 2x

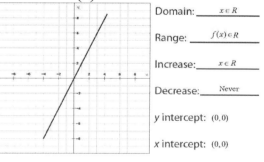

Domain: $x \in R$
Range: $f(x) \in R$
Increase: $x \in R$
Decrease: Never
y intercept: (0, 0)
x intercept: (0, 0)

10. $y \leq 3x - 5$

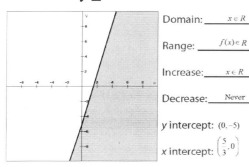

Domain: $x \in R$
Range: $f(x) \in R$
Increase: $x \in R$
Decrease: Never
y intercept: $(0,-5)$
x intercept: $\left(\frac{5}{3}, 0\right)$

11. $f(x) = 3 - 2x$

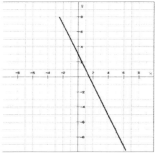

Domain: $x \in R$
Range: $f(x) \in R$
Increase: Never
Decrease: $x \in R$
y intercept: $(0,3)$
x intercept: $\left(\frac{3}{2}, 0\right)$

12. $f(x) = \frac{x}{3}$

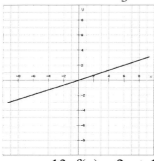

Domain: $x \in R$
Range: $f(x) \in R$
Increase: $x \in R$
Decrease: Never
y intercept: $(0,0)$
x intercept: $(0,0)$

13. $f(x) = 2x + 1$

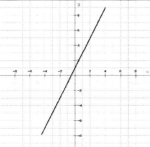

Domain: $x \in R$
Range: $f(x) \in R$
Increase: $x \in R$
Decrease: Never
y intercept: $(0,1)$
x intercept: $\left(-\frac{1}{2}, 0\right)$

14. $f(x) = 2x - 2$

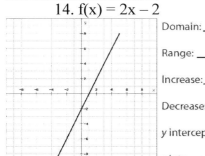

Domain: $x \in R$
Range: $f(x) \in R$
Increase: $x \in R$
Decrease: Never
y intercept: $(0,-2)$
x intercept: $(1,0)$

15. $f(x) = 3x+5$

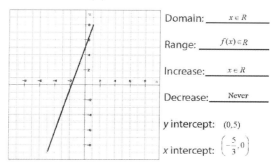

Domain: $x \in R$
Range: $f(x) \in R$
Increase: $x \in R$
Decrease: Never
y intercept: $(0,5)$
x intercept: $\left(-\frac{5}{3}, 0\right)$

16. $f(x) \leq \frac{x}{2} - 5$

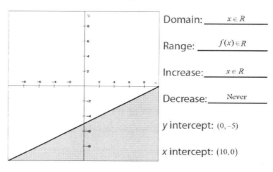

Domain: $x \in R$
Range: $f(x) \in R$
Increase: $x \in R$
Decrease: Never
y intercept: $(0,-5)$
x intercept: $(10,0)$

17. $f(x) = \frac{x}{4} + 6$

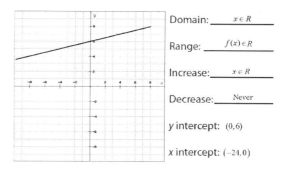

Domain: $x \in R$
Range: $f(x) \in R$
Increase: $x \in R$
Decrease: Never
y intercept: $(0,6)$
x intercept: $(-24,0)$

18. $f(x) \geq \frac{3x-10}{2} = \frac{3x}{2} - 5$

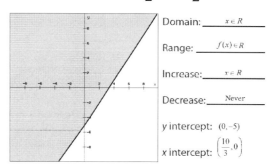

Domain: $x \in R$
Range: $f(x) \in R$
Increase: $x \in R$
Decrease: Never
y intercept: $(0,-5)$
x intercept: $\left(\frac{10}{3}, 0\right)$

19. $f(x) = -\dfrac{3}{2}x - \dfrac{3}{2}$

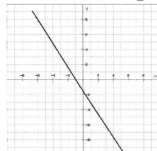

Domain: $x \in R$

Range: $f(x) \in R$

Increase: Never

Decrease: $x \in R$

y intercept: $\left(0, -\dfrac{3}{2}\right)$

x intercept: $(-1, 0)$

20. $f(x) = -\dfrac{1}{2}x - \dfrac{3}{2}$

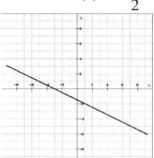

Domain: $x \in R$

Range: $f(x) \in R$

Increase: Never

Decrease: $x \in R$

y intercept: $\left(0, -\dfrac{3}{2}\right)$

x intercept: $(-3, 0)$

21. $f(x) = \dfrac{7}{2}x - \dfrac{1}{4}$

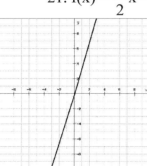

Domain: $x \in R$

Range: $f(x) \in R$

Increase: $x \in R$

Decrease: Never

y intercept: $\left(0, -\dfrac{1}{4}\right)$

x intercept: $\left(\dfrac{1}{14}, 0\right)$

22. $f(x) = -\dfrac{9}{5}x + \dfrac{8}{3}$

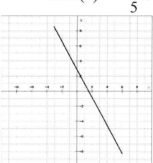

Domain: $x \in R$

Range: $f(x) \in R$

Increase: Never

Decrease: $x \in R$

y intercept: $\left(0, \dfrac{8}{3}\right)$

x intercept: $\left(\dfrac{40}{27}, 0\right)$

23. $3x + 2y = 2$

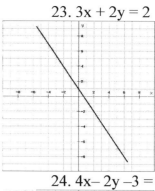

Domain: $x \in R$

Range: $f(x) \in R$

Increase: Never

Decrease: $x \in R$

y intercept: $(0, 1)$

x intercept: $\left(\dfrac{2}{3}, 0\right)$

24. $4x - 2y - 3 = 1$

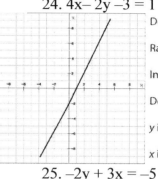

Domain: $x \in R$

Range: $f(x) \in R$

Increase: $x \in R$

Decrease: Never

y intercept: $(0, -2)$

x intercept: $(1, 0)$

25. $-2y + 3x = -5$

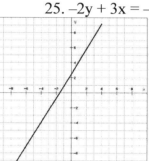

Domain: $x \in R$

Range: $f(x) \in R$

Increase: $x \in R$

Decrease: Never

y intercept: $\left(0, \dfrac{5}{2}\right)$

x intercept: $\left(-\dfrac{5}{3}, 0\right)$

26. $y - x \leq 2$

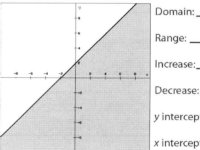

Domain: $x \in R$

Range: $f(x) \in R$

Increase: $x \in R$

Decrease: Never

y intercept: $(0, 2)$

x intercept: $(-2, 0)$

27. $y + 2x - 3 \geq 1$

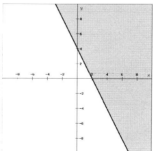

Domain: $x \in R$

Range: $f(x) \in R$

Increase: Never

Decrease: $x \in R$

y intercept: $(0, 4)$

x intercept: $(2, 0)$

28. 5y + 5x = 5

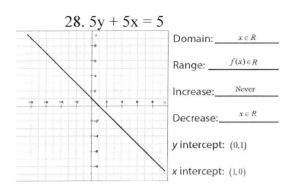

Domain: $x \in R$
Range: $f(x) \in R$
Increase: Never
Decrease: $x \in R$
y intercept: (0,1)
x intercept: (1,0)

29. 2x − 2y −3 = 1

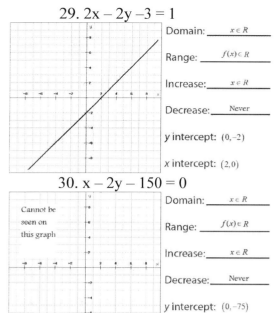

Domain: $x \in R$
Range: $f(x) \in R$
Increase: $x \in R$
Decrease: Never
y intercept: (0,−2)
x intercept: (2,0)

30. x − 2y − 150 = 0

Cannot be seen on this graph

Domain: $x \in R$
Range: $f(x) \in R$
Increase: $x \in R$
Decrease: Never
y intercept: (0,−75)
x intercept: (150,0)

31. $y = 2x; 2x - y = 0$

32. $y = \frac{1}{2}x - 2; x - 2y - 4 = 0$

33. $y = -\frac{5}{2}x - \frac{1}{2}; 5x + 2y + 1 = 0$

34. $y = 3x - 2; 3x - y - 2 = 0$

35. $y = \frac{8}{5}x - \frac{17}{5}; 8x - y - 17 = 0$

36. $y = x + 6; -x + y - 6 = 0$

37. $y = 5x + 9; -5x + y - 9 = 0$

38. $y = -\frac{1}{2}x + \frac{9}{2}; x + 2y - 9 = 0$

39. $y = -\frac{1}{5}x + 2; x + 5y - 10 = 0$

40. $y = x; y = 2x; y = -3x; y = -x; y = -\frac{1}{2}x; y = -\frac{1}{3}x$

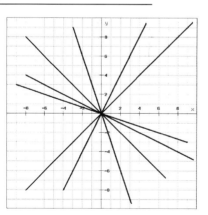

41. $y = -3x - 3$

42. $y = 2x - 4$

43. $y = -\frac{1}{2}x - 1$

44. $y = 2x + 10$

45. $2x - 3 = -5x - 2 \quad x = \frac{1}{7} \quad \left(\frac{1}{7}, -\frac{19}{7}\right)$

46. No intersection, lines are parallel.

47. $\left(\frac{7}{2}, 4\right)$

48. No intersection, lines are parallel.

347

49. $-12x-13=15x+20 \quad x=-\dfrac{33}{27} \quad \left(-\dfrac{33}{27},\dfrac{5}{3}\right)$

50. $2a=-5; a=\dfrac{-5}{2}$

51. The same line, all the points of the line are the intersection.

52. $3m-5=10; m=5$

53. $2-b=7; b=-5$

54. The same line, all the points of the line are the intersection.

55. Sketch the line $f(x)=\dfrac{-x}{2}+3, -4 \leq x < 8$

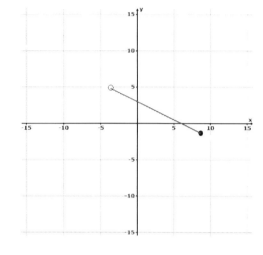

DISTANCE AND MIDPOINT BETWEEN 2 POINTS

56. Distance $=\sqrt{16+36}=\sqrt{52}$
    Midpoint $=(3,5)$

57. Distance $=\sqrt{64+64}=\sqrt{128}$
    Midpoint $=(1,-4)$

58. Distance $=\sqrt{16+25}=\sqrt{41}$
    Midpoint $=\left(-3,-\dfrac{7}{2}\right)$

59. Distance $=\sqrt{(a-5)^2+16}=5; a_1=2; a_1=8$
    Midpoint(1)$=\left(\dfrac{7}{2},1\right)$; Midpoint(2)$=\left(\dfrac{13}{2},1\right)$

60. Distance $=\sqrt{(c+4)^2+16}=10; a_1=-4+2\sqrt{21}; a_2=-4-2\sqrt{21}$
    Midpoint(1)$=\left(3,-4+\sqrt{21}\right)$; Midpoint(2)$=\left(3,-4-\sqrt{21}\right)$

61. This equation describes a circle $x^2+y^2=4$

62. This equation describes a circle $(x-2)^2+(y+1)^2=25$

63. $c^2=100; c=\pm10$ Midpoint $=(0,\pm5)$

64. Distance $=\sqrt{196+49}=\sqrt{245}$ Midpoint $=\left(-1,-\dfrac{5}{2}\right)$

PERPENDICULAR LINES ($m \cdot m_\perp = -1$)

65. A slope perpendicular to 1 is $\underline{-1}$. A slope perpendicular to 2 is $\underline{-\dfrac{1}{2}}$

   A slope perpendicular to k is $\underline{-\dfrac{1}{k}}$ A slope perpendicular to $\dfrac{a}{b}$ is $\underline{-\dfrac{b}{a}}$

66. $y = -\dfrac{1}{3}x + 13$

67. $y = \dfrac{1}{3}x + b \qquad y = \dfrac{1}{3}x + 2$

68. $y = \dfrac{5}{2}x - \dfrac{9}{2}$

69. Given the points (–2, 5) and (4, 2).

   a. $f(x) = -\dfrac{1}{2}x + 4$

   b. No: $f(5) = -\dfrac{5}{2} + 4 = \dfrac{3}{2} \neq 1$

   c. $f(x) = 2x + b \qquad$ Midpoint: $(1, \dfrac{7}{2}) \qquad f(x) = 2x + \dfrac{3}{2}$

   d. Points: $(x, 2x + \dfrac{3}{2}) \quad d = \dfrac{1}{2} = \sqrt{(0-x)^2 + \left(2 - \left(2x + \dfrac{3}{2}\right)\right)^2}$

   $x_1 = 0 \quad x_2 = \dfrac{5}{2} \quad$ Points are: $(0, \dfrac{3}{2}), (\dfrac{5}{2}, \dfrac{13}{2})$

70. Find a point on the x axis that is $\sqrt{5}$ units away from the line $y = 2x + 4$
   Points: $(a, 0), (x, 2x + 4)$

   distance $= 5 = \sqrt{(a-x)^2 + (0 - (2x+4))^2}$

   Perpendicular Slopes: $-\dfrac{1}{2} = -\dfrac{2x+4}{a-x}$,

   Solving system for a: $(\dfrac{1}{2}, 0), (-\dfrac{9}{2}, 0)$

71. Find a point on the y axis that is 5 units away from the line $y = 3x + 2$
   Points: $(0, a), (x, 3x + 2)$

   distance $= 5 = \sqrt{(0-x)^2 + (a - (3x+2))^2}$

   Perpendicular Slopes: $-\dfrac{1}{3} = \dfrac{3x+2-a}{x}$,

   Solving system for a: $a \approx 14.65$

72. Given that the slope of one of the lines is 3 and that the lines are perpendicular, find the **exact** coordinates of the point of intersection of the two lines.

Increasing line (plug (1,0): $y = 3x - 3$

Decreasing line: $y = -\dfrac{1}{3}x + 2$

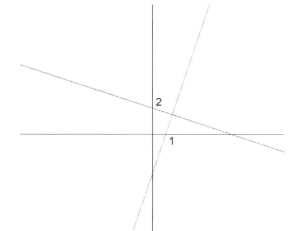

Intersection: $3x - 3 = -\dfrac{1}{3}x + 2$

$x = \dfrac{3}{2}$ $\left(\dfrac{3}{2}, \dfrac{1}{2}\right)$

SLOPE – INTERCEPT FORM OF A LINE

73. The line $y - 3 = 2(x + 1)$ passes through the point $(-1, 3)$ and has a slope of 2
74. The line $y + 5 = -3(x - 51)$ passes through the point $(51, -5)$ and has a slope of -3
75. The line $-y + 1 = (x + 3)$ passes through the point $(-3, 1)$ and has a slope of -3
76. The line $2y + 5 = -6(x + 7)$ passes through the point $(-7, -2.5)$ and has a slope of -3
77. The line $y + a = m(x + b)$ passes through the point $(-b, -a)$ and has a slope of m
78. The line $y - a = m(x - b)$ passes through the point (b, a) and has a slope of m
79. The line $y - a = m(x + b)$ passes through the point $(-b, a)$ and has a slope of m
80. The equation of $y - 3 = 2(x + 1)$ in the explicit form $y = 2x + 5$
81. The equation of $y + 5 = 2(x + 6)$ in the explicit form $y = 2x + 7$
82. The equation of a line passing through (5, 2), slope 1 $y - 1 = 1(x - 2)$
83. The equation of a line passing through (–4, –3), slope –2. $y + 3 = -2(x + 4)$
84. The equation of a line passing through (6, 3), slope $\dfrac{2}{3}$. $y - 3 = \dfrac{2}{3}(x - 3)$
85. The equation of a line passing through (–2, –5), slope $-\dfrac{2}{5}$. $y + 5 = -\dfrac{2}{5}(x + 2)$
86. The equation of the line passing through (–2, –5), (–7, –5), $y + 5 = 0(x + 2); y = -5$
87. The equation of the line passing through (–1, –3), (6, 5), $y + 3 = \dfrac{8}{7}(x + 1)$
88. The equation of the line passing through (–1, 5), (7, –2), $y - 5 = -\dfrac{7}{8}(x + 1)$

APPLICATION

1. The price of a new TV (in US$) is $P(t) = 500 - 20t$, t given in months.
   a. Sketch the corresponding graph.
   b. The initial price of the TV?   500$
   c. The price of the TV after 10 days   300$
   d. The domain of the function, argument the answer, $t \in [0, 25]$ Price cannot be negative.
   e. The range of the function? $P \in [0, 500]$
   f. What is the meaning of 20? Does it have units? What are they? $20\$/month$, it is the monthly reduction of the price.

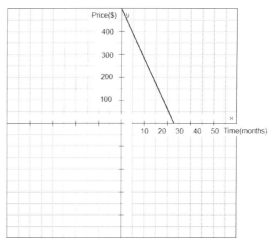

2. A certain computer has 10000 MB (Megabytes) of memory occupied by the operating system and it can store information at 200 MB per second. It is known that the Hard disk of the computer is full when 500000 MB (500 GB) is reached.
   a. The function to describe the amount of memory occupied as a function of time while the computer stores information
      $M(t) = 10000 + 200t$
   b. State its domain and range.
      $500000 = 10000 + 200t \quad t = 2450s$
      $t \in [0, 2450] \quad M \in [10000, 500000]$
   c. What are the units of the slope?
      $MB/\sec ond$
   d. How long will it take the computer to store a 700 MB file? $\dfrac{700}{200} = 3.5s$
   e. In case it took the computer 5 seconds to store a file, find the size of the file?
      $5 \cdot 200 = 1000 MB = 1GB$

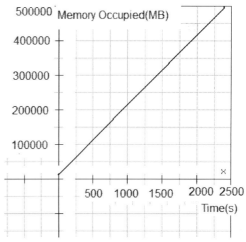

3.
   a. The functions to describe the cost C as a function of the number of products n for both machines. Indicate the domain and range of both functions. What are the units of the slope?
      C1(n) = 250 + 2n   C2(n) = 200 + 4n
      Domain: $n \in [0, 200]$ Domain: $n \in [0, 200]$
      Range: $C1 \in [250, 650]$ Range: $C2 \in [200, 1000]$
   b. Graph the functions, use appropriate scale, variables and units. Calculate the coordinates of important points on the graph.
      250 + 2n = 200 + 4n
      n = 25, C1(25) = C2(25) = 300$
   c. Discuss in which case each machine is best.
      If $0 \leq n \leq 25$ Machine 1, If $25 \leq n \leq 200$ Machine 2

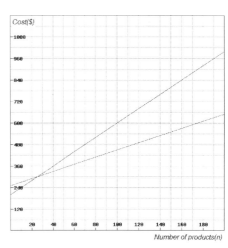

351

4. A parking lot with 1200 parking is full after 5 hours.

   a. Write the function to describe the number of cars N as function of time t in hours. Indicate the domain and range of the function. What are the units of the slope?
   $N(t) = 240t \quad t \in [0,5]$
   $N \in [0,1200]$ Units of slope : cars/hour

   b. If the parking opens at 7, Find the number of free spots at 8:30.
   $N(t) = 240 \cdot 1.5 = 360$
   $1200 - 360 = 840$ free spots

   c. In case the owner needs 400 free spots after how long should he close the parking?
   $800 = 240 \cdot t \quad t = 3.33h \quad (3h:20\min)$

   d. Graph the function, use appropriate scale, variables and units.

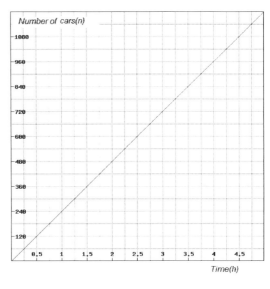

5. You need to rent a car for one day and to compare the charges of 3 different companies. Company I charges 20$ per day with additional cost of 0.20$ per mile. Company II charges 30$ per day with additional cost of 0.10$ per mile. Company III charges 60$ per day with no additional mileage charge.

   a. Write the cost function for each one of the companies.
   $C_I = 20 + 0.2x$
   $C_{II} = 30 + 0.1x$
   $C_{III} = 70$

   b. Sketch all 3 graphs on the same axes system.

   c. Comment on the circumstances in which renting a car from each one of the companies is best.
   The black line represent the cheapest price:
   It is important to find the intersection points between: lines I, II and lines II, III.
   I, II: (100, 40)
   II, III (400, 70)

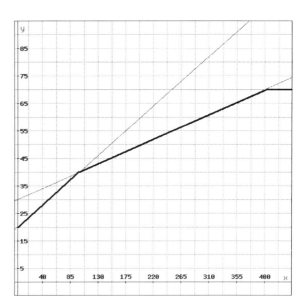

   If we travel less than 100 miles Company I is best.
   If we travel between 100 and 400 miles Company II is best.
   If we travel more than 400 miles Company III is best.

6. A container filled with water is being emptied as can be seen in the diagram. The following graph describes the water level in the container as a function time:

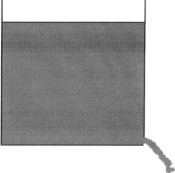
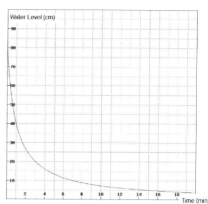

   a. The water level in the beginning? 80cm
   b. It takes the water level to go down by 50% 1 minute (to 40 cm)
   c. It takes the water level to go down by 75% 3 minutes (to 20 cm)
   d. The water level went down after 7 minutes by $\dfrac{70}{80} = \dfrac{7}{8} = 0.875 = 87.5\%$
   e. The water level went down after 15 minutes by $\dfrac{75}{80} = 0.9375 = 93.75\% \approx 94\%$
   f. According to the graph, how long do you think it will take the container to be emptied completely? An infinite amount of time
   g. Is this a linear function? Explain. This is not a linear function since it does not have a constant slope

7. The height of a ball above ground as a function of time (t) in seconds is given by the following function: $Height(t) = -t(t-4)$.

   a. Fill the table:

Time(s)	0	1	2	3	4	5	6
Height(m)	0	3	4	4	0	−5	−12

   b. Draw the corresponding points on the graph: Include the corresponding numbers. Is this motion linear? Explain

   This is clearly not a linear function as the ball goes up and then down, there is no constant slope.

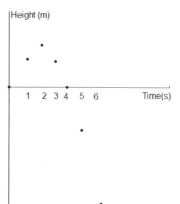

8. The cost of making a certain product ($) is given by the function
   $Cost(n) = \dfrac{100}{n} + 5$ where n is the number of products made in thousands.

   a. Fill the table:

Number of products made(n)	1	2	4	5	10	20	50	100
Cost($)	105	55	30	25	15	10	7	6

   b. Draw the corresponding points on the graph. Include the corresponding numbers. Is this graph linear? Explain
   This graph is not linear as can be seen the slope is not constant

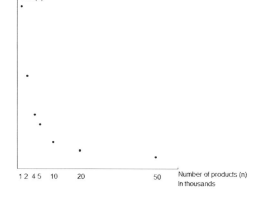

TRAVEL GRAPHS

1. Describe the motion of the train, the vertical axis represents the distance from its objective: <u>Since the distance does not change it means the train is not moving.</u>
2. Describe the motion of the object, the vertical axis represents the distance from its objective: <u>The train is moving towards its objective at a speed of 1 km/min</u>
3. Describe the motion of the following object; the vertical axis describes the distance of the object from point A. Is this motion a realistic one? Explain.
   <u>The object is moving away from point A, then stays still for a while, the moves towards point A, reaches it and stays still, finally moves away from point A and then stays still. The motion is not realistic because the change from motion to non-motion is instantaneous and that is not possible.</u>
4. Determine if the following graph can describe a motion of an object, explain and describe the motion if possible. <u>The following graph cannot describe the motion of an object because it implies that the distance of an object from another object is different at the same time.</u>
5. Determine if the following graph can describe a motion of an object, explain and describe the motion if possible. <u>The following graph cannot describe the motion of an object because it implies that there are 2 possible distances of an object from another object at the same time.</u>
6. Determine if the following graph can describe a motion of an object, explain and describe the motion if possible. <u>Yes, it can describe the motion of an object. The object moves towards the reference until hour 7 and then stops and starts moving away from the reference.</u>
7. Given the following graph describing the motion of a certain object. Describe the motion providing the speed of the object in each part of the trip. Object moves away from reference (A) at about 40/3 km/h, suddenly starts moving towards it at about 50/3 km/h until it reaches the reference (B) at t = 6h. It immediately starts moving away from it (C) for 1 hour at about 10 km/h, then stops for 2 hours (D) and suddenly continues moving away from it at 20 km/h (E). Lastly it increases the speed to 50 km/h as it gets away from the reference (F).

CHAPTER 4 - STATISTICS

4.1. – STATISTICS

1. The set of objects that we are trying to study is called population. the number of elements in the population can be finite or infinite.
2. Usually the population is too big and therefore we obtain a sample. This process is called sampling.
3. We use the sample to obtain conclusions about the population.

Types of DATA

4. Categorical data.
5. Numerical data that can be divided to continuous or discrete.
6. Numerical discrete can be counted while numerical continuous data can be measured.
7. Give 3 examples of Categorical data:
   Eye color (blue, green, brown etc.)
   Favorite food (meat, pasta, ice cream etc.)
   Preferred website (whatever.com, whatsup.com etc.)
8. Give 3 examples of numerical discrete data:
   Number of students in a classroom
   Shoe size
   Number of rabbits in the forest
9. Give 3 examples of numerical continuous data:
   Height of people
   Amount of energy in a laser beam
   CO_2 level in the atmosphere
10. Given the following variables, classify them in the table:

Categorical	Numerical Discrete	Numerical Continuous
Eye color	Shoe size	Height
Type of fruit	Number of cars in a parking lot	Weight
Name of writer	Number of apples sold a day in a store	Velocity of the wind
	Numbers of pages in a book	Temperature
	Number of students in a school	

11. In a certain class the favorite dessert of students was studies. The following results were obtained:

Ice cream, fruit, Ice cream, coffee, cake, fruit, fruit, cake, cake, Ice cream, fruit, cake, cake

   a. How many students participated? <u>13</u>
   b. What kind of data is this? <u>Categorical</u>
   c. Organize the information in a table (use technology)

Type of food	Ice cream	Fruit	Coffee	Cake
Number of times selected	3	4	1	5

   d. Represent the information in a Bar Chart (use technology)

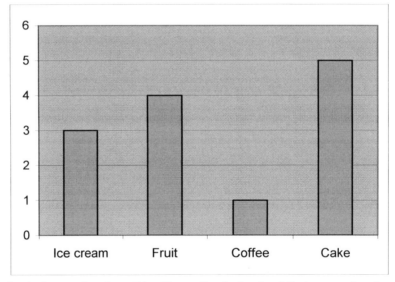

   e. Represent the information in a Pie Chart (include the %) (use technology)

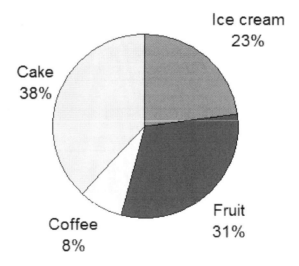

12. In a certain math class the following grades were obtained:

    70, 70, 70, 70, 70, 70, 70, 80, 80, 80, 80, 90, 90, 90

    a. How many students in the classroom? 14
    b. What kind of data is this? Numerical discrete
    c. Represent this information in a table (group) (use technology)

Grade	70	80	90
Number of times repeated	7	4	3

    d. Use the table to create a bar graph (use technology)

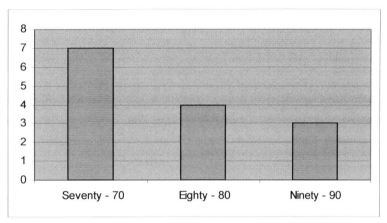

13. In a certain math class the following grades were obtained:

    65, 72, 85, 89, 52, 71, 89, 68, 63, 76, 61, 86, 98, 79, 79, 91, 74, 89, 77, 68, 78

    a. How many students participated? 21
    b. What kind of data is this? Numerical discrete
    c. Suggest a method to represent this information in a table. By grouping

    d. Use the table to create a bar graph

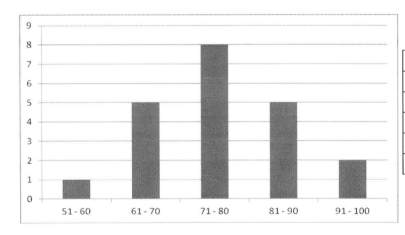

Grade	Number of students
51 - 60	1
61 - 70	5
71 - 80	8
81 - 90	5
91 - 100	2

14. In a certain zoo the length of a certain type of animal (in meters) was studied.

   a. How many animals participated? 14
   b. What kind of data is this? Numerical continuous
   c. Represent the information in a Bar Chart. In this case we must choose Intervals
   d. Use the table to create a bar graph (use technology)

[1.50, 1.60)	3
[1.60, 1.70)	4
[1.70, 1.80)	4
[1.80, 1.90)	2
[1.90, 2.00)	1

Wider or narrower intervals could have been chosen

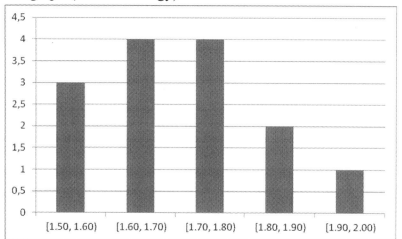

15. In a certain group shoe size was studied and the following results obtained:

    45, 36, 44, 38, 41, 42, 48, 39, 40, 42, 43, 41, 38, 45, 41, 38, 42, 44, 41, 41, 46

   a. How many students participated? 21
   b. What kind of data is this? Numerical discrete
   c. Suggest a method to represent this information in a table. By grouping
   d. Use the table to create a bar graph

Shoe size	Number of people
[36, 38]	4
[39, 41]	7
[42, 44]	6
[45, 47]	3
[48, 50]	1

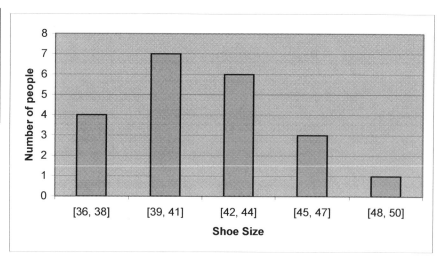

16. The number of imperfections in a certain product was studies and the following results obtained in a group of products:

    0, 1, 0, 0, 1, 2, 0, 2, 0, 3, 0, 0, 2, 1, 0, 0, 0, 1, 1, 2, 0, 3, 0, 1, 1, 0, 0, 0, 1, 0

    a. How many products were tested? <u>30</u>
    b. What kind of data is this? <u>Numerical discrete</u>
    c. Suggest a method to represent this information in a table (use technology)

Number of imperfections	Zero	One	Two	Three
Number of times appeared	16	8	4	2

    d. Use the table to create a bar graph (use technology)

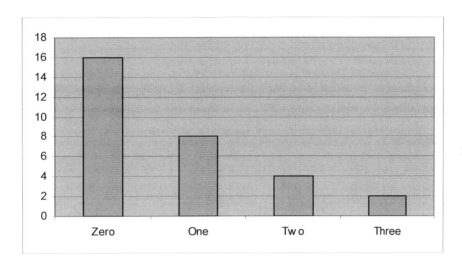

17. Choose a variable to collect information about in your classroom, state its kind, represent the information in a table and create a bar graph. (use technology)

4.2. – BIVARIATE DATA AND SCATTER PLOTS

1. In many occasions variables may be related to each other, for example:
   - Age – Height
   - Level of education – Average income
   - Resistance to wind – gasoline consumption

   Give 3 other examples; discuss the kind of relation that exists between the variables:
   - Age – Weight,
   - Age – Shoe size
   - Height – Weight
   - Percentage of HW done – Grade
   - Time – Position of an airplane
   - Month unemployement level – Amount of taxes collected in that month

   The relation between variables is called: <u>correlation, it can be positive, negative, strong, weak, etc.</u>

2. Given the following data about a group of students and the corresponding graph:

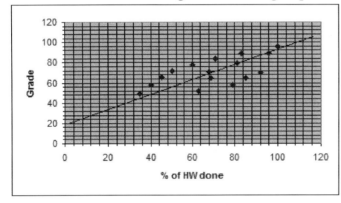

Student	% of HW done	Grade
Helena	71	84
Alexandra	68	71
Alicia	95	89
Ben	45	66
Sofia	85	65
Blanca	63	52
Anabel	35	49
Elena	40	58
Isabella	77	78
Elia	83	82
Raquel	100	96
Núria	92	70
Pablo	69	70
Martim	81	79
Iris	67	72
Carlota	79	58

   a. Sketch an approximate straight line that best fits the data.
   b. Find the equation of the line.
      Selecting 2 points approximately on the line:
      $(100, 95)$, $(20, 35)$
      $$y - 35 = \frac{100-35}{95-35}(x-20)$$
      $$y = \frac{13}{12}x + \frac{170}{3}$$
   c. Comment on the correlation between doing HW and obtaining grades. <u>There is a positive strong approximtley linear correlation between the percentage of HW done and the grade.</u>

360

3. Life expectancy of different animals was studies and the following data obtained:

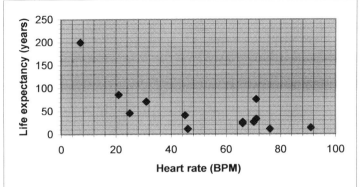

Heart rate (BPM)	Life expectancy (years)
7	200
25	46
71	76
31	71
21	86
66	26
66	23
45	41
76	11
91	14
46	11
71	33
70	26

Discuss the nature of the correlation between the heart rate and life expectancy of animals. There is a strong negative non-linear correlation between hear rate and life expectancy. It is clear that the lower the heart rate is the higher life expectancy is.

4. Kinetic energy of an object is given by the expression: $E = \frac{1}{2}mv^2$ where m is the mass of the object and v is the speed of the object. Given an object of 4 kg, fill the following table:

v (m/s)	0	1	2	3	4	5	6	7
E (J)	0	2	8	18	32	50	72	98

Add the corresponding points to the graph and discuss the nature of this correlation. There is a strong positive non-linear correlation between velocity and energy.

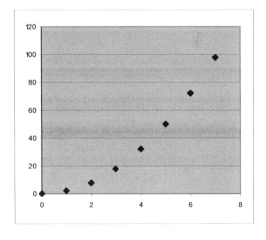

5. The relation between variables is called: correlation and if it is linear it can be classified in the following way..
6. This correlation is characterized by a certain number called correlation coefficient (r).
7. In case of a perfect positive correlation the value of r is 1
8. In case of a perfect negative correlation the value of r is –1
9. In case of a no correlation the value of r is 0
10. Finally r is between –1 and 1

11. In a certain math class the following data about students was found:
    a. Represent the data on a graph (choose an appropriate scale)

Name	John	Dean	Elisa	Marc	Heather	Alicia	Raquel	Kevin	Alex	Deena
HW Done %	58	90	75	50	40	95	100	85	75	82
Grade(%)	70	80	80	65	55	78	86	89	82	70

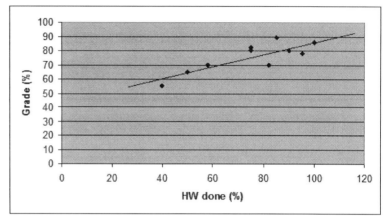

b. Is there correlation? <u>Yes there is</u>, what kind? It seems <u>approximately linear</u>.
c. Sketch a line that best fits the data and find its equation. <u>Using 2 points on the graph:</u>
$(40,60)(100,85)$
$y - 60 = \frac{25}{60}(x - 40)$
$y = \frac{5}{12}x + \frac{130}{3}$

d. Use your equation to predict the grade of a student that did 72% of the HW.
$y = \frac{5}{12}72 + \frac{130}{3} \approx 73.3\%$

e. A student obtained a grade of 77, find the percentage of the HW she did.
$77 = \frac{5}{12}x + \frac{130}{3} \qquad x = 80.8$

12. In a group of students, height and weight correlation was studies. The results are given by the table below.
    a. Represent the data on a graph (choose an appropriate scale)

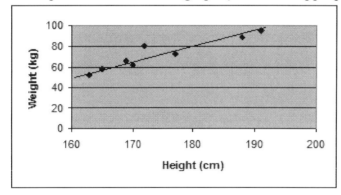

Height (cm)	Weight (kg)
165	58
170	62
172	80
169	65
188	88
163	52
191	95
177	72

b. Is there correlation? <u>Yes there is</u>, what kind? It seems <u>approximately linear</u>.
c. Sketch a line that best fits the data and find its equation.
$(160,50)(190,90) \qquad y - 50 = \frac{40}{30}(x - 160) \qquad y = \frac{4}{3}x - \frac{490}{3}$

d. Use your equation to predict the weight of a student whose height is 180 cm
$y = \frac{4}{3}180 - \frac{490}{3} \approx 76.6 kg$

e. A student's weight is 78 kg, find his height.
$78 = \frac{4}{3}x + \frac{790}{3} \qquad x = 181 cm$

13. In a group of students the reading speed was studied in relation to age of the student. The results are given by the table below.

a. Represent the data on a graph (choose an appropriate scale)

Age (years)	Spelling errors in a 1000 words
15	3
12	10
17	2
19	3
18	2
16	5
19	2
17	3
13	8
14	9
14	7
15	6

b. Is there correlation? <u>Yes, there is.</u> What kind? <u>It seems approximately linear although maybe becomes more flat in later years.</u>

c. Sketch a line that best fits the data and find its equation.

$(12,10)(20,0) \quad y - 0 = \dfrac{-10}{8}(x - 20) \quad y = -\dfrac{5}{4}x + 25$

d. Use your equation to predict the number of spelling errors of a student who is 13 years old.

$y = -\dfrac{5}{4}13 + 25 = 8.75 \, errors$

e. Use your equation to predict the age of a student who made 4 spelling errors.

$4 = -\dfrac{5}{4}x + 25 \quad x = 16.8 \approx 17 \, years$

TWO WAY TABLES

1. In a certain study the following data was obtained:

	Smokers	None-smokers	Total
Male	27	56	83
Female	35	78	113
Total	62	134	196

   a. Fill the missing parts of the table.
   b. This type of tables is called: Two way tables
   c. Write down the number of participants in the study: 196
   d. Find the percentage of smokers in the sample: $\frac{62}{196} \approx 0.32 = 32\%$
   e. Find the percentage of non-smokers in the sample: $\frac{134}{196} \approx 0.68 = 68\%$
   f. Find the percentage of male smokers in the sample: $\frac{27}{196} \approx 0.14 = 14\%$
   g. Find the percentage of female smokers in the sample: $\frac{35}{196} \approx 0.18 = 18\%$

2. In a certain study the following data was obtained:

	High Blood Pressure	Normal Blood Pressure	Low Blood Pressure	Total
Overweight	50	56	25	131
Normal weight	35	78	44	157
Total	85	134	69	288

   a. Fill the missing parts of the table.
   b. This type of tables is called Two way tables
   c. Write down the number of participants in the study: 288
   d. Find the percentage of overweight in the sample: $\frac{131}{288} \approx 0.45 = 45\%$
   e. Find the percentage of normal weight in the sample: $\frac{157}{288} \approx 0.55 = 55\%$
   f. Find the percentage of high blood pressure in the sample: $\frac{85}{288} \approx 0.30 = 30\%$ normal blood pressure in the sample: $\frac{134}{288} \approx 0.47 = 47\%$ low blood pressure in the sample: $\frac{69}{288} \approx 0.23 = 23\%$

3. Some students were asked about their favorite subject. The following information was obtained

   a. Fill the missing parts of the table.

	Math	History	English	Total
Male	123	86	102	311
Female	x	109	100	209 + x
Total	123 + x	195	202	520 + x

   b. It is known that the percentage of male in the sample is 50%, find x

   $$\frac{311}{520+x} = 0.5 \qquad x = 102$$

   c. Find the percentage of female students who prefer math: $\frac{102}{622} \approx 0.16 = 16\%$

   d. Find the percentage of male students who prefer math: $\frac{123}{622} \approx 0.20 = 20\%$

   e. Draw a conclusion from your results: It seems that in this sample more males prefer math than females.

4. A new medicine called "Unbroken heart" for heart diseases is being tested and the following results obtained:

	Used "Unbroken heart"	Did not use "Unbroken heart"	Total
Cured	77	y	77 + y
Not Cured	43	45	88
Total	120	45 + y	165 + y

   a. Fill the missing parts of the table.
   b. It is known that the percentage of patients who did not use "Unbroken heart" is 40%, find y

   $$\frac{45+y}{165+y} = 0.4 \qquad y = 35$$

   c. Find the percentage of cured patients who used "Unbroken heart" in the sample:
   $$\frac{77}{200} = 0.385 = 38.5\%$$

   d. Find the percentage of cured patients who did not use "Unbroken heart" in the sample:
   $$\frac{35}{200} = 0.175 = 17.5\%$$

   e. Draw a conclusion about the medicine "Unbroken heart": The medicine seems to work as the percentage of cured patients using it is much higher than the percentage of patients who were cured without using.

4.3. – MEAN, MEDIAN, MODE AND FREQUENCY DIAGRAMS

1. The mean is <u>the arithmetic "average", adding the numbers and dividing by the number of elements.</u>
2. The mode is <u>element that repeats most.</u>
3. The median is <u>the value of the element such that the number of smaller than it and elements and bigger than it is equal (the element "in the middle")</u>
   If the number of elements is <u>odd</u> the median will be the element in the $\frac{n+1}{2}$ position. If the number of elements is <u>even</u> the median will be the <u>mean</u> of the elements in the positions $\frac{n}{2}$ and $\frac{n}{2}+1$
4. In a certain club the number of visitors per days was studied during 1 week and the following results obtained: 50, 52, 51, 55, 55, 70, 65

   a. State the number of elements in the set: 7
   b. What kind of data is this? <u>Numerical discrete</u>
   c. Find its mean: $\frac{398}{7} \approx 56.9$ Find its mode: 55
   d. Write the data in an increasing order: 50, 51, 52, 55, 55, 65, 70
   e. Find its Median: 55

5. In a certain restaurant the amount of meat (kg) consumed per day was studied and the following results obtained: 11.5, 12.2, 14.6, 15.0, 23.2, 21.2, 10.1, 13.1

   a. State the number of elements in the set: 8
   b. What kind of data is this? <u>Numerical continuous</u>
   c. Find its mean: $\frac{120.9}{9} \approx 15.1$ Find its mode: None
   d. Write the data in an increasing order:
      10.1, 11.5, 12.2, **13.1, 14.6**, 15.0, 21.2, 23.2,
   e. Find its Median: $\frac{13.1+14.6}{2} = 13.85$

6. In a certain math class the number of exercises per day given for HW is the following: 5, 6, 6, 6, 4, 4, 5, 5, 4, 5, 6, 6, 7, 3, 0, 3

   a. State the number of elements in the set: 16
   b. What kind of data is this? <u>Numerical discrete</u>
   c. Find its mean: $\frac{75}{16} \approx 4.69$ Find its mode: 6
   d. Write the data in an increasing order:

      0, 3, 3, 4, 4, 4, 5, **5, 5**, 5, 6, 6, 6, 6, 6, 7

   e. Find its Median: $\frac{5+5}{2} = 5$

7. In the following data: 2, 2, 3, 3, 9, 9, 9 one natural number is missing. It is known that the median with the missing number is 3. Find all the possible values of the missing number.

    The number can be 1:   1, 2, 2, **3, 3**, 9, 9, 9   (median 3)
    The number can be 2:   2, 2, 2, **3, 3**, 9, 9, 9   (median 3)
    The number can be 3:   2, 2, 3, **3, 3**, 9, 9, 9   (median 3)

So the missing number is either 1, 2 or 3.

8. In a certain math class the following grades were obtained:

68, 79, 75, 89, 54, 81, 88, 62, 67, 75, 64, 85, 97, 77, 79, 90, 75, 89, 76, 68

   a. State the number of elements in the set: <u>20</u>
   b. What kind of data is this? <u>Numerical discrete</u>
   c. Find its mean: $\mu = \dfrac{1538}{20} \approx 76.9$ Find its mode: <u>75</u>
   d. Write the data in an increasing order:
      54, 62, 64, 67, 68, 68, 75, 75, 75, 76, 77, 79, 79, 81, 85, 88, 89, 89, 90, 97
   e. Find its Median: $M = \dfrac{76+77}{2} = 76.5$ Q1 = <u>68</u>   Q3 = <u>86.5</u>
   f. Fill the table:

Grade	Mid – Grade (Mi)	Frequency (fi)	fi x Mi	Cumulative Frequency (Fi)	Fi (%)
[51, 60]	55.5	1	55.5	1	5
[61, 70]	65.5	5	327.5	6	30
[71, 80]	75.5	7	528.5	13	65
[81, 90]	85.5	6	513	19	95
[91, 100]	95.5	1	95.5	20	100
Total		20	1520		

   g. Use the table to find the mean: $\mu = \dfrac{1520}{20} = 76$ Comment on the result compared to the previous mean obtained. <u>Since the data was grouped the mean obtained is very similar but not identical to previous one.</u>
   h. Discuss the advantages and disadvantages of organizing information in a table. <u>The big advantage is that the data is much easier to read and understand, analyze. The disadvantage is that some accuracy is lost.</u>
   i. Is this the only possible choice for the left column of the table? Why? Discuss the advantages and disadvantages of organizing information in such a way.
      <u>No it is not the only possibility. Narrower or wider intervals can be chosen. Narrower interval implies higher accuracy but information may be harder to understand and/or analyze. It also implies more work. Wider interval implies lower level of accuracy but information may be easier to understand and/or analyze. It also implies less work.</u>

j. Design a new table with a different interval

Grade	Mid – Grade (Mi)	Frequency (fi)	fi · Mi	Cumulative Frequency (Fi)	Fi (%)
[51, 55]	53	1	53	1	5
[56, 60]	58	0	0	1	5
[61, 65]	63	2	126	3	15
[66, 70]	68	3	204	6	30
[71, 75]	73	3	219	9	45
[76, 80]	78	4	312	13	65
[81, 85]	83	2	166	15	75
[86, 90]	88	4	352	19	95
[91, 95]	93	0	0	19	95
[96, 100]	98	1	98	20	100
Total		20	1530		

k. Use the table to find the mean: $\mu = \dfrac{1530}{20} = 76.5$ Comment on the result compared to the previous mean obtained. Since more intervals are used the result is more accurate.

l. The mean of the population is denoted with the Greek letter mu: μ and typically it is unknown The mean of the sample is denoted by $\bar{x}$

m. Find the modal interval in both tables: 1st: [71, 80] 2nd: [76, 80], [86, 90]

n. In general this method of organizing information is called grouping

o. The 1st column is called class with upper interval boundary and lower interval boundary.

p. The 2nd column is called Mid - Class

9. In a certain class the following heights (in m) of students were collected:
   a. State the number of elements in the set: 14
   b. What kind of data is this? Numerical continuous
   c. Find its mean: $\mu = \dfrac{23.99}{14} \approx 1.71m$ Find its mode: 1.70, 1.77 (bimodal)
   d. Write the data in an increasing order:
      1.51, 1.54, 1.60, 1.65, 1.66, 1.67, 1.70, 1.70, 1.73, 1.77, 1.77, 1.86, 1.89, 1.94
   e. Find its Median: $M = 1.70m$.   Q1 = 1.65m   Q3 = 1.77m
   f. Fill the table:

Grade	Mid – Grade (Mi)	Frequency (fi)	fi x Mi	Cumulative Frequency (Fi)	Fi (%)
[1.50, 1.60)	1.55	2	3.1	2	15.4
[1.60, 1.70)	1.65	4	6.6	6	46.2
[1.70, 1.80)	1.75	5	8.75	10	76.9
[1.80, 1.90)	1.85	2	3.7	12	92.3
[1.90, 2.00)	1.95	1	1.95	13	100
Total		14	24.1		

g. Use the table to find the mean: $\mu = \dfrac{24.1}{14} \approx 1.72 m$. Comment on the result compared to the previous mean obtained. <u>Since the data was grouped the mean obtained is very similar but not identical to previous one.</u>

h. Discuss the advantages and disadvantages of organizing information in a table. <u>The big advantage is that the data is much easier to read and understand, analyze. The disadvantage is that some accuracy is lost</u>
Is this the only possible choice for the left column of the table? Why? Discuss the advantages and disadvantages of organizing information in such a way. <u>No it is not the only possibility. Narrower or wider intervals can be chosen. Narrower interval implies higher accuracy but information may be harder to understand and/or analyze. It also implies more work.
Wider interval implies lower level of accuracy but information may be easier to understand and/or analyze. It also implies less work.</u>

10. In a certain class students eye color was collected:
   Brown, Black, Brown, Blue, Brown, Blue, Green, Brown, Black, Green
   a. State the number of elements in the set: <u>10</u>
   b. What kind of data is this? <u>Categorical</u>
   c. Fill the table:

Eye Color	Mid – Color (Mi)	Frequency (fi)	fi x Mi	Cumulative Frequency (Fi)	Fi (%)
Brown	N/A	4	N/A	N/A	N/A
Blue	N/A	2	N/A	N/A	N/A
Green	N/A	2	N/A	N/A	N/A
Black	N/A	2	N/A	N/A	N/A
Total	N/A	10	N/A	N/A	N/A

   d. Obtain the mean: <u>N/A</u>
   e. State the mode of the set: <u>Brown</u>
   f. Find the modal interval: <u>N/A</u>
   g. Find the Median using the original data: <u>N/A</u>
   h. Find the median using the table, discuss your answer. <u>N/A</u>
   i. Represent the data in a histogram:

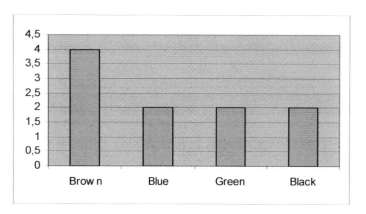

STEM AND LEAF DIAGRAM

1. The following stem and leaf diagram gives the heights of a group of high school students (in cm):

Stem	Leaf
15	7 7 9
16	4 5 6 7 7 8
17	1 3 3 4 8 8
18	2 3 4 8 9 9
19	0 1 3

   a. Find the number of students in the classroom: 24

   b. Mean = $\dfrac{4203}{24} \approx 175 cm$

   Median = $\dfrac{171+173}{2} = 172 cm$ Mode = None

   c. Min = 157cm   Max = 193cm

   d. What percentage of students is less than 165cm tall? $\dfrac{4}{20} = 20\%$

   e. What percentage of students is more than 182cm tall? $\dfrac{8}{20} = 40\%$

2. The following stem and leaf diagram gives the grades of a group of high school students in math:

Stem	Leaf
5	1 3 5 5 8
6	0 1 3 5 6 6 7
7	1 3 4 7 8
8	0 1 1 3 7 8 8
9	2 6 8

   a. Find the number of students in the classroom: 27

   b. Mean = $\dfrac{1967}{27} \approx 72.9$ Median = 73 (element number 14)

   Mode = None

   c. Min = 51   Max = 98

   d. 60 is the passing grade in the class room. How many students failed? 5 students

   e. What percentage of students obtained 85 or more? $\dfrac{6}{27} \approx 22\%$

4.4. – PROBABILITY

Probability is the science of chance or likelihood of an event happening
If a random experiment is repeated n times in such a way that each of the trials is identical and independent, where n(A) is the number of times event A occurred, then:

$$\text{Relative frequency of event A} = P(A) = \frac{n(A)}{N} \quad (N \to \infty)$$

Exercises

1. In an unbiased coin what is P(head) ? <u>0.5</u>
   This probability is called <u>"theoretical probability"</u>
2. Explain the difference between theoretical probability and "experimental" probability.
   <u>Theoretical probability is calculated, predicted. "experimental" probability is measured in an experiment. The probability for head is theoretically 0.5, we would need to repeat an experiment an infinite number of times to make sure it is. In reality the coin has some small probability to lend on its thin side (more than 0) so it is not really 0.5 for head…</u>

3. Throw a drawing pin at least 15 times and fill the table:
   <u>This experiment should be done in class</u>
4. The definition of probability is:

   $$P(A) = \frac{\text{Number of times A ocurred}}{\text{Total number of times experiment repeated}}$$

Properties of probability $\quad 0 \leq P(A) \leq 1 \quad\quad P(U) = 1$

5. Given the sentence "Good morning grade eight". Find the following probabilities in case the choices are being made in a random way:
   a. P(choosing a vowel) = $\frac{8}{21}$
   b. P(choosing a "o") = $\frac{3}{21}$
   c. P(choosing a "e") = $\frac{2}{21}$
   d. P(choosing a "z") = $\frac{0}{21} = 0$
6. In case a student is chosen randomly in your classroom. Find the probability it's a girl. <u>This should be done in class</u>
7. Find the probability of getting a prime number sum on tossing 1 dice. $\frac{3}{6}$ (1 is not considered prime)
8. Find the probability of getting a sum of 7 on tossing 2 dice.
   $1+6, 6+1, 2+5, 5+2, 3+4, 4+3 \quad \frac{6}{36} = \frac{1}{6}$
9. Find the probability of being left handed in your classroom. <u>This should be done in class</u>
10. Find the probability of obtaining a sum of 4 on tossing 2 dice.
    $1+3, 3+1, 2+2 \quad \frac{3}{36} = \frac{1}{12}$

11. Find the probability of obtaining 2 tails on tossing 2 coins.
    $\{HH, HT, TH, TT\}$ $P(TT) = \dfrac{1}{4}$

12. Find the probability that a 2 digit number divides by 10
    There are 90 2 digit numbers and 9 of them divide by 10, so $P = \dfrac{9}{90} = \dfrac{1}{10}$

13. Find the probability of choosing the letter b in the word probability $P = \dfrac{2}{11}$

14. Find the probability of choosing a number that contains the digit 8 in the first hundred numbers (1 to 100). The numbers: 8, 18, 28..98 and the numbers 80,81…89, careful not to count 889 twice, so: $P = \dfrac{19}{100}$

15. Find the probability of choosing a number that contains only odd digits in the first thousand numbers (1 to 100).
    5 in the first ten: 1,3,5,7,9
    5 in the next ten and all the tens that start with an odd numbers so $P = \dfrac{55}{100}$

16. Find the probability of choosing a palindrome number <u>between</u> 100 and 200. A palindrome number is one that is read the same from left to right is at is from right to left, for example 12321.
    101,111,121,131..191. $P = \dfrac{10}{99}$

CHAPTER 5

5.1. – INTERNATIONAL SYSTEM OF UNITS

1. Meter (m) is a unit of <u>length/distance</u> Other units of <u>length/distance</u> are: <u>mile</u>.

2. Meter square (m^2) is a unit of <u>area</u> Other units of <u>area</u> are: <u>mile^2</u>

3. An area has units of m^2 A length has units of <u>m</u>

4. Kilo = <u>1000</u> Mili = $\dfrac{1}{1000}$

Convert the units, use scientific notation in at least one of each type of exercises:

5. How many metres in 2.5 km?

   <u>2500m</u>

6. How many metres in 0.5 km?

   <u>500m</u>

7. How many metres^2 in $\dfrac{1}{3}$ km^2?

   $\dfrac{1000000}{3} m^2$

   Ffg

8. How many metres in 56 km?

   <u>56000m</u>

9. How many metres in 2500 km?

   <u>2500000m</u>

10. How many km^2 in 26 m^2?

    $\dfrac{26}{1000000} km^2 = 0.000026 km^2$

11. How many km in 75 m?

    <u>0.075km</u>

12. How many km in 1000 m?

    <u>1km</u>

13. How many m in $5.2 \cdot 10^7$ km?

    $5.2 \cdot 10^{10} m$

14. How many km^2 in $5.12 \cdot 10^8$ m^2?

    $\dfrac{5.12 \cdot 10^8}{10^6} = 512 km^2$

15. How many mm in 3.04 m?

    <u>3040mm</u>

16. How many mm^2 in 0.5 m^2?

    $\underline{0.5 m^2 = 0.5 \cdot 10^6 mm^2 = 5 \cdot 10^5 mm^2}$

17. How many mm^2 in 1 m^2?

    $\underline{1 m^2 = 10^6 mm^2}$

18. How many mm in 2 m?

    <u>2000mm</u>

19. How many mm in 2.5 m?

    <u>2500mm</u>

20. How many mm^2 are 1.35 m^2?

    $\underline{1.35 m^2 = 1.35 \cdot 10^6 mm^2}$

21. How many cm in $\frac{1}{3}$ m?

    33.3cm

22. How many cm² in 56 m²?

    $56m^2 = 56 \cdot 10^4 cm^2 = 5.6 \cdot 10^5 cm^2$

23. How many cm in 3.1 km?

    310000cm

24. How many mm² in 0.5 cm²?

    $0.5cm^2 = 0.5 \cdot 10^2 mm^2 = 50mm^2$

25. How many cm in in 120 m?

    12000cm

26. How many mm² in 5.1 cm²?

    $5.1cm^2 = 5.1 \cdot 10^2 mm^2 = 510mm^2$

27. How many cm in 17 km?

    1700000cm

28. How many m in 12392 km?

    12392000m

29. How many mm² in 5.1 m²?

    $5.1m^2 = 5.1 \cdot 10^6 mm^2$

30. How many m² in 2.2 mm²?

    $2.2mm^2 = 2.2 \cdot 10^{-6} m^2$

31. How many cm in 13.12 m?

    1312cm

32. Complete the table:

mm	cm	m	km
14	1.4	0.014	0.000014
650	65	0.65	0.00065
3000	300	3	0.003
5000000	500000	5000	5
12.5	1.25	0.0125	0.0000125
37	3.7	0.037	0.000037
4780	478	4.78	0.00478
1310000	131000	1310	1.31
8000	800	8	0.008

mm²	cm²	m²	km²
14	0.14	$0.14 \cdot 10^{-4} = 1.4 \cdot 10^{-5}$	$0.14 \cdot 10^{-10} = 1.4 \cdot 10^{-11}$
6500	65	0.0065	$0.0065 \cdot 10^{-6} = 6.5 \cdot 10^{-9}$
3000000	30000	3	$3 \cdot 10^{-6}$
$5 \cdot 10^{12}$	$5 \cdot 10^{10}$	$5 \cdot 10^6$	5
12.5	0.125	$0.125 \cdot 10^{-4} = 1.25 \cdot 10^{-5}$	$0.125 \cdot 10^{-10} = 1.25 \cdot 10^{-11}$
370	3.7	0.00037	$0.00037 \cdot 10^{-6} = 3.7 \cdot 10^{-10}$
4780000	47800	4.78	$4.78 \cdot 10^{-6}$
$1.31 \cdot 10^{12}$	$1.31 \cdot 10^{10}$	$1.31 \cdot 10^6$	1.31
$8 \cdot 10^9$	$8 \cdot 10^7$	8000	0.008

5.2. – COMMON ERRORS

1. $\sqrt{A+B} = \sqrt{A} + \sqrt{B}$ True / **False**, Give an example to show your answer.
   $\sqrt{16+100} \neq \sqrt{16} + \sqrt{100}$

2. $\sqrt{A^2 + B^2} = A + B$ True / **False**, Give an example to show your answer.
   $\sqrt{4^2 + 10^2} \neq 4 + 10$

3. $(A+B)^2 = A^2 + B^2$ True / **False**, if false write the correct version.
   $(A+B)^2 = A^2 + B^2 + 2AB$

4. $(A+B)(A-B) = A^2 + B^2$ True / **False**, Give an example to show your answer.
   $(3+7)(3-7) \neq 3^2 + 7^2$

5. $(A+B)(A-B) = A^2 - B^2$ **True** / False, if false write the correct version..

6. $(x+2)^2 = x^2 + 4x + 2$ True / **False**, if false write the correct version.
   $(x+2)^2 = x^2 + 4x + 4$

7. $(A-B)^2 = A^2 - B^2$ True / **False**, Give an example to show your answer.
   $(3+7)^2 \neq 3^2 - 7^2$

8. $(2x-3)^2 = 4x^2 - 6x + 9$ True / **False**, if false write the correct version.
   $(2x-3)^2 = 4x^2 - 12x + 9$

9. $(\sqrt{a} - 3)^2 = a^2 - 6a + 9$ True / **False**, if false write the correct version.
   $(\sqrt{a} - 3)^2 = a^2 - 6\sqrt{a} + 9$

10. $x^2 x^3 = x^6$ True / **False**, if false write the correct version.
    $x^2 x^3 = x^5$

11. $(x^2)^3 = x^{(2^3)}$ True / **False**, if false write the correct version.
    $(x^2)^3 = x^6$

12. $\dfrac{x^{10}}{x^2} = x^5$ True / **False**, if false write the correct version.

$\dfrac{x^{10}}{x^2} = x^8$

13. $x^1 = 1$ True / **False**, if false write the correct version.

$x^1 = x$

14. $x^0 = 0$ True / **False**, if false write the correct version.

$x^0 = 1$

15. $-3^2 = (-3)^2$ True / **False**, if false write the correct version.

$-3^2 = -3 \cdot 3 = -9;\ \ (-3)^2 = (-3)(-3) = 9$

16. $(4x^2) = (4x)^2$ True / **False**, if false write the correct version.

$(4x^2) \neq (4x)^2 = 16x^2$

17. $\sqrt{7x} = 7x^{\tfrac{1}{2}}$ True / **False**, if false write the correct version.

$\sqrt{7x} = \sqrt{7} \cdot \sqrt{x} \neq 7x^{\tfrac{1}{2}} = 7 \cdot \sqrt{x}$

18. $\dfrac{0}{2} = \dfrac{2}{0}$ True / **False**, if false write the correct version.

$\dfrac{0}{2} = 0 \neq \dfrac{2}{0} = Undefined!$

19. $\dfrac{14+x}{14} = x$ True / **False**, if false write the correct version.

$\dfrac{14+x}{14} = \dfrac{14}{14} + \dfrac{x}{14} = 1 + \dfrac{x}{14} \neq x$

20. $\dfrac{7-x}{7} = x - 1$ True / **False**, if false write the correct version.

$\dfrac{7-x}{7} = \dfrac{7}{7} - \dfrac{x}{7} = 1 - \dfrac{x}{7} \neq x - 1$

21. $\dfrac{a+b}{a} = 1 + \dfrac{b}{a}$ **True** / False, if false write the correct version.

22. $\dfrac{14+x}{14} = x + \dfrac{x}{14}$ True / **False**, if false write the correct version.

$\dfrac{14+x}{14} = \dfrac{14}{14} + \dfrac{x}{14} = 1 + \dfrac{x}{14} \neq x + \dfrac{x}{14}$

23. $\dfrac{1}{x+y} = \dfrac{1}{x} + \dfrac{1}{y}$ True / **False**, if false write the correct version.

$\dfrac{1}{x+y} \neq \dfrac{1}{x} + \dfrac{1}{y} = \dfrac{y+x}{xy}$

24. An **expression** and an **equation** is the same thing.   True / **False**

25. $\dfrac{\left(\dfrac{a}{b}\right)}{c} = \dfrac{a}{\left(\dfrac{b}{c}\right)}$ True / **False**, if false write the correct version.

$\dfrac{\left(\dfrac{a}{b}\right)}{c} = \dfrac{a}{bc} \neq \dfrac{a}{\left(\dfrac{b}{c}\right)} = \dfrac{ac}{b}$

26. $-a^2 = (-a)^2$ True / **False**, if false write the correct version.

$-a^2 \neq (-a)^2 = a^2$

27. $a^{-2} = (-a)^2$ True / **False**, if false write the correct version.

$a^{-2} = \dfrac{1}{a^2} \neq (-a)^2 = a^2$

28. $a^{-2} = -a^2$ True / **False**, if false write the correct version.

$a^{-2} = \dfrac{1}{a^2} \neq -a^2$

29. $a^{-2} = -\dfrac{1}{a^2}$ True / **False**, if false write the correct version.

$a^{-2} = \dfrac{1}{a^2} \neq -\dfrac{1}{a^2}$

30. $a^{-2} = \dfrac{1}{a^2}$ **True** / False, if false write the correct version.

31. $a^{-1} = -\dfrac{1}{a}$ True / **False**, if false write the correct version.

$a^{-1} = \dfrac{1}{a} \neq -\dfrac{1}{a}$

32. $\dfrac{1}{2} + \dfrac{1}{3} = \dfrac{1}{2+3}$ True / **False**, if false write the correct version.

$\dfrac{1}{2} + \dfrac{1}{3} = \dfrac{5}{6} \neq \dfrac{1}{2+3} = \dfrac{1}{5}$

33. $a^{-1} + a^{-1} = a^{-2}$ True / **False**, if false write the correct version.

$a^{-1} + a^{-1} = \dfrac{1}{a} + \dfrac{1}{a} = \dfrac{2}{a} \neq a^{-2} = \dfrac{1}{a^2}$

34. $a^{-1} a^{-1} = a^{-2}$ **True** / False, if false write the correct version.

35. $a^{-2} a^{-3} = a^{-6}$ True / **False**, if false write the correct version.

$a^{-2} a^{-3} = \dfrac{1}{a^2} \cdot \dfrac{1}{a^3} = \dfrac{1}{a^5} = a^{-5} \neq a^{-6}$

36. $a^{-2} + a^{-3} = a^{-5}$ True / False, if false write the correct version.

$a^{-2} + a^{-3} = \dfrac{1}{a^2} + \dfrac{1}{a^3} = \dfrac{a+1}{a^3} \neq a^{-5} = \dfrac{1}{a^5}$

Made in the USA
San Bernardino, CA
07 July 2018